AMERICAN INDIANS AND THE URBAN EXPERIENCE

CONTEMPORARY NATIVE AMERICAN COMMUNITIES
Stepping Stones to the Seventh Generation

Despite the strength and vibrancy of Native American people and nations today, the majority of publications on Native peoples still reflect a public perception that these peoples largely disappeared after 1890. This series is meant to correct that misconception and to fill the void that has been created by examining contemporary Native American life from the point of view of Native concerns and values. Books in the series cover topics that are of cultural and political importance to tribal and urban Native peoples and affect their possibilities for survival.

SERIES EDITORS:
Troy Johnson
American Indian Studies
California State University, Long Beach
Long Beach, CA 90840
trj@csulb.edu

Duane Champagne
American Indian Studies Center
3220 Campbell Hall, Box 951548
University of California, Los Angeles
Los Angeles, CA 90095
champagn@ucla.edu

BOOKS IN THE SERIES
1. *Inuit, Whaling, and Sustainability*, Milton M. R. Freeman, Ingmar Egede, Lyudmila Bogoslovskaya, Igor G. Krupnik, Richard A. Caulfield and Marc G. Stevenson (1999)
2. *Contemporary Native American Political Issues*, edited by Troy Johnson (1999)
3. *Contemporary Native American Cultural Issues*, edited by Duane Champagne (1999)
4. *Modern Tribal Development: Paths to Self Sufficiency and Cultural Integrity in Indian Country*, Dean Howard Smith (2000)
5. *American Indians and the Urban Experience*, edited by Susan Lobo and Kurt Peters (2001)
6. *Medicine Ways: Disease, Health, and Survival among Native Americans*, edited by Clifford Trafzer and Diane Weiner (2000)

AMERICAN INDIANS AND THE URBAN EXPERIENCE

EDITED BY
SUSAN LOBO & KURT PETERS

ALTAMIRA PRESS
A Division of Rowman & Littlefield Publishers, Inc.
Lanham • Boulder • New York • Toronto • Plymouth, UK

ALTAMIRA PRESS
A division of Rowman & Littlefield Publishers, Inc.
A wholly owned subsidiary of The Rowman & Littlefield Publishing Group, Inc.
4501 Forbes Boulevard, Suite 200
Lanham, MD 20706
www.altamirapress.com

Estover Road
Plymouth PL6 7PY
United Kingdom

British Library Cataloguing in Publication Information Available

Library of Congress Cataloging-in-Publication Data

American Indians and the urban experience / edited by Susan Lobo and Kurt Peters.
    p. cm. — (Contemporary Native American communities ; v. 5)
    Includes bibliographical references and index.
    ISBN 0-7425-0274-0 (cloth : alk. paper) — ISBN 0-7425-0275-9 (pbk. : alk. paper)
    I. Indians of North America—Urban residence. 2. Indians of North America—Social
conditions. 3. Rural-urban migration—United States. 4. City and town life—United States.
5. Urbanization—United States. I. Lobo, Susan. II. Peters, Kurt, 1939– III. Series.

E78.U72 A54 2000
973.04'9701732—dc21

                                                                                    00-040162

Printed in the United States of America

♾™ The paper used in this publication meets the minimum requirements of American
National Standard for Information Sciences—Permanence of Paper for Printed Library
Materials, ANSI/NISO Z39.48-1992.

CONTENTS

Foreword

DONALD L. FIXICO

T HE FACT THAT more than two-thirds of the total American Indian population of 2.1 million lives in urban areas is a revelation to many people who still believe the stereotypes about Indians. American Indians have migrated to towns and cities since the early decades of the twentieth century, and now the urban Indian constitutes an unseen, little understood Indian identity. Communities and enclaves of Indian people dwell in Chicago, Seattle, Gallup, Denver, Oklahoma City, Albuquerque, Minneapolis-St. Paul, and Los Angeles, which has the largest concentration of urban Indians in the United States. Urban Indians live in other cities as well.

The impetus for this demographic shift from reservations to urban areas occurred following World War II with the introduction of the federal relocation program, which offered jobs and housing in cities for Indians. Promising a better way of life, including economic improvement and a lifestyle similar to most other Americans, the United States government planned to assimilate Indians into the mainstream via urbanization. This did not happen as the federal government had anticipated. Culturally a communal people, urban Indians found other Native Americans and formed new Indian communities, usually starting in ghettoes.

The story of the urban Indian is told in the following pages and it could not be told soon enough. Indian people have struggled to learn a new culture of mainstream urbanization, but rather than becoming absorbed into the process, they have survived to form a new identity of their own. Hence, urban Indians have managed to control their own lives, although federal Indian policy and bureaucrats have worked to nullify the spirituality of Native Americans and their determination to be their own people. Their inherent sovereignty has been battered and abused, but in spite of the propaganda and colonization, American Indians have adapted as they have always done. The greatest quality of Indian people has been adaptability when necessary, and the dilemma of choosing between reservation and urban life has been a relatively mild problem for urban Indians, although the federal government has thought otherwise. Urban Indians have opted to live in cities at will and to return to reservations when they felt compelled to do so.

However, in the early years of relocation, during the 1950s and 1960s, urban Indians were not so much in control of their lives. Economic pressure and the cultural alienation of city life frustrated the early generations of urban Indians who were miserable living in run-down apartments and feeling lost in the city. Some Native people gave up and returned home to reservations and traditional homelands, but a hearty group remained in the cities. Learning the ways of the street and finding comfort in identifying with other Indians, tribal barriers began to dissolve as urban Indians learned about each other and helped in the forming of urban Indian centers and urban Indian organizations. Based on this newfound brand of "Indianness," urban Indians learned about survival, adaptation, and organization beyond the tribal level. By the late 1960s, they found more success controlling their own lives. In what was sometimes called the "second removal," urban Indians found a new home in the city, one representing modern traditions of an urban Indian culture that the following chapters describe very well. Such a book is overdue, for American Indians have been in urban areas much longer than the mainstream society realizes, and they are thriving based on new values that very much resemble traditional ways.

Introduction

SUSAN LOBO

"INDIANS IN CITIES?! YOU MUST BE KIDDING." No, just trying to set the record straight—that is what this book is all about. Those of us living, working, or carrying out research about Indian life in urban areas became aware that there is very little focused attention, research, or writing that relates to urban Native topics. Many of us had worked on these topics in one way or another for years, some of us have lived them our entire lives. But essentially we were thinking about these things in isolation from each other, wondering why, with more than half of all Indian people now living in urban areas, there is so little urban-focused interest among researchers, writers, poets, and artists, and why there are so few books on urban themes and contexts.

The small number of publications on urban themes and topics is particularly striking when compared to the vast and active interest and literature on other American Indian topics and contexts. Perhaps, we reasoned, writing about, thinking about, and otherwise exercising creativity regarding the urban Indian scene really has been out there, but it has been scattered. It needed to be pulled together into a book such as this one in order to be recognized and acknowledged by the world outside the many urban Indian communities that now flourish in towns and cities throughout the Americas. This book, then, conveying something of the spirit, the history, the context, dynamics, and voice of Indian life in cities, is, we believe, long, long overdue.

There have been significant signposts along the way that have galvanized some thinking about urban issues and, to an extent, have served to bring some of the contributors to this volume together. These include the 1990 U.S. Census, the special 1994 "Alcatraz Revisited" issue of the *American Indian Culture and Research Journal*, and the panel "Being Indian in the City: Reflections on Urban Identity and Community" at the American Anthropological Association meetings in San Francisco in 1996. In addition, many of us who live and work in urban Indian communities, teach in Native American or American Indian studies or related departments, or exhibit art and participate in poetry readings come into contact with one another on a frequent basis, and we increasingly have begun to "think urban."

The 1990 census, in spite of problems with undercount, reaffirmed that large numbers of Indian people live in urban areas. Also the process of carrying out the census demonstrated the lack of understanding by this governmental agency, and by extension other governmental agencies, regarding the very nature of urban Indian populations and communities. Issues arose during the 1990 census concerning the dynamics of residency, age, gender, education, and income that made it clear to those of us living and working in urban areas that the Census Bureau was not making an accurate count. This miscount not only fueled continued misperceptions regarding Indian life in cities, but also justified reduced funding for the many greatly needed social services for Indian people living in cities. The word was even circulating in some circles that this was a form of "statistical genocide," yet another and modern burden from the government for Indian people to deal with. Many of the contributors to this volume have taken note of the many ramifications of the urban miscount by the Census Bureau. Terry Straus and Susan Lobo, who have chapters in this book, participated in a census-sponsored research project of "hard to count populations"—Straus in Chicago and Lobo in Oakland. During the course of this census project it became evident that the methodology utilized by the Census Bureau, based on a series of premises that are not relevant to understanding Indian people and the structuring of urban Indian communities, was a major factor contributing to the miscounting of Indian people living in urban areas.

The 1994 special issue of the *American Indian Culture and Research Journal* "Alcatraz Revisited: The 25th Anniversary of the Occupation, 1969–1971" was significant in bringing together writers and community activists who discussed a number of themes, including the impact of the Alcatraz occupation and its aftermath in urban and rural areas of Indian Country.[1] This occupation, like many others during the late 1960s and 1970s, was a catalyst, affecting the life decisions of people, many of whom have continued over the past twenty-five years to live and work in urban areas. Jack Forbes has written about the impact of the occupation of Alcatraz and is one of the contributors to this book. Teweah Garcia, whose poem "My Uncle" is included here, is the daughter of a long-term occupier of Alcatraz who continues to be a community activist and leader in the educational field in her urban community.

A third event that was a catalyst for the development of this book was the panel on urban Indian topics organized by Deborah Jackson at the American Anthropological Association 1996 annual conference. A number of contributors to this book, including Deborah Jackson, Kurt Peters, Terry Straus, Joan Weibel-Orlando, and myself, participated in this panel, which was attended to overflowing and generated intense interest. Duane Champagne, editor of UCLA's *American Indian Culture and Research Journal*, participated as well. This event was yet another indication of the need to recognize the existing research, to connect with other scholars, writers, and visual artists in order to publish the results of our work. During the hours of discussion following this panel we were joined by Darby Price and Renya Ramirez—other contributors to this volume—and finalized the plan to put together a special urban issue of the *American Indian Culture and Research Journal* (Vol. 22:4, 1988, edited by Lobo and Peters). We even began talking about The Book. The reality and vitality of continuing Indian life is urban, rural, and everything in between. For Indian people these varied settings are interrelated in multiple ways. Why, then, has an urban focus taken so long to come into being? The rigid rural/urban dichotomy is not a true expression of Indian reality, yet it has been one of the molds and barriers that has continued to shape research, writing, and, to a lesser extent, creative expression. A brief overview of the legacy of the fields of urban studies and American Indian studies gives insight into influences at the root of why American Indian urban studies have not been more actively carried out in the past. We also discuss here the ways in which this legacy has contributed in a positive way to shaping some of the thinking reflected in this book.

A prominent and very influential early approach to urban and urbanization studies from the 1940s and 1950s was that of Redfield and his "folk-urban continuum."[3] He juxtaposed rural "folk" and their communities with "urbanites" and their communities. While he ostensibly proposed a continuum, his work has generally been interpreted as a dichotomous model. Although most of his work was in Latin America, his influence, via his students and colleagues at the University of Chicago, was far-reaching in shaping later rural to urban migration studies, as well as in defining and emphasizing the concepts of acculturation and assimilation in urban areas.

Closely associated with urban studies of that period and also very influential in establishing the urban research themes and tone was the work of Wirth.[4] His theories associate urbanization with "social disorganization" and "cultural breakdown," thematic concepts that continue to influence urban sociological studies. This approach focuses on social problems on an individual psychological level, leading to an emphasis on urban loneliness, despair, anomie, and the effects of alcoholism, racism, and poverty. On a practical basis, these are themes and approaches within the domain of social welfare, and they continue to be many of the issues that urban Indian community-based social service organizations deal with in creating and maintaining community well-being.

Another related variant on the theme of "disorganization" is the thesis of the "culture of poverty" originated by Lewis.[5] Although criticized with good reason, this concept continues even today to influence both research and political and economic policy in often subtle ways. The creation of these urban research theories, methodologies, and approaches during the 1940s, 1950s, and 1960s, dovetailed with and influenced the development and implementation of policy affecting Indian lands, resources, and economic and social options. This is seen most prominently in the termination-relocation policies of the 1950s and their aftermath into the 1970s. These policies were major catalysts for Indian people to migrate in large numbers into urban areas, thereby intensifying the process of establishing urban communities. Journalistic accounts of Indians living in cities reflected the "lo, the poor Indian" tone of the times, and cities came to be depicted as the modern variant of "the end of the trail." But wait! There must be more to urban life for Indian people. Yet it has taken another almost thirty years for that varied voice of urban life to emerge, depicted vividly here, for example, in the photographs of Pena Bonita, in the poetry of Joy Harjo, and in the writing of Julian Lang.

These pre-1980s research approaches, and the models regarding urban life for Indians and non-Indians alike that they generated, reflected and validated long-standing stereotypes regarding the causes and nature of poverty, migration into cities, and social organization of those living in cities. In turn, these models and theories have affected the current state of research, writing, and creative reflections regarding American Indians living in urban settings. Why is that so?

Parallel with yet functionally distinct from urban studies have been the massive amounts of research, writing, and creative expression related to American Indian history, culture, and politics. Most of this scholarship and writing has had an almost exclusively rural focus. There are three particularly prominent reasons for this rural focus. One is that Native homelands have overwhelmingly been in rural areas, so that many American Indian research themes including genocide, loss and control of land and resources, and the relationship with the federal government have, for practical and historical reasons, focused on non-urban areas.

A second reason for the emphasis on rural rather than urban areas stems from the strong influence of anthropology on American Indian studies. Urban settings remained almost exclusively the domain of sociologists. A desire to avoid turf wars led to an unspoken code by academics that anthropologists could "have" Indians, while sociologists could "have" urban studies. One of the results was that the two topics were not deemed as appropriate to be considered in the same sentence in academically polite company. An additional barrier created by the link between anthropology and research and writing regarding American Indian topics has been the traditional anthropological stance emphasizing the static model of the "ethnographic present." This model often has been criticized for its idealized frozen-in-time effect. The ethnographic present, almost exclusively rural in context, created a mindset, generated by anthropologists and historians, but embraced by the general public, that has been very difficult to set aside.

A third reason for the rural emphasis stems from the weight of generalized popular stereotypes stressing that everything Indian is set on a rural stage, and very frequently colored by romantic views of the past. Both the media and the educational system reinforce these popular stereotypes throughout contemporary Indian and non-Indian society, making them very difficult to discard. American Indian fiction writers such as Momaday and Silko, who have not been constrained by social science and research orientations, took an important step in breaking out of the restrictive rural, past-tense mode, as discussed by Miller in this volume. They have been able to more freely and creatively reflect on Indian realities, aspirations, and visions, wherever they might be taking shape. Bomberry, Ramirez, and especially the poets and artists whose work appears in this book, have likewise successfully laid aside these constraining stereotypes.

Although the title of this book is *American Indians and the Urban Experience*, it is evident that there exists not one experience, but many experiences and multiple perspectives. We think of this book as a patchwork, modeled after the star quilts and many other patterns created by the Indian women of the northern Plains and elsewhere. It includes many facets, united to create a patterned whole; not the only whole by any means, but one that is a valid expression of one aspect of Indian reality.

There are a series of themes that are linked and woven together throughout this book. Although the focus is on urban contexts, both in terms of looking at specific cities and also in a general way, there is also an underlying holistic approach that views Indian urbanism on a hemispheric scale and that links urban areas to rural, suburban, and reservation areas. The emphasis in the book is on contemporary urban experiences, yet there is strong acknowledgement of the historical and traditional roots of that experience. While there is some emphasis on the migration of Indian people into cities, there is also consideration of rural communities that have become engulfed by urban areas, and migration from city to city nationally and internationally, as well as return migration or intermittent movement from cities to more rural homelands. The book is divided into three sections that overlap in content and theme: an overview of urbanism, the structuring and dynamics of urban communities, and individuals and families in urban contexts.

This book represents a fresh start—one that is aware of and, in many cases, stems from the historical, theoretical roots of past researchers, writers, and creative thinkers; one that is equally immersed in and deeply cognizant of the role of "The Cid," as Julian Lang says here, in American Indian lives. We appreciate the research legacy of the past and see many elements and themes from these studies reflected in current research and writing. We further believe that the words and images brought together in this book are effectively unbounded from the restraints and research agendas of the past. Although the writers and artists whose work has been brought together for this book come from many fields, including literature, anthropology, Native American and ethnic studies, visual arts, social welfare, education, history, political science, and economics, here, in this book, the lines between these fields have become blurred. The fundamental motivation in creating this book is the thematic focus of American Indian urban life and experiences, viewed from a wide array of perspectives and presented in diverse ways that are engaging to everyone who would like to join the circle to "set the record straight."

It has been exciting to have worked with the authors and artists included in this book. In addition to all of the contributors to this volume who put their hearts and a lot of hard work into their contributions, we owe a particular debt of gratitude to Duane Champagne, editor of the *American Indian Culture and Research Journal* for his encouragement throughout, and to Pamela Grieman, managing editor of the journal, whose inspiration and hard work made possible the publication of the special urban issue. Jennifer Collier, our brilliant editor at AltaMira Press, has been unfailingly helpful with clear-headed critique at crucial junctures. To Kelina Lobo for her patience; to Mike Gray for cutting wood for the stove; to Marilyn St. Germaine for lots of good times; to Joyce Keoke and the Community History Project board; to Janeen Antoine; to Theresa Harlan; to Wes Huss; and to all the many others, friends and family at Intertribal Friendship House, we say "thanks." As Julian Lang says, "May we all live to be a long time!"

Notes

1. See *American Indian Culture and Research Journal* 18, no. 4 (1994).

2. See Robert Redfield, *The Folk Cultures of Yucatan* (Chicago: University of Chicago Press, 1941).

3. Louis Wirth, "Urbanism as a Way of Life," in *Reader in Urban Sociology*, ed. Robert Hatt and John Reiss (Glencoe, New York: The Free Press, 1951).

4. See Oscar Lewis, "The Culture of Poverty," in *Scientific American* 215, no. 4 (1966).

The Path to the Milky Way Leads through Los Angeles

JOY HARJO

There are strangers above me, below me and all around me and we are all
strange in this place of recent invention.
This city named for angels appears naked and stripped of anything resembling
the shaking of turtle shells, the songs of human voices on a summer night
outside Okmulgee.
Yet, it's perpetually summer here, and beautiful. The shimmer of gods is
easier to perceive at sunrise or dusk,
when those who remember us here in the illusion of the marketplace
turn toward the changing of the sun and say our names.
We matter to somebody,
We must matter to the strange god who imagines us as we revolve together
in the dark sky on the path to the Milky Way.
We can't easily see that starry road from the perspective of the crossing of
boulevards, can't hear it in the whine of civilization or taste the minerals of
planets in hamburgers.
But we can buy a map here of the stars' homes, dial a tone for dangerous love,
choose from several brands of water, or a hiss of oxygen for gentle
rejuvenation.
Everyone knows you can't buy love but you can still sell your soul for less
than a song, to a stranger who will sell it to someone else for a profit until
you're owned by a company of strangers in the city of the strange
and getting stranger.
I'd rather understand how to sing from a crow who was never good at singing
or much of anything but finding gold in the trash of humans.
So what are we doing here I ask the crow parading on the ledge of falling that
hangs over this precarious city?
Crow just laughs and says *wait, wait and see* and I am waiting and not seeing
anything, not just yet.
But like crow I collect the shine of anything beautiful I can find.

OVERVIEW OF URBANISM I

Introduction

SUSAN LOBO

T HIS SECTION GIVES A general overview of some of the essential themes found throughout the book. One is the hemispheric consideration of migration and urbanization. Although the focus of the book is on cities in the United States, Forbes's chapter here and, later in the book, Julca's chapter remind us that Native people have made and continue to make their homes throughout the entire hemisphere, in urban areas that include not only the modern, European-derived cities, but also those ancient cities that are truly indigenous to this hemisphere. Forbes sets the tone, demonstrating that prior to the relatively recent incursion into this hemisphere by peoples from across the seas, this entire hemisphere, in all of its urban and more rural forms, was (and, to many, remains, as Zig Jackson's cover photograph asserts) all the Native homeland. Geographically, it is Forbes's chapter that takes the broadest hemispheric approach in the book.

Related to this hemispheric approach is the question of borders, both international and state, that now often separate and divide Indian homelands and affect both migration and urbanization. Trujillo outlines Yaqui history and the many ways that migration and changing international borders between the United States and Mexico, and even the Phoenix city limits, have imposed barriers to movement and also have been factors in shaping a tribe's history and group identity. And, like Forbes, she maintains that a fundamental aspect of understanding urbanism is that "the social adaptation of Native Americans to an urban context . . . is much older than the history of Native American/non-indigenous American contact." She also discusses the ways in which education and language learning establish a people as being considered by the world external to the tribe or as belonging on one side of the border or the other. As Abel Silvas asserts in Price's chapter, "Since we were here before the border, we didn't cross the border—we were crossed by the border."

In her chapter, Miller addresses the more abstract representation of cities and their many connotations. She provides insights into the ways that contemporary Indian fiction writers utilize their works to counter stereotypes, especially those of invisibility and victimization, existing in the non-Indian imagination. As Miller finds, these images are reversed in the literature that provides an Indian perspective, expressing cultural vitality in settings of positive change that include the many faces of urban experience. This analysis shows the contrast between European-based and -derived notions of place and relationship with those of Native peoples. Concepts such as "urban" and "community" are introduced and considered from an Indian perspective. She raises the questions "How alien is an urban environment?" and "What are the foundations of 'civilized' behavior?"—two themes that continue to emerge throughout this book. Reflections of these questions are especially evident here in the poetry of Revard and Butler, in the depiction by Manriquez of "Coyote as a Simple Man"—watching cowboys and Indians on TV no less—and in Larry Rodriguez's "Kokopeli Gigging in the City." Dugan Aguilar's photograph "Two Worlds" presents yet another abstracted and symbolic view of The City.

The Urban Tradition among Native Americans I

JACK D. FORBES

U RBANIZATION IS AN EXTREMELY IMPORTANT CONCEPT because virtually all European writers imagine that "civilization" arises only with cities. Indeed, the very word *civilization* is derived from the Latin *civitat* and *civitas*, citizenship, state, and, in particular, the City of Rome, which is in turn from *civis*, a citizen. The word *city*, as well as the Castilian *ciudad*, is derived similarly.

A people that does not have cities or urban centers will ordinarily not be viewed as being "civilized" by Eurocentric writers and, indeed, the dualistic split between "nature" and "culture" in much of Eurocentric thinking is also a "country" versus "city" split, as I discuss elsewhere.[1]

Most European writers picture Native Americans as peoples living in the countryside, in jungles, forests, on the plains and pampas, or in small villages surrounded by mountains as in the Andes. Naturally, then, it becomes problematic for them when they discover that huge numbers of First Nations people reside today in cities such as Buenos Aires, Lima, La Paz, Quito, Guatemala City, Mexico City, Toronto, Denver, Chicago, Los Angeles, San Francisco–Oakland, and so on. What many non-Native writers do not realize is that the First Americans have, in fact, gone through periods of deurbanization and reurbanization on various occasions in their history and that urban life has been a major aspect of American life from ancient times.

In fact, it may well be that the Americas witnessed a greater process of urban development in pre-1500 C.E. times than did any other continent, with the growth of the most elaborate planned cities found anywhere. In fact, the evidence seems to indicate that from about 1600–1700 B.C. until the 1519–1520 C.E. period, the largest cities in the world were often located in the Americas rather than in Asia, Africa, or Europe.

Before discussing ancient urbanization, however, we should say something about what constitutes an *urb* (Lat. for city) or *odena* (Otchipwe for town or city; *otana* in Powhatan). The archaeologist John H. Rowe, in discussing ancient urbanization in Peru, states that

> an urban settlement is an area of human habitation in which dwellings are grouped closely together. The dwellings must be close enough to

leave insufficient space between them for subsistence farming, although
. . . gardens may be present.[2]

Rowe distinguishes several kinds of urban settlements, including the *pueblo*, where all
of the residents are engaged in subsistence activities at least part of the time, and the
city where some residents are engaged in other activities such as manufacturing, trade,
service, administration, defense, crafts, etc. He also differentiates between cities and
pueblos where all of the people are gathered in the settlement and the surrounding
countryside is basically empty, and cities or pueblos with a scattered rural population
around them (somewhat like ceremonial or market centers can exist with rural settlements scattered around them).

Rowe proposes to refer to urban settlements with fewer than two thousand inhabitants as small and to those with more than two thousand as large. (The U.S.
census regards any place with 2,500 or more persons as being urban.) Of course,
I would add that the density of surrounding areas must be considered also, since
one might find a series of hamlets separated by fields or forest that together form
a close-knit economic and social unit. In any case, the population of American
cities frequently far exceeds two thousand, and metropolitan areas (such as around
Goleta in Santa Barbara County, California) could have many pueblos of a thousand residents each in a rather small area.

We can also analyze *urbs* in other ways. Let us note the following distinctions:
(1) multiethnic (multitribal, multilingual, multiracial) *urbs* as opposed to single-
ethnic *urbs*; (2) *urbs* organized in *calpulli*-style kinship neighborhoods as opposed to
cities with dispersed kinship; (3) metropolitan areas that include areas of countryside
and villages or barrios associated intimately with a ceremonial or market center as opposed to distinctly separated urban-rural zones; (4) megacities such as Chan Chan or
Tenochtítlan as opposed to smaller cities.

It is very possible that many ancient American cities were organized into *calpulli*-
like kinship-based divisions. *Calpulli* is the Nahuatl word for a semi-self-governing
neighborhood or unit comprised of related persons—that is, a tribe, band, or other
kinship group. It also would appear that many of the greatest *urbs* in America were
multilingual. Even in areas where one language family predominated over a wide area,
there are clear examples where many different dialects were spoken in the *urbs* as well
as occasional unrelated tongues (such as Nahuatl in the Maya area). In the urban traditions of Mexico and Guatemala, groups speaking various Maya, Mixe-Zoque,
Nahuan, and other languages are frequently mentioned as living in the same city or region or as migrating together into some other group's territory. Incidentally, it is in
the Olmeca-Tulapan region on the coast of the Gulf of Mexico that the oldest date
of the Mesoamerican calendar seems to be grounded, a date of 3113 B.C. or 3114 B.C.
(August 11, 13, or 20 or September 8 according to the anthropological interpretation
of the long count found on Maya monuments, or March 20 as found in the Tepixic

Annals). This date is probably related to the process of urbanization in the Olmeca-Tulapan region, perhaps marking the founding of a complex or community there or at the very least marking the period when maize agriculture provided the dietary basis for intensive population concentrations. On the other hand, it might refer to a great astronomical event.

But before discussing the period of year I A.C. (American Calendar), let me return for a moment to the classification of urban areas. One of the special characteristics of American life in such diverse regions as Peru, Mesoamerica, and the Mississippi Valley is the very early development of ceremonial centers, usually featuring mounds or pyramidlike structures. I interpret these mounds as being symbolic breasts of Gahesina Haki (Mother Earth), especially when a structure is placed on top of the mound, as was usually the case. Such breasts would serve to link Americans spiritually with the nurturing power of Gahesina Haki.

Many of these mounds become huge (as at Cahokia, Teotihuacan, Cholula, and Moche), rivaling the largest pyramids of the ancient Kemi (Egyptian) people. In any case, these ceremonial structures are not always surrounded by a dense civilian settlement or city but are often surrounded by farmlands and unpopulated areas, in which small to medium towns or hamlets are located. It would appear that the ceremonial center and the dispersed settlements together form a unit, that is, that they are part of a single social unit that can be seen as being urban without being concentrated. Is that possible? Can we conceive of a large area with many small towns or hamlets working together to support a market center/ceremonial center/educational center as a kind of city? Indeed we must, because otherwise we cannot explain the erection of such centers (with all of the immense amounts of labor involved) or their enlargement and management over hundreds of years.

We also must come up with a new term for this type of urban development, one that resembles some modern "garden cities" but has at its hub a communal center with spiritual as well as secular purposes. I propose that we speak of "heart circle" to describe a region where one finds a long-enduring association between many small communities and a spiritual "heart." Such a circle has many urban characteristics, but the productivity of its landscape is not marred by the intensive and continuous erection of streets and structures. Such heart circles may, indeed, reflect a profound wisdom and a benign socialist democracy. They ensure an adequate protein base for all persons in the region, with so-called wild animals, trees, and plants being preserved and protected from exploitation, while at the same time being harvested on a regular but respectful basis.

One of the problems for all early *urbs* is to insure that large concentrations of people can indeed obtain a balanced diet. Some scholars believe that some American cities collapsed because their populations became too large and concentrated to allow for an adequate food supply, and, in particular, a balanced one with sufficient nonmaize sources of protein.

In any event, not all American *urbs* evolved as heart circles. In fact, there is an immense variety among early American towns, in part because of the great variety of geographical settings. Marine environments sometimes provided sufficient food for population growth without horticulture, as among the Calusa of Florida, the Chumash of the Santa Barbara Channel, and some Pacific Northwest nations. Likewise, the careful management of nondomesticated animals, plants, and trees, as found with the eco-managing peoples of California, sometimes led to substantial population growth. Nonetheless, the evolution of agriculture was a major step toward urbanization in many regions from the Mississippi Valley southward.

Seeds of cultivated squash found in an Oaxaca cave have been dated at 9975 B.P. (before the present). By 8000 B.P. the squash rind had the orange color of modern pumpkins (*cucurbita pepo*). In any case, American horticultural science has been pushed back to almost ten thousand years ago, a date comparable to the origins of domestication in Africa and Asia.[3] In the eastern area of the United States the domestication of cucurbits, sunflowers, and other plants (except maize) goes back to about 4500 B.C. Maize was domesticated in Mexico by about 5000 B.C. and spread into the southwest U.S. by 2000–1500 B.C. By 700–900 C.E. the widespread production of maize began to revolutionize Mississippi Valley lifeways.[4] In coastal Peru the cultivation of cotton and other crops may have begun as early as 3500 B.C., contributing along with marine resources to urban developments after 2000 B.C. when maize culture becomes evident.[5] The continued study of plants by Native people illustrates their intellectual vitality during these many millennia, since at least a hundred and fifty plants were adapted to horticulture in the Americas, in addition to the management and/or regular use of hundreds of unaltered species.

It is interesting that weaving with cotton seems to develop about the same time as ceramic manufacturing, but apparently in different regions. The earliest ceramics found thus far are from the mouth of the Amazon, along the north coast of Colombia, and from Valdivia, Ecuador, dating between 3600 and 3000 B.C. (about the same time as fired clay objects were being produced in Louisiana). In Mexico, bowls and jars of stone appear by 3400–2300 B.C. and ceramics by 2300–1500 B.C. A soapstone bowl industry developed in the southeast U.S. between 3000 and 1000 B.C., preceding ceramic bowls. Specialized manufacturing seems to have existed at Huaca (Waka) Prieta in Peru after 3000 B.C., where thousands of fabrics made of cotton and other fibers have been found.[6]

Since 4000 B.C., America has had many shared developments. For example, recent work has demonstrated that Louisiana is home to the earliest dated human-built mounds in the hemisphere, one complex (Watson Brake) being dated at 5400–5000 years ago, with other sites yielding dates in the 3500–4000 B.C. range. The Monte Sano mounds near Baton Rouge had a permanent structure and charcoal dating to circa 3500 B.C. The Watson Brake complex forms a series of linked mounds, shaped like a doughnut around a central area. The people of these early mounds were fisherfolk as well as eco-managers of game, trees, and plants (or what some writers like to call "hunter-gatherers"). To the east is another complicated series of mounds (Poverty Point) dated to circa 1700 B.C. or 1500 B.C., depending on the source. All of these mounds were preceramic except for the numerous fired clay blocks noted above.[7]

The American determination to construct mounds or raised platforms and other ceremonial structures can also be seen in Mesoamerica and the Andean region, with mounds appearing along the Peruvian coast after 2600 B.C. and especially after 2000 B.C. Callejon de Huaylas near Huaricoto began about 2800 B.C. It has thirteen ceremonial hearths of a type subsequently found elsewhere in the highlands of Peru. Aspero, a huge preceramic center by about 2000 B.C. has seven known mounds and six other structures. Work began there by 2600 B.C. and continued on for several hundred years.[8]

In Mexico earthen constructions appear in the 1200–900 B.C. period in Olmeca-Tulapan (southern Vera Cruz-Tabasco) at San Lorenzo, a major ceremonial center located near the Rio Coatzacoalcos. There a mesa was artificially altered with large amounts of fill and ridges were constructed outward on three sides. But the major feature of this site is its huge basalt heads, eight of them, the largest weighing some twenty tons. The site is also very rich in Olmeca-type art works and figurines whose style has led to wild speculation on the part of European-American scholars. It is thought that San Lorenzo was destroyed in 900 B.C., but the cultural tradition continued on at La Venta. Mounds or pyramids as such seem to appear after 900 B.C., as at Cuicuilco near Mexico City where a circular pyramid was erected, 60 feet high and 370 feet in diameter, with four tiers and four other structures nearby (all buried beneath lava prior to discovery). About the same time the people called the Olmeca erected pyramids of clay in the region of Tollan or Olmeca-Tulapan, as at La Venta. There during the 900–400 B.C. period the Americans built a giant pyramid that stood some thirty meters high, containing perhaps more than two hundred thousand cubic meters of fill. Estimates indicate that its construction required eight hundred thousand man-days and a supporting population of at least eighteen thousand.[9] In Oaxaca the Zapotec (or Binizá people, meaning People of the Clouds)also began the construction of their great centers of Monte Alban and Mitla (circa 800–500 B.C.). Great Kaminaljuyú, near Guatemala City, evolved after 1700 B.C., with several hundred great temple mounds and some large clay temple mounds completed by 500 B.C. at the latest. On the Pacific Coast at Izapa large numbers of earthen mounds were also built. This site was occupied from the 2000–1000 B.C. period and reached its peak after 500 B.C. Izapa is interesting because of its connections with the Olmeca area and also because, located on the Pacific, it could have had connections with South America.[10]

The eagerness of many Americans to devote huge amounts of labor to building "breasts" soon spread. After 800–500 B.C. they appeared northward among the so-called Adena peoples of the Ohio Valley and vicinity. There immense numbers of mounds were constructed which were also used for burial purposes, thus they are often known as burial mounds. (A mound of this kind was excavated in Virginia, incidentally, by Thomas Jefferson.) During this same period the earliest large Maya cities (Nakbe, 600–400 B.C., and Tikal, a bit later) were the sites of platform and higher mounds. And far to the south at Qaluyu, near Pucara in the Lake Titicaca region of Peru-Bolivia, Americans were building a low mound several acres in size in 1000–500 B.C., with a later one, reportedly shaped like a catfish, after 700 B.C.[11]

John Rowe would probably not regard the mound complexes or heart circles as being urban unless they were surrounded by a certain number of dense structures leaving no room for farming in between. But is this structural density really the key to urbanness? I must argue that the key to urbanness is not the presence of closely spaced structures but rather the intimate interaction of substantial numbers of people in a given geographical space. In other words, urbanness is a form of association where communication and networking, as opposed to isolation, are the norm. I will also argue that mounds (as well as the trading of goods, diffusion of art styles, and spread of technical knowledge) are strong evidence for communication and social interaction.

The early period of medium-size or small villages, coupled with common public works projects in the areas mentioned above, such as the mounds, signified the gradual development of greater population densities and the concomitant expansion of agriculture. This led to the development of cities along the lines envisioned by Rowe (but often of much greater size). Many European archaeologists also imagine that this period was accompanied by the development of nondemocratic political systems (command systems) and by hierarchical social structures. They often use terms such as *chiefdom* to refer to political units and they see social hierarchy in every grave with gift offerings, just as every executed person becomes a human sacrifice, and so on. Basically, these are all projections from their own European and Middle Eastern historical experiences, projections that may have no validity at all for Americans.

Knowing something about contemporary indigenous Americans would lead me to suspect that the mounds and other great works were constructed voluntarily by devoted persons whose spiritual values took precedence over other considerations. I would imagine the republics that constructed these ceremonial (and perhaps educational) centers as being large cooperative systems of together-living persons. But, of course, this is not the perspective of most of my colleagues of European background, who see incipient kingdoms, tribute-states, and empires in the heart circles, and who regard the development of hierarchy and oppression as necessary steps in the long bloody trail of becoming "civilized."

We can turn to the Andes for the earliest large cities in the Americas, and especially to the coast where rich maritime resources coupled with trade led to population concentrations in narrow river valleys. After 3000 B.C. small urban settlements became very common, as at Huaca Prieta in Chicama, where what are assumed to be public buildings have been identified. Rio Seco has two mounds about four meters high to create a raised substructure for an important building. By about 2500 B.C. there were towns with permanent buildings both along the coast and in the highlands, many of which have monumental architecture. The early structures were small, but by the 2000–1500 B.C. period some were enormous.

Rowe describes the site of Aspero as a "huge preceramic center by about 2000 B.C.," with seven mounds, as noted above. No population estimates are given for Aspero, but Las Haldas, north of Lima along the coast, is described as a very large city with perhaps ten thousand or more people. Its area covers a site of two kilometers by one kilometer, and it features a complex and imposing temple structure with sunken circular courts. A date of 1631 B.C. has been obtained for Las Haldas. It was probably the largest city in the Americas at that time (1700–1400 B.C.) and very possibly one of the largest in the world, outside of Kem (Egypt) or Mesopotamia.[12]

Another early *waka* (sacred site) was Chiquitanta (El Paraiso) at the mouth of the Chillon River, Peru. Dating from 1600 B.C., it is considered the largest preceramic complex of monumental architecture yet known in South America, with at least six mounds. The two largest mounds are over three hundred meters long, being built of cut stone, plastered over with clay. In between is a patio with a temple structure at one end. Clearly, such a center required a large population nearby to construct and maintain it.[13] Other urban developments continue to appear thereafter along the Peruvian coast, as at a site in Acarí, dated about 1297–997 B.C. The site may include public buildings and could be a city according to Rowe. By 1000 B.C. the Americans there were cultivating cotton, gourds, lima beans, squash, guava, and peanuts. During this same era, from about 1200–200 B.C., a cultural tradition known as Chavín spread to many centers throughout a great part of Peru. The site after which the culture was named, Chavín de Huantar, is dated from 850–200 B.C., but the tradition itself is worth commenting upon here because of the cat motifs that remind one of similar themes in Olmeca art of the same period. It strongly suggests ideological contact between Mesoamerica and the Andean region, but also contact with Amazonia. Scholars have suggested that Chavín iconography shows an Amazonian tropical forest influence, which is quite understandable since the city is located on a branch of the far-flung Amazon River system.[14]

At this point, it is wise to note that ancient urbanization along the alluvial plains of the Amazon, as well as on the eastern slopes of the Andes, is very likely, but data seems hard to come by. This may, however, ultimately prove to be a key area for American cultural evolution because of the nature of the environment along the rich rivers. In any case, cities of two thousand persons are quite possible along the Amazon, and one Apinayé village had 1,400 persons as late as 1824, even after the effects of disease and slave raids. Robert L. Carneiro has calculated that tropical forest agriculture, centered on manioc, can be extremely productive in the alluvial areas. He states that the Kuikuru, with whom he studied, have an agriculture that is "more productive than horticulture as practiced by the Inca." The average Kuikuru gardener spends only about two hours per day in manioc cultivation, leaving quite a lot of leisure time, and making possible food surpluses.[15] Thus, there are many areas of the Americas where we cannot, as of yet, make any certain statements about urban experiences in ancient times.

The next place where urban developments seem to begin is in the Tollan region of Mexico, along the Gulf Coast but in reach of the Pacific Coast via the Strait of Tehuantepec. The center of San Lorenzo has already been described (1200–900 B.C.) as a major ceremonial and artistic center. But it also required a large adjacent population to aid in all of the earthwork and artistic productions, which included such architectural innovations as U-shaped basalt storm drains with the individual pieces laid end-to-end. (It is noteworthy that a somewhat analogous drain system existed at Chavín in Peru). About two hundred house mounds at San Lorenzo have been located, which could mean a resident population of some size.[16] If this was one of our early American universities, then, of course, these houses could have been for students and faculty.

The period beginning about 900–800 B.C. is fascinating because urban developments and mound building moved forward in many parts of the Americas, from the Andean region north to the Ohio Valley. Is this because there was regular communication, perhaps by maritime and river routes? To my knowledge, no one has adequately studied the tendency of many Native Americans to travel vast distances both for trade (the *pochteca* of Mesoamerica are well known as traders) and for such purposes as learning about new things, seeing new places, and studying under new teachers. Until such a study is carried out we cannot know much about American ancient travelers, but we do know that navigation, both in the Caribbean Atlantic and the Pacific Coast sectors was extremely well developed before 1492 C.E.

About 850 B.C. Chavín in Peru evolved into a major city and center, with an occupation area of about one kilometer by one-half kilometer. Its ruins include a great temple which is considered by some to be one of the most remarkable surviving monuments of American antiquity. As noted, the city has cat motifs and a great pyramid, a north pyramid, a great plaza, and the temple site. Canals were created to run fresh water through the temple. Chavín seems to have reached its peak in 400–200 B.C. Later it survived as a ceremonial center, with habitation areas abandoned.[17]

Farther north, urban developments also occurred in the regions of Guatemala (at Izapa and Kaminaljuyú, for example) and Tollan or Great Tula on the Gulf. Gordon Brotherston tells us that in ancient Mesoamerican texts Tula "is most often presented as the city with which recorded political history itself begins."[18] It is also described as having four parts with twenty towns, which leads me to believe that Tula, Tollan, or Olmeca-Tulapan was a region and not a single city. This is, I believe, borne out by the introduction of Adrian Recinos to the *Popol Vuh*, in which he identifies many cities in Tula including Zuiva and Nonohualco.[19] In any case, Tollan plays a major role in the later history of peoples speaking many different languages (Mayan languages, along with Nahuatl and others) who trace their origins, at least in part, to the many cities of the region.[20] Though the people of the region are called Olmeca they probably were not a single group at all, but rather a cultural tradition. Some archaeologists believe that an Olmeca state or empire existed, but there is no evidence to support any particular theory about social structure. European scholars often interpret the huge basalt heads as being portraits of specific rulers, and other statues are also supposed to be kings or leaders, but numerous other interpretations are possible. For example, if it is true that the American calendar, a writing system, and written mathematics evolved here (which is not certain), then why not imagine that the heads and statues are of great thinkers, inventors of the new tools for recording events and for calculating solar movements?

As noted earlier, La Venta (900–400 B.C.) was one major Olmeca site, among many that have still not been studied or located. A large population was doubtless living in the region, judging from the public works constructed. About the time of La Venta's decline, the *urb* of Tres Zapotes, further north, became significant and maintained cultural connections with Izapa along the Guatemalan Pacific Coast. But also much urbanization was taking place in interior Mexico, as at Cholula where, around 500 B.C., people are said to have arrived from the Olmeca region. The pyramid constructed at Cholula possesses a greater volume than the Cheops pyramid in Kem (Egypt). Its base was 440 meters long and it was formerly higher than 210 feet. This became one of the largest solid single structures in the world. Interestingly, the later great pyramid at Cahokia is 1,080 feet long—compared with 1,440 for Cholula— and at least 100 feet high—about half as high. But both possess a greater mass than the Cheops pyramid.[21]

At about the same time as the growth of Cholula, the Biniza (Zapotec) people began to quicken the pace of urbanization at Monte Alban in Oaxaca. The early period saw the construction of a temple platform with drawings of the "dancers," figures thought by some to portray conquered enemies (but which, of course, could represent a great many other things). The most significant aspect, however, is the presence of hieroglyphs associated with each of the figures. Current knowledge regards this as "the earliest body of writing in Mesoamerica," leading to the idea that "it may be that it was the Zapotec who invented writing and the Mesoamerican calendar." On the other hand, it is quite arguable that Monte Alban was one of the great centers of learning of its day and that scholars of many nations resided there in order to study calendrics and associated disciplines. Eventually, Monte Alban became "a truly urban civilization" with an estimated population of twenty to forty thousand residents. Its ruins cover about nineteen square miles, an area comparable to Thebes in Kem and larger than Rome at its peak.[22]

During this same period, trends towards urbanness accelerated to the south in the Peten region of Guatemala and adjacent areas of Mexico and Belize. The people living in this area are largely Maya-speakers today, but in earlier times there may have been other languages spoken as well. Many smaller towns developed, along with great population density, after about 2000 B.C. Some of these towns may not have ever come to exceed a thousand residents, but people from surrounding hamlets seem to form part of their together-living circles.

On the other hand, large cities and ceremonial centers also appear somewhat later than Izapa and Kaminaljuyú. The latter is considered by some to be one of the greatest of all archaeological sites in the Americas, with a sophisticated culture by 800 B.C. It must have been an extremely large city but, sadly, it has been largely destroyed by the growth of modern Guatemala City.[23]

Further north, cities such as Nakbe and Tikal, to name but two, grow greatly beginning in the 600–500 B.C. period. Some believe that that Nakbe was established first, but Tikal seems to have exceeded it in importance. The latter was built in the midst of a heavily populated countryside covering an area of fifty square miles. In this region "family compounds" are said to be seldom further than five hundred yards apart. Estimates of Tikal's population range from twenty to eighty thousand, making it, without a doubt, one of the world's largest cities prior to its abandonment soon after 889 C.E.[24]

During roughly the same period (600–150 B.C.) the Valley of Mexico was becoming ever more densely populated with many urban settlements such as Cuicuilco. However, it was lacking in major cities in comparison to areas in the south. But another wave of great city-making was soon to begin, preceded slightly by a similar surge in southern Peru and Bolivia.

Rowe tells us that many Andean towns qualify as urban in the period after 700 B.C., but all appear to have been deserted by 3100 A.C. (B.C./A.D. I), with people spreading out in farming communities in fertile river valleys. The one exception was Tiahuanaco (Paypicala) at Lake Titicaca, which may have already been a city in Early Horizon times. Dates indicate its existence from circa 239 B.C. to at least circa 800 C.E.—about eleven hundred years. Tiahuanaco became a great city, with a core area of at least one and one-half by one and one-quarter kilometers. One author states that the Aymara (Colla) people believed that Paypicala (their name for the city) was the middle of the world. In any event, Tiahuanacan cultural influences gradually spread over a vast area.

Another important urban settlement with imposing public buildings was Pucara, located in the Titicaca basin. In the region were several other Pucara-like cities as well. In the Ica Valley along the coast a few "very large urban settlements" also appeared at about the same time (circa 100 B.C.). The Callango (Media Luna) site is one kilometer across with fifteen small adobe mounds (probably public buildings or temples). Later, irrigation canals were built to serve the agricultural needs of the area.[25]

To put things in perspective, we can regard Tiahuanaco, Tikal, Monte Alban, and Cholula as being among the great "new" cities of the post–500 B.C. period. They also were contemporaries of Teotihuacan, Taxim (El Tajin), El Pital, Huari, and other cities that began perhaps slightly later (150 B.C. to 100 C.E.). Interestingly, many of these great cities declined or were abandoned after about 800 C.E. This issue of abandonment is extremely significant, and quite clearly must be examined from a hemispheric perspective. Some scholars focus only upon abandonment in the Valley of Mexico, or in the Peten, or in Peru and Bolivia, when, in fact, the issue is perhaps a continental one.

In any case, from about 3100 A.C. until about 3900 A.C. (800 C.E.) America was home to an incredibly large number of great cities and urban regions, including many that I have not mentioned or that scholars have not even described yet. There is no doubt but that America was far more urbanized than was Europe in this era, especially since Rome and Athens had become much reduced in size after the German invasions.

Far to the north, population densities were increasing in all of the river valleys of Sinaloa, Sonora, and Arizona. An example of gradual urban development is Skoaquik (Snaketown), a Hohokam town along the Gila River. Skoaquik commenced in about 400 B.C. and lasted until 1100–1200 C.E. It went through many phases, often reflecting influences from Mesoamerica including ball courts, irrigation canals, and the construction of a platform mound in circa 500 C.E. It seems to have had about a hundred houses at any given time, thus yielding an in-town population of a thousand or more.[26] The construction of at least three miles of hand-dug canals by 300 B.C. (or earlier) would indicate a large, supportive population in the area, as well as direct contact with Mesoamerica.

About 150 B.C. major urban development commenced in the Valley of Mexico with carefully planned designs featuring avenues and plazas arranged in a systematic manner totally unknown in most European cities of the time. Teotihuacan, soon to be the largest city in the world, came to possess a ceremonial area of seven square miles. It eventually had a population between 125 and 250 thousand persons. The total urbanized zone covers over twenty square kilometers (five times larger than Rome within its walls), but evidence indicates that the entire valley was utilized as a food-producing area for the city, with highly efficient chinampa horticulture around the great lake in the center.

Teotihuacan commenced cityhood with about seventy-five hundred people, but by 150 C.E. it had become much larger (forty-five thousand or more), and impressive public monuments such as the gigantic Pyramid of the Sun had been completed, along with the complex of major north-south and east-west avenues. The discovery that there are seven caves or caverns under the Pyramid suggests that Teotihuacan was connected with the ancient city of Seven Caves in Tabasco (Olmeca-Tulapan). Recinos mentions Vucub-Pec (Seven Caves in Maya) along with Tulan-Zuiva and Vucub-Zivan (Seven Ravines) as being places visited by the Quiché and the Yaqui (a Nahuatl-speaking group) in their migrations. A tradition relating to the origin of the people who established themselves in Anahuac (central Mexico) has them coming from Chicomoztoc, which is said to mean seven caves or ravines also. Thus Teotihuacan was perhaps selected as a sacred site from early times.

Clearly, Teotihuacan became a major spiritual and educational center for Meso-america, as well as a center for trade and manufacturing. In addition to pilgrims and students who were probably attracted from great distances, large numbers of the local people of the Valley of Mexico came to be housed there in some four thousand apart-mentlike dwellings, perhaps exchanging farming for craft activities as the food pro-duction system in the countryside became ever more efficient.

Teotihuacan was a multilingual city, with a barrio of Oaxacan (Zapotec) people, a barrio of people using Early Classic Maya pottery from the Peten, and probably people who spoke Mixtec and Nonohualco languages, the latter from Tabasco. The dominant language of this fantastic City of the Great Spirit (Deity) was perhaps Nahuatl, but this is not certain. Teotihuacan "outposts" existed as far away as Mata-capan on the Vera Cruz coast and at Kaminaljuyú in Guatemala. The influence of the city's lifeways reached virtually throughout Mesoamerica.[27]

Some archaeologists speak of a Teotihuacan "empire" but evidence for such a command state is lacking or ambiguous. Europeans seem to love to discover em-pires, perhaps because Euro-Asian history is so replete with an emphasis on one great command society after another. The fact that cities come to share certain physical similarities is insufficient to establish the existence of a common com-mand state, as one can readily see by comparing Shanghai, Singapore, New York, and Toronto. The appearance of similar features in New York and London, such as subways and tall buildings, does not prove that both belong to the same empire, although they clearly share material traits.

The period from about 3100 A.C. to 3200 A.C. is remarkable for the evolution of several extremely significant cities in both Mesoamerica and South America. It is al-most as if the two areas were following the same rhythm of growth. In the coastal re-gion of Vera Cruz the great centers of Taxim (El Tajin) and El Pital developed. The latter is located on the Nautla River, accessible by small boat from the Gulf of Mex-ico. It is forty miles south of Taxim and features some two hundred structures, in-cluding earthen pyramids more than eighty feet high, most of them covered with stucco. The city center covers almost one mile square but is surrounded by about forty square miles of outlying settlements with raised fields and sophisticated irrigation sys-tems. The population must have been as dense as that of Taxim (which had tens of thousands of residents). Little is known about El Pital because the area was still un-restored and unstudied as of three years ago.[28]

Taxim may have evolved slightly later, but it certainly became a uniquely beautiful center with a remarkable style of architecture, related to that of Maya country in cer-tain respects. It is located on the Tecolutla River, near sites going back to 2900 B.C. Taxim covers 2,550 acres (about four square miles) and seems to have become a ma-jor administrative and religious complex. The city had at least ten ball courts with large-scale irrigation projects and terraced hillside agriculture in the vicinity. Taxim en-dured until about 1100 C.E.[29]

Along the coast of the Andean region many cities developed or grew during the period after 3200 A.C. (100 C.E.). There were large urban sites in the southern valleys of Pisco, Ica, Nasca, and Acarí. Tambo Viejo was the largest urban site in the latter valley, with an area of about one kilometer by one-half kilometer. The greatest city in the southern region was Huari, located twenty-five kilometers to the north of present-day Ayacucho. "The site of Huari is enormous," according to Rowe. The Huari culture included the "construction of very large building complexes consisting of plazas, corridors, and . . . rooms laid out according to a formal plan." Rowe believes that Huari was an imperial city. According to Rowe, "It represents the formation of an imperial state with a well organized administration."[30] Regions that came under Huari influence tended to have a large part of the population concentrated in large cities. This is similar to what was happening at Teotihuacan at the same time.

After about 800 C.E. both Huari and Tiahuanaco were abandoned, although their cultural influences continued to exist until circa 1100 in northern Peru. In any case, "in a large part of southern Peru and Bolivia the abandonment of cities was general." Virtually no new cities were established in the region and "the entire pattern of settlement in large cities was eliminated." Nonetheless, the Ica Valley continued to have imposing ceremonial centers after 800, but settlements were small. Apparently, heart circles had replaced concentrated urban centers.[31]

Further north, however, cities such as Pachacamac continued to thrive until gradually declining in the period between 1100 and the Inca conquest (the fifteenth century). Pachacamac was "a very large city" in circa 800, with a beginning in the 3200 A.C. era. It and Cajamarquilla were already large *urbs* in the 100–800 C.E. period.[32]

Along the north coast of Peru the early pattern had been heart circles, that is, ceremonial centers rather than concentrated cities. This pattern continued, for the most part, during the Moche or Mochica period (about 100 to 750–800 C.E.). The Moche lifeways (named after a single settlement also known as Early Chimu) involved advanced irrigation systems, heavy use of crops such as maize, beans, avocados, squash, chili peppers, manioc, potatoes, coca and peanuts, heavy reliance on seafood, and the use of tamed llamas, guinea pigs, and muscovy ducks. The people built huge pyramids, including the famous Huaca (*waka*) del Sol, a massive adobe brick structure with 50 to 140 million bricks used in the construction. The mound is 135 feet high and covers about twelve and a half acres (450 feet wide by 1,200 feet long). It is comparable to those at Cholula and Cahokia.

The Mochica peoples were sophisticated metalworkers and wonderful artists, producing unique portraitlike ceramics of the finest possible quality. They traded in all directions. The population was very dense, in spite of the absence of large cities. One place, Pampa Grande in the Lambayeque Valley, had pyramids surrounded by an expansive urban center supporting ten thousand people. Some scholars think that the Mochica were highly warlike, since armed men are often illustrated in their art. Interestingly, the archaeologists seldom comment upon the highly erotic nature of Mochica art.

In any event, the Mochica lifeways were modified in the 750–900 period when influences from the south, called Tiahuanacoid by some and Huari by others, became dominant. The southern ways included the introduction of cities, and Rowe notes that there were many large and imposing cities as a result. But by 1100 C.E. local lifeways began to revive, leading into the Chimu culture.[33]

During this general period, the Calusa people (or their predecessors) in southern Florida were constructing mounds along the coast. One was first inhabited in 50 C.E. while others were built in stages between 600 and 1400. Significantly, these mounds have yielded papaya seeds and chili pepper seeds, the first in the U.S. (dated about 3100 A.C.). This illustrates direct contact with the Caribbean and, via the Caribbean, perhaps with South America as well.[34]

The region of northern Central America and southern Mexico, similar to Peru, Bolivia, and central Mexico, was going through a great period of urban development in the period of 250–900 (3350–4000 A.C.), so much so that this has been referred to for years as the Classic Period. There were numerous great cities in addition to Nakbe and Tikal, such as Copan, Palenque, Becan, and Dzibilchaltun, to name but a few. The latter is said to have had forty thousand people at its peak, while Tikal may have had up to 125 thousand. Perhaps some three million persons were living in the lowlands of Peten, Yukal-Peten (Yucatan), and adjacent areas. One might consider the entire region urbanized or, at least, consider all areas urban-linked. Cobá, an important city in Yucatan, with a twelve-tiered pyramid, has a dated monument of November 30, 780, which also counts back 1,422,000 days to the date of August 11, 3114 B.C., or what I am calling year 1 A.C. In any case, the great cities in much of the area were abandoned around 900 (4000 A.C.) just as in southern Peru and Bolivia. No one knows why such abandonments occurred in either region, although many theories exist including one focused on revolts by the *macewalob* (the *macehuales*, or common people).[35]

Some of the Maya-like people seem to have moved north for a time into central Mexico. The city of Cacaxtla, near Cholula and Tlaxcala, is thought to have been founded by Olmeca-Xicalanca from the Gulf Coast, perhaps being the Xicalanca capital after 650. The city features elaborate murals of a Maya type (but, of course, art knows no ethnic boundaries and always transcends language distinctions). Cacaxtla seems to have been very carefully abandoned in about 900 (4000 A.C.).[36] Various chronicles of Maya peoples, such as the *Popol Vuh*, indicate many migrations during this era, primarily from Olmeca-Tulapan (Tabasco) into Yucatan, Peten, and highland Guatemala, perhaps. Some of the migrants were possibly non-Maya in origin, such as Ah Zuytok Tutul Xiu (987–1007) who took up residence at Uxmal and whose group remained dominant there until the Spanish invasion. The Tutul Xius were said to be from Nonoual (or Nonoualco) in Olmeca-Tulapan by one chronicle.

It would seem that at about this time, a group of Toltecas (people from Tollan or Olmeca-Tulapan) migrated into the Valley of Mexico. There they joined forces with some Chichimec people led by Mixcoatl (Cloud Serpent) and founded the new city of Tula to the north. The spiritual figure of Quetzalcoatl is intimately connected with this new Tula and, indeed, with old Tollan as well. One source tells us that Quetzalcoatl was associated with the Nonoalco people of Tabasco, and, as we shall see, that is where Topiltzin Quetzalcoatl returned after the fall of this new Tula (in 1064 according to the Cuauhtitlan Annals, but perhaps later according to some scholars). Tula became a very impressive city, with an art style that later influenced Chichén Itzá. Some scholars believe that Tula was the capital of a kingdom or empire and that the Toltecas were quite warlike, but other evidence suggests exactly the opposite type of culture. In any case, Topiltzin Quetzalcoatl was forced eventually to flee to the Gulf coast and from thence to Tabasco and Yucatan.[37]

Significantly, during this period, when the new Tula existed and many cities were being abandoned in Mesoamerica, there was a quickening of the pace of urbanization in the north. In southern Arizona the Hohokam entered into the so-called colonial period from 500 to 900 C.E., during which their area of cultural influence expanded. The prevalence of Mesoamerican ball courts, which were played upon using rubber balls, shows direct trade with the rubber-producing regions of the Mesoamerican tropical lowlands. Between 900 and 1100 the Hohokam culture reached its peak, with villages concentrated near the Gila and Salt Rivers. More irrigation canals were dug and pottery manufacturing reached the stage where thirty-gallon jars could be produced. Pottery was traded widely, and copper balls from Mexico were obtained. At the same time, the size of towns in northern Arizona, New Mexico, and Sonora was increasing, while a similar process was occurring in the Mississippi Valley and its tributaries. This stage was probably due to increased mastery and/or adoption of maize horticulture, along with resultant population increases and perhaps the acceptance of an urban way of living.[38]

The origins of what is known as Mississippian culture are not entirely clear, but by the period of 700–1000 the major elements of the way of life seem to have emerged. Typically, social units seem to have included a major town and ceremonial center with a number of outlying hamlets, a still larger number of farmsteads, and resource gathering locations, such as quarries and fishing locations. The larger towns had platform mounds around an open plaza, with structures located on top of the mounds in the southern Mesoamerican style. The larger mounds were built over a period of three hundred years or more, thus indicating stability as well as devotion. According to James B. Griffin,

> Towns vary in size, but a population of three to five hundred would probably be the norm. A population of over one thousand would have indicated a major town, while sites like Cahokia, Moundville (Alabama), or Angel in southwestern Indiana are unusual with populations of two to five thousand or perhaps even ten thousand for the central Cahokia area at its peak.[39]

In the Ohio Valley region a tradition known as Hopewell preceded Mississippian influence and spread outward between 900 and 1300. This tradition featured large communal projects such as burial mounds and great earthworks. One site has an elevated circular platform five hundred feet in diameter, reached by a graded six-hundred-foot-long road. At the other end of the road is an oval area enclosed by a low earthen rampart twenty feet wide. Inside are burial mounds. The Hopewell people are said to have been the finest metalworkers in pre-European North America. They traded very widely, with a network covering all of eastern North America and extending as far west as the Rocky Mountains.[40]

In the Southwest and northwest Mexico, urbanization increased rapidly after about 900 (4000 A.C.), with the construction of large towns that are often in the form of row houses or apartments arranged in an arc or in a rectangle, or in the shape of an E. Generally, most towns at this time were compact masses of contiguous rooms (from twenty to about a thousand). During this period many of the Great Pueblos of Arizona and New Mexico were built including Pueblo Bonito (919–1130), Aztec (1110–1121), Mesa Verde area (1073–1262), White House (1060–1275), Showlow (1174–1393), and Yellowjacket (southwest Colorado, 950–1300). Yellowjacket was the largest city in Colorado and it contained the highest density of ceremonial structures found in the Southwest. Also included in the city were 182 kivas, a great kiva, 17 towers, and a great tower. Some room blocks were three stories high. About thirty thousand persons may have resided at Yellowjacket and in the adjacent fertile Montezuma Valley at its peak in the mid-1200s, whereas about four thousand persons are estimated to have been living in the nearby Mesa Verde cliff dwellings at about the same time.

It is clear that many of the pueblos of the Southwest were ceremonial centers in the same sense as were the centers of the Mississippi, Mesoamerica, and Andean regions. The difference seems to be the use of kivas going down into the earth rather than breasts going up into the sky. But both made use of plazas, apparently for ceremonial activity, even as they do today. One also should not overlook the educational functions of such large centers. Recently scholars have begun to examine the elaborate system of trails leading in virtually all directions from the great Chaco Canyon centers and have also begun to question whether some of these towns were not primarily religious or educational centers.

Pueblo Bonito, built in an arc shape, had at least eight hundred rooms and many stories. Aztec, also related to the Chacoan tradition, had at least three stories with 221 rooms in the lower story, 119 in the second, and 12 in the third, but much has been destroyed over the years. Strangely, Aztec was abandoned about 1130 and then reoccupied in 1220–1260, perhaps in response to environmental factors. In 1276–1299 tree-rings indicate a severe drought in the region, and at about that time most of the large cities were abandoned.[41]

New towns began to be established in the Rio Grande Valley as well as to the south of the Chaco region. An example is San Marcos (1100–1680), south of

Santa Fe. Immigrants, perhaps from the Four Corners, swelled its population along with that of other pueblos in the vicinity. San Marcos had two or more stories, with twenty-two room blocks surrounding five large plaza areas. It had about two thousand ground-floor rooms, with perhaps five thousand rooms in all (although not necessarily occupied at the same time). Clearly, the population was very substantial. In 1680, after Spanish oppression and diseases had taken a toll, six hundred persons were still residing there.[42]

Many of the new towns established after 1300 (some went back to 1150 and just grew after 1300) were—and are—quite large. They frequently were multistoried, some going up to four stories in height. These cities had streets and plazas and good-sized populations, with many exceeding a thousand residents. Pecos, a very large pueblo, had perhaps two thousand residents and was four stories high in 1590. In modern times the populations of such survivors as Isleta, Laguna, Santo Domingo, and Zuni have all exceeded a thousand, while many others have been close to that figure. Among these are our oldest continually occupied cities, including such places as Acoma, Oraibi, and Taos.[43]

During the same era, peoples of the Mogollon-Mimbres tradition inhabited many pueblos in Arizona and vicinity, eventually building Casa Grande and Pueblo Grande near Phoenix. Casas Grandes, Chihuahua, and Sahuaripa, Sonora, were large pueblos in north Mexico.[44] Most of the towns were abandoned after 1400–1450, in a trend similar to what happened in many parts of the Mississippi Valley.

Turning to South America, the period of 1200–1400 witnessed the growth of the great city of Chan Chan, whose ruins still cover an area of up to eleven square miles and whose population was estimated at between fifty thousand and two hundred thousand persons (probably making it larger than any other city in the world, outside perhaps of eastern or south Asia, until the rise of Tenochtítlan). Chan Chan had a harbor at its west wall, with docks that could be closed with gates. It had a well-laid-out plan of residential districts with gardens, pyramids, and extensive irrigation canals (one seventy-three miles long). The Chimu culture possessed great engineers, indicating an advanced educational system. They were able, for example, to construct a huge dam in the Nepeña Valley. Chan Chan is said to have been the largest premodern city in South America, but the great metropolis declined before the rise of the Inca State.[45] The latter's culture did not favor large cities, organizing the people instead into smaller cities with granaries and intensive agricultural zones. The major exception was Cuzco, the capital, which was a carefully planned city laid out in the form of a puma. In the early 1500s Cuzco had some four thousand residential buildings, along with neighborhoods serving particular social functions in keeping with the Incan "welfare state" system of production and rational planning.

Further north, large cities continued to exist in Mexico, as at Mayapan in Yucatan (1250–1350) where eleven to twelve thousand people lived, and at Dzibilchaltun, with even a larger population, as noted.[46] Many cities had disappeared throughout

Mexico, but in the central area, Cholula, Atzcapotzalco of the Tepanecas, Culhuacan, Texcoco, and others remained fairly large. In 1325 the people known as the Aztecs or Mexicas founded Tenochtítlan on an island in the Lake of Texcoco and during the 1400s it became, with its close neighbor Tlaltelolco, the greatest city in the world, perhaps the greatest city ever created by human beings anywhere.

Much can be written about Tenochtitlan, but I will be very brief. Its population is variously estimated at from one hundred thousand to two hundred thousand (or much more), but all agree on the incredible beauty and "modernity" of the city—with its geometrical arrangement of both streets and canals, its causeways and freshwater aqueduct to the mainland, and its some two hundred thousand canoes operating on the lake and along the canals. It was a thoroughly planned city with public health concerns of a startlingly advanced nature. The removal of hazardous trash and feces and the provision of fresh water and plentiful food supplies made Tenochtitlan a model city. However, we should note that it was probably patterned in this respect after earlier cities in the Americas. All of this was destroyed by the invading Spaniards.[47]

In many parts of America, large settlements existed. Unfortunately, time and space does not allow for a careful documentation of cities in the Caribbean or in many other areas. One example will suffice to show, however, that many Americans were town-dwellers, even in regions we might normally think of as being rural. Scholars have found that a Mandan town in North Dakota in the 1550–1675 period covered 3.43 hectares and had 103 dwellings, surrounded by a ditch and palisaded earthwork on three sides (with the river on the fourth). Long rectangular houses were aligned in rows, with an open plaza in the center and a large rectangular structure located therein, probably a ceremonial building. Ethnographic data supports a population of some ten to fifteen persons per dwelling, and so the town very much resembles many small cities located in other regions, such as the Mississippi and Ohio Valleys. After European contact the size of northern plains towns declined greatly.[48]

Meanwhile, in the Mississippi Valley and throughout much of the southeastern U.S. the Mississippian tradition reached its peak of development after 1100–1200. Many large and impressive ceremonial centers and associated cities typify the period, represented especially by huge centers in such places as Moundville (Alabama), Angel (Indiana) and Cahokia (Illinois). The largest and probably the greatest was Cahokia, a city that not only featured its own group of impressive mounds, but that also stands at the center of hundreds of other mounds within a radius of seven miles. One of its early visitors compared its population with that of Philadelphia in 1811 (a city of fifty thousand). But it was more than simply a residential, commercial, and ceremonial metropolis. It appears also to have been a major calendric and astronomical center with many "circles" designed to record solar movements precisely. A beaker found in an offertory pit near a winter solstice sunrise position has on it a cross symbol remarkably like the Maya symbol for sun and time. Cahokia is also thought to have been a political center, controlled by a ranked, hierarchical society, but such opinions simply do not jibe with the political behavior of the people who are descended from the Cahokians, namely many Siouan-speakers (and perhaps others, including Iroquoians and Algonkians).

A decline seems to have occurred after 1300–1400 for many of the large cities, especially north of Memphis. The end is said to be abrupt in southeastern Missouri (c. 1350) but perhaps a bit later elsewhere. To the south, however, some areas showed new growth, and large towns still existed in 1541 when the Spaniards invaded the southeast and caused a massive decline in population. For example, the city of Etowah in Georgia, founded around 1200, reached its peak of about three thousand persons just before 1500. Some mounds and associated villages continued in use until the eighteenth century in the lower Mississippi Valley, as among the Natchez and Choctaw.[49]

Over vast areas of America the Native peoples lived highly urbanized lives for many millennia. Other Americans lived in sizable towns of a permanent character, usually with many other nearby towns in the region. Often ceremonial centers and heart circles were associated with these cities and towns. Much of this was destroyed by the European invasions and by the resulting population declines and dislocations. But we need to be able to study the earlier centuries if we are to fully comprehend our aboriginal American heritage. Our concepts should not be formed wholly by the period of European intrusion.

Notes

1. Jack D. Forbes, "Nature and Culture: Problematic Concepts for Native Americans," *Ayaangwaamizin: The International Journal of Indigenous Philosophy* 1, no. 1 (Winter 1997): 3–22.

2. John H. Rowe, "Urban Settlements in Ancient Peru" in Daniel R. Gross, ed., *Peoples and Cultures of Native South America* (New York: Doubleday, 1973), 51–4.

3. David Perlman, "Mexican Cave's 10,000 Year-Old Surprise," *San Francisco Chronicle*, May 9, 1997, A2. See also Michael Coe, Dean Snow, and Elizabeth Benson, *Atlas of Ancient America* (New York: Facts On File, 1989), 89–90.

4. James B. Griffin, "Comments on the Late Prehistoric Societies of the Southeast," in David H. Dye and Cheryl Anne Cox, eds., *Towns and Temples Along the Mississippi* (Tuscaloosa: Univ. of Alabama Press, 1990), 5–7.

5. Peveril Meigs, "Peru's Coastal Deserts," *Unesco Courier*, March 1966, 14; Coe, Snow, and Benson, *Atlas*, 178; Brian Fagan, "Maize, the Staff of Life," *American Archaeology* 1, no. 2 (Summer 1997): 10–11.

6. Coe, Snow, and Benson, *Atlas*, 90, 177–8; "Atlanta's Earliest Industry," *American Archaeology* 1, no. 2 (Summer 1997): 24–5.

7. *The Archaeological Conservancy Newsletter*, Fall 1996, 4–5. See also Martha Ann Rolingson, "The Toltec Mounds Site," in Bruce D. Smith, ed., *The Mississippian Emergence* (Washington: Smithsonian, 1990), 45.

8. Coe, Snow, and Benson, *Atlas*, 173, 175, 177; Rowe, "Urban Settlements," 54–5, 72.

9. Michael D. Coe, *The Maya* (New York: Praeger, 1966), 46; Frederick A. Peterson, *Ancient Mexico* (New York: Capricorn, 1962), 33; Coe, Snow, and Benson, *Atlas*, 94–102.

10. Howard La Fay, "The Maya, Children of Time," *National Geographic* 148, no. 6 (December 1975): 733; *The Archaeological Conservancy Newsletter* (Spring 1992): 6; Coe, *The Maya*, 47–8; Coe, Snow, and Benson, *Atlas*, 100, 102, 114.

11. Rowe, "Urban Settlements," 56; *The Archaeological Conservancy Newsletter,* Winter 1996–97, 3; C.W. Ceram, *The First American* (New York: Harcourt, Brace, Jovanovich, 1971) 212–19; Thomas H. Maugh, Jr., "New-Found Site in Jungle May Be First Maya City," *Los Angeles Times,* November 14, 1989, sec. A, p. 31.

12. Rowe, "Urban Settlements," 54–5; Coe, Snow, and Benson, *Atlas*, 54–55.

13. Coe, Snow, and Benson, *Atlas*, 175.

14. Rowe, "Urban Settlements," 55–6, 61, 72–3; Coe, Snow and Benson, *Atlas*, 178–81.

15. Robert L. Carneiro, "Slash and Burn Cultivation Among the Kuikuru and Its Implications . . ." in Daniel R. Gross, *Peoples and Cultures of Native South America* (New York: Doubleday, 1973), 104–8, 122n.

16. Coe, Snow, and Benson, *Atlas*, 100.

17. Rowe, "Urban Settlements," 61, 72–3; and Coe, Snow and Benson, *Atlas*, 178–81.

18. Gordon Brotherston, "Tula: Touchstone of the Mesoamerican Era," New Scholar, 10 (1986): 26.

19. Adrian Recinos, *Popol Vuh*, trans. by Delia Goetz and Sylvanus G. Morley (Norman: Univ. of Oklahoma Press, 1950), 62.

20. Brotherston, "Tula," 21–4, 26, 28; Recinos, *Popol Vuh*, 62–5.

21. Brotherston, "Tula," 22, 25; Peterson, *Ancient Mexico*, 48, 56–7, 63; Coe, *The Maya*, 46; Ceram, *First American*, 216; Coe, Snow and Benson, *Atlas*, 94–101.

22. Coe, Snow and Benson, *Atlas*, 102, 113; *The Archaeology Conservancy Newsletter*, Spring 1992, 6.

23. Coe, *The Maya*, 47–8; La Fay, "The Maya," 733; Norman Hammond, "Unearthing the Oldest Known Maya," *National Geographic* 162, no. 1 (July 1982): 128–30, 133.

24. William R. Coe, "The Maya, Resurrecting the Grandeur of Tikal," *National Geographic* 148, no. 6 (December 1975): 793, 795; Maugh, "New-Found Site," sec. A, p. 2, 31.

25. Rowe, "Urban Settlements," 56–7, 59–61, 64, 69, 74; Cottie Burland, Irene Nicholson, Harold Osborne, *Mythology of the Americas* (London: Hamlyn, 1970), 326.

26. Emil W. Haury, "The Hohokam," *National Geographic* 131, no. 5 (May 1967): 674, 676–7, 682, 685, 690–91, 695.

27. Recinos, *Popol Vuh*, 62; Peterson, *Ancient Mexico*, 51, 61; Coe, Snow and Benson, *Atlas*, 104–6, 109, 112; Thomas C. Patterson, *America's Past* (Glenview: Scott, Foresman, 1973), 76, 78, 86, 88–9.

28. John Rice, "Ancient Ruins Discovered on Coast of Mexico," *Yakama Nation Review* (February 11, 1994): 4.

29. S. Jeffrey K. Wilkerson, "Man's Eighty Centuries in Vera Cruz," *National Geographic* 158, no. 2 (August 1980): 204, 213–20; Peterson, *Ancient Mexico*, 59.

30. Rowe, "Urban Settlements," 56.

31. Rowe, "Urban Settlements," 62–4, 67–70.

32. Rowe, "Urban Settlements," 65, 68, 71.

33. Rowe, "Urban Settlements," 65, 68, 71; Richard P. Schaedel, "Mochica Murals At Pañamarca," in John Rowe and Dorothy Menzel, *Peruvian Archaeology* (Palo Alto: Peck, 1967), 105–6, 108, 110–12; Gerdt Kutscher, "Iconographic Studies as an Aid in the Reconstruction

of Early Chimu Civilization," in Rowe and Menzel, *Peruvian Archaeology*, 115–16, 118–19; Burland, *Mythology*, 297, 342; Walter Alva, "New Tomb of Royal Splendor," *National Geographic* 177, no. 6 (June 1990): 2, 6; Christopher B. Donnan, "Masterworks of Art Reveal a Remarkable Pre-Inca World," *National Geographic* 177, no. 6 (June 1990): 17–33, 41; Michael E. Moseley and Carol J. Mackey, "Chan Chan, Peru's Ancient City of Kings," *National Geographic* 143, no. 3 (March 1973): 332–3, 336.

34. Arden Arrington, "Learning From the Fierce People," *American Archaeology* 1, no. 2 (Summer 1997): 21–2; *The Archaeology Conservancy Newsletter*, Fall 1996, 3, 5.

35. La Fay, "The Maya," 729, 732–3, 760, 762; Coe, Snow, and Benson, *Atlas*, 124, 127; George E. Stuart, "The Maya, Riddle of the Glyphs," *National Geographic* 148, no. 6 (December 1975): 773, 785; Peterson, *Ancient Mexico*, 52–3.

36. George E. Stuart, "Mural Masterpieces of Ancient Cacaxtla," *National Geographic* 182, no. 3 (September 1992): 123, 134, 136.

37. Coe, Snow, and Benson, *Atlas*, 134; La Fay, "The Maya," 763; Brotherston, "Tula," 21; Recinos, *Popul Vuh*, 63–5.

38. Paul S. Martin, George I. Quimby, and Donald Collier, *Indians Before Columbus* (Chicago: Univ. of Chicago Press, 1947), 174, 182.

39. James B. Griffin, "Comments on the Late Prehistoric Societies in the Southeast," in Dye and Cox, *Towns and Temples*, 5, 7–8. See also Rolingson, "Toltec Mounds," 45.

40. Ceram, *First American*, 222; Martin, Quimby, and Collier, *Indians*, 267, 272, 277.

41. "Saving the Anasazi Heartland," *American Archaeology* 1, no. 2 (Summer 1997): 23; Martin, Quimby, and Collier, *Indians*, 124, 129; Ceram, *First American*, 83–7, 132.

42. *The Archaeological Conservancy Newsletter*, Fall 1996, 1–2.

43. Ceram, *First American*, 52, 71; Martin, Quimby, and Collier, *Indians*, 149–50, 162.

44. Martin, Quimby, and Collier, *Indians*, 188, 196. Francisco de Ibarra was impressed by Sahuaripa in 1565.

45. Pál Kelemen, *Art of the Americas* (New York: Crowell, 1969), 38; Meigs, "Costal Deserts," 14–15; Michael E. Moseley and Carol J. Mackey, "Chan Chan, Peru's Ancient City of Kings," *National Geographic* 143, no. 3 (March 1973): 318, 320–22, 324, 328; Patterson, *America's Past*, 74–5.

46. Coe, Snow, and Benson, *Atlas*, 136.

47. Patterson, *America's Past*, 74; Coe, Snow, and Benson, *Atlas*, 145, 150.

48. James Brooks, "Household Archaeology on the Middle Missouri," ms. 1989, 2.

49. Melvin L. Fowler, "Mound 72 and Early Mississippian at Cahokia," in James B. Stoltman, *New Perspectives on Cahokia, Views From the Periphery* (Madison: Prehistory Press, 1991), 1, 3, 8–9; Ceram, *First American*, 216; Martin, Quimby, and Collier, *Indians*, 283, 353–4, 409, 411; Griffin, "Late Prehistoric Societies," 14–15. George J. Armelagos and M. Cassandra Hill, "An Evaluation of the Biocultural Consequences of the Mississippian Transformation," 27–8; James E. Price and Cynthia R. Price, "Protohistoric/Early Historic Manifestations in Southeastern Missouri," 59; Dan F. Morse, "The Nodena Phase," 76, 94–6; R. Barry Lewis, "The Late Prehistory of the Ohio-Mississippi Confluence Region . . . ," 54–5; Stephen Williams, "The Vacant Quarter," 173–7, 179; Gerald P. Smith, "The Walls Phase," 167–8; David H. Dye and Cheryl Anne Cox, "Introduction," i; all in Dye and Cox, *Towns and Temples*. George E. Stuart, "Etowah: A Southeast Village in 1491," *National Geographic* 180, no. 4 (October 1991): 61.

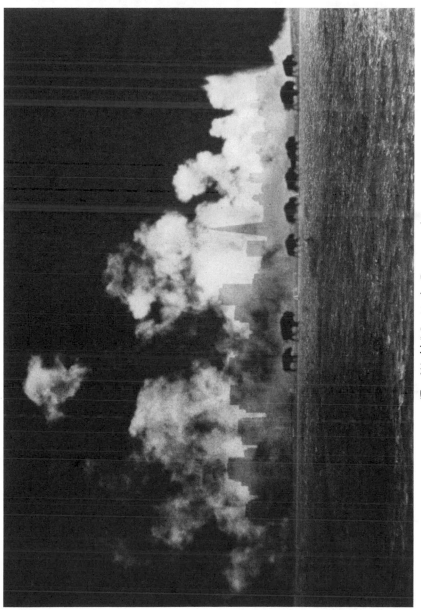

"Two Worlds" © 1993 by Dugan Aguilar

Telling the Indian Urban

Representations in American Indian Fiction

2

CAROL MILLER

⊞

END-OF-CENTURY DEMOGRAPHIC INFORMATION reveals that a surprisingly large number of Indian people—almost half of the approximately two million who identified themselves as Native American in the last census—now live away from reservation and trust lands. Except for the fact that the American Indian population is significantly younger and growing more rapidly than that of the nation as a whole—a fact that has been true for decades but is confounding to presumptions of doom and vanishing—a descriptive profile reveals information that mostly confirms what Indian people already know: our population is significantly poorer and at greater risk than the nation's at large. The proportion of American Indian families living below the official poverty level is, in fact, almost three times that of all families taken together, and the per capita income of Indians is less than half that of whites. Indians also have higher death rates attributable to accidents, suicides, and homicides; and the second leading cause of death for Native young adults is directly linked to the effects of alcoholism.[1]

Frequently motivated by poverty at home and the promise of greater economic opportunity elsewhere, Indian people, especially since World War II, have congregated in growing numbers in urban areas, where the particularities of their lived experience are either largely unexamined by non-Native American society or understood only within the broad categories of stereotype. In popular culture, images of Indianness are seldom associated with town and city spaces, and yet for many individuals and families, those spaces are where they live out their lives—as they have done for several generations. What does urbanization mean for cultural identities and tribal communities? How do ideas of homeland and ancestral values maintain themselves or shift their shapes when they are transformed within urban environments? To what degree, if at all, may this movement be understood as a "(re)taking place"—a double breaking out—both from federally designated boundaries historically intended to isolate and contain Native people and from an equally pervasive confinement within the anachronistic fantasy-wildernesses of the white imagination?

These questions have been consistently addressed by American Indian writers, who have long grappled with postcontact cultural interactions in all the settings—including towns and cities—where they have been acted out. Exploring some of these fictional representations, especially in their relation to one another, is instructive for several reasons. In addition to providing significant information about a consequential and ongoing Native American diaspora essentially ignored by mainstream white society, narratives about urban America as Indian country also reinforce the link between contemporary and ancestral storytelling traditions. And in doing so, they provide an important medium not only for sustaining culture but for creating a significant illustrative resource about the pragmatic business of "going along" in the world, just as the old stories always have done. Imaginative print-language "tellings" that explore intersections of Indianness and urbanization share the serious functionality of traditional Native storytelling, a functionality made even more important because of five hundred years of cultural disruption. The power of stories to influence actuality is certainly what Leslie Marmon Silko asserts in the poem that begins her 1977 novel *Ceremony*:

> I will tell you something about stories,
> [he said]
> They aren't just entertainment,
> Don't be fooled.
> They are all we have, you see,
> all we have to fight off
> illness and death.[2]

This essay argues that American Indian storytellers writing about urban Indian experience participate in specific struggles against illness and death by constructing increasingly diverse and transcendent accounts that counter images of invisibility and victimization. Moreover, in doing so, they frequently reassert a particularly Native American idea of urbanness that expresses positive change and cultural vitality. And viewed within the context of the broader American literary canon, these storytellers contribute significantly to a function of literature that Elizabeth Cook-Lynn has recently lamented as having been left mostly unaddressed in the twentieth century: the power of narrative to "stir the human community to a moral view which would encompass all of humanity, not just selected parts of it."[3]

Even as Native writers represented them in early manifestations, towns were emblematic of both cultural alienation and physical risk or danger. For example, in *Cogewea the Half-Blood*—published in 1927 and credited as one of the earliest novels by an American Indian woman—Mourning Dove (Okanogan) constructs the town as a dehumanizing "othered" space that exposes her Indian characters to degradation and physical threat. Much of the novel, which concerns the conflicted identity and resulting life choices of Mourning Dove's mixed-blood heroine, is set in the already disrupted middle ground of the privately owned ranch belonging to Cogewea's sister and her white husband. Juxtaposed against this culturally mediated space, ancestral home and values are represented by two metonymical sites: the tepee of Stemteema, Cogewea's traditional grandmother, and Buffalo Butte, the girl's favorite haunt—an unspoiled natural space in which spirit voices still have the power to speak.[4] The central problem of the novel is cast in the terms of post-Victorian domestic romance. Will Cogewea be seduced by the urbane but villainous Densmore, her fortune-hunting white suitor, or will she choose Jim, the mixed-blood foreman who loves her? Beneath the surface of melodramatic plotting, the novel's imagined physical spaces take on symbolic significance in their exploration of cultural conflict and integrity.

The town is significant as symbolic space at two narrative moments. In the first, Cogewea visits the town in order to compete in both the "Squaws'" and "Ladies'" horse races, which are part of the white community's annual Fourth of July celebration. Her victory in both races precipitates confrontations that call into question the supposedly civilized behavior of white society while foregrounding the alienating terms of Native and non-Native cultural conflict. Town is the place where, subjected to the sexual insults of the "gentleman whites," Cogewea reflects with regret on "the passing of an epoch, when there were no 'superiors' to 'guide' her simple race to a civilization so manifestly dearth of the primitive law of respect for womanhood" (65). Town is also the place where the breakdown of Native traditions of communality is made evident by the bitterness directed at Cogewea by other Native women because of her mixed-blood status. And town is the place where blatant white racism cheats Cogewea of her deserved recognition as winner of the Ladies' race and threatens Jim with imprisonment and physical violence when he speaks up for fair treatment.

Later, in another suggestion of urban place as symbolic space, the city is the intended destination of Densmore's and Cogewea's disastrous elopement. When the villain's plans are thwarted by the discovery that Cogewea has no wealth of her own, the city is the place to which the exploitative and abusive Densmore flees. It represents an alienated way of living that Cogewea rejects when she ultimately chooses Jim and reinserts herself into the "splendid world" (284) of Buffalo Butte.

In this early representation, therefore—and also in almost every subsequent fictive intersection of Indianness and Euro-American urbanity—town and city spaces are, for Indian people, places of risk, separation, disillusion, and dissolution. Why? Perhaps because Euro-American urban spaces have evolved as sites in which genuinely fundamental differences between Native and non-Native conceptions of place, culture, and relationships of power are brought into sharpest relief. Historian Inga Clendinnen has pointed to the destructive contemporary consequences of centuries of what she identifies as "unassagueable" cultural otherness.[5] Such worries might seem confirmed by the quite distinct and contending ideas held by colonizers and Native people about nature in relationship to civilization and civilized behavior. Within the earliest images of the colonizers' appropriation of the American landscape—their "errand into the wilderness" to construct an idealized "city upon a hill"—there is an implicit tension between nature and civilization and a resulting projection of the need for transformation and cultural imposition. This tension is written indelibly on both the practical outcomes of colonization and on its resulting intellectual and artistic production. The American wilderness represented, after all, a complicated dichotomy within the white imagination: freedom, renewal, and unlimited possibility at one polarity, and anarchy, error, and disappointment at the other. From the beginning, the European sensibility both romanticized and abhorred the "New World" as at once paradisiacal and primitive—but in either case conceived in opposition to Western ideas of civilization. Among those already in residence in this world, there was apparently no such dichotomy. Inverting the categories of civilized and primitive by means of the hindsight of several centuries of postcontact experience, Luther Standing Bear would write, "Only to the white man was nature a 'wilderness' and only to him was the land 'infested' with 'wild' animals and 'savage' people."[6]

In its most fundamental character, the very act of "westering"—the European and later Euro-American drive toward the western horizon—involved aspects of separation, isolation, and disillusion that reinforced the dichotomous perspective of migrants to the "New World." The Jeremiad tradition of lamentation of unworthiness as accompaniment to exultant conquest, so apparent in the writings of so many early colonizers, is a reflection of this sense of dividedness. It is present as well in the symbolic and actual dysfunction of the colonizers' first attempts at urbanness. Howard Kushner argues that this dysfunction explains the surprisingly high mortality rate among settlers in Jamestown, one of the earliest "urban" settings established by English settlers, many of whom were apparently so disillusioned by a frontier that was supposed to provide effortless wealth that they starved to death unnecessarily. From an Indian point of view, there is an intriguing irony in Kushner's suggestion that the settlers' appropriation of serotonin-inhibiting maize as their undiversified dietary staple contributed to their dysfunction: "When the vision fell short of its promise, they became depressed and lethargic. Unable to return to a rejected past, they found in self-destruction a viable alternative."[7]

On the one hand, then, were the physical and psychological separations the colonizers imposed upon themselves in order to bring about their objective of establishing a purer civilization than that they were leaving behind. Even more consequential to tribal people of the time were the separations imposed on those already in possession of the American "wilderness" as they were systematically dispossessed of their precontact homelands. The resulting history of contention between the ideals of democracy and the interests of nationalism translated into a permanent psychological dualism that Dolores Hayden has called a "despair about placelessness . . . as much a part of American experience as pleasure in a sense of place."[8]

Such a history of dividedness and contradiction is summed up by D. H. Lawrence's assertion that "the American landscape has never been at one with the whiteman."[9] It is manifested throughout much of the canon of several centuries of "masterwork" American literature predicated upon recursive versions of heroic alienation from place and culture. James Fenimore Cooper's ambivalent idealization of the heroic individualism integral to opening and civilizing the frontier, for example, could never quite be reconciled with his protagonist's elegiac nostalgia for primitive America as an unspoiled natural space. Thoreau, credited as the founder of American nature writing (ironically, from an American Indian perspective), promotes in *Walden* and other journal writing a self-reflexive model of the vision quest derived directly from an appropriated aesthetic authority he establishes at the cost of erasing prior Native presence and possession.[10] Hawthorne's finely drawn tension between the repressiveness of Puritan town life and the liberating lure of the demonic forest creates another field for contradiction, in which the cosmopolitan is set against the "primitive," with characters such as Hester Prynne and Young Goodman Brown paying the price for daring to negotiate a morally and intellectually ambiguous middle ground. Melville's Ishmael survives Ahab's monomaniacal challenge of the natural world perched upon Quequeg's highly metaphorical coffin. And Twain's Huckleberry Finn, navigating the moral currents of the symbolically charged Mississippi, finally rejects his North-South exploration of the border between the frontier and the ethically flawed, "civilized" territory of nineteenth-century America. Carrying on the "westering" fantasy of his progenitors, he strikes out alone toward an imaginary, untrammeled future in California. In the perpetual wilderness of the mythical West, he is the archetypal American cousin of Peter Pan, free from the obligations both of civilization and adulthood.

Moby Dick and *The Adventures of Huckleberry Finn* are both representative American "great books," constructed upon alienated sensibilities and set in action within fragmented landscapes where nature and civilization can never be fully reconciled. Reconciliation, made even less possible by the exacerbated insecurities of twentieth-century modernism and postmodernism, is also largely unattainable within the pantheon of more contemporary "masters"—for example, Faulkner, Fitzgerald, Hemingway, Salinger, and Pynchon—whose most indicative works focus on the failures of individuals to come to terms either with each other or with the corrupted natural, urban, and even entropic galactic landscapes that surround them. Their storytelling offers a vicarious projection of the alienation that results when individualism cannot be integrated into community, or when community is finally imagined but fails to mesh with the actual shortcomings of lives lived within it.

Our Indian ancestors who might have been contemporaries of Ishmael or Huckleberry Finn, and who were engaged in life and death struggles to preserve the integrity of their own particular communities, would surely have considered such contradictory being as pathological—some form of soul sickness. They would not have understood a view that considered individuals unconnected to their societies, or that divided the human world from the natural one or from that of the other sentient beings, human or otherwise, who "peopled" the immediate environment. This is the distinction critic William Bevis introduces in his examination of "homing" as a distinctive structural and thematic feature of many contemporary narratives by American Indian writers. "Native American nature is urban," Bevis writes.

> The connotation to us of 'urban,' suggesting a dense complex of human variety, is closer to Native American 'nature' than is our word 'natural.' The woods, birds, animals, and humans are all 'downtown,' meaning at the center of action and power, in complex, unpredictable and various relationships.[11]

If human and natural worlds are unified rather than divided, traditional cultures have no impetus for conceiving nature as wilderness or as in any sense primitive. Within the relational epistemologies of most Native peoples, the earth is almost universally mother; the sun may be father; the moon, grandmother; and human and non-human entities are bound together in ancestral kinships and clan connections based upon interdependence and obligation. Place and person are inextricably bound. The elements constituting place are as much character as setting, participants in complex and unifying systems of kinship that help to define how civilization itself is constructed and maintained. Culture exists within what Keith Basso has called a "place-world," significant because "what people make of their places is closely connected to what they make of themselves as members of society and inhabitants of the earth." [12] It is not illogical then, that traditional Indian communities situated in their natural settings of complex activity and interrelationship would have considered that very quality of culturally determined and specialized urbanness an essential component of their conception of themselves as civilized.

Dakota writer and ethnologist Ella Deloria presents exemplary portraits of the traditional Dakota camp circle as urban in precisely Bevis's sense of dense and varied social constructions in two books, *Speaking of Indians* and *Waterlily*, both apparently drafted in the 1940s but published more than forty years apart. In the former, Deloria describes an ideal community based on a "scheme of life that worked," a community that understood itself to be highly civilized, that prized its civilization as crucial to functional existence, and that had developed sophisticated social codes to maintain that civilization.[13] "I can safely say," Deloria writes,

> that the ultimate aim of Dakota life, stripped of accessories, was quite simple: One must obey kinship rules; one must be a good relative. . . . Without that aim and the constant struggle to attain it, the people would no longer be Dakotas in truth. They would no longer be even human. To be a good Dakota, then, was to be humanized, civilized. And to be civilized was to keep the rules imposed by kinship for achieving civility, good manners, and a sense of responsibility toward every individual dealt with. Thus only was it possible to live communally with success; that is to say, with a minimum of friction and a maximum of good will (25).

Deloria had been a field worker for Franz Boas, and she uses the skills of both sto-ryteller and ethnographer to show how this ultimate aim of civilized behavior was pragmatically attained in people's everyday interactions. In the extended fictional narrative *Waterlily*, unpublished until 1988, the voice is the teller's. The story cen-ters on the personal, family, and community interrelationships of a young Dakota woman residing in a traditional camp circle seemingly untouched by cultural dis-ruption. As such, it presents a detailed portrait of the complex and indissoluble in-terdependencies of individual and communal well-being based on an unshakable premise of biological and social kinship relations and an economic system of dis-tributing wealth by "giving to get." Significantly, in the cosmology of the observ-ing Dakotas, it is whites who are considered primitive because of their inhumane treatment of their own children. And when small pox introduced by whites deci-mates the tightly bonded social circle that cannot imagine the necessity of isolat-ing those who are ill, the epidemic works as a figure foreshadowing broader philo-sophical tensions between individualism and communality that distinguish non-Native and Native cosmologies. Deloria's narrative illustrates how the very essence of civilized conduct within traditional Native societies derives from that particularized sense of communal urbanness in which, Bevis argues, identity be-comes "for a Native American, . . . not a matter of finding 'one's self,' but of find-ing a 'self' that is transpersonal and that includes a society, a past, and a place."[14]

What happens, however, when this exemplary idea of indigenous urbanness grounded in the matrices of communality, tradition, and homeland is exposed to the stresses of Westernized urbanization? Deloria addressed that question in *Speak-ing of Indians*, published in 1944, toward the end of World War II, which dramati-cally accelerated the urbanization of Indian people as large numbers of Native men and women entered the armed services or moved to the cities to work in war in-dustries.[15] Speaking of—talking about rather than to—Indians, Deloria attempts to predict the impact of these changes from the perspective of an insider and to speculate about their effects both on those left in traditional communities and those who have "moved into the cities and are meeting problems they have never faced before" (145). Her purpose is not merely to valorize the traditional past but to contextualize that past by referencing it against the present and future of post-war America. She imagines a model of sojourning rather than of permanent mi-gration, since "many Indians cannot yet feel complete with just their little family, their spouse and children"(146). Of those who had become city dwellers, Deloria argues that their traditional backgrounds include virtues that make them excellent workers. Demands non-Natives take for granted, however—paying rent, handling larger amounts of money than have ever been available before, securing child care—are foreign and discomfiting. Acknowledging and to some degree even wel-coming intensified pressures to assimilate, Deloria also imagines new demands for agency and authority as Native people claim what their recent investment in the preservation of democracy has earned them:

> the right to talk the common language of America, and I don't mean just literally, but figuratively as well. That is to say, they will want to participate in the larger thought and life of the land and not be given special work scaled down to their abilities, as if those abilities were static, or to their needs, as if those needs must always be limited to tribal life (148).

Successful adaptation will depend upon white society's willingness to forego paternalism and to provide genuinely equal opportunity and participation. But it will also depend upon a transposition of the elemental parts of that Dakota scheme of the life that worked—those qualities of civilized and fully human community—into the new locations of contemporary experience. Native people, Deloria asserts, must be allowed the motivation of their own values—especially ancestral allegiances to kinship and to the well-being of future generations. Deloria's representation of movement from tribal to urban communities is important for its perception that the culturally specific urbanness of the traditional past offers an effective foundation to create a coherent and productive urban present. But writing at yet another diasporic moment for Indian people, what she cannot or perhaps chooses not to anticipate in any detail is a future in which that foundation is continually undermined by a materialist environment of sustained racism, poverty, and cultural denigration.

Succeeding generations of American Indian writers would address that future. Two of the most successful, writing from the empowered center of what has been called a renaissance of American Indian narrative, undertake constructions of the city in relation to Indianness that may seem on the surface to reiterate each other but more accurately illustrate an evolution of narrative purpose upon which other writers continue to build. Both Scott Momaday, in *House Made of Dawn*, and Leslie Marmon Silko, in *Ceremony*, present post-World War II America as a critical moment of dislocation. Both tell highly intertextual stories engaging the questions posed at the beginning of this discussion. In their contemporary representations, what happens when Indian people leave their traditional communities for new lives in the city? What does city life mean—for them and for the communities they leave behind or to which they return? Momaday, acknowledging the centrality of oral traditions upon which Silko draws in *Ceremony*, has called her book a telling, but he might as correctly have called it a retelling, since, at the surface, the plots and protagonists of Silko's novel and his own seem to echo each other. It may seem, in fact, that in many ways the two stories are actually the same story. The points of plotting and characterization at which they converge, however, suggest older storytelling traditions and employ deliberate recursion to mark the importance of the story both writers choose to tell. Extending from those convergences, Momaday and Silko ultimately draw quite distinct, though complementary, conclusions.

For Momaday, the city represents a site of ultimate exile, the place where his protagonist Abel hits a rock bottom even more destructive than his experience in prison, which Momaday doesn't describe at all. One of Momaday's targets is "relocation"—the federal policy that supposedly attempted to hasten assimilation but resulted instead in the accelerated development of an urban Indian underclass. In Los Angeles, surely among the most alien of alien environments for tribal people, Abel, his friend Benally, and Tosamah, Momaday's urban trickster/Priest of the Sun, each represent aspects of the dysfunction resulting from this dis/relocation. Abel and Benally are assigned dead-end jobs that lead neither up nor out. Tosamah preaches to his displaced "congregation" that they have come to live in the white man's world and on that ground they are "as children, mere babes in the woods."[16] In the reverse-wilderness of the city, they are bombarded by white ways conveyed by the white "Word," which is empty, incomprehensible, and devoid of truth. Benally describes downtown in just those terms—as an alien space where "it's dark . . . all the time, even at noon" (140); where the old men who sell papers are always yelling at you but you don't understand what they're saying. "You know, you have to change," he says. "That's the only way you can live in a place like this. You have to forget about the way it was, how you grew up and all" (148).

Benally has internalized contradiction, separating himself from place and its associations of family and home. He wants—at least he tells himself he does—what the city seems but actually fails to offer—"money and clothes and having plans and going someplace fast" (158). He tries to convince himself that in the tribal place he has left behind, "there's nothing there . . . just the land, and the land is empty and dead. Everything is here. Everything you could ever want. You never have to be alone" (181). Benally seems oblivious of the values Bevis associates with the older indigenous urbanity, attaching his aspirations instead to the material version he finds in L.A. But his life in the city is actually despairingly lonely and hopeless, forcing escape into alcohol and pipe dreams. Occasionally, however, another sort of escape is possible when he allows himself to call up childhood memories of his grandfather telling stories in the firelight of his family's sheep camp. There, he had been "right there in the center of everything, the sacred mountains, the snow-covered mountains and the hills, the gullies and the flats, the sundown and the night, everything—where you were little, where you were and had to be" (157). For Benally, the city is an infectious and deadening environment of alienation.

Momaday refuses to present, however, an image of urban Indianness in unequivocal or stereotypical terms of victimhood. Abel's experience of urbanization appears potentially even more injurious than Benally's since it accelerates a virulent soul sickness already established by a lifetime of disrupted attachments of both family and traditional community. But Abel, the Longhair, resists the city. His time in the city, in fact, brings on a crisis that can only be resolved through resistance and will lead either to annihilation or to reintegration with his traditional world. Far away from his desert home, beaten almost to death by a sadistic cop, lying in a liminal space where he is reached by the sounds of both the sea and the city, Abel feels, hears, and sees something else as well: a restoring vision of the runners after evil who, within the traditional belief system that he has previously found impenetrable, give design and meaning to the universe. This vision will eventually turn him homeward, away from the city. But it does more, suggesting a transcendent cultural and spiritual agency with the power to link landscapes that are tribal and urban, ancient and contemporary.

Even in the city, Momaday insists, visions are possible, people come together to chant and pray, peyote rituals are conducted and, amidst the cacophony of brassy music and street traffic, the Priest of the Sun serves notice that "something holy was going on in the universe" (114). Tosamah preaches that, within the white world, the word, ubiquitous and unreliable, has "as an instrument of creation . . . diminished nearly to the point of no return" (95). His remembering of his grandmother as storyteller illustrates, however, that for Native people, consummate being may yet be derived from the uses of language. Story is the medium that allows the past and those who lived within it to take hold of the imagination so that the listener may confront that which is sacred, eternal, and timeless. Momaday's novel is itself just such an instrument of creation and it points the way to other stories that may function similarly to show Native people how to, as Tosamah says with only partial cynicism, "get yours" (98).

If, in Momaday's cosmology, language is potently creative, it may also be an instrument of destruction, an idea Leslie Marmon Silko takes up in her 1977 novel *Ceremony*. Witchery—a human capacity for destruction and violence in dimensions both personal and political—is the name Silko gives to what she sees as an escalating threat to the survival of all living things. The origins of this capacity are unknowable, but it is set in irrevocable motion by Destroyers who imagine it first in a story—the particular story of the European conquest of the New World. Once in play, Silko imagines, witchery is carried forward in an expansive design of accelerating violence deriving from personal, transpersonal, and transnational culpability. The novel's central narrative strand concerns how this design must be countered by a process of ceremonial regeneration that rejects violence and internalized guilt and restores ancestral balance within human and natural worlds.

Silko's story is set mostly in and around the pueblo community to which her protagonist Tayo returns after his service in World War II, but some of the story unfolds in city spaces—this time Gallup and Albuquerque—presented as dehumanizing outlands that pervert and destroy those who are attracted to them. Tayo's mother is one of those who is destroyed, and Tayo's memories of his time with her living in a tin shelter thrown together in a vagrant camp in Gallup are nightmarishly sordid: a toddler's bewildered endurance of neglect, alcoholism, promiscuity, and violence. In the bars of Gallup where his mother leaves him, "He could not remember when he first knew that cigarettes would make him vomit if he ate them.

He played for hours under the tables, quiet, watching for someone to drop a potato chip bag or a wad of gum" (108).

The meanness of Gallup is far removed from the civilized society Deloria describes—a society based, at least in the ideal, upon the premise of striving to treat everyone as a relative and motivated by its dedication to future generations. Dakota or Pueblo, the fundamental tenets of civilized behavior have been dependent upon communality. Over thousands of years, Silko explains, Pueblo people had shared the same consciousness. "The people had known, with the simple certainty of the world they saw, how everything should be" (68). But the entanglement of tribal and European values has resulted in many kinds of separation:

> All creation suddenly had two names: an Indian name and a white name. Christianity separated the people from themselves . . . because Jesus Christ would save only the individual soul; Jesus Christ was not like the Mother who loved and cared for them as her children, as her family. (68)

Gallup is a foreign, removed site in which the radical breakdown of traditional communality is acted out. But remnants of that shared ancestral consciousness are still strong enough to engender an individual and collective internalization of guilt. Tayo's mother internalizes what the teachers and missionaries tell her about "deplorable ways of the Indian people" (68) and is ashamed enough to break away and go off with the white men in Albuquerque who smile at her as if she were white. Shame deepens her isolation and seals her destruction, but, significantly, it is a collective guilt that will infect not only her family, but the entire community that wants her back. "For the people," Silko writes, "it was that simple, and when they failed, the humiliation fell on all of them; what happened to the girl did not happen to her alone; it happened to all of them" (69). The novel's narrative movement is about how this internalized guilt and humiliation must be purged by a process of ceremonial reintegration. A detail of significance and irony, however, is that one of the principal agents of this reintegration, the mixed-blood medicine man Betonie, resides tenaciously in the hills directly above Gallup. "It strikes me funny," the medicine man says, "people wondering why I live so close to this filthy town. But see, this hogan was here first. Built long before the white people ever came. It is that town down there which is out of place. Not this old medicine man" (118). Like Momaday, Silko is not willing to surrender place, even urban place, as a domain in which ancestral authority is without power and provenance. Like Momaday too, however, her resolution involves her protagonist's necessary return to a contained tribal community. Only the murderous Emo stays outside, migrating to California, which is, we are told, a good place for him. "Westering" for Silko clearly suggests something Mark Twain wouldn't have imagined: a destination of poetic justice for those who perpetuate witchery.

In the more recent *Almanac of the Dead*, Tucson, where Silko herself lives, has become an even more surreal location of perversion and violence, an unredeemable "city of thieves."[17] For Silko, however, the ultimate urban metaphor of postcolonial devastation is real estate developer Leah Blue's dream city: Venice, Arizona. Leah Blue and the capitalist establishment she represents don't care that their faux-Venice, intended for the wealthy and complete with canals and waterways, will require deep-water drilling—the ultimate penetration and despoiling of the Mother for profit. Silko elevates the imagery of urban America to the level of parody—a decadent city of the future imagined as a baldly materialist resuscitation of the European past. In doing so, she undercuts centuries of nationalist exceptionalism and illustrates her largest theme. The compounding destructive synergy of the original theft, which implicated the colonizers' first images of virgin territory made to give way to a city on a hill, can be averted only by a reversal of history and a restoration of tribal land. In *Almanac of the Dead*, Silko's representations of the intersections of Indianness and urban America serve a larger visionary purpose engaged with the preservation of the sacred earth.

Momaday and Silko have created influential representations in which urbanization is essentially figurative: a destructive process culminating in an ultimately universal fatality. Cities in these foundational novels are places to go home from if you can because your own life and those of others depend on it. As the demographics remind us, however, more and more Indian people are living urban lives. Many others have established a pattern of movement between tribal and urban communities. Many do not come from contained tribal communities, do not perceive themselves as sojourners but rather as permanent city dwellers, and may in fact be several generations into complex urban experience in which identity, tribal connections, and notions of culture are shaped anew. Fifty years from the post-war moment of Ella Deloria's gaze, other narrative representations are beginning to emerge that acknowledge that staying within or reintegrating with traditional homeplaces are not the only options for the preservation of viable personal and cultural lives. This discussion concludes by examining two alternative views of how traditional Indian urbanness is transformed within contemporary city spaces.

Ojibway writer Ignatia Broker's little-known narrative *Night Flying Woman* is a genre-stretching blend of fiction and memoir whose central subject is the process of postcontact change and adaptation endured by her several-generations-removed Ojibway ancestors. Broker asserts the ties of the traditional past to a personal/transpersonal urban present by re-membering that past but finally returning to the context of the contemporary moment. Her narrative strategy is deceptively simple. She uses a series of sequential flashbacks to slip the reader back in time as she recalls the stories her grandmother told her, which her grandmother in turn heard from her grandmother. These stories center upon the lives of Oona and her family as they first flee from, but eventually have to negotiate, experiences of cultural disruption that begin with relocation to reservation villages and are then compounded by conversion to Christianity, boarding school experience, and loss of language and traditional practice. Broker's strategically important narrative springboard for this story of the past, however, is a prologue—a brief description only a few pages in length—about the quality of post-war urban life for Indian people in Minneapolis and St. Paul. *Night Flying Woman* problematizes stereotypes of vanishing and victimhood, in part by its use of this prologue to counter the essentializing tendencies of previous urban representations.

The prologue's title, "The Forest Cries," appears to point to the woodland past of Broker's Anishinabe forebears, suggesting familiar themes of dislocation and loss while simultaneously recalling the animate urban complicity of human and natural worlds. But since the prologue is set not in the forest but in the city, where Broker lived for more than forty years, the title actually works to contextualize present time and place by suggesting its connection to the time and place of the ancestral past. Referring to her more recent personal past, Broker acknowledges the power relationships affecting life in the urban neighborhood to which she brought her children in the 1950s:

> That day thirty years ago when we moved here, me and my children, we were the aliens looking for a place to fit in, looking for a chance of a new life, moving in among these people, some of whose "forefathers" had displaced my ancestors for the same reason: looking for a new life.[18]

However alien the city might make Indian newcomers feel, it is potentially a location of opportunity. Over time, their urban neighborhood stops representing contamination or danger for Broker's family. It becomes the place where her children go to school and church and marry. Even though, as adults, they may be "in faraway places, they seem to have their roots here, for they had lived in no other place while growing up" (2).

Broker's initial experience of the city might be viewed as providing a more detailed account of Deloria's suppositions about war-industry migrants. Moving from the reservation in 1941, she writes that she worked in a defense plant by day and took classes to supplement inadequate schooling at night. But if the city offered opportunity, it also subjected Indian people to all sorts of discrimination, especially in housing, where they were often turned down by landlords or forced to share illegal rentals of substandard housing in over-crowded conditions. Broker refuses, however, to emphasize the victimization of urban Indian experience, concentrating instead on traditional values of communal sharing and respect and the economic system of "giving to get" that could still be sustained and nourished.

> I think now that maybe it was a good thing, the migration of our people to the urban areas during the war years, because there, amongst the millions of people, we were brought to a brotherhood. . . . And because we, all, were isolated in this dominant society, we became an island from which a revival of spirit began. (5)

New communities, "vibrant with sharing," (6) began to be formed, and they stimulated activism and agency.

> After that, the tide of Indians moving to Minnesota's urban areas increased, and today there are ten thousand of us. As the number grew, newfangled types of Indian people came into being: those demanding what is in our treaties, those demanding service to our people, those working to provide those services—and all reaching back for identity. (7)

Although Broker does not ignore aspects of alienation and inequity in city life, she does assert the good of urban migration. Her larger story may be about how her people's present evolved from and maintains relationship with its past. Her book also provides an overview, if not a detailed examination, of the creation of urban pockets of community where political and cultural power can be nurtured and where the meanness of contemporary urbanization may be mitigated by traditional values.

That more detailed examination, although drawn from another geographic and cultural landscape, is what Greg Sarris provides in *Grand Avenue*, a first novel about the tangled lives of Pomo families living in "the Hole," the worst part of Santa Rosa, California, fifty miles from San Francisco. Grand Avenue is far from grand; it's the synecdochic marker of an Indian ghetto, and Indian people would easily be able to substitute other such street names for similar neighborhoods in any city or town in America with a significant Indian population. Like most of those other neighborhoods, Grand Avenue is a racial mix—Indians, African Americans, Mexicans—of those on the lowest rungs of the economic ladder. One feature of the neighborhood is a park frequented mutually by old people, children, and gangs; another is a slaughterhouse whose owner uses it at night as a place of assignation for the neighborhood girls he recruits into prostitution. Work for most of those who live on Grand Avenue is seasonal, low paying, and punishing—picking fruit in the apple fields or packaging in the local cannery. Indian families form and re-form as economic needs demand in overcrowded "apartments" that are actually refurbished army barracks separated by mud tracks. Sarris's portraits of dysfunction—alcohol, drugs, promiscuity, family breakdown—are a realistic representation of the circumstances of many Americans, whatever their ethnicity, race, or economic circumstances. But it is a distinctly Indian—distinctly Pomo—version of contemporary life that Sarris constructs. Within this version, there are new complications attached to the possibilities of separation and reintegration, and new circumstances to factor into equations describing the values of culturally determined concepts of urbanness.

In some of the ways Sarris's stories detail and reinforce the destructive toxicity to which these characters are exposed, they may seem reiterations of already established cultural parameters. Sarris's "poisoners," for example, converge with Silko's notions of destroyers and their witchery. As in Silko, the struggle between the poisoners and those who use their medicines to heal rather than hurt has been carried on from time

immemorial. Both writers invest this struggle with an ironic agency, decentering whiteness as neither cause nor effect. Another feature that Sarris's portrayal of contemporary community shares with those previously imagined by Momaday and Silko is the
exercise of a hybridized spirituality. In *Grand Avenue*'s opening story, "The Magic
Pony," for example, the mother paints on her living room wall a mural that appears to
conflate traditional and Christian symbolism: a green forest demarcated by fingernail-
polish pink crosses to protect her family against the sources of trouble and poison.[19]

In other ways, however, Sarris destabilizes conventional expectations about the features of Indianness. Sarris's Indians are far from universally sharing a sense of rever-
ence for and relation with the natural world. "I'll leave you in the woods, you hear! I'll
leave you with the white people" (34), one mother threatens her daughter, indicating
the degree to which nature and whiteness have taken on a similar bogeyman alienness.
How could such a breakdown have occurred? Significantly, for Sarris's Pomo families
there is no ancestral homeplace, no traditional tribal community to return to. Santa
Rosa Creek is the home from which, generations ago, these clans were dispersed, split
up, driven out; and contemporary Santa Rosa is where they have returned to a present
now bewildering in the ways it intermingles with the past. Sarris's interweaving stories
of five generations build a composite allowing him to feature complicated contemporary issues—the consequences of mixed-race identity, cross-group racism, internal exploitation, even inadvertent incest resulting from the breakdown of kinship systems in
an urban setting. On Grand Avenue, rare are those who do not make hate and insecurity "best friends" (39), who do not open their hearts to poison, the "misuse of
power" (21), who overcome loneliness to find even temporary tenderness, who reject
the escapes offered by alcohol, sex, violence, or fantasy.

For Sarris no less than for other Native writers, the past impinges on the present,
but the intersections of cultural transformation and permanent urbanization he addresses seem to preclude previous outcomes, which involved reintegration in traditional homeplaces or acknowledgment of shared communal consciousness. Particularly in the last three stories in his collection, however, we begin to see how older values
reconfigure themselves as the tools that might be used to construct a more hopeful
contemporary urban place-world.

The first of these, "The Indian Maid," is told from the point of view of Stella
who, in order to make a better life for herself, has to struggle against the grain of her
sisters' envy and her mother's failures. Leaving Santa Rosa for a good job in even more
urban Tucson is for Stella a sign of possibility rather than betrayal, but a mishap on
the eve of her departure helps her to recognize the depth of her connections to family. Stella will be able to leave, but she will take with her a clear understanding of the
content of her mother's dream on the night, years before, when she had returned to
her own family: "They were all happy, I might have told my mother that night. They
didn't fight. It was simple, a lesson an eight-year-old could discern. Appreciate one another. Get along. Share" (183).

In "Secret Letters," the apparent success of Steven, a postal carrier, and his wife Reyna, a teacher, in securing a good life away from Grand Avenue—one that includes acknowledgment of their cultural ties—is threatened by Steven's concern for Tony, an illegitimate son conceived unknowingly years before with his own sister. Contradictory loyalties lead Steven to deceive his wife and children about why he wants to move back to Grand Avenue where the boy lives. A disastrous attempt to shore up the boy's self-esteem by sending him a series of letters in which Steven pretends to be an anonymous admirer precipitates a brush with the law and the revelation of his secret. Sarris offers no easy solutions to the entanglements of Steven's past and present, but the final scene allows a reconciliation of Steven's divided loyalties and an assertion of the power of love over blame and betrayal:

> At the dinner table tonight my two children, Shawn and Raymond, seem unusually calm, given what happened. . . . I must tie up the story for them. But how do I begin? Where?
> "What's the lesson in this story?" I ask, unable to think of anything else. But my children are way ahead of me.
> "When's Tony coming to dinner?" Shawn asks.
> "Tomorrow," my wife says.
> "Tomorrow," I say. (208)

And finally, in "The Water Place," the healer Nellie Copaz, ostracized by her family because of her medicine powers and marriage to a white man, is able to form a bond with Alice, her gentle, overburdened young relation, which revitalizes ancestral power and passes it forward in the service of simple happiness and the cessation of recrimination. If the city has been an ultimate site of triumph of the machine over the garden, in this story, Nellie's riotous garden is a reversal of that triumph, a symbolic evocation of the tenaciousness of nature—and the first thing that attracts Alice to Nellie's door. Even—and especially—in the blight of Grand Avenue, Nellie exhorts Alice, "It's important to talk. Us Indians here are all family. That's the trouble, no one talks. Stories, the true stories, that's what we need to hear. We got to get it out. The true stories can help us. Old-time people, they told stories, Alice. They talked. Talk, Alice, don't be like the rest" (219). Alice does talk, but Nellie comes to value something else as more important: Alice's gift for making and creating new designs for the baskets that are one of the traditional sources of Pomo tribal identity and power. In the midst of a dispiriting town/city environment, which breeds anger, self-loathing, and fear among the young and the old, Alice is "as clear as water, as open as the blue sky" (222).

No matter how mean the streets, how deep the wounds of separation, how far removed from their original time and place contending conceptions of wilderness and civilization, these evolving representations converge on the power that remains in relational being, in family, and in the stories by which these are conveyed. In that convergence is a healing functionality that can indeed help to build the resilience that urban

Indian people need to challenge the demographics. More universally, these stories of the Indian urban answer Elizabeth Cook-Lynn's call for narratives capable of stirring the human community to an encompassing moral view.

Notes

1. "We the . . . First Americans," *1990 Census of Population and Housing*, Racial Statistics Branch, Population Division, Bureau of the Census (Washington, D.C., 1990), 1. All demographic data cited is based on the 1990 Census.

2. Leslie Marmon Silko, *Ceremony* (New York: Penguin Books, 1977), 2. Succeeding page references are given in the text.

3. Elizabeth Cook-Lynn, *Why I Can't Read Wallace Stegner and Other Essays* (Madison: University of Wisconsin Press, 1996), 64.

4. Mourning Dove, *Cogewea the Half-Blood* (1927; reprint, Lincoln: University of Nebraska Press, 1981), 280. Succeeding page references are given in the text.

5. Inga Clendinnen, "'Fierce and Unnatural Cruelty': Cortes and the Conquest of Mexico," in *New World Encounters*, ed. Stephen Greenblatt (Berkeley: University of California Press, 1993), 41.

6. Luther Standing Bear, *Land of the Spotted Eagle* (1933; reprint, Lincoln: University of Nebraska Press, 1978), 50.

7. Howard I. Kushner, *Self-Destruction in the Promised Land: A Psychocultural Biology of American Suicide* (New Brunswick: Rutgers University Press, 1989), 184.

8. Dolores Hayden, "The American Sense of Place and the Politics of Space," in *American Architecture: Innovation and Tradition*, ed. David G. DeLong et al. (New York: Rizzoli International, 1986), 185.

9. D. H. Lawrence, *Studies in Classic American Literature* (1923; reprint, New York: Penguin, 1961), 56.

10. Don Scheese, "Thoreau's Journal: The Creation of a Sacred Place," in *Mapping American Culture*, ed. Wayne Franklin and Michael Steiner (Iowa City: University of Iowa Press, 1992), 139.

11. William Bevis, "Native American Novels: Homing In," in *Recovering the Word*, ed. Brian Swan and Arnold Krupat (Berkeley: University of California Press, 1987), 601.

12. Keith H. Basso, *Wisdom Sits in Places: Landscape and Language among the Western Apache* (Albuquerque: University of New Mexico Press, 1996), 6–7. Succeeding page references are given in the text.

13. Ella Deloria, *Speaking of Indians* (New York: Friendship Press, 1944), 24. Succeeding page references are given in the text.

14. Bevis, "Native American Novels," 585.

15. Alison R. Bernstein, *American Indians and World War II* (Norman: University of Oklahoma Press, 1991), 68.

16. N. Scott Momaday, *House Made of Dawn* (New York: Harper and Row, 1968), 94. Succeeding page references are given in the text.

17. Leslie Marmon Silko, *Almanac of the Dead* (New York: Penguin, 1991), 610.

18. Ignatia Broker, *Night Flying Woman* (St. Paul: Minnesota Historical Society, 1983), 2. Succeeding page references are given in the text.

19. Greg Sarris, *Grand Avenue* (New York: Penguin, 1994), 9. Succeeding page references are given in the text.

Yaqui Cultural and Linguistic Evolution through a History of Urbanization

3

OCTAVIANA V. TRUJILLO

HE VALLEY OF THE SUN is a large basin in which two major Sonoran Desert water systems, the Salt and Gila Rivers, converge, enabling large-scale human settlement in central Arizona. The agricultural potential of this natural resource has sustained a stable population base since prehistoric times. Today the valley is home to a number of small cities that comprise the Phoenix metropolitan urban sprawl and more than half of the residents of the state of Arizona. Located at the far eastern foot of South Mountain, the southern natural boundary of the valley, is Guadalupe, an urban anomaly that seems strangely juxtaposed against this widely spread, low-density urban landscape fashioned by the advent of the automobile culture.

Founded by Yaqui refugees from Sonora just after the turn of the century, the small, one-square-mile desert settlement was no more than a refugee camp, an innocuous cluster of extremely humble dwellings on the lightly populated valley's periphery. This was about to change. Just two years after Guadalupe came into being, the small but significant city of Phoenix became the capital of the new state of Arizona. Guadalupe's peripheral location was symbolic of the Yaquis' lack of cultural and social integration in their new homeland. As the twentieth century progressed, so did the urban sprawl, eventually threatening to envelop their community, as would the social and cultural pressures of the dominant society.

The urban cultural adaptation of the Yaqui people of Guadalupe to that force is a unique story that has unfolded over centuries. Most indigenous groups, to be sure, have had to undergo pronounced bilingual and bicultural adaptation, particularly in the urban setting, as a result of their proximity to a dominant European American cultural presence. The Yaqui experience in Guadalupe has had an additional intercultural variable—interaction with Mexicans and Mexican Americans—resulting in the manifestation of a trilingual and tricultural character.

To understand the underpinnings of this unique cultural setting, it is imperative to briefly retrace the historical antecedents of both the cultural region in general, and of the direct ancestors of the Yaqui founders of Guadalupe to their traditional homeland in the southern region of the state of Sonora, Mexico.

Urban, socially interdependent communities, characterized by a high degree of cooperation and specialization, have been found historically throughout the Americas. While this socioeconomic milieu has not been a predominant one, the exceptions are as striking as they are noteworthy. The sites of the Maya, the Toltecs, the Zapotecs, and, most recently, the Aztecs are some of the better-known examples. Snaketown, Casas Grandes, and Chaco Canyon further north, however, were also home to highly integrated societies.

The phenomenon of the social adaptation of Native Americans to an urban context, therefore, is much older than the history of Native American–nonindigenous American contact. This contact has, in fact, characterized a relatively short period in the Native American urban social experience. A consequence of this contact, which has been, indeed, unique in Native American history, is the profound cultural and linguistic diversity that informs the contemporary urban landscape.

Changes in the Yaqui Social Landscape from Their First Contact with Nonindigenous American People

The first nonindigenous influence in North America was a result of the establishment of the Spanish colony in the Valley of Mexico, from which the Yaqui steadfastly maintained a virtually singular isolation. Yet significant inroads were made into traditional Yaqui culture as a result of their adoption and adaptation of Catholicism, initially introduced to them by the Spanish Jesuit missionaries during their long journeys north into the present-day western U.S.[1] This also provided the common thread that would eventually link them culturally, if not socially, to the growing Mexican population neighboring their homelands.

In the early 1600s the Jesuits convinced the Yaquis to organize and settle in eight pueblos, similar to European towns, by having them build eight mission churches across the length of their country, which straddles the Rio Yaqui in the south of the present day state of Sonora.[2] They proposed to gather the Yaqui dwellings close to these ceremonial centers. This gradual process was easily facilitated by distributing the churches without moving their residence. Whatever the rate of movement to the ceremonial centers and whatever number of families that preferred at first not to participate in this Jesuit-led urbanization, there is no doubt that by 1700 a new settlement pattern had been created. So firmly did this pattern become established among the Yaquis, they came to believe that it was sacred and supernaturally mandated, thereby conceptually intertwining history and legend.[3] The new communities consisted of from three to four thousand inhabitants instead of the three to four hundred that had comprised the traditional *rancherias*. With this new urban landscape came significant social change, as Yaquis found themselves compelled by circumstance to accept a common governmental system, and a realignment of family groups.

With so few missionaries—never more than ten—in Yaqui territory to accomplish the tasks of the church, the government, and business operations, it became necessary to rely on Yaquis who were trained as assistants. Since Yaqui territory was devoid of any Spanish settlement or even any Spanish presence save the Jesuits, intercultural relations with nonindigenous people outside of the few missionaries were essentially nonexistent. This resulted in the development of a new urban sociopolitical cultural milieu, as a cadre of Yaqui officials emerged to administer the new towns. Even as Christianity began to have an ever-greater impact on the culture, this new urban society remained wholly indigenous in composition if not character, as direct interaction with the colonists was not a factor in Yaqui lifeways. This simultaneous enhancement of social organization and restriction of self-determination was inherently paradoxical. The evolving paradigm provided Yaquis the opportunity to develop administrative leadership in support of these more integrated urban communities, guided by a persuasive and, indeed, coercive missionary policy. It also created a psychological openness among the Yaqui toward the acceptance of social change of which they were the implementers, if not the masters.[4]

The increased urbanization of the Yaqui communities and the pressure for change in the areas of government and agriculture that it necessitated were driven to a large degree by the pressure for conversion that these changes would facilitate. The constant focus of each missionary on religious instruction and the maintenance of church ritual brought about the rapid introduction of Christian verbal and behavioral forms. In order to disseminate these forms outward among the townspeople at large, the missionaries depended on trained Yaqui associates. This process inadvertently promoted a much wider acceptance, as the associates blended them with traditional Yaqui forms (which the Jesuits had not intended), making them far more relevant and accessible to the people.

Undoubtedly the Jesuit religious ideas constituted alternatives for most Yaquis during this period. The new conception of the supernatural world, with its centralization of power in the mysterious Trinity, its division of an afterworld into good and bad regions, and its separation of men and animals, must have taken considerable reconciling with their earlier conception of the supernatural world.[5] Although some Christian rituals coexisted as alternatives to Yaqui ritual, others were complementary to traditional Yaqui beliefs. The close link between church and government also created a complementary form of governance. Yaqui governors were elected by the people. In major decisions the governors and church officials deliberated together.

This complementary and supplementary form of cultural change was also reflected in the Yaqui language. To accommodate these cultural innovations, not only did Yaqui acquire loan words, but its morphology and syntax were also influenced by the Spanish language.[6] Yaqui speakers directly incorporated Spanish words and grammatical structures to accommodate new concepts, rather than coining new Yaqui terminology or even attempting translations into Yaqui. This phenomenon characterizes the early intercultural period, before the Yaqui began to feel the oppression of cultural coercion.[7]

This period of gradual, peaceful cultural change through Spanish cultural traits such as beliefs, practices, clothing, and tools slowly replacing or coexisting with traditional Yaqui ones, came to an end in 1740. With the gradually but steadily increasing encroachment of Spanish colonists and opportunists into Yaqui territory and their desire to gain more control over the Yaqui towns, the Yaquis finally joined with their neighbors, the Mayos, in revolt. During the ensuing months they killed or drove out all Spaniards from the river towns and the adjoining territory, sparing only the Jesuits. Then toward the end of 1740 at a spot called the Hill of Bones, five thousand Yaquis were killed and their resistance crushed. Their leaders were executed, and a Spanish presidio was built at the eastern edge of Yaqui country to control the towns.[8]

A dominant Yaqui preoccupation during the remainder of the Spanish period was the struggle to maintain control over their own affairs and the resistance to Spanish political and economic domination in their territory. Shortly after the revolt of 1740, the Spanish soldiers were withdrawn to fight other neighbors of the Yaquis, the Seris. The Jesuits were also withdrawn, expelled from the "New World." A few Franciscan priests subsequently attempted to work with the Yaquis, but this effort was unsuccessful. Eventually their newfound autonomy permitted the Yaquis to form their own religion and socioreligious form of government.

The constant threat to local autonomy and to the traditional communal control of the land, however, necessitated a continual defensive preparedness. Just as the Yaquis were gaining more control of their affairs, there was a considerable decline in population. Significant numbers of Yaquis had removed themselves from the strife with the Spanish government by moving out of Yaqui country. The break-up of the Jesuit agricultural operations also resulted in an increasing number of Yaquis seeking new economic opportunities and wage work elsewhere. Some assumed seasonal work on the haciendas or in the mines. Yaqui identity was maintained, even in the face of necessary relocation, through a strong awareness of the Yaqui homeland and through sustained Yaqui socioreligious institutions and practices in their new locales.

As the Spanish influence spread throughout the population with the growth of both the size and the power of the colony, many indigenous groups were drawn in to a large-scale "mestizification" through intermarriage with the Europeans. This trend continued, contributing to a marked increase in the size of the nonindigenous population, until today only a minority of Mexican nationals can be said to be purely indigenous racially or ethnically, and even fewer purely European.

After the 1770s, ever-greater numbers of Yaquis found it necessary to work outside Yaqui country. Although corn, wheat, beans, watermelons, pumpkins, and squash were still raised through the traditional method of flooding rather than irrigation, from the 1820s onward, warfare caused a decline in agricultural activity. Gradually the Yaquis became more dependent upon the Mexican economy for manufactured goods.

Pressures on Yaqui Community Integrity
from the Emerging Mexican Republic

Soon after Mexican independence was established, the federal government and, later, the Sonoran state government assumed a role similar to that of the Spanish before them. With time they would increasingly attempt to impose political and economic control upon the Yaquis. In response, the Yaquis—united with the Mayos, Opatas, and Pimas—conceived of the notion of an independent indigenous nation in the region. Under the leadership of a literate Yaqui, Juan Banderas, who was reported to have had a vision of the Virgin of Guadalupe, the outsiders were expelled from the territory, until Banderas was finally defeated and executed in 1833.[9]

In the late 1870s a new leader appeared. Cajeme had had wide experience in the Mexican army and had been a mayor, the highest civil authority of the Yaqui towns. In 1885–86 he fought a brilliant campaign using both Mayos and Yaquis against federal and state troops. His defeat and execution in 1887 ended organized Yaqui military operations, although various guerrilla activities continued from mountain strongholds for another twenty years.[10]

Yaqui oral history now included the conflicts with the Spaniards and the Mexicans, combining them with the growing myths of the time such as the founding of the towns through prophetic vision. Gradually some Yaquis became literate both in Spanish and Yaqui. Yaqui leaders wrote to their Mexican contemporaries in Spanish and to their literate Yaqui friends who had relocated to other parts of Sonora in Yaqui. As church ceremonies were written in Spanish and Yaqui for all to use, a Yaqui written record appeared.[11] The majority of Yaqui were literate, although with little formal schooling, and many spoke several languages.[12] The Yaquis considered themselves more civilized than Mexicans and other indigenous groups, and equal, except in technical skills, to European Americans.

The atrocities perpetrated by both sides during warfare greatly reduced the likelihood of Yaqui assimilation into Mexican society. A group of Yaquis at Guymas in 1914 even had the dubious distinction of being history's first recipients of aerial bombardment. This historical animosity continues to be a factor in Mexican–Yaqui relations to this day.[13]

The period of unrest that culminated in the Mexican Revolution affected Yaqui society in a variety of ways. First, it implanted in the Yaqui ideology an even firmer concept of Yaqui sacred territory. Even though the geography of the Yaqui towns changed drastically during this period, the notion of the homeland remained constant. The greatest force informing the development of Yaqui cultural adaptation since the coming of the Spanish was the steady growth of the Mexican nation around them. The ever-increasing population of non-Native peoples in their immediate environment brought with it, like the earlier presence of the Spanish missionaries, a major impetus for cultural adaptation that was beyond their control.

Yaqui Social Realignment and Emigration in the Face of Increasing Adverse Contact with Mexicans

During the warring years of Spanish colonialism in Mexico, the Yaqui culture had begun to develop a form of adaptation in the face of adversity that was to persist to the present day. By the time the Yaqui began to migrate across the border into the United States in the late 1800s, their lifeways had undergone drastic changes from earlier times. Cultural adaptations continued as Yaquis established small communities in Arizona.

The Yaqui struggles against Mexican encroachment, particularly the Mexican government's effort to forcibly evict them from their traditional homeland, provided the context for both the greatest trauma and the most profound cultural adaptation ever faced by the tribe. This crisis precipitated a diaspora through which a considerable number of tribal members rapidly experienced cross-cultural interaction under duress, as hundreds were exported against their will to the opposite end of the Mexican republic to work as forced laborers on the *henequen* plantations of the Yucatan. Meanwhile, others seeking to avoid such a fate began clandestinely making their way across the U.S. border into Arizona and into a life of self-imposed exile, also wrought with peril, but at least safe from the threat of annihilation.

Yaquis began to cross the border into the United States as early as the mid-1880s, so they were not strangers to the northern region. Yaqui oral history tells of their presence in the area of what is today the southwestern U.S. from time immemorial.[14] The major migration of the historical era came during the years 1900–1910. The Yaqui uprising of 1927 in Mexico led to another wave of northerly migration. By the 1950s, there were approximately four thousand in Arizona. For the most part, they were escaping deportation to Yucatan or seeking employment when conditions in Sonora had become extremely difficult. As many Yaquis in Sonora were doing, those coming to Arizona established themselves in barrios at the edge of cities or in work camps, neither assimilating into the dominant society nor returning to their homeland permanently.[15] This historical turn of events was accompanied by the ironic transformation of their principal geopolitical reality from the former homogeneous Yaqui urban community characterized by home rule under foreign dominion to the relative laissez-faire autonomy of the benignly neglected, culturally segregated American ghetto.

The Yaquis were now refugees with no legal status and their earliest settlements bore universal refugee characteristics. Primary among these were inadequate food, shelter, and sanitation. They owned no land and were forced to establish themselves as squatters. During the early years, they were fearful of being identified as Yaquis and being sent back to Sonora, so they operated primarily within their own cultural enclave as a defense against the perceived threat of deportation. Because of this, Yaqui identity, language, and religious practices were outwardly suppressed. They had as little contact as possible with government officials, so nearly fifteen years passed before the Yaquis became aware that they had been afforded political asylum and that in the United States religious freedom was upheld regardless of political or social status.

Most Yaquis came to the U.S. as individuals without any kin or social grouping to help them survive. During the early years of residence in Arizona, they gradually developed new family groupings through the reunion of separated families and the starting of new families. Ritual kin groups, based upon baptismal godparents and ceremonial sponsors further extended the basic family organization.

Among the earliest Yaqui settlers in the Valley of the Sun were freedom fighters who were fleeing the guerrilla war after the execution of Cajeme, but who planned to return home eventually. This was never to be, as the Mexican government subsequently appropriated their land. These defiant Yaquis supplied rebels back in their homeland with food staples and, when necessary, helped them to escape by sheltering them in this northern camp.[16]

Within a decade, the Western Canal camp had grown so as to warrant the residence of a Franciscan friar. In the years before Friar Lucius arrived in 1904, sporadic Yaqui rituals had been held, but the consistent demands of membership within a ceremonial society were difficult, if not impossible, to maintain for men whose employment kept them away from camp for even brief periods of time.

Most of the men were employed as agricultural workers on the farms within the large basin area and they were entirely dependent upon their Anglo employers. Others found work on outlying ranches, but such jobs entailed prolonged absence from the Yaqui camp. Some of the men who left to work on ranches were able to take along their immediate families, but most went alone, returning whenever possible to their families and friends.

As field workers, the Yaquis gained an impressive reputation as diligent and conscientious laborers. Employers usually separated workers into ethnic groups, not only in residential camps, but also in the field. Cotton farmers claimed that they could identify rows picked by the Yaquis at a glance by the neat and thorough method of their work. Agricultural laborers were separated into four major groups: Indians, Mexicans, Negroes, and Anglos. Although this perpetuated the concept of social stratification, it did serve to reinforce Yaqui linguistic and cultural continuity in their new land.

The atrocities witnessed by those Yaquis who had been caught up in the bloodiest fighting in the Rio Yaqui campaigns were bitterly remembered by those who fled. These memories formed the basis for deep-seated hatred and justified anxieties. Fearing their vulnerability to potentially hostile Mexicans in Arizona, some fleeing Yaquis denied their ethnicity by posing as either O'odham (formerly known as Papago) or Mexicans according to their physical characteristics and any positive contacts they may have had with either of these two groups.

The Reemergence of a Yaqui Urban Community in Guadalupe

By 1910, Friar Lucius had acquired forty acres for the Yaquis to build a permanent settlement.[17] The constant complaints from neighboring towns about the proximity of the culturally different "squatters" underscored the need for these people to have a place of their own. The friar was unable, however, to secure for them the land beside the Western Canal because of its potential value as farmland. Instead, he acquired forty acres on high ground west of the Highline Canal granted by a United States government patent and signed by President Woodrow Wilson on November 14, 1914.[18] The new site was elevated enough to be worthless as farmland since it could not be irrigated. The legal transaction was not completed until recorded by the County Recorder at the request of M. J. Dougherty on July 20, 1915.[19] This cultural transformation found the Yaquis once again in a homogeneous urban community characterized by an enclave of Yaqui home rule within an area of sociopolitical hegemony of others. The difference this time was that they were no longer in their traditional homeland.

Upon the arrival of Friar Lucius with the symbolic *santa* of the Virgin of Guadalupe, the Western Canal camp came to be known as Guadalupe. After the move to higher ground, the former settlement, which continued to serve as a burial site, was referred to as Old Guadalupe and the new settlement simply as Guadalupe.

The decade comprising the last five years of Old Guadalupe and the first five years of Guadalupe on high ground was a period of intense cultural renaissance. In 1915 the first Catholic Church, a small adobe structure, was built facing onto a traditional open plaza. The move from Old Guadalupe to the new site covered only one mile but altered the lives of all involved. Along the Western Canal the Yaqui camp was self-sufficient in its food production by gently irrigating the fertile land immediately adjacent to the settlement. On the high ground this was not possible. The Yaquis now were dependent upon a cash economy—labor for wages as hard currency—in order to purchase every basic need.

In the 1920s, Mexican Americans began to settle the area adjacent to the forty acres but remained a minority of the settlement's population. Interaction between Guadalupe and the other neighboring settlements was still minimal. Due to its proximity, Tempe was the most accessible town. More Yaqui men were gradually employed as manual laborers by the Water Users Association.[20] Young women either walked or rode into Tempe, about four hours round trip, to work ten-hour days as seamstresses. Merchants from Tempe peddled their wares in Guadalupe at elevated prices to cover the cost of delivery.

A Presbyterian mission comprising one hundred acres was set up adjacent to the *Cuarenta* at the eastern side of the original acreage.[21] On January 17, 1924, Jennie Biehn, a missionary widow, gave most of this land to the Presbyterian Church to be used as "homesites for Yaqui Indians." The ambiguity of the original bequest, known as the Biehn Colony, was to lead to future strife.

Yaqui women Americanization class, Guadalupe, Arizona, 1926. (CP SPC 123:1, Arizona Collection, Arizona State University Libraries)

Yaqui men Americanization class, Guadalupe, Arizona, 1926. (CP SPC 123:2, Arizona Collection, Arizona State University Libraries)

The renaissance of Yaqui traditional culture had included an elected *kobanao* (governor) to administer justice in the community. As the Military Society faded away due to inactivity and emigration, a major foundation of Yaqui society waned. The traditional orientation of this society had served as a guiding force in re-establishing the *kobanao* administration in 1910. The loss of the Military Society coupled with the expansion of the community into the Biehn Colony diminished the political base of the *kobanao*. The community was fiercely divided on the issue of maintaining this office. Some families left Guadalupe rather than live under the administration of the *kobanao*. By 1925, the office of the *kobanao* had disappeared. The leading Yaqui positions were now those of the *maestro* and the *capitan de los Fariseos*.[22] Non-Yaqui authorities handled civil matters. As elsewhere in Arizona, justice was administered in courts of law.

The Depression was heavily felt in Guadalupe throughout the 1930s. Displaced English-speaking farmers from the dust bowl farther to the east, whose farms had been repossessed, were intent on reaching California. Some of these farmers, upon reaching the fertile Salt River Valley, decided to settle there, further crowding the Yaquis as field laborers. The number of Mexican-American families settling adjacent to the forty acres continued to grow, finally equaling the Yaqui population. In the mid-1930s many Yaqui families returned to the Rio Yaqui, drawn to the relative peace in their homeland and driven away by the difficult conditions of the Depression. Despite this emigration, the population of Guadalupe was steadily increasing. Agricultural labor or canal maintenance, however, was the only work consistently available.

The Guadalupe community volunteered most of its able-bodied men to the U.S. armed services during World War II. Those servicemen fortunate enough to return from the war brought back hard currency and such practical knowledge as was required to operate motor vehicles. Previously, transportation had been restricted to horseback or mass transport in the bed of a large truck. Although transportation by horseback was still common at the end of World War II, the privately owned automobile became the predominant mode of transportation in the community. Though few Yaqui households owned cars, they shared this resource—as they did all resources—with their relatives and friends.

By the end of the Korean conflict, Yaquis comprised a distant and rapidly diminishing minority of the overall population of Guadalupe, although their numbers continued to dominate the barrios of the *Cuarenta* and the Biehn Colony, the two oldest neighborhoods. With the growth of the aviation and defense industries in the metropolitan Phoenix area, Guadalupe was no longer so isolated from its neighbors.

The political activism of minority people that characterized the United States in the 1960s took root in Guadalupe as well.[23] The political consciousness rose over the issue of land. The economic base of the Guadalupano Yaqui had become diversified. The number of agricultural workers, including the canal maintenance workers, had been reduced due to the automation of the agricultural industry. Only one out of four households had members working in the fields. The manufacturing and construction industries had become the dominant employers, offering higher paying jobs for more sophisticated menial labor. The Yaqui successfully adapted to that change. Economic security was a threat that could be handled within the *compadrazgo* system, since employment was found through personal contacts rather than through any sort of job service program.[24]

The construction of the Interstate-10 highway on the west boundary of Guadalupe was begun in 1962. At this time, the streets of Guadalupe were unpaved dirt; heavy rains left them impassable. All mailboxes were lumped together on the main road, Fifty-Sixth Street. In 1964 the streets were paved, and each individual house relocated its mailbox along the street in front of the house. Still there was no sewage system, few septic tanks, and many Yaqui homes had no running water. Political activity had brought about changes, but many more improvements were needed. The greatest obstacle to progress was the factionalism within the community. Not only was the Mexican-American community at odds with the Yaquis, but also opposing factions within the Yaqui society had emerged. A pronounced rift between the Catholic and Protestant groups further exacerbated this situation. Each group tended to criticize the actions of the other groups as it vied for hegemony.

By 1974, the population of Guadalupe had reached nearly five thousand. The growth of Tempe, to the very edges of Guadalupe, led to consideration of the annexation of the smaller community. Local action was taken in an attempt to register the community as a historic site with the State Parks Department and to list it on the National Register of Historic Places in order to preserve its special character. As the threat of annexation increased, the Citizens Committee to Incorporate Guadalupe was formed to begin action that would secure the community from rules and regulations imposed by the ordinances of other cities. In February 1975 the residents voted to incorporate.

Thus the Yaquis of Guadalupe continue to survive in spite of internal factionalism and economic and legal pressures without disrupting the stable way of life that has evolved during one hundred years of adversity as residents of Arizona. Anselmo Valencia of Tucson demonstrated this tenacity by shepherding congressional legislation to grant federal tribal recognition to the Pascua Yaqui Tribe of Arizona on September 18, 1978.[25] As in Mexico, Yaquis were faced with the cultural diversity that was anything but democratic. While the Mexican majority in Sonora had essentially relegated them to second-class status in their homeland, in the U.S. their social status was diminished yet a further level by the Mexicans there who were, themselves, already enduring a second-class status relative to the white population. The trilingual characteristic of the contemporary Arizona Yaqui community is a cross-cultural legacy of the dynamics of living many decades in proximity to ever increasing numbers of nonindigenous-language-speaking neighbors flanking both their original Mexican and current U.S. communities.

Despite considerable success in trilingual and tricultural adaptation, the Yaqui continue to be the poorest of any single population in southern Arizona. This is largely attributable to extraordinarily low levels of formal education. Only some two-thirds have completed the eighth grade, fewer than 20 percent have completed

"La Cuarenta," original Guadalupe Yaqui town site, squeezed by the Phoenix urban sprawl, March 18, 1990. (Photo by Mike Ging, courtesy of *The Arizona Republic* © Phoenix Newspapers, Inc.)

high school or the equivalency, and fewer than one percent have graduated from an institution of higher education. Economic indicators show that over 60 percent are unemployed, and that of the employed, less than a quarter are employed full-time. Based on national standards, approximately 85 percent of the tribal population lives below the poverty level.[26]

The Role of Bilingualism in Yaqui Urbanization: The Acquisition of a Foreign Language

In stark contrast with North Americans of today, the vast majority of Mexicans can trace some percentage of their ancestry to indigenous roots. The development of a Mexican national consciousness, nevertheless, has paralleled a commensurate disassociation with an exclusively indigenous identity for much of the population. Probably no one historical trend has been more significant to this phenomenon, with the possible exception of the advent of Christianity, than the development of Spanish as a national language and an intercultural lingua franca throughout the country and most of the hemisphere.

Although it was not uncommon for Yaquis in the traditional homeland to know other languages, Spanish was the first truly *foreign* language with which they would be compelled to contend in terms of cultural adaptation. By the time of the founding of Guadalupe, it was widely used by the Yaqui residents in all their dealings, economic and social, with the population of Mexicans and Mexican Americans that surrounded them.

Spanish is the dominant language today in Guadalupe, even among the Yaqui. It is spoken in virtually all Yaqui homes, roughly 70 percent of the time on average. Yaqui is spoken approximately 20 percent of the time on average (usually by older family members), with the remainder consisting of English (usually younger family members). These three languages coexist in most households, however, with a high degree of lexical interchange and code switching among them.[27]

The children of today typically learn Spanish as their first language, since this is the predominant lingua franca of Guadalupe. The trend is, nevertheless, toward children learning English as their first language, which is reinforced in the schools, so that it is now common for parents to speak to their children in Spanish and for the children to respond in English. Elders are the predominant speakers of Yaqui today, and they use it primarily intragenerationally, using Spanish far more commonly with those who are younger.

The Role of Bilingualism in Yaqui Urbanization: The Acquisition of a Second Foreign Language

The Yaquis had adapted to the changes in Mexico by learning the "cultural vocabulary" as well as the vernacular of the Mexicans. These skills served them well when they arrived in the U.S., enabling them to readily interact with the Mexicans and Mexican Americans of Arizona when necessary. But a new cultural vocabulary and vernacular had to be acquired to survive in the Anglo-dominant society. Until the late 1950s, Yaquis in Arizona remained primarily bilingual in Yaqui and Spanish. The third generation, coming of age during that decade, was beginning to speak English as well as the two other languages.

The population of Guadalupe Yaquis today is young; almost half are in school. Their language abilities are mixed. Most over age fifty speak at least some Yaqui— and a dialect of Spanish—in which they have steadily become dominant. Most of the school-age population is dominant in a regional Spanish dialect and also has acquired a nonstandard English dialect, while a few enter school knowing no English at all. A very few adolescents maintain at least a passive knowledge of spoken Yaqui, although virtually none continues to speak Yaqui fluently. An ever-increasing number of children speak only English, with varying degrees of receptive knowledge of Spanish.

The particular character of the linguistic competence of Yaquis is unique. They, as most Native Americans, speak a dialect variant of English that bears a strong influence from the native language. Since individuals who are raised in an indigenous or minority community usually learn English from other members of that community, the linguistic patterns of their English dialect continue that influence.[28]

In the case of the Yaqui of Guadalupe, however, there exists another dimension to their linguistic culture, since they have gone through this same process earlier in learning Spanish as a second language. The majority of these people acquired English as dominant Yaqui-dialect *Spanish* speakers. That is, many of the grammatical patterns and items of vocabulary differ in form and meaning from those used in the standard form of both English *and* Spanish.[29]

Impact of Public Education on the Cultural Adaptation of Guadalupe Yaquis

Frank School, the Tempe public elementary school in Guadalupe, enjoys a favorable image in the community, largely due to the practice of employing aides from the community, which has engendered a widespread identification with the school. This bridge between the school and the community has helped to increase communication between these two groups. This has been accomplished both by providing a sense of community–school continuity, as well as providing a linguistic bridge between the mostly Spanish-speaking students and the mostly European American, English-speaking instructional staff. Such a bridge has been essential since language is more than an instrument of communication; it is an inseparable and inexorable part of culture.[30] It provides a complex set of categories that determine the capacity to decipher and manipulate complex structures, a sort of intellectual literacy.

The community–school communication, however, has not been historically bilateral in that aides disseminated information to the community, but significantly less input has gone from the community to the school. Although the outreach endeavors of the local school district have been well received in the community, the closed nature of traditional Yaqui society has continuously acted to inhibit interaction outside the community. This is a historically conditioned response that has served to protect the people and the culture, albeit to a limited degree, from external elements that have forced change upon them.[31]

At the core of the discontinuity between the school and the community is the institution's implicit hidden curriculum, which is predicated on the age-appropriate skills and knowledge native English-speaking European American students typically bring with them to school. From this presupposition follows a deficit model of the Yaquis as learners. This is generalized to both language and culture and the Yaquis are, therefore, assumed to be linguistically and culturally deficient. If learning is fostered in a context of positive interaction, mutual intelligibility, and shared meaning, then the dominant assumptions of the institution's hidden curriculum serve only to marginalize the Yaquis.

The school, even though it is located in the community and outwardly attempts to communicate with the parents of the Yaqui students, has nevertheless perpetuated both the social distance and the school–community discontinuity. It has done this by assuming that this discontinuity is a result of the educational and social "deficiencies" of the students and their community. That attitude has justified the lowering of expectations for Yaqui learners, and, in turn, hindered their attainment of educational benefits commensurate with their potential capabilities in a manner consistent with that of those students who are envisioned in the "hidden" curriculum. To be sure, as part of their education Yaqui students need to be guided toward the *additive* skills of dominant culture linguistic and cultural competency in order to maximize their future personal and economic options. That this hasn't happened to any greater degree is largely due to the failure of educators to perceive the dynamics of cultural "literacy," to recognize the variability of how it manifests itself in different cultures, and to understand the implications that it has for education.[32]

For many years Tempe Elementary School District provided no bilingual instruction, nor did it do appropriate assessment to ascertain the educational needs of the Yaqui and Mexican children. Three decades ago, over 67 percent of the children in special education classes were Yaqui and Mexican, although they constituted only 17 percent of the district student population. In August 1971, the community-based Guadalupe Organization (GO) took action to correct the situation of misdiagnosing and mislabeling Guadalupe's non–English-proficient students by filing a class action lawsuit against the school district.[33]

In 1972, the district was ordered to develop a desegregation plan as a result of the U.S. Office of Civil Rights (OCR) finding racism and school segregation at the local elementary school in Guadalupe. This action immediately precipitated a row between the community and the school district. The desegregation plan for Guadalupe included the busing of students to seven elementary schools in Tempe. Guadalupe parents argued that they had not been allowed to contribute to the plan, which seemed to them inadequate. They had favored a plan in which a second school would be built nearby that would attract children from European American neighborhoods.

Some Guadalupe residents felt the school district was trying to destroy the power of the community by scattering the more than seven hundred Guadalupe children among seven different schools where they would constitute minority enclaves. They felt, furthermore, that the school district was overtly attempting to assimilate the kids into the majority culture. Both Guadalupe and Tempe school parents resisted the busing plan. Guadalupe parents, through GO, began to take a critical look at the educational services provided to their children at the secondary level as well.

During the height of the busing boycott in 1973, the Guadalupe Organization opened *I'tom Escuela*, "Our School" in Yaqui and Spanish, in a church community center with fifteen volunteer teachers and two hundred students.[34] Many in the community charged that the inability of public education to meet the needs of

Yaqui and Mexican students was one of the prime reasons for the prolonged economic plight in Guadalupe.[35]

I'tom Escuela was financed by rummage and bake sales, car washes, contributions from community groups, and fund-raising campaigns. Its teachers were paid through money received from Volunteers in Service to America (VISTA). The alternative school prided itself on building on the cultural heritage students brought from home. The instructional program was not oriented to test or grade outcomes; rather it helped students establish positive self-concepts through learning about their culture and those of others. Three languages were taught—English, Spanish, and Yaqui.

The curriculum included the unseen components of language that structure the way people view themselves, each other, and the world around them by presenting content area instruction from the perspective of, and with respect for, the cultural background of the community. It also addressed many injustices—the most glaring being the placement of children in classes for the mentally challenged on the basis of IQ tests administered in English—by seeking more appropriate measures for ascertaining student abilities that were free of cultural and linguistic biases.

After ten years of providing a trilingual-tricultural curriculum for the students of Guadalupe *I'tom Escuela* finally closed its doors due to financial instability. A primary barrier to their seeking federal funds for continuing this unique school was, ironically, their action in resisting busing and boycotting the Civil Rights Plan for Desegregation.

The 1973 lawsuit against the Tempe Elementary School District by the Guadalupe Organization brought about change in respect to language and student assessment. The *Guadalupe Decision* was incorporated into Arizona Department of Education policy on assessment, which now states that the primary language of each student must be determined and the student's proficiency must be tested in that language. As a class action suit, the *Guadalupe Decision* ensured that all children in the state of Arizona would be assessed in their native language.[36] The Tempe Elementary School District appealed the ruling, but seven years later, in 1978, the U.S. Supreme Court refused to hear an appeal of a lower court decision in favor of the community.[37]

In 1977, while awaiting their final appeal to the high court, the district announced its OCR compliance plan. Numerous changes were put into effect, including more responsive and comprehensive assessment of children whose first language was not English. This included conducting home language surveys to ascertain what language the children spoke at home, assessment of the children's language proficiency in Spanish, utilizing instruments in Spanish and Spanish-speaking testers, and a teacher/aide instrument for ascertaining student language usage and patterns in the classroom, in the lunchroom, and on the playground. Provision was also made for providing training to administrators, instructional, support, and assessment personnel to better prepare them for meeting the needs of the language minority students.[38]

Yaqui Perceptions and Attitudes toward Linguistic and Cultural Adaptation

The possession of multiple operating cultures is the ability to act and behave appropriately in accordance with alternative sets of standards as determined by a specific situational context. To be able to engage multiple operating cultures constitutes a wider field of shared cultural experience as one's original set of cultural standards is expanded to accommodate alternative sets. The Yaquis distinctive identity within their respective communities in both countries, where they must coexist with dominant cultures, has been reinforced as a consequence of both positive and negative factors.

Languages are generally not viewed by the Yaqui community as systems of communicative competence, but rather as vehicles of access to the socioeconomic cultural domains they symbolize. The Yaqui language is perceived more as a repository for culture and heritage in a static sense rather than an equally valid and viable medium for intellectual and contemporary social development. English, however, is imbued with these latter qualities and thereby becomes the gatekeeper for success in the European-American–dominated national culture.[39]

A study of Yaqui viewpoints on language and literacy conducted in 1989 found that cultural conflict exists in the contexts of both education and language learning. For Yaquis, cultural conflict in education results from the dichotomy of cultural survival (preservation) versus functional survival within the multiple operating cultures (adaptation).[40] According to the study, Yaquis often attribute the decline of the Yaqui Language in Arizona to cultural change as well as to adaptation to the dominant culture.[41] Yet, paradoxically, their historical marginalization by the dominant society and its institutions such as the schools, as well as by the Mexican American community, has served to keep that identity strong.

The educational expectations of the Yaqui are embedded in the need, as indigenous people, to adapt and to change in order to exist in the context of a dominant society. These expectations spring from their participation in multiple alternative cultural standards, that is, the Yaquis' multiple cultural "literacies." Some of their experience and learning is shared with the majority, some is shared with other minorities—especially Mexicans and, to a lesser degree, Mexican Americans—and some is shared as a unique aspect of being Yaqui in the Guadalupe cultural setting. All the resulting cultural change and adaptation occurs under conditions of sustained contact in this milieu.

Situational interaction, however, can override the effects of cultural differences, as acculturation is not unimodal.[42] It is evident that many Yaquis share cultural similarities with others, but in different ways. Social experiences, or the effects of "primary and secondary networks," greatly diversify their existing range of operating culture. This has gone largely unnoticed by the educational institutions that serve them.

The importance of language to the participatory development and transmission of culture is paramount. Education as cultural transmission implies a set of basic assumptions about a society's cultural interests. It is not the individual, but rather a human group that shares a common cultural system. Although information comes from individuals based upon their social perceptions and interactions, it suggests how social structures and functions inform and define the accepted patterns for transmitting culture.[43] Since this is not happening in the classrooms attended by Guadalupe Yaquis, their native language skills in Yaqui or Spanish are not being developed. Neither is their primary language skill being exploited to assist them with their acquisition of English. Their overall linguistic development is being compromised as a consequence.

Inner conflicts are also a by-product of multiculturalism, in that individuals are likely to experience a greater degree of role conflict in a multicultural setting. This is particularly true for minority individuals who may be caught in a conflict between the expectations of the dominant culture and those of their own primary culture. In addition, role conflict can be expected to arise between the personal aspirations of an individual and appropriate behavior as defined by the person's cultural group.

Language is generally acknowledged in our society as a critical aspect of cultural pluralism, and study of the languages of developed societies—especially those deemed significant to the global economy—is widely encouraged. There continues to be a stigmatization, however, associated with indigenous languages or—as in the case of Spanish—with languages that are locally associated primarily with culturally and economically marginalized groups. Spanish study is viewed favorably, on the other hand, for native English-speaking European American students who may, for example, seek to participate in an exchange program in Spain. Yet it is viewed quite differently when it is offered for minority students who come from Spanish-speaking homes.

Few people will regularly choose to use a stigmatized language without a strong ideological commitment. This has provided a strong impetus for many Guadalupe Yaquis to seek to ensure that their children learn English as a primary language as early as possible. Often this is done even to the detriment of commensurate Spanish and/or Yaqui skills development.

Development and maintenance of language skills demands the use of the language in significant and useful ways as part of normal, real-life activities, not just in structured language lessons. Full language acquisition necessitates availability of the total range of communicative possibilities by which the learner may selectively re-create the language in a natural order.[44] This is why dominant languages always prevail while minority languages are continually retreating in their path.

This is the situation Guadalupe community leaders face as they attempt to develop community educational programs that address the Yaqui language and culture. Historically, their cultural and linguistic adaptation has been primarily reactive, in an effort to ensure that they would survive. The focus has now shifted with the awareness that in a democratic multicultural society it is the right of every culture, as with every individual, to thrive.

Notes

1. Andres Perez de Rivas, *My Life Among the Savage Nations of New Spain*, trans. in condensed form by Tomás Antonio Robertson (Los Angeles: Ward Richey Press, 1968); Herbert Eugene Bolton, *Rim of Christendom* (New York: Russell and Russell, 1960).

2. Evelyn Hu-DeHart, *Missionaries, Miners, and Indians: Spanish Contact with the Yaqui Nation of Northwestern New Spain, 1533–1820* (Tucson: University of Arizona Press, 1981); Christopher Vecsey, *On the Padres' Trail* (Notre Dame: Notre Dame University Press, 1996).

3. Larry Evers and Felipe Molina, "The Holy Dividing Line: Inscription and Resistance in Yaqui Culture," *Journal of the Southwest* 4 (Summer 1992).

4. Bolton, *Rim of Christendom*; Hu-DeHart, *Missionaries, Miners, and Indians*.

5. Larry Evers and Felipe Molina, *Yaqui Deer Songs: A Native American Poetry* (Tucson: Sun Tracks and the University of Arizona Press, 1990).

6. Edward H. Spicer, "Linguistic Aspects of Yaqui Acculturation," *American Anthropologist* 45 (1943): 3, 409–26.

7. Edward P. Dozier, "Two Examples of Linguistic Acculturation: The Yaqui of Sonora and Arizona and the Tewa of New Mexico," *Language* 32 (1956): 1, 146–57.

8. Edward H. Spicer, *Cycles of Conquest* (Tucson: University of Arizona Press, 1962).

9. Evelyn Hu-DeHart, *Yaqui Resistance and Survival: The Struggle for Land and Autonomy, 1821–1910* (Madison: University of Wisconsin Press, 1984).

10. Frank Hillary, "Cajeme, and the Mexico of His Time," *The Journal of Arizona History* 8 (1967): 120–36.

11. Carroll G. Barber, "Trilingualism in an Arizona Yaqui Village," in *Bilingualism in the Southwest*, ed. Raul R. Turner (Tucson: University of Arizona Press, 1973), 295–318.

12. Edward H. Spicer, *The Yaquis: A Cultural History* (Tucson: University of Arizona Press, 1980), 26.

13. Sam Aaron Brewer, Jr., "The Yaqui Indians of Arizona: Trilingualism and Cultural Change" (Ph.D. diss., University of Texas, 1976), 116.

14. Senate Committee on Indian Affairs, *Pascua Yaqui Tribe Extension of Benefits. Hearing before the Committee on Indian Affairs*, 103rd Cong., 2nd sess., 27 January 1994, 11.

15. Edward H. Spicer, *Perspectives in American Indian Culture Change* (Chicago: University of Chicago Press, 1961), 7–93; Edward H. Spicer, *People of Pascua* (Tucson: University of Arizona Press, 1988).

16. Dane Coolidge, "The Yaqui in Exile," *Sunset: The Magazine of the Prairie and of All the Far West* 23 (September 1909), 299–302.

17. Lucius Zittier, letter to Catherine Drexel, Sisters of the Blessed Sacrament Archives, Cornwell Heights, Penn.

18. Patent Number 442696.

19. Ibid.

20. Leah S. Glaser, "Working for Community: The Yaqui Indians at the Salt River Project," *Journal of Arizona History* 37 (Winter 1996): 337–56.

21. *Cuarenta*, forty in Spanish, is the term used by locals of Guadalupe to refer to the original forty acres.

22. *Maestro* means teacher in Spanish. Jesuit missionaries utilized them as associates during the Christianization of the Yaqui. Capitan de los Fariseos (Soldiers of Rome) leads the community during the Lenten ceremonies.

23. Eric Meeks, "Cross-Ethnic Political Mobilization and Yaqui Identity Formation in Guadalupe, Arizona," in *Reflexiones 1997: New Directions in Mexican American Studies*, ed. Neil Foley (Austin: CMAS Books, 1998).

24. *Compadrazgo* is a system of ceremonial sponsorship.

25. Mark E. Miller, "The Yaquis Become American Indians: The Process of Federal Tribal Recognition," *The Journal of Arizona History* 35 (1994): 183–204.

26. Yaqui Family Literacy Partnership Program, *Needs Assessment* (Tucson: Pima Community College, 1989).

27. Tempe Elementary School District 3, *Culture: A Way to Reading* (Tempe, Arizona: 1979); Octaviana V. Trujillo, "A Tribal Approach to Language and Literacy in a Trilingual Setting," in *Teaching Indigenous Languages*, ed. J. Reyhner (Flagstaff: Northern Arizona University, 1997), 10–21.

28. William Leap, "The Study of American Indian English: An Introduction to the Issues," in *Papers in Southwestern English II: Studies in Southwestern Indian English*, ed. William Leap (San Antonio: Trinity University, 1977), 33–41.

29. Leap, "Study of American Indian English."

30. Ward Goodenough, *Culture, Language, and Society* (Menlo Park, Calif.: Cummings Publishing Co., 1981), 102.

31. Tempe Elementary School District 3, *Culture: A Way to Reading*.

32. John H. Chilcott, "Where Are You Coming From and Where Are You Going?: The Reporting Of Ethnographic Research," *American Educational Research Journal* 24 (1987): 199–218; John H. Chilcott, "Yaqui World View and the School: Conflict and Accommodation," *Journal of American Indian Education* 2 (1985): 21–32.

33. *Guadalupe Organization, Inc. v. Tempe Elementary School District No. 3*, No. Civ. 71–435 (Phoenix, August 10, 1971).

34. Cathryn Retzlaff, "Guadalupe Kids Celebrate Town's Pride," *Arizona Republic*, 10 February 1982, extra.

35. Cathryn R. Shaffer, "Trilingual School Keeps Hanging On During Hard Times," *Arizona Republic*, 12 October 1983, extra.

36. Octaviana V. Trujillo, "Guadalupe: Conflict and Civil Rights in a Tricultural Setting," in *Living the Dream in Arizona: The Legacy of Martin Luther King Jr.*, ed. G. M. Bataille and A. L. McHenry (Tempe: Arizona State University, 1992), 21–5.

37. Editorial, "Seven Year War Rages On Still Unsettled," *The Arizona Forum*, March 1978.

38. Tempe Elementary School District 3, *A Compliance Plan of Educational Strategies for Eliminating Educational Practices Ruled Unlawful under Lau vs. Nichols for Non-English Speaking Students of the Tempe Elementary School District #3* (Tempe, Ariz: 1977).

39. Tempe Elementary School District 3, *A Compliance Plan*.

40. Octaviana Trujillo, "Yaqui Views on Language and Literacy," (Ph.D. diss., Arizona State University, 1991), 123–48.

41. Ibid.

42. R. Erickson and J. Shultz, "When Is a Context? Some Issues and Methods in the Analysis of Social Competence," in *Ethnography and Language in Educational Settings*, ed. J. Green & C. Wallat (Norwood, N.J.: Ablex, 1981), 106–12.

43. John Singleton, "Implications of Education as Cultural Transmission," in *Education and Cultural Process: Towards an Anthropology of Education*, ed. G. O. Spindler (New York: Holt, Rinehart, and Winston, Inc., 1974), 26–38.

44. Noam Chomsky, *Aspects of the Theory of Syntax* (Cambridge: Massachusetts Institute of Technology Press, 1965).

STRUCTURING AND DYNAMICS OF URBAN COMMUNITIES

II

Introduction

SUSAN LOBO

THIS SECTION EMPHASIZES the overall nature of urban Indian communities: their structuring, the dynamics within these communities, and some of the ways that linkage and interaction take place with surrounding nonurban areas. Just what is a "community" and what are some of the ways it is both defined and conceptualized by its members? This is a tricky question—as I comment in my contribution to this section—the often-used concept of community may not be as "simple or one-dimensional as it appears." I characterize the urban Indian community as "a widely scattered and frequently shifting network of relationships with locational nodes found in organizations and activity sites of special significance." While reflecting the reality of urban Indian communities, this definition emphasizes the less evident forms that relationships take, rather than adhering to the frequent definitions of community that stress ethnically contiguous neighborhoods. Weibel-Orlando focuses on the role of the Southern California Indian Center and the structural, administrative, and philosophical basis for what has been a very successful and long-standing core institution in the Indian community. Throughout this book, other authors, including Jackson, Lowery, and Gonzales, stress that community is not essentially a place, but rather it is characterized by relationships that bond people together and is therefore one of the ways that identity is established.

This section also clarifies and defines a number of other seemingly simple terms and concepts that are often used, but whose meanings and connotations are rarely discussed in depth. These include "urban," "tribe," and "Indian." Straus and Valentino particularly emphasize that "tribalness" is not lost in urban contexts, as some feared and predicted, but rather has been redefined and augmented. In this section, Peters, Straus and Valentino, Lang, and Beck take a careful look at the multiple ways in which urban Indian communities have reconnected to more rural "tribal" homelands and, in so doing, have often redefined or enriched what it is to be Indian.

Another theme that emerges in this section is gender roles in urban settings. Hoikkala writes on "American Indian Women and Political Activism in Phoenix, 1965–1980," focusing on the modes of women's leadership in building and sustaining the community. Using the example of the Phoenix area, Hoikkala says,

"Women accepted the tasks assigned to them in the gender systems of their societies but, by the same token, they demanded the rights that their obligations entailed." This comment is echoed regarding both men and women in other parts of the book: in Garcia's poem "My Uncle," and in Thompson's about Tina Deschenie, in the diligent Peter and Dereck waiting at the bus stop that Manriquez depicts, and in Beck's discussion of the women and men who use their urban ties to influence the protection of tribal land-based resources.

How are urban communities linked to more rural tribal homelands, and how do individuals relate both to cities and homelands? Introduced in this section, this question reemerges repeatedly throughout the book. Peters talks about the relationship between Laguna Pueblo railroaders in Richmond, California, and the Atchison, Topeka, and Santa Fe railroad company. He discusses how establishing a village at the railhead created, in a sense, an outlying urban colony linked to Laguna Pueblo. Beck, Lang, and I describe some of the forms that relationships take that likewise create ties between "back home" and the City. Westerman's lyrics to "Quiet Desperation" convey the emotion when one is in the city but the heart recalls the smell of sweet grass on the plains.

Is Urban a Person or a Place? 4
Characteristics of Urban Indian Country

SUSAN LOBO

⊞

IS URBAN A PERSON OR A PLACE? Urban is a place, a setting where many Indian people at some time in their lives visit, "establish an encampment," or settle into. Urban doesn't determine self-identity, yet the urban area and urban experiences are contexts that contribute to defining identity. The intent of this chapter is to delineate some of the general structural characteristics of urban Indian communities in the United States and to indicate the ways that urban communities interplay with individual and group identity. While most of the focused research for this discussion has been carried out since 1978 in the San Francisco Bay Area and the principal examples are specific to this region, many of the comments are also applicable on a general level to other urban Indian communities such as those found in Seattle, Los Angeles, and Chicago. The work, for example, of Garbarino and Straus in Chicago, Liebow in Phoenix, Shoemaker in Minneapolis, Bramstedt and Weibel-Orlando in Los Angeles, Danziger in Detroit, and Guillemin in Boston indicate parallels and counterpoints to the regional focus of this chapter.[1]

Each Indian community throughout the United States and Canada has its unique character, yet traveling from one to another, visiting friends and family, and participating in events around the country, it is evident that there are also many underlying similarities that characterize urban Indian Country and that these fundamental similarities create a setting that is "like home" in the city. Some of the significant factors influencing the parallels among different urban Indian communities (as well as each community's unique qualities) include the historic role played by the relocation program and other types of policy-driven external influences; the degree of proximity and ease of travel and communication between cities and tribal areas, reservations, and homelands; and the availability of employment, housing, and educational opportunities. An in-depth comparative study of various urban Indian communities is long, long overdue.

This chapter is based on long-term applied work, research, and personal engagement in the San Francisco Bay Area American Indian community. I began in 1978 as a co-founder and have continued as the coordinator of the Community History Project located at the Oakland American Indian Center, Intertribal Friendship House (IFH). The Center was established in 1955 and is, along with the Chicago Indian

Center, one of the oldest urban Indian centers in the United States. It was founded in response to the federal relocation program and to the incipient demographic shift toward the city by Indian people that was then getting underway. As one of the early urban Indian institutions nationally, Intertribal Friendship House and the Bay Area Indian community overall continue to loom large on the Indian Country cognitive map. It is remarked by many Bay Area Indian residents that wherever one goes, no matter how remote, how seemingly unlikely, you can bet that whoever you may be talking to will say in effect, "Sure, I know Oakland. We used to go to the Wednesday night dinners at IFH all the time," or, "We were there for a while when I was young and I remember my Mom took me over to see the buffaloes at the San Francisco zoo when I was six, for my birthday. Boy, they were sure in bad shape. I still remember her saying that they didn't know how to really take care of them." IFH is identified by many as the emotional "heart" of the Bay Area Indian community. It is the ideal urban Indian community crossroads where the Community History Project, a photographic and oral history archive, has developed. This is a collection of contemporary, urban-focused historic materials that is referred to as a community resource archives because of the active involvement of the community in formulating, building, and using the archives for purposes identified by the community itself.

The IFH Community History Project, which started as a narrowly defined oral history project, has grown into an extensive Indian-controlled and community-based research unit and archive of taped oral histories, photographs, videos and films, documents, and ephemera focusing on the Bay Area American Indian community from the 1940s to the present. This is, to my knowledge, one of the very few, and also the most extensive, archive emphasizing contemporary Indian history within an urban area. It is also a working archive, open to the Indian community as well as to outside researchers. It is actively circulated, added to, reformulated, interpreted, and used for a wide array of educational and advocacy purposes. My experience immersed in this material, participating in the continual flow of community events and activities, and working jointly with Indian community members on an ongoing basis on a variety of community projects is the foundation for the description and analysis that follows.

Methodologically, this kind of deep, long-term, and unabashedly personal involvement in a community allows for an understanding of both those aspects of the community that change and those that persist over time, sometimes stretching across generations. For example, there are those delicate balances of power, informed by kinship and tribal affiliation, or the routes that leadership and alliance formation take, all continually shifting and yet simultaneously unfolding fluidly over long periods of time.

The Community

For American Indians living in the Bay Area, and for our definitional purposes here, the Indian community is not a geographic location with clustered residency or neighborhoods, but rather it is fundamentally a widely scattered and frequently shifting network of relationships with locational nodes found in organizations and activity sites of special significance. It is a distinct community that answers needs for affirming and activating identity; it creates contexts for carrying out the necessary activities of community life; and it provides a wide range of circumstances and symbols that foster "Indian" relationships at the family and community levels.

The American Indian community in the San Francisco Bay Area is characterized here on a general level as a social group in which:

1. community members recognize a shared identity;
2. there are shared values, symbols, and history;
3. basic institutions have been created and sustained; and
4. there are consistent features of social organization such as those related to social control and the definition of distinctive and specialized gender- and age-related roles.

There are geographic markers around the Bay that set the stage for community activities: the enclosing hills, the Bay, the bridges that connect the East Bay with San Francisco and San Francisco with Marin County. However, these geographic features only set the stage for the "Indian map" of the area. This "map" charts the shared abstract connotations of people who speak of "going to the Healing Center," a residential treatment center for women and their children, or nodding with the head to the north of downtown Oakland and saying, "over by CRC," an American Indian family and child assistance agency. People in the Indian community know where these points of reference are; those not participating in the community would not know. Another example of such shared connotations is when an Indian person comments, quite possibly totally out of context, "You going to Stanford?" the question is not, "Do you attend Stanford University?" but rather, "Will I see you at the Stanford pow-wow this May?" Or when someone says, "I saw your niece up at Hilltop," the reference is to a high-profile Indian bar, not to be confused with a shopping mall of the same name. Each of these examples illustrates one of the ways in which Indian people in the Bay Area talk about or interpret their environment as both a setting for community as a place and also as deeply intertwined with the network of relatedness that ties members together as a community. Theodoratus and LaPena express this idea well in reference to Wintu sacred geography: "[This paper] is about topographical features that are the embodiment of Wintu expression of an ordinary and nonordinary world. It is about a concept of land and interpretations of that natural universe that translate into a coherent world."[2] In the case of the Bay Area Indian vision of community, both the topographical features and the built environment are a part of creating this "coherent world."

The physical environment, while the backdrop and the grounding for much of the community activity, is not "the community," which instead finds its focus in relationship dynamics and the more abstract realm of shared knowledge that informs and shapes actions. An urban Indian community is not situated in an immutable, bounded territory as a reservation is, but rather exists within a fluidly defined region with niches of resources and boundaries that respond to needs and activities, perhaps reflecting a reality closer to that of Native homelands prior to the imposition of reservation borders. For example, with the development and flourishing of D-Q University, an Indian-controlled community college, the conceptualization of the Bay Area Indian community extended sixty miles to the north to include this institution as an outlying entity.

On tribal homelands a major source of identity is embodied in the land, and often in the old stories and songs that tie personal reality to time and place. As Basso notes, "Knowledge of place is therefore closely linked to knowledge of the self, to grasping one's position in the larger scheme of things, including one's own community, and to securing a confident sense of who one is as a person."[3] Yet in an urban community there is essentially no land base, except for those few recently purchased buildings and properties. Or, on the other hand, as someone recently pointed out to me, "all of it is our urban territory." In this urban context, the Indian organizations come to powerfully represent Indian "space" or "a place that is Indian" and are intimately tied to identity. Consequently, the control, the programs, and the guiding values of these organizations are under constant scrutiny, negotiation, and adjustment by core community members who act as arbitrators.

To many outside the urban Indian community it is an invisible population, both because of the abstract and nongeographically clustered nature of the community, but also because of the continued existence of a series of stereotypes regarding Indian people. A widespread and mistaken assumption held by the general public is that American Indians have "vanished" or live overwhelmingly on reservations in rural areas. In reality, this is an expanding population, and the majority of Indian people now live in urban areas. In much of the social science literature and federal and state policy, as well as in criteria frequently utilized by funding sources, there is a mindset that imposes a dichotomy between urban and rural, based on the lingering stereotype that "Indian" is synonymous with rural and that urban is somehow not genuinely Indian. While there are certainly differences in these two types of settings, establishing rural/ urban as the defining characteristic of identity is not realistic from an Indian point of view and serves to further officially alienate Indian people from homelands. One of the most notorious recent policies reflecting this attitude was Relocation, initiated in the 1950s and based on government assumptions that Indian people, once removed or relocated from tribal homelands, would become urban . . . definitively. Conversely, for many Indian people the urban areas are visualized more as an extension of home territory, or as one person put it, "our urban encampment out here." For those living in the city, even those a few generations removed from tribal homelands, these strong linkages to "back home" are, for the most part, not broken. One simply extends the sense of territory, often keenly aware, for example, that sacred places are found at home and that after death one will very likely be buried there. For third- and fourth-generation urban people, this connection to Home may change and take new forms but nevertheless continues.

The underlying Native sense of community—if viewed fundamentally as a network of relatedness that has become subsequently structured in many tribal homelands into formalized, federally prescribed tribes—reemerges in the city as the rigid, bounded "tribe" demanded by the government of federally recognized tribes falls away. In this volume Straus also discusses this aspect of urban communities. The federal government's image of a tribe as a bounded entity within a geographically rigid, demarcated territory or reservation, governed by a body of elected officials, and with stringently designated criteria for membership is not transferred to urban Indian communities. In contrast, here in cities, the social entity is reconstituted with a structuring based on a network of relatedness. The fluid territory has changing outer limits, there is no over-arching formalized governing body, and membership is defined by a series of strongly situational and to some degree negotiable criteria.

The most striking urban parallel to the tribal political structuring found on rural reservations is the legal non-profit status of many urban Indian organizations in which there is a governing board of directors, by-laws, and possibly membership lists. However, Indian people in the city, in contrast to the situation in a reservation tribal setting, are not governed by these organizations, nor do the organizations establish and enforce criteria for community membership. In the city, people may choose whether to become active in any particular organization at any specific time.

Although structured differently, the urban community comes to hold many connotations for Indian people that are similar to those of the tribe. The urban community gives a sense of belonging, meets a need to look inward to this social entity, and fosters a feeling of responsibility to contribute to the well-being of the members via support of the continuity and flourishing of urban institutions. In the Bay Area one occasionally hears joking reference to the Indian community as "The Urban Tribe."

One of the underlying objectives of the federal relocation program initiated in the 1950s was the assimilation of American Indians into an envisioned mainstream. Yet to many Indian people in the Bay Area, the existence and resiliency of the Indian community is an expression of resistance to pressure and domination by the non-Indian world. One factor in this persistence is the fluid, network-based social structure. As Indian people often explain it, the community itself has the potential for regeneration. The community is ephemeral in nature, as Coyote has taught people to appreciate, with the power to continually take new forms and thus endure. Or it is described as being like the old-time warrior's strategy to disperse, vanish, become invisible, and then to regroup to fight again another day. This dynamic is a familiar one to Indian people, who throughout the history of Indian–White relations and before have sought ways to persist as individuals and as peoples. The institutions in the Indian community are in continual flux, able to disassemble and reassemble. Yet through all of this motion, there is an underlying network structure that allows for persistence.

The urban community, in addition to having become the doorway to urban jobs and education, also functions as a doorway and a refuge for those who have unsolvable problems or who are deemed undesirable in their home reservation areas. Emo, the villain in Silko's classic novel *Ceremony*, is last mentioned leaving New Mexico, "'They told him to never come back around here. The old man said that. I heard he went to California.'. . . 'California,' Tayo repeated softly, 'that's a good place for him.'"[4] The urban community is also a gateway for those, such as Jackson discusses in this volume, who have been alienated from their tribal roots and who wish to reidentify as Indian.[5] There are also those with hazily defined, distant Indian ancestry who create a niche for themselves in the urban Indian community and who are generally accepted if they make a substantial contribution to the community wellbeing. Increasingly the urban community is a doorway into Indian Country for Indian people who were "adopted out" in infancy—that is, raised in foster care or adopted by non-Indian families—and who seek to reestablish their Indianness in adulthood. Snipp has discussed some of these mechanisms of reidentification in regard to the increasing U.S. census count of American Indians.[6]

The American Indian community is also characterized by a geographic mobility as people move in and out of the city, make return visits to their rural home territories or reservations, or sometimes return there for good. People speak of circulating through, or of establishing a temporary urban living situation as a way of indicating that living in the Bay Area is viewed by some as an extension of their original territory. At the same time, people often speak longingly of "back home," and there are shared in-group and tribally specific understandings of the connotations that "back home" holds. These are expressed in jokes ("You know that one about the Doggy Diner down on East Twelfth and the two Sioux guys who just come into town?"), in music (rap group WithOut Rezervation–WOR's CD cover speaks of the group's tie to "the mean streets of Oakland"), and in reference to aspects of the natural world. Movement through space, as movement through time, is a part of living.

In addition to increasing dramatically in population over the past fifty years, the Bay Area Indian community, as characteristic of many urban Indian communities, has become increasingly diverse and complex in the following ways.

1. *There has been a proliferation of organizations*, the crucial nodes on the network of community. This array of organizations has become increasingly specialized as community needs become apparent and funding and human resources become available. For example, the generalized multiservice Indian Center has spawned a now-separate preschool and a number of other educational efforts, as well as many specialized cultural arts and social activities and social-service–focused organizations and projects.

2. *The community is now multigenerational.* Whereas the first generation to come to the Bay Area through relocation in the 1950s was primarily young single people and young families, the infant fourth generation is now often seen playing at their mothers' feet during meetings. This generational layering means that experiences, urban personal histories, and orientation toward both urban and rural contexts have become increasingly varied. The urban angst expressed in the now-classic Floyd Red Crow Westerman songs of the 1970s such as "Quiet Desperation" and "Going Home" are contrasted with the more hard-hitting contemporary urban Indian music.

3. *The community is multitribal.* And, as intertribal marriages continue to occur, the children and grandchildren are themselves often multitribal. This has the potential to enrich each child's identity, but also to create complexities related to tribal enrollment and tribally based cultural knowledge. Recent research in the Bay Area in which 290 women were interviewed indicated 90 tribes represented, 35 in-state tribes and 57 from out of state.[7]

4. *The community is linked* in increasingly diverse ways to often geographically distant people and places in Indian homelands. The term *Indian Country* has come to include the urban communities. Family members visit from home and visits to home are made to attend funerals, see relatives, or to take children there for the summer. Many people return home for personal and spiritual renewal. Some return home to avoid problems with the law. Some older people decide to retire back home. Medicine people frequently come out to the city for ceremonies, or people return home for ceremonies. There is the recent and increasing presence in the city of the nearby "Casino Tribes" via their in-town offices and staff. There are also those living on the streets who follow an annual seasonal route between various cities and rural areas.

5. *There is increased economic and class diversity* in the Bay Area Indian community, with some resulting from educational opportunities that first became available in the late 1960s, and some the result of business and professional successes. There are those living hand-to-mouth on the streets, and there are those arriving in splendor at the gala annual American Indian Film Festival at the Palace of Fine Arts in San Francisco. Those living on the streets are not excluded from the community; nor are those living in the hills of Berkeley. In fact, they may all sit at the same long table at the Indian Center during a community feast. There are the many whose education does not include high school graduation and there are those completing their doctorates in ethnic studies, anthropology, or education at the University of California at Berkeley or Stanford, or those taking advanced computer courses at the community-based United Indian Nations in Oakland.

6. *There is now a recognized urban history,* and a community persona that is frequently referenced and that creates a framework for shared identity. A series of events

and people, tied to dates, is shared in the minds of community members as being symbolically significant. For example, particularly memorable are the occupation of Alcatraz, the Bay Area Princess competitions, the old Intertribal Friendship House music festivals, and the annual Stanford pow-wow. Everyone knows who is being referred to when there is mention of Floyd or Bill within specific contexts. And the old-timers have full recollections of Walter and Mrs. Carnes. Remembrances are filled with shared connotations. "Remember when they drew the ticket for that raffled car, there was standing room only, and it was the director's girlfriend who got it!" Ah, yes. And what about the meeting twenty-three years ago, "And your grandmother stood up and, in front of everyone, said *that* about my aunt at that board meeting." Everyone gives "that look," remembering this event well; if they weren't there they certainly heard about it in detail. A well-known activist leader recalled recently to a group, "And we started right here. We started the Longest Walk to Washington D.C. right at this door." Many nodded in agreement and remembrance. These are parables of life in the city and a means of validating the shared historical content of urban living as a community.

Identity

With their implications of inclusion and exclusion, the defining of who is Indian and the issue of who does the identifying are complicated and emotion-laden topics any-where in Indian Country. For example, there is self-identity, there is identity externally imposed, there are the situationally appropriate shifts in identity, and there are the shifts in identity that may occur over a lifetime. In urban areas, although no roles exist com-parable to tribal roles, there are a number of other ways by which one is identified by self and others as a community member and as Indian. Gonzales also discusses many of the nuances related to the question of identity in this volume. The urban Indian community is most frequently invisible to the non-Indian world, both informally in the general public mind that has not discarded the stereotype that everything Indian is ru-ral and in the past, but also formally via institutions such as the U.S. Census Bureau that has yet to adequately count urban Indian people.[8] Likewise, the federal emphasis on an-cestry as the outstanding defining criteria, represented in a "blood quantum" model, is a much narrower and limiting criteria than that found in urban Indian communities.

Within the urban community there is a very different perspective regarding mem-bership from that found on those tribal homelands structured by federally imposed criteria. As with the fluidity of defining the urban "territory," membership in the ur-ban Indian community and the link to Indianness as defined by the community is like-wise fluid. Membership in the Indian community is known and agreed upon through informal consensus. Indian people feel comfortable with this approach. This is the way it is, through consensus, rather than written on a piece of paper, a document.

There is a shared understanding by participants of the social boundaries of the American Indian community, as well as the membership within the community. These boundaries and sense of membership are fluid, however, and always under review and negotiation. Those non-Indians who do not participate, who are external to the community, are not aware of these dynamics that tie the community together and mark who is "in the community" and who is not. Defining Indianness in the city is therefore essentially released from the burden of the formalized documentation imposed on federally recognized tribes. For example, as a strategy to channel the outcome of the board election at one of the urban organizations in the Bay Area, a board member recently sent out a letter indicating that in order to vote, community members should bring documentation proving they were Indian. Many people—those who could bring forward documentation and those who could not—were acutely offended. The strategy backfired and the board member was roundly criticized for taking an inappropriate stance. Her request was ignored at the polls.

Another example of the rejection and disdain in an urban setting for federally imposed tribal formulae, emanating from governmental demands for enrollment numbers, was demonstrated by a group of Bay Area Indian artists in protest of laws requiring proof of Indianness in order to exhibit their art as Indian artists. One artist, Hulleah Tsinhnahjinnie, took a series of defiant photographs of herself with numbers painted across her forehead. In essence, these people are asserting, "I am Indian because I say I am," "I am Indian because you know me and my family and see me participate in the community," and "I am Indian because I know what it is to be Indian: the protocols, the jokes, the knowledge of shared history, the racism and struggle that are a part of who we all are." "Trying to identify me as a number is fucked."

Thus, in urban areas Indian identity is defined through:

1. *Ancestry*: Does a person have Indian relatives and ancestors, and function as a member of an Indian extended family?
2. *Appearance*: Does a person look "Indian"?
3. *Cultural knowledge*: Is the person knowledgeable of the culture of their People and of those pan-Indian values and social expectations shared within the urban Indian community?
4. *Indian community participation*: Does the person "come out" for Indian events and activities in the Indian community and contribute to the community well-being?

The weight and combination given to these elements to determine Indian identity vary situationally and, to some extent, are always under community assessment, shifting with the changing times. For example, there are many people well accepted in the Bay Area Indian community who may not "look very Indian," who may not have verifiable documented Indian ancestry, yet—through a long history of actively participating in and contributing to the community well-being, as well as demonstrating a thorough understanding of Indian values and protocols—will be deemed without hesitation to be a member of the Indian community . . . until a conflict arises, then this combination may be critically scrutinized.

In an urban area there is an element of choice as each individual determines to what degree and in what circumstances tribal membership and urban Indian community participation is actualized. Thus, situationally, individuals may choose which criteria of Indianness may be activated and when. Some Indian people living in the Bay Area are affiliated with a home tribe but do not choose to participate in or identify with the urban Indian community during a particular time in their life. Others are actively engaged as members of their home tribes, and are also participants in, and identify with, the Bay Area American Indian community. Others may not be enrolled or active participants in their home tribes, yet they may be very involved and active in the urban community. Logically there are also some people who, though identifying as Indian, do not participate in or identify with either the urban community or a home tribe. There are some people who have chosen at some point in their life as a result of racism, assimilation pressures, or out-marrying, to pass as a non-Indian—for example as Mexican, Italian, or White. Increasingly, many of these individuals are choosing to reevaluate their racial self-identity, and often to reestablish their American Indian identity by reintegrating into and becoming active in an urban Indian community.[9]

The position of children in the urban community is a telling one. In an urban community as tribally diverse as that of the Bay Area, there may come to be, after two or three generations, a number of children who, while undeniably Indian genetically, may have difficulty becoming enrolled in any one particular tribe due to mixed tribal ancestry and tribally specific criteria for enrollment. There is also the consideration that some children with a mother from a patrilineal tribe and a father from a matrilineal tribe may not be recognized by or enrolled in either tribe. These children of mixed tribal heritage and those of Indian/non-Indian heritage who may have difficulties related to formal tribal enrollment are, nevertheless, often active and accepted participants in the urban Indian community. Indian parents who are involved in the Bay Area community and whose children, for one of the reasons sketched here, do not have strong ties to a home tribe, often express concern that their children will lose their identity as American Indians and anguish over the problems that may be associated with tribal enrollment. A major theme of activities in the Bay Area Indian community is that participation validates and heightens Indian identity, and parents frequently facilitate their children's participation, knowing that this participation will foster a strong sense of Indian identity, as well as acceptance by the community. For example, children may join in special educational efforts such as attending Hintil Ku Caa's preschool and after-school programs, participate with the family in pow-wows and other activities, or come with their families to events such as the Wednesday night dinner at Intertribal Friendship House.

Concluding Remarks

This chapter raises the caution that a much used concept such as "community" may not be as simple or as one-dimensional as it appears. It is important to pay close attention to the ways that people and communities of people perceive and define their environment, in terms of both its physical and social aspects.

Some of the fundamental ways in which the complex urban Indian community in the San Francisco Bay Area has constituted itself and, in turn, how this community structuring relates to identity, have been delineated here. Conceptually, the community here is primarily abstract, based as it is on a series of very dynamic relationships and shared meanings, history, and symbols, rather than on the more commonly assumed clustered residential and commercial neighborhood. It is particularly noteworthy that, although most Indian people living in the San Francisco Bay Area take advantage of the recreational opportunities the parks offer, live in a wide range of apartments and houses, and are, by and large, adept users of the roads and freeways, this physical environment, while the backdrop and the physical grounding for much of the community activity, is not "the community." The community instead finds its focus in relationship dynamics and the more abstract realm of shared knowledge that informs and shapes actions.

Notes

1. See Merwyn S. Garbarino, "Life in the City: Chicago," in *American Indian in Urban Society*, ed., J. Waddell and R. Watson (Boston: Little, Brown, and Co. 1971); Terry Straus, "Retribalization in Urban Indian Communities" (paper presented at the American Anthropological Association Meetings, San Francisco, 1996) and *Native Chicago* (Chicago: University of Chicago Press, 1998); Edward B. Liebow, "Urban Indian Institutions in Phoenix: Transformation from Headquarters City to Community," *Journal of Ethnic Studies* 18, no. 4 (1991); Nancy Shoemaker, "Urban Indians and Ethnic Choices: American Indian Organizations in Minneapolis, 1920–1950," *The Western History Quarterly* (November 1988); Wayne G. Bramstedt, *Corporate Adaptations of Urban Migrants: American Indian Voluntary Associations in the Los Angeles Metropolitan Area* (Los Angeles, Ph.D. diss., University of California, 1977); Joan Weibel-Orlando, *Indian Country, L.A.: Maintaining Ethnic Community in Complex Society* (Urbana: University of Illinois Press, 1991); Edmund Jefferson Danziger Jr., *Survival and Regeneration: Detroit's American Indian Community* (Detroit: Wayne State University Press, 1991); and Jeanne Guillemin, *Urban Renegades: The Cultural Strategy of American Indians* (New York: Columbia University Press, 1975).

2. Dorothea J. Theodoratus and Frank LaPena, "Wintu Sacred Geography," in *California Indian Shamanism*, ed. Lowell Bean (Menlo Park, Calif.: Ballena Press, 1992), 211.

3. Keith H. Basso, *Wisdom Sits in Places: Landscape and Language among the Western Apache* (Albuquerque: University of New Mexico Press, 1996), 34.

4. Leslie Marmon Silko, *Ceremony* (New York: The Viking Press, 1977), 260.

5. Deborah Jackson, *Urban Indian Identity and the Violence of Silence* (paper presented at the American Anthropological Association Meetings, San Francisco, 1996). Another version of this paper appeared in the *American Indian Culture and Research Journal* 22, no. 4, 1998, and as a chapter in this book.

6. C. Matthew Snipp, *American Indians: The First of This Land* (New York: Russell Sage Foundation, 1989).

7. Dorie Klein, Elaine Zahnd, Bohdan Kolody, Sue Holtby, and Loraine T. Midanik, *Pregnant and Parenting American Indian Study* (Berkeley: Western Consortium for Public Health and San Diego State University Foundation, 1995).

8. For discussion of the Indian undercount in the Bay Area see Susan Lobo, *Oakland's American Indian Community: History, Social Organization and Factors that Contribute to Census Undercount* (Washington, D.C., Center for Survey Methods Research, Bureau of the Census, 1990). *American Indians in the San Francisco Bay Area and the 1990 Census, Ethnographic Exploratory Research Report #18* (Washington, D.C.: Center for Survey Methods Research, Bureau of the Census, 1992).

9. C. Matthew Snipp, *American Indians.*

Retribalization in Urban Indian Communities 5

TERRY STRAUS and DEBRA VALENTINO

I N THE 1970s, the late Bob Thomas (Cherokee) of the University of Arizona warned that Indian people were becoming "ethnic Indians" with no tribal knowledge or connection, especially in the intertribal, interethnic urban environment. "There is now a whole generation of Indians," he argued, "who have been born, raised and socialized in the city. . . . A great many city-raised Indians are not distinctively Indian in the way that they behave or the way that they think about things";[1] and later, "I'm not so sure in my mind if Indians can exist as city people. The city really cuts one off from the 'natural' world. Can the Indian's sacred world continue in a world of concrete and automobiles?"[2] Social relations of Indians in cities, moreover, take place primarily with non-Indians: "American Indians do not live in old-style, bounded, ethnic neighborhoods as did earlier immigrants, but are scattered throughout the population," which means that "there is very little of an Indian community in most cities. There are Indians living in cities and there are Indian centers in cities . . . and you see some Indians involved with Indian centers. But they are a minority of the Indians who live in cities."[3]

In this view, quite common in the 1970s, pan-Indianism was understood inevitably to displace tribal knowledge, identity, and connection for Native Americans in urban areas. Urban residence was thus seen as a major threat to Indian people. Pan-Indianism, an artificial foil invented to facilitate federal policy, was seen gradually and insidiously to become accepted by Indian people as their own identity. On the one hand, Thomas got "the uneasy feeling that we have come to believe the slogans that we present to the non-Indian public,"[4] such as, Indian people were increasingly accepting dominant definitions of themselves as an "ethnic group" and a "racial minority." "Along with all of the emotional problems that come with viewing one's self and group as a racial minority of a larger society, rank considerations, negative definitions, social acceptance, subtle discrimination, etc."[5] This assumption of dominant-society definitions is a central aspect of what Thomas called the "internal colonialism" that had become a serious "impediment to analysis" by Indian people.

Thomas warned against urban residence and generic, intertribal pan-Indianism. Like much of what he wrote, these warnings were intended for Indians, presented in

Indian gatherings, and rarely published. Like most of what Thomas wrote, it was insightful, sincere, and straightforward.[6] Here, as elsewhere, he demonstrated an understanding of the interplay of internal and external stereotypes and of essentialized and fluid constructs in the process of identity creation, which other anthropologists are only just now, a quarter of a century later, beginning to apprehend and acknowledge. He spoke, however, to Indian people, not to anthropologists, warning against the external imposition and internal invention of intertribal "Indian" identity. In his view, the extent to which Indian people accepted their Indianness and participated in pan-Indian culture and communities, especially urban Indian communities, was the extent to which tribal identity culture and self-determination would be lost. Many came to agree with this perspective.

Twenty-five years later, and with the advantage of hindsight, we suggest here that the process Thomas and many others recognized and resisted has taken an unexpected turn, especially in urban Indian communities. To develop the argument, however, we need to clarify its conceptual base, specifying what we mean by "urban," "tribe," and "Indian."

"Urban" is not a kind of Indian. It is a kind of experience, one that most Indian people today have had. There are urban areas on or closely bordering many reservations; there is a lot of movement between urban and reservation communities; and in today's world, telephones, television, and the Internet expose every reservation to the problems and perks of urban life. The rift between urban and reservation Indian people is artificial and imposed. It derives in large part from the federal policy that excluded off-reservation Indians from tribal treaty rights, as clearly acknowledged in Title 8 (Urban and Rural Non-Reservation Indians) of the American Indian Policy Review Commission.

"Tribe" must also be understood in the context of federal policy. "Tribe" was neither a Native concept nor a Native political reality. Instead, the concept of "peoplehood" is often used to define the sense of commonality and relationship among those who speak the same language, share the same lands and lifeways, and participate in common ceremonies and celebrations. "Tribes" began, if we accept Cornell, in the conflict and negotiation with non-Indian governments. Political units and political leaders were established for the purpose of treaty negotiations. Those political units became associated with specific, defined territories and special legal and political status within the federal government.[7] Federal policy also required the counting of Indians as tribal members and the establishment of membership criteria.[8] "Tribalism" was fostered by the Indian Reorganization Act, which established reservation political units as corporate groups eligible for federal loan programs and democratic republics that were to be the basis of Indian "self-government." Original or assigned reservation lands, once considered temporary halfway houses for assimilation, became redefined as tribal homelands, critical features of tribal identity. While some recognized the ill fit between the idea of a "tribe" and their own sociopolitical reality and therefore resisted "tribalization," "tribe" became the recognized political unit in Indian Country. It is also the unit of ethnic identity and enumeration.

"Indian" is taken here to mean pan-Indian or intertribal: an identity likewise derived from the interplay of external and internal definitions. While it is popular, politically correct, and in many ways important to note that Indian people did not think of themselves as Indians until they were so identified by others, it must be simultaneously asserted that intertribal exchange of items, ideas, and individuals occurred long before European presence in the "New World." Today, Native peoples on reservations as well as in urban areas identify as Indian and as members or affiliates of a particular tribe or tribes. These variant identities are situationally determined and differ at different points in the life cycle.

When Thomas predicted that Indian people in urban areas would become generic "Indians," he intended to sound the alarm against what he called detribalization. Urban Indians, inventing community in the urban setting, necessarily engaged in the project of acknowledging and creating common ground, common culture, and common identity. In Chicago, for example, the first organizations bore names such as Indian Council Fire and All Tribes American Indian Center, affirming awareness of the project implied in the creation of community in the city.

But Chicago has been a meeting ground for Indian people since before the fur trade. The Illini and Miami people, the earliest known historic residents of the area, were not tribes but confederations of Algonquian-speaking communities. Many of these people left the area when Potawatomi, Chippewa, and Odawa moved in under fur trade pressure. Those who did not leave joined the new Indian communities. (The fur trade founders of early Chicago, men such as Beaubien, Robinson, Mirandeau, Caldwell, and LaFramboise, were mostly half breed Potawatomis whose mothers were full-blood tribal people and whose fathers were white traders and trappers.) Sixty years after the Treaty of Chicago by which the Potawatomis relinquished their claim to the land, the World's Columbian Exposition was held there, bringing yet other Indian people into a much changed city. The Dawes Act was in full swing and boarding schools, extolled in one exhibit, were firmly incorporated: "Indianness" was already well established. World War I caused some movement of Indian people, including movement into cities. The first intertribal Indian organization in Chicago, the Indian Council Fire, established in 1923, incorporated those new "urban Indians." When the city population grew significantly in response to World War II and the postwar relocation program, generations of Indian people had already imagined and worked towards the development of an urban Indian community.

Federal relocation "terminated" individual Indians, distinguishing Indians in cities from those on reservations. Tribal programs and privileges focused on reservation residents; tribal elections excluded off-reservation voters; tribal culture was intricately bound up with tribal land; tribal language could remain vital only in tribal communities. Lame Deer and others proclaimed, "The city is not a good place for a ceremony," while Thomas worried that "you can't have any personal spiritual power or medicine if you live in the city," and tribal traditions that could not be practiced or taught there would disappear in the concrete jungle.[9] Those who believed with Thomas that they should return often and for long periods of time to their reservations were often thwarted. Transportation was difficult and phones were expensive. Intertribal marriage became more and more common in urban areas and the offspring of those unions frequently did not qualify for enrollment in either (or any) tribe. This is what Thomas meant when he predicted the decline of tribal cultures and identities in the city, a decline he considered to be hastened by the growth of pan-Indian culture and institutions.

Indian activism, from Alcatraz on, found its origins in the city and served to strengthen urban intertribal communities. From Thomas's perspective, it therefore catalyzed the loss of tribal identity and integrity. Many of the young people who provided the founding energy for the American Indian Movement (AIM) and other Red Power groups had scant or distant tribal/reservation experience. Joane Nagel writes, "The American Indian Movement was founded in Minneapolis in 1968, with chapters quickly established in several U.S. cities (Cleveland, Denver, Milwaukee). AIM's membership was drawn mainly from urban Indian communities, and its leadership and membership tended to be drawn from the younger, more progressive ranks of the urban Indian population."[10] In part because of this social profile, the 1972 Trail of Broken Treaties "magnified strains between urban and reservation Indians," as well as between older and younger generations.[11]

Despite their urban origins, activist efforts soon became reservation centered. "Red Power protest activity shifted after the 1972 BIA occupation from mainly symbolic, short-term actions to longer, more violent events, often on or near reservations. Thus, what was initially an urban Indian movement, eventually returned to its reservation roots."[12] Apparently, the rift between urban and reservation Indians was not unbridgeable. The result of urban-initiated, intertribal political action in the era of the Great Society was increased funding, expanded programming, and enhanced self-determination for tribes and reservations.

Great Society–Office of Economic Opportunity programs had a different effect in urban Indian communities themselves. Indian and other monies that did filter into urban communities supported intertribal programs and organizations—Indian health services and Indian alternative schools, for example. In Chicago, this was a period of organization growth and vitality which saw the development of American Indian Health Services, the Native American Committee, several important educational projects (O-Wai-Ya-Wa Elementary School, Little Big Horn High School, Native American Educational Services College [NAES]), Indians for Indians (CETA), the American Indian Business Association, and the Indian Child Welfare Program at Saint Augustine's Center. Each of these organizations served Indian people of all tribes residing in the Chicago area; each faced the challenge of negotiating common ground among intertribal staff and clientele. The leadership in these new programs and organizations came predominantly from second-generation urban residents, individuals who had been raised and even born in the city, although they had reservation experience as well.

One result of increased federal funding and related organizational growth in urban areas is that urban Indian communities became conscious of themselves as such. Opportunities for interacting with other Indians increased, and while, as Thomas noted, bounded ghettos did not develop, Indian communities did. In Chicago, it was at this time that community members began to refer to themselves facetiously as "Chicagojos." Community came, in some sense, to replace tribe in individual orientation and motivation. "The Community" became personified and spoken of as if it had thoughts and desires, likes and dislikes, preferences and sensitivities. As awareness of community was growing and informing the consciousness of its members, a conference was held in 1981 (the Chicago American Indian Community Organizations Conference) which sought to define the community and articulate common goals within it. Tribal enrollment was irrelevant to community membership, and, indeed, many in the community were not enrolled and/or had not enrolled their children. Tribal affiliation was assumed and understood to enhance the urban community, but common history, culture, and concerns were emphasized.

While fiscally empowered tribal self-determination proceeded on reservations, urban Indian communities were indeed "detribalized" in the sense that they focused on "Indian" rather than "tribal" identities. The federal wedge between urban and reservation communities became entrenched. Even the Red Power shift to reservation issues "seemed to increase tensions between urban and reservation individuals and groups."[13] Indians in urban areas were negatively stereotyped by reservation people as "fallen" or diminished Indians, "sell-outs" who abandoned tribal homeland, practice, politics, and problems for the good life in the city. Such stereotypes affected communication between members of urban and reservation communities and made it difficult for urban residents to return to their home reservations. John, the "Indian Killer" in Sherman Alexie's novel of that name, represents the confusion and despair commonly associated with the internal oppression of the urban Indian experience. Not surprisingly, the literature on urban Indians in the 1970s and 1980s reads like a social work manual, overwhelmingly detailing social, medical, and psychological problems.

Thomas was right. Indian identity, born in the fur trade, defined by federal policy, and nurtured in boarding schools and military service, found fruition in urban communities. But that is only part of the story. Politically, economically, and organizationally, urban Indian communities are now experiencing retribalization, and Indian people in cities are reconnecting with their tribes.[14]

With the majority of Indian people now living in cities, tribal governments have been forced to become more sensitive to their urban membership and have begun to establish offices in cities where they have significant membership. The first such office in Chicago is the Ho-Chunk Nation office, headed by Dmitri Abangan. The Ho-Chunk Nation also maintains an office in Milwaukee, as does the Oneida tribe of Wisconsin. Recently, a delegation of Oneidas from Chicago attended a tribal budget committee hearing in Milwaukee, and separate hearings on the revision of the Oneida tribal constitution were held in Chicago at the American Indian Center. Such offices activate and symbolize the connection between tribe and city.[15]

Demographic shifts that have located an increasing percentage of the Indian population in cities compel a shift in campaign strategies as well as in political representation. Tribal members residing in Chicago and other urban areas are potential voters. In most cases, enrolled members must return to the reservation to register their votes, but for members of neighboring tribes, it is only a few hours' drive to do so. Recently, moreover, absentee ballots have been developed and accepted by a number of tribes, facilitating voting by off-reservation members. Tribal members running for political office campaign in Chicago and Milwaukee as well as on the reservations, as do tribal politicians lobbying for a particular vote on a specific program or issue.

More than sixty different tribes have been represented in Chicago. Clearly, not all tribal members are close enough to their reservations to run home to vote, and not all tribal governments schedule meetings in the city. In regard to the topic at hand, however, the political retribalization of urban residents of neighboring tribes establishes the expectation of political representation and consideration by other tribes of their off-reservation urban membership. This is a new development.

The downside might seem to be that off-reservation residents are uninformed voters and noninvested decision-makers. Some might question the wisdom of their political incorporation by the tribe. But this is the 1990s—communication is easy and continuous, visiting is frequent if not necessarily as extended as it was fifty years ago, and tribal newspapers circulate throughout the country, providing a common source of political education for all tribal members. The broad circulation of tribal newspapers is fairly new and, interestingly, seems to have followed in the aftermath of the success of intertribal presses (*The Warrior* from the AICC, *Wasaja*, and *Akwesasne Notes*). Off-reservation tribal members and others look to their tribal newspapers as a source of tribal news and personal connection, but also as the primary resource for announcements of upcoming conferences, celebrations, powwows, and so on, which they may plan to attend.

Demographic changes and the associated political changes are only part of the retribalization in urban Indian communities. Tribal economic development has recently reached out into urban areas as well. Gaming is probably the best illustration of this trend, but it is not the only possibility. Seeking markets for casino gambling, tribes have purchased land and established Indian Country in urban areas. The success of this effort has led to a new concept of urban communities. As Chicago considers the possibility of casino gambling on land as well as on the rivers, city officials have already contacted the Sault Sainte Marie Chippewa in regard to developing the industry. Other recent tribal economic development proposals include the development of tourism. Two years ago, when Defense Department cuts caused the closing of the Glenview Naval Air Station north of the city, Ron Bowan, as director of the Chicago American Indian Center, researched and proposed the return of this land to the Prairie Potawatomi tribe from whom it had originally been taken, with a view towards establishing a museum and cultural center there. Subsequently, as Mayor Daley and Governor Edgar argued over the small lakefront airport called Meigs Field, the spirit of Simon Pokagon shone on as Chicago residents reconsidered his claim that the Potawatomi people really owned that land. The Treaty of Chicago outlined a specific and well-defined cession of land. Land not specified for cession—in this case, land created after the treaty by build-up along the lakeshore—was not ceded and was thus reserved for the Potawatomi. In these and other endeavors, Chicago Indians have looked towards the Milwaukee model, where recently purchased Potawatomi tribal land in the city includes a school, a gym, a temporary residence, a ceremonial lodge, two sweat lodges, and powwow grounds on the old campus of Concordia College. Is this the new colonialism: reservation colonies in urban areas?

The other side of tribal development in cities is tribal economic support for urban Indian communities' members and organizations. The Ho-Chunk Nation has supported the American Indian Center in Chicago, and the Oneida tribe of Wisconsin and Menominee tribe also have provided grants to Chicago Indian organizations for the first time ever within the past three years. Tribal educational support for off-reservation residents has increased significantly as tribal revenues and management have increased. Off-reservation residents used to receive only the leftovers, if there were any, from education funds distributed to reservation residents.[16] Today, tribal support of urban residents is well established. Tribal investment in its own members, wherever they may reside, is presumed to encourage tribal development generally.

Over the years, every Indian organization in the Chicago community has assisted eligible community members to become enrolled and to enroll their children in the tribe. Enrollment certainly encourages interest in tribal histories and cultures and involvement in tribal affairs. It is not all about per capita payments, as we so often hear; it is mostly about family and identity. The Indian community organizations serve members of all tribes, recognized or not, enrolled or not, but they work with and through tribal organizations as well.

In addition to the community-wide organizations in Chicago, tribal clubs and less formal tribal groups have also experienced something of a rejuvenation in recent years. Chicago has seen a recent revitalization of the Oneida, Menominee, Winnebago, and Lakota tribal clubs, which have experienced greater interest, greater attendance at meetings, and greater support. These clubs originated quite early on, became quiescent, and are now experiencing revitalization. At first, perhaps, they served as support in the transition to pan-Indian community. Today, however, they serve to sustain and enhance tribal affiliation and identity for urban Indian people. Tribal club activities and celebrations are commonly shared within the community, but the sponsorship and work are provided by the individual clubs. Each of these clubs has sponsored tribal language programs. Interest in tribal languages is high throughout the community, and those who are fluent in their tribal language are respected for their knowledge.

There is ample political, economic, and organizational evidence of retribalization in Chicago and other urban Indian communities. The most compelling evidence, however, is found in personal stories. Considering her connection to the Chicago Indian community and to the Oneida tribe, Debra Valentino reconstructs her own identity process in a story that moves past the void Thomas predicted. A founding director of one of the newest organizations in the Chicago Indian community and head of the revitalized Oneida Club, Mrs. Valentino points out that, when growing up in Chicago, she did not connect significantly with the Indian community or with her own Indian identity: "Since I was a child, I knew I belonged to a wonderful family, but outside that immediate family and its protection, there was no real connection to anything or anyone else. This is a sad state for an Indian person, especially when it still exists today. I know, because I can see its existence in some of the people I work with and talk to on a daily basis."

Mrs. Valentino had family, but she also had a sense of disconnection, anomie. She was Indian, but with little understanding of what that meant in her life. She lived in the community and "every day . . . encountered lots of people who knew their culture and their language," while she did not. These were people she could have asked, people she could have known, but she avoided contact. She "often found [herself] wanting to shrink up in a corner whenever anyone wanted to know about her." Alcohol, already part of her environment, became a part of her life, exaggerating her isolation from culture and community. As a mother, she began to work towards her own recovery and to develop important new relationships with other Indian people.

Like many others in the Chicago community, her initial, positive involvement in the community came through the American Indian Center, where she volunteered and participated in a variety of activities, always including her family. Community members began to rely on her as a responsible recovering person for various things and involve her more and more. Accepting increasing responsibility, she came gradually to identify with the community and to reinvent herself as Indian. She included her husband and four daughters in that process. In the next few years, as a student of Dr. Lola Hill (Chippewa) at NAES College, she began to use writing as a way to work through a lot of remaining family and personal issues. She wrote poetry, and was encouraged by other Indian poets to share her work in community and other gatherings. She also became involved in the Women's Leadership Group and in the Indian Parent Committee for Audubon School, a public receiving school for Indian children that her own children attended. In the space of just a few years, she moved from anomie to positive Indian identity and community involvement. As it turned out, this was a step towards, not away from, tribal identity.

An enrolled member of the Oneida tribe of Wisconsin, married to another enrolled Oneida, Debra had lots of family on the reservation. She visited occasionally and especially enjoyed the July 4 pow-wow, but she had been raised primarily in the city and had little consistent experience of Oneida culture or community. As she became seriously engaged in the pan-Indian community in the city, other tribal members in the city and on the reservation started to take notice of her. Today, as coordinator of the Oneida group in Chicago and recipient of Oneida education funding and of a significant tribal grant to her organization, she serves informally as a representative from Chicago to the Oneida tribal council. Last winter, she, her husband, and their daughters traveled to Oneida by invitation to participate in the mid-winter longhouse ceremonies for the first time. They returned to Chicago with Oneida names to signify their new status, new paths in life, and new engagement in the tribal as well as Indian community.

Mrs. Valentino moved from anomie through recovery and community involvement to "Indianness," and from a strong Indian base to a reconnection with her tribe. For her, as for Jeanne LaTraille, another Chicago Oneida forty years her senior, Indian identity was the necessary antecedent to, not the death knell of, tribal identity and involvement. Ms. LaTraille, a self-described "born again Indian," married a non-Indian and lived much of her adult life away from other Indian people. Returning to Chicago from Florida after several decades of absence, she visited the American Indian Center, which encouraged her connection to the Indian community and her interest in Indian activities and issues. She became, in fact, the oldest person to represent the Chicago Indian community in demonstrations on the boat landings in the conflict over Lake Superior Chippewa fishing rights several years ago. From her newly formed Indian base and Indian identity, Ms. LaTraille has also reconnected with the Oneida tribe, subscribing to the tribal newspaper, attending Oneida language classes, studying Oneida history and traditions, and visiting the reservation often. Mrs. Valentino describes this as "many good things . . . coming full circle." The creation of identity is a process, not an event. It is dynamic and different at different points in the life cycle. For these Oneida women, Indian and tribal identities were and are sequentially and positively related, allowing for the possibility of "good things coming full circle."

The path from anomie to community and from community to tribe is a common one in urban Indian communities. It is also relatively new. Earlier generations of Indian people who lived for extended periods of time in urban areas faced the daunting task of creating common community and identity, a task that presupposed the backgrounding and downplaying of tribal differences. By what is now the third and even fourth generation of urban residence, the context is different. Now, Indian people growing up in a city, always aware and respectful of tribal affiliation, may look first to a positive Indian identity, supported by connection with Indian organizations and community, and, from that base, move forward to a real connection with tribe, often selecting among the several that comprise their heritage.

Certainly, Indian and tribal identities are jointly conceived and represented by all Indian people today. What seems particularly interesting in the urban Indian context is that strong community involvement and related Indian identity may anticipate and serve as a foundation for a reinvented tribal identity.

Unfortunately, Bob Thomas did not live long enough to see this begin to happen.

Notes

1. Robert K. Thomas, "New Sacred Nationalism," paper held in archives at Native American Educational Services College, Chicago, Illinois Archives, 3; see also Thomas's "The Sacred Nationalism," Proceedings of the Conference on Indian Issues of the Eighties (Claremore College, Oklahoma, 1980).

2. Ibid., 5.

3. Ibid., 22, 3.

4. Robert K. Thomas, "Impediments to Analysis," paper held in archives at Native American Educational Services College, (Chicago, Illinois, 1966), 4. Subsequently printed in *Americans Before Columbus* 13, no. 3 (Albuquerque, NM: National Indian Youth Council, 1985).

5. Ibid., 6.

6. For an extended discussion of the life and work of Bob Thomas, see Steve Pavlik, ed., *A Good Cherokee, A Good Anthropologist: Papers in Honor of Robert K. Thomas* (Los Angeles: UCLA American Indian Studies, 1998).

7. Stephen Cornell, *Return of the Native* (London and New York: Oxford University Press, 1988).

8. For a detailed discussion of the history of blood quantum, see Paul Spruhan, "Quantum of Power: Historical Origins of Blood Identification in U.S. Indian Policy" (M.A. thesis, University of Chicago, 1996).

9. John Fire Lame Deer and Richard Erdoes, *Lame Deer, Seeker of Visions* (New York: Simon and Schuster, 1973), 133; Robert K. Thomas, "Cherokee Prophecy," paper held in archives at Native American Educational Services College (Chicago, Illinois, n.d.), 267.

10. Joane Nagel, *American Indian Ethnic Renewal* (New York: Oxford University Press, 1996), 166.

11. Ibid., 138.

12. Ibid., 170.

13. Ibid., 170.

14. I am indebted to Don Fixico for loaning me this term. He says he borrowed it, too, but is not sure from where.

15. The Ho-Chunk example is particularly interesting, since the 1961 American Indian Chicago Conference was the major impetus for the former Wisconsin Winnebagos' push for federal recognition. We are used to thinking about the importance of reservation communities to urban Indian life, but seldom consider the impact of urban communities on tribal affairs.

16. Tim Murphy, financial aid officer at Native American Educational Services College, personal interview with author, May 1996.

And the Drumbeat Still Goes On . . .   6
Urban Indian Institutional Survival into the New Millennium

JOAN WEIBEL-ORLANDO

O N RESERVATIONS, the sovereignty of tribal governments and institutions is the political and legal foundation upon which the distinctiveness and vitality of Indian peoples will stretch from the immemorial past far into the future. Simultaneously, this book demonstrates that the large and growing presence of Native Americans in urban settings does not constitute assimilation or a weakening of this cultural and political autonomy. The writers and artists depict both networks of communities and individuals crossing and disrupting the rural/urban dichotomy, and the many ways in which Native Americans create unique and distinctively Native spaces in the city. Susan Lobo has pointed out in chapter 4 some of the similarities and differences between corporate tribal structures on rural reservations and legal, nonprofit urban Indian organizations. One important parallel has been the extent to which both of these types of institutions have fought to weather vast changes in federal, state, and local conditions that threaten their existence. By examining one of the oldest and most widely known urban Indian institutions in the twentieth century, this chapter will offer insights and strategies for other Indian community organizations fighting for survival in the twenty-first.

What is today known as the Southern California Indian Center, Inc., has precedence in two urban southern California Indian organizations. The first was the Los Angeles County–based Indian Centers, Inc. (ICI), established in 1935.[1] With the onset of the Johnson Administration's War on Poverty programs in the late 1960s, ICI provided an increasing number of federally funded social services to the Native American residents of the Los Angeles Basin. By 1977 ICI was described as "the most widely known Indian institution in Los Angeles," having "existed longer and [being] more of a focal point of sentiment among [Los Angeles] Indians than any other Indian organization, past or present."[2]

ICI-L.A. was already a venerable institution in 1967, when the founding families of the Orange County Indian Center (OCIC) began to store their collections of food and clothing for distribution among "our less fortunate Indian friends and neighbors in Orange County" in John and Louise Knifechief's Stanton, California, garage.[3] Both ICI and OCIC had begun to receive federal employment and training funds and other federal social service grants at about the same time (1968–69), though ICI had always been the more heavily and diversely funded, primarily as a result of census figures that characterized the proportion of Native American residents in each county.[4] Then in 1986, amid charges of fiscal mismanagement and unethical administrative procedures, the Los Angeles Indian Center, Inc. officially closed its doors. Its demise constituted a major community crisis. Means by which the largest urban Indian population in the United States and its representatives interacted with funding and service agencies at all levels of government had been truncated. Meanwhile, however, the OCIC had, from its relatively modest origins, experienced a meteoric rise propelled by the transfer to OCIC of the Department of Labor's Job Training Partnership Act (JTPA) grant that had previously been awarded to ICI. In 1987 OCIC changed its name to Southern California Indian Centers, Inc. (SCIC) to reflect its regional, rather than Orange County–specific service territory. By 1996, with satellite offices throughout the region, SCIC had become the largest, most comprehensive social service program for urban Indians in Los Angeles and Orange Counties.

The years since the closing of ICI-L.A. and the emergence of SCIC as the area's primary Native American social service organization were characterized by continuous socioeconomic upheaval in the Los Angeles and Orange Counties' Native American social services community. An initial period of organizational retrenchment was followed by political realignments and stabilization, only to be followed by further retrenchments in response to the dramatic cuts in social service grants generally and in urban Indian set-aside funds, particularly after the results of the 1990 census were published.[5]

Nevertheless, throughout this fiscal and political instability, SCIC demonstrated an extraordinary aptitude for institutional survival. How is it that, after suffering devastating yearly cuts in its funding portfolio—cuts that have become yet more intensive since 1995—SCIC has been able to continue to survive? How does SCIC manage to keep its social services drumbeat alive? Could an analysis of SCIC's perception of its institutional survival strategies provide an operational model for other and equally threatened urban Indian community organizations? These were the issues I had in mind when I contacted the SCIC administrative officers in October 1996.

On January 22, 1997, I met with John Castillo (Apache), the then-executive director, and Paula Starr (Southern Cheyenne and Arapaho), the then assistant executive director of SCIC in their Garden Grove, California administrative offices.[6] These two well-educated veterans of urban Indian organizational life shared their understandings, earned on the front lines, as to what accounts for SCIC's impressive survival profile. The following outline of survival strategies is theirs. The discussion and analysis sections are syntheses of the thoughts of the three of us regarding the relative utility of such strategies and their place within more abstract models of organizational process and maintenance.

Funding Sources in the 1990s:
Of Censuses, Balanced Budgets,
and Legal/Rational Bureaucracies

John first explained that the federal government's balanced budget rhetoric of the last few years had created a climate of fiscal retrenchment and attempts to "downsize" social service programs throughout the nation that were perceived to be fiscally flabby.[7] Localization of funding decision-making, as a consequence of the block grant funding policy of the past decade, had created a further disruption of their organization's well-established network of national and state funding agency relations.

The unexpected underreporting of Native Americans in Los Angeles and Orange Counties in the 1990 U.S. census count, however, was a "double whammy" for social services, and an even more profound setback to attempts to "grow the SCIC."[8] First, the Los Angeles and Orange Counties' Native American population figures actually represented a loss of residents between 1980 and 1990—45,508 for Los Angeles and 12,165 for Orange County.[9] Second, and equally devastating, was the comparative rise in socioeconomic status of those Native Americans in the two counties who did fill out and return their census forms.[10] After a year-long campaign by an all–Native American census task force to encourage Native Americans to fill out and return their census forms so "that our voices be heard," those Los Angeles and Orange County residents who did so were predominantly from the upwardly mobile, educated middle class—politically aware and active segments of the urban Native American community.[11] In other words, the community members who would have benefited most by filing a census report were not approached by census workers, did not see the purpose in filling out the form when it did arrive, or held such antipathy for and/or suspicion of all U.S. government agencies that refusing to fill out a census form became the equivalent of political statement and protest.

Most federal funding agencies make their distribution decisions based on a formula that includes population size and documented need among their several allocation indices. The 1990 census profiles of the Los Angeles and Orange County Native American populations were apparently interpreted by Federal and State funding agencies as indicating a shrinking ethnic community with fewer needs for publicly funded social services. The forces of urban migration and acculturation, as far as the social services funding agencies could determine, had worked their economic and assimilative magic for the Native American population in Southern California.

The 1990 census findings were made public in July 1992. Subsequently SCIC experienced sweeping cuts across most of its programs starting with fiscal year 1995 (as did many other social service agencies in ethnic communities). In 1997, SCIC was operating with a budget that had been reduced approximately 40 percent since 1994. Although its staff uniformly presented a confident and well-directed posture to its community, SCIC was still reeling from a continuing series of blows to its fiscal stability.

Running a Tight Corporate Ship:
Tradition, Adaptation, and
Rational Bureaucracy

On reservations, corporate tribal governments have by necessity woven together traditional and non-Native forms of leadership and social organization for institutional survival. In cities, Indian organizations must also develop multiple cultural sensibilities—they too are "surviving in two worlds."[12] Nevertheless, it should not be assumed that organizational strategies in the urban nonprofit sector are entirely unknown to Native tradition. The readiness of a Native American organization to accept and function well within the tenets of legal/rational bureaucracy has to be understood in its historical context. A reading of Wallace's description of eighteenth-century Seneca governing structure or Moore's insightful structural/functional analysis of Hoebel's description of nineteenth-century Cheyenne tribal organization informs that the efficacy of bureaucratization as a governing and managerial form was well established in both theory and practice among Native American tribal groups before contact and not solely superimposed by Western Europeans.[13]

In contemporary Los Angeles, the executive directors of SCIC are convinced that solid organizational structure and sound managerial practices are crucial factors in the success and survival of their organization. Interested in learning about SCIC's administrative style, I asked John how the relationship between the board of directors, the staff, and he work. "The way it's supposed to work!" he returned with unanticipated energy. John explained that the staff works with him and the community and, through him, with the board. And the executive director works at the direction of the board.

After the SCIC board of directors reaches its decisions, the president of the board informs the executive director of them. He is then responsible for ensuring that those decisions are carried out by the appropriate SCIC staff members. The executive director meets with the SCIC staff every other week to communicate the board's decisions as well as to listen to staff members' suggestions about how to improve and/or increase SCIC services. Such suggestions usually find their way, via the executive director, onto future board meeting agendas.

A delineated chain of command with well-defined lines of communication up and down that chain sounded like pure, unadulterated, legal/rational bureaucracy to me. John explained his adherence to this formal administrative structure.

> A breakdown in the structure slows down the process of providing good services and programs. We ensure that this process of information flow and control takes place. [The board members] are the policy makers of the agency.[14] My role as an employee is to follow their decisions. The board provides the vision. My job is to implement that vision. The staff provides the front-line services. We understand each other's roles in the organizational structure and try not to circumvent or undermine them.

John firmly believes in the rationality of clearly articulated divisions of labor. Paula proudly confirmed, "He's a great delegater!" John accepted his colleague's pronouncement. "It's important to learn to let go, to trust that the other person can do it, and to know who can and cannot [be trusted] to do [the job]." Paula added, "This is an area of John's expertise—keeping us on track, organizing us, assuring that we follow through on our own assignments and objectives."

Both of the executive directors are sensitive to the social distance that the misapplication of their considerable authority could produce between the staff and them. John said, "We don't want to be [so authoritative] that the people feel they can't approach us, walk into our office and talk with us. I moved furniture last week in our Carson office. I didn't have to do that. But I want to lead by example." Paula added, "I'm not everybody's friend. Wish I was. Sometimes, you can't be. I understand that negative reinforcement has to take place at times. But I'd rather not do [that]. My preference is to reward people in a positive way [for good performance]."

Paula was unrelenting in her praise of John's stewardship of SCIC. "He's an example of what makes a director a good one. He's complimentary and supportive to our staff. We know he's always going to be there for us. He allows us to pick his brain. John is action oriented. He doesn't just talk about doing [something for the community]. He finds a way for us to do it." Agreeing with his leadership style and seeing parallels between it and the cultural values she learned as a member of her tribal community, Paula attempts to emulate it in her own staff and client interactions.

> A lot of people who come to us are homeless, trying to get back on their feet. [They may have problems with] alcohol and/or substance abuse. [We accept that and say] "OK, what's the next step?" We do a lot of peer counseling. I'm never too busy to talk with them when they come through my door. We operate from the values instilled in us during our childhood—to ensure that the whole village and community are well. We try to do that by being positive with everyone.

Even the flurry of alternative management models of the last three decades—"organized anarchy," "loose-tight properties," and "informated organizations," or Osborne's and Gaebler's insistence in the "bankruptcy of bureaucracy"—have not weakened a generally held belief in the managerial efficacy of legal/rational bureaucracy.[15] Many still perceive it as "the most efficient, the hardiest and . . . the most natural structure ever devised for large organizations."[16] Strict adherence to the tenets of legal/rational bureaucratic structure and practices has become the SCIC modus operandi. John summarized it in this way: "We try to run a . . . tight operation here. We don't want to be brought down by bureaucratic or fiscal carelessness as other urban Indian organizations have in the past. We try to do things by the book."

Subtle shifts in the more rigid demands of formal bureaucratic structure have occurred at SCIC in the name of adherence to Native American cultural values of equality, humility, and community cohesiveness and well-being. The SCIC managerial style, therefore, has evolved its own ethnical quality. Just as tribes and tribal governments are extremely varied in character, the organizational and leadership styles developed by urban Indian institutions will depend on specific conditions. However, a strategic and appropriate combination of tradition and innovation seems crucial to survival and stability.

Staff and Volunteers: Education, Commitment, and the Dedication Factor

> People decisions are the ultimate—perhaps the only—control of an organization. . . . No organization can do better than the people it has.
>
> —PETER F. DRUCKER,
> *MANAGING THE NON-PROFIT ORGANIZATION: PRINCIPLES AND PRACTICES*

In the early 1970s, a bachelor's or graduate degree was considered a rare and wonderful, but certainly not necessary, criterion for staff or executive placement in the Indian Centers in Los Angeles. Hiring criteria included Indian ancestry, high and positive visibility in the L.A. Indian community, a critical mass of friends and/or family who would "put in a good word for you" to hiring panels and boards of directors, and the fuzzy notions of "eligibility" and "qualifiability." Those days when tribal affiliation, family or personal connections, and community popularity were actual (although rarely stated) hiring criteria are clearly over. Today academic credentials are common requirements—and not only for SCIC's top management. Both of the SCIC administrators have bachelor's degrees and have completed or are working toward the completion of graduate degrees. Increasingly, applicants for mid-level service providers, program directors, and site supervisors are expected to have some college education when they apply for employment.[17] By 1997, the SCIC hiring process and sets of employment criteria were fully rationalized. John explained, "We choose the person who is the best for the job. The Indian Preference in Hiring Act [allows] us to advantage an Indian applicant." But we operate under the assumption that we want the very best person for the job and hopefully, [he or she will be] Indian."[18]

The struggles and fluctuations faced by the center are eased by staff continuity, and SCIC prides itself on its employee loyalty. Management expert Peter Drucker writes, "I have never seen anything being done well unless people were committed."[19] Several staff members have worked at SCIC for ten or more years. Incentives for longevity include bonuses for staff members who wish to continue their education and a policy of promotion from within. Some staff members who started as participants in the Center's JPTA training program have gone from program participants to SCIC employees. Paula underscored the sagacity of this employment strategy by sharing that "we have always seen education as a solution for our people."

In addition to committed core staff, volunteers are vital to any urban Indian community organization. In southern California, the philanthropic impulse of Delmar Nejo (Digueño), a much decorated World War II veteran and tribal spokesman, and his circle of Indian friends in Orange County in 1967 eventuated in the official formation of OCIC on February 25, 1969.[20] Today that same impulse prompts more than four hundred Native Americans to continue to pay their SCIC membership dues and provide volunteer services to the organization each year.

Both Paula and John underscored certain altruistic and psychological factors that also contribute to SCIC's continuing viability as a social services organization. They view the continuing high level of the SCIC members' personal commitment to group goals and their willingness to volunteer time and energy toward that end as particularly critical human resources in this period of fiscal retrenchment. Board membership, for example, is an entirely voluntary endeavor. Paula said, "Most [of the board members] are elderly and retired. So they have the time to do board work. Plus they have been with it since the beginning. They have a vested interest in what we do and how we do things here. They have commitment." Volunteerism extends itself into all aspects of SCIC activity. Paula continued, "Ninety percent of the people involved with ongoing activities at the center are volunteers of some form or another. Even paid staff will sometimes volunteer extra time on a center project without getting paid for it. [I call it] the dedication factor."

An energized volunteer base also reflects the vitality and importance of an organization's presence in the community. The spirit of volunteerism at SCIC is most fully expressed during preparations for its annual pow-wow. Every member has a clearly defined role to play in this activity—the largest fundraising event of the year. John explained how the pow-wow is organized:

> The Orange County Pow-wow has been going on for twenty-nine years. [The executive directors'] role is to make it better, make it grow. [It's our] responsibility to put the organizational elements into a pow-wow so that it runs smoothly and allows more people to attend, to raise funds for our programs in a time when there are a lot of cuts in our grants. We [provide] the organizational abilities and skills. . . . Our board and our pow-wow families are involved to maintain the traditional values of our pow-wow so that it doesn't become a commercial thing that has no meaning.

An institution that supports the well-being of its urban Indian constituency and is truly integrated in the community provides its own rewards, which in turn create commitment on the part of staff and volunteers. For example, the responsibilities of SCIC executive leadership have resulted in fifty- to sixty-hour work weeks for its directors. Staff, committee, and board meetings, grant deadlines, legislative crises, weekend community activities, and "take home" work dictate that they remain involved in "Center business" long past the traditional nine-to-five

Tom Phillips (Kiowa/Creek), center, a nationally known powwow announcer, emcees the 1996 SCIC powwow at the Orange County Fair Grounds in Costa Mesa, California. The sign below the speakers' dais graphically illustrates SCIC's continuing outreach to local as well as international sponsors. The juxtaposition of a Plains-style coup stick and the United States flag underscores the symbiotic relation of the sociopolitical groups they represent. (Photo © Paula Starr.)

work day and Monday–Friday work week. "I look at it [this] way," said John. "The things that we both do help people eat, help people get jobs, help our kids get educated—that's what . . . we are both here for. That's what the Indian Center is here for. That drives us."

Paula concurred:

> John and I [love to attend] the graduation of our GED and continuation high school students. It is a real ceremony with diplomas, a procession, [we all wear academic] robes, the dean of the school leads the procession. [There is an] invocation. We have a[n] [Indian] drum. And hearing [the students'] testimony about getting through and how many times it took them, the care [SCIC gave them]—that's what gives us the energy back, ignites us. And when we see foster children get reunited with their families, a person getting a job, [a woman] who was homeless and who now has her own apartment—that's what keeps us going.

A few of the hundreds of traditional dancers and more than thirty thousand attendees of the 1996 SCIC powwow at the Orange County Fair Grounds in Costa Mesa, California. (Photo © Paula Starr.)

Institutional Survival Strategies

> Fund development is *people* development. You're building a constituency . . . understanding . . . support.
>
> —PETER F. DRUCKER

Networking and information exchange at local, state, and national levels of policy development and social service funding are critical institutional survival strategies. The executive directors pointed to their untiring attempts to build bridges of communication between SCIC and its funding sources as essential elements of their organization's fiscal and executive survival. In the 1980s and 1990s, and especially with the escalation of the mandated balanced budget rhetoric, there has been continuous debate and rumor in Washington, D.C., about the discontinuance of ethnic minority program set-asides. John credited his lobbying skills and knowledge of whom to approach for help in Washington and Sacramento for having helped save the urban Indian component of JTPA from being folded into the national job training budget lines.

As SCIC's executive officer, John regularly telephoned, faxed or went to call on "pro-Indian" legislators to deliver the following message:

> Training programs that do not acknowledge and respond to the special needs of ethnic minority JTPA participants are not culturally sensitive. Indians learn best when involved in an Indian-fostered educational environment. If the U.S. government believes its own rhetoric (all welfare recipients and, by extension, all Indians need to be brought to self-sufficiency), then those people who are not now self sufficient must be given the educational and technological skills necessary to make them competitive in the current job market. Employment is at the root of self-sufficiency. It doesn't make sense to have cut the Indian employment programs not once but twice in the last two years and expect that Indians will still be able to gain self-sufficiency.

John's continuous attempts to educate and convince legislators of the short-sightedness of the proposed amalgamation of several programs paid off.

SCIC's executive directors are in touch with their contacts and supporters in Washington and Sacramento at least weekly. During periods of a bill vote or when threatened by program cancellation, however, the executive directors are on the phone daily to their legislative contacts. Both directors have presented white papers or delivered speeches to the state and federal legislators on behalf of proposed or threatened Indian set-aside programs. They attend information sharing conferences at local, state, and national venues two or more times a year. They deal with legislators, program directors, and attorneys on a daily basis. John commented:

> It's a[n educational] process. [We] provide the linkages [between SCIC's board of directors] and the legislators. It's our job to build this network. We keep [the legislators and SCIC board] informed about issues and concerns. We also provide suggestions to [the both of] them [about] programs we offer or things that are coming up that we'd like to see for our community. We try to keep them as informed as possible.

Networking is a never-ending process, and the California State Assembly is especially vulnerable to network breakdown. "California's new limited term appointments are [a case in point]. Every time there is a change of legislator or staff we have to go back in there and reeducate the new legislators . . . establish a new rapport," John explained.

The SCIC executive directors are both reactive and proactive in their attempts to maintain their far-flung network of political supporters. An Indian education bill was due to be debated on the U.S. Senate floor sometime during the 1997 spring session. Paula described the lobbying process:

> [We] Indian educators met . . . [and decided], "Let's pool our moneys, [call a] strategy meeting, [do some] fact finding [find out] who's friendly with

whom, talk to the person who is going to introduce the bill on the senate level." Yes, you have to have friends. We have to be the ones to say, "This is our concern. This is what we are worried about." [The legislators] need [to be] educated by us about the special needs of American Indians because they really don't know.

Being Politic and "Playing the Game"

These networking strategies—identification of potential advocates in position to shape policy, implementation of strenuous lobbying efforts, and ongoing reeducation—little resemble the American Indian Movement's (AIM) property-destroying occupation of the BIA offices in Washington, D.C., and its several politically motivated "camp-ins" and "takeovers" of the late 1960s and early 1970s.[21]

Both executive directors were clearly advocates of artful persuasion rather than strong-armed, ethnically toned political confrontation. In John's opinion, "In order to get to [a desired] goal, you just don't go in there and knock a door down. There are other ways to go about it—and be sophisticated about it. Other ethnic groups have done that and have achieved certain goals. [Now] we just have to be even better [at it]." Paula added, "I just call it 'playing the game'. . . . The game is knowing who's friendly with whom, who's educated [about Indian affairs] and knows that there is a history [of U.S. and Native American political relations], that we're dealing with treaties and peoples' histories. And we have to play *their* game."

Networking, information dissemination and retrieval, and alliance-building are essential building blocks of power, control, and institutional viability. The SCIC executive directors have raised the practice of these skills to high art. The lesson to be learned here is that no service institution can survive in isolation. "Getting the message out" and "making friends in high places" are vital survival strategies and are best learned through their continuous practice.

Doing Almost as Much with Substantially Less

For the last four years since the findings of the 1990 census were fully realized we have been in a defensive posture. We dug in, moved back, did not hire other people when staff left. We consolidated [our efforts]. We prepared ourselves for the time when the monies would be less.

—JOHN CASTILLO

The funding climate of the 1990s forced SCIC to make hard decisions about continuing to offer certain underfunded programs and grants. Paula described one such situation:

> There is so much bureaucratic hassle dealing with [a certain government funding agency that shall remain nameless]. For the amount of money we get from them we get more headaches than we do running a larger program run by the federal government's Department of Labor. . . . They monitored us so much . . . [there was] so much paper work, we said, "Take your grant back." It just got to be cost ineffective for us to continue to provide the insufficiently funded services.

SCIC used to receive Federal Emergency Act (FEMA) grants and federal Indian shelter funds. These monies provided supplies but no funds for administering the program. John explained, "With a million dollar cut in our budget we don't have the luxury of doing 'freebies' for the government anymore. Doing vouchers for hotels when dealing with two counties took a half-time staff position. It wasn't cost effective to continue this service. We still provide some shelter when we have the funds, but not as before."

SCIC's initial response to the funding cuts of 1995 was to reduce its physical plant and service locations. The board of directors agreed to consolidate the Van Nuys facility into the L.A. office early in 1996. In mid-January 1997, the Carson site was closed, and its service programs relocated to the commerce office. "This way SCIC still provides some services to the South Bay area without the luxury of having an office there," John explained.

Other overhead reduction strategies have included the search for "free" space (city and county facilities, churches, people's homes) throughout the L.A. County basin and especially in the South Bay area. Because of the dispersed residential patterns of the Southern California urban Indian population, historically the Indian centers have maintained a number of "easy access" equipped vans. The expense of maintaining this resource has prompted SCIC to advocate the use of public transportation by its members and program participants and a subsequent reduction of its former van fleet.

The decision to reduce its physical plant allowed SCIC to use the larger portion of its reduced budget for direct services. Cutting costs, however, did not end with physical plant reduction. The directors and their staff researched alternative, less costly education venues for their clients. "We [are now working with] schools like the Regional Occupational Program or the Federal Skills Centers. We still provide the education but not at the same expense as before. We're looking at more cost effective processes to help our people. . . . Actually we are servicing, more or less, about the same number of people. We just cut our overhead," said John.

Doing the Possible: Shifting from Service Provider to Service Facilitator

No SCIC program component was as drastically reduced in the 1990s as was its BIA Indian Child Welfare Act grant. At one point SCIC had received more that two hundred thousand dollars in ICWA grants. In 1997, SCIC received just a quarter of that amount. To continue to offer these critical community services SCIC uses the funds the BIA provides in conjunction with a patchwork quilt of grants from eight other funding sources.

In the 1970s urban Indian service organizations throughout the nation made "separate but equal" service facilities for ethnic minorities their political mantra.[22] During the recent retrenchments the notion of urban Indian social service organizations as cultural liaisons, gatekeepers, and service facilitators working in conjunction with mainstream providers has surfaced as an expedient, rather than ideal, social services delivery structure. Programmatic flexibility and accommodation now dictate service provision decisions. Paula offered one example:

> We coordinate and direct applicants to other, mainstream programs and services. We attempt to build on each other. For example, we have [established] a collaboration with La Plaza [a local service agency with a large Latino clientele]. We subcontract with them to do "family preservation." Sometimes that doesn't work and children have to be placed in foster homes. Originally we thought that Indian children should only be placed in Indian foster homes. Well, today, how many foster homes do we have that are Indian? Maybe twenty. But there's over three hundred Indian children who need foster home placement.[23] The board voted to let us train non-Indian [foster] families to be culturally sensitive. So, this way, we can place Indian children in homes were there is some sensitivity to their cultural backgrounds, expectations, behavior, and needs. We have to take such steps these days. [Otherwise] these kids [would stay] on a waiting list for Indian foster homes that are not there anyway and [they would eventually] go into non-Indian homes with no cultural sensitivity training.

Doing the possible is accomplished by knowing how to make use of available general resources in creative ways. "We do a lot of referrals. With the de-funding of the American Indian Free Clinic by IHS, there was a void. So we [began] to refer [community members who needed medical treatment] to the Irvine Medical Center and to clinics [run by] various Southern California tribes," Paula explained. The SCIC administrators have also increased their networking activities with local service providers and suppliers. The food and toy distribution programs are examples of SCIC's increasing associations with local commercial and industrial benefactors. SCIC ensures its continuing relationship with local and, often, non-Indian groups through an efficient redistribution program. As an example, SCIC'S Supportive Services staff food collection efforts are often overzealous. SCIC routinely donates surpluses to churches and other charitable organizations that service non-Indian populations. Paula said:

> We have a computer list of service centers throughout the Counties that can make use of our surpluses. They can call us if they are having an event. We can give them our day-old bread and other surpluses [that] they use for their dinners. That way it doesn't get wasted. And [the surpluses don't go] just to Indians. That's important and a part of our outreach to the larger community.

As with thousands of both public and private organizations and corporations across the United States, "downsizing" has been the perceived panacea to institutional survival in the 1990s. "Downsizing" SCIC took many forms. Its board of directors chose to maintain services as much as possible at the expense of its developed infrastructure and physical plant. The notion of entrepreneurial government (and, by extension and fiscal dependence, social service organizations) has been introduced recently as an alternative to dependency on public funds for organizational survival.[24] John candidly offered that "we run SCIC like a business." This operational standard has resulted in both the hard-nosed downsizing decisions just described and in the creative ways in which the SCIC administrators have gone about locating new operating capital. "We're at a place now where we can begin . . . to build again," said John. "We've protected, as much as possible, the service structure we had. Now we can be aggressive in securing additional funds and staff and services." As SCIC's principal fundraisers, the executive directors make a concerted effort to locate nontraditional forms of funding.

"[Our] funding strategy mode right now [is] to go beyond being dependent upon government grants and programs that have been established for Indians. We are transitioning into private and foundation monies, [and] personal, commercial and industrial contributions. We even are [being funded by] the United Way and its donor designation grants," said Paula. John concurred. "Four or five years ago, we didn't have any foundation money. Now we receive grants from ten foundations."

Matching Social Services with Contemporary Community Needs

The mood of SCIC's executive directors in 1999 was decidedly more upbeat and hopeful than it had been in 1997.[25] A number of new projects had either been initiated or were in early stages of development. They included programmatic responses to determined needs of the community.

Chief among these projects was the development of a comprehensive housing and social services community for their aging and single-parent members. Residences that accommodate their particular social, financial, and health needs have become the foci of the Community Housing Development Project. Importantly, this urban Indian–

initiated project has gained the interest and sponsorship of at least one of the fiscally empowered rural Southern California Native American bands. "Indians helping Indians" is now a rallying cry of this pan-California Native Americans movement.

Recently SCIC initiated a training program for cultural impact monitors. Its seventeen graduates were mostly indigenous Californian Native Americans (Gabrieliños and Juaneños). Deemed so successful and needed, SCIC planned to offer a second such training session in 2000. Another perceived urban Native American need for which SCIC has successfully located service funds is diabetes and heart disease detection, referral, and nutritional intervention. Finally, there were plans in late 1999 to locate and secure funds and infrastructural support for a culture-sensitive charter school.

SCIC 2000: Costs, Conflicts, Coalitions, and Campaigns

Urban Indian social services institutions face an uncertain future. While in 1997 SCIC was poised to take aggressive steps and innovative approaches to institutional preservation and alliance building, old and new complications and conflicts continued to impede the process. In the decade between 1987 and 1997 SCIC developed and perfected a number of operational strategies for continuing to provide needed social services to their constituents in both Orange and Los Angeles Counties despite diminished resources and increased attempts by public funding agencies to devalue and (ultimately) to defund ethnic-specific social service programs. While a number of Los Angeles–based Native American social service organizations were forced to close for lack of funding during this period, SCIC managed to sustain services to its urban Indian clients. Focal community redefinition, institutional reorganization, leadership and staff skills development, creative approaches to securing funds, building new alliances, and maintaining loyal advocates at all levels of public funding policy development are among the institutional survival strategies that have established and sustained SCIC as one of the most successful regional Native American social service organizations.

In 1999 SCIC was characterized by its maintenance of a stable, well-delineated hierarchical structure, an able, informed, and equally stable administration, a handpicked staff of capable and committed paid and volunteer community members, and an emphasis on the comprehensive delivery of needed services to a widely dispersed community.

Urban/Rural Cooperation: Toward an Operational Model of Urban Indian Institutional Survival in the Next Millennium

In chapter 5 of this volume Straus and Valentino describe the dissipation of rural/ tribal versus urban/pan-Indian program rivalries in the Chicago area. Such rivalries continue to thwart a Southern California rural/urban Indian united front from mounting effective challenges to federal and state funding policy proposals and decisions perceived as antithetical to Indian community needs. The SCIC administrators continue to network with both funding agencies and rural Indian groups in order to maintain or develop future coalitions. They argue that 62 percent of the American Indian population now lives in urban settings. If legislators and foundations wish to have services provided to an optimum number of Native Americans, they must distribute their grants accordingly. Most legislators and foundation staff understand and are sympathetic to this argument.

Rural tribal entities, however, continue to suspect and resist such arguments. Rather, they see themselves as being in direct competition with their urban brothers and sisters for already insufficient Native American entitlement funds. The SCIC administrators have attempted to persuade rural tribal groups of the logic of cooperation and mutual support. They argue, "Your extended family is here in the city. And we're servicing them. We need some portion of the available social service funds to do it." Unfortunately, and unlike the results in Chicago, their efforts to effect a rural/urban Indian coalition have been met with limited acceptance among rural tribal groups.[26]

The SCIC directors see a greater potential for alliance-building with other urban Indian groups in California—a process they were able to bring to fruition around the issue of the 2000 census count. John described SCIC's strategy: "All Indian groups in California should work together to get the figures up in the next census. Population figures form the basis for grant allotments. I was able to develop a coalition of California urban Indians two years ago. Two people from other Indian centers up north will be coming down in February [1997] to strategize with us about our roles in the 2000 census."

SCIC's purpose in continuing to encourage statewide cooperation among Indian groups with regard to the 2000 census count is twofold. First, a full count of California's urban Indian population could reverse the notion of urban Indian out-migration and socioeconomic self-sufficiency as suggested by the 1990 census figures. Second, avoidance of another major undercount of Native Americans in California would thwart efforts to use census figures and demographics to deny ethnic minority groups access to federal and state funding consideration. As Paula Starr points out, "There are over three hundred thousand Native Americans in California today. California leads the Nation in Indian residents. The funding allocations for Native American programs in our state should reflect these statistics."[27] In the coming millennium, the development, strength, and survival of Native institutions will depend on their ability to serve all American Indians—urban, rural, and everything in between.

Importantly, while SCIC has successfully adopted the legal/rational organizational structures and processes demanded of block grant recipients, it retains, in important and cohesive ways, its traditional Native American community character. Respect of one's elders and their experience-derived wisdom is still a cultural imperative as illustrated by the mentor-facilitator relationship of the SCIC board of directors and its executive directors. The belief that the health of an organization (or community) is the responsibility of all of its members is another dynamic of Native American community relations that remains a driving force in the maintenance of SCIC institutional integrity. Nowhere is the subordination of individual desires to group needs more clearly demonstrated than in the SCIC members' donation of thousands of hours of service to ensure the success of their annual powwow.

The SCIC executive directors optimistically continue to forge new funding campaigns and program initiatives. In January 1997 the administrators, at the direction and sanction of their board of directors, were involved in building a comprehensive legal aid program at SCIC. Within the year SCIC had initiated a training program for cultural impact monitors. In early 1998 SCIC initiated a mobile health survey, assessment, and referral program. In 1999 that program had been awarded a grant that doubled its previous operating budget. The SCIC education budget had also been substantially increased that year. In fact, SCIC's 1999 budget rivaled its pre-1995 budget cut profile. And the drumbeat goes on . . .

Notes

1. This anthology about the Native American experience in several urban centers across the nation underscores several parallel personal and group reactions to diverse urban milieus, as well as sociostructural processes within and across them. Straus and Valentino, for example, identify in chapter 5 of this volume the equally early development of multitribal social organizations such as the Indian Council Fire (1923) and the All Tribes American Indian Center in Chicago. Lobo, in her outline of defining characteristics of the American Indian community in the San Francisco Bay Area in chapter 4, lists sustained basic institutions as one of the four critical elements of that ethnic community. The same can be said of the Native American communities in Los Angeles (Weibel-Orlando, *Indian Country, L.A.* [Champaign: Illinois University Press, 1999]) and Chicago (Arndt, "'Contrary to Our Way of Thinking': The Struggle for an American Indian Center in Chicago, 1946–1953," *American Indian Culture and Research Journal 22*, no. 4 [1999], 117–34).

2. Wayne G. Bramstedt, "Corporate Adaptations of Urban Migrants: American Indian Voluntary Associations in the Los Angeles Metropolitan Area" (Ph.D. diss., Department of Anthropology, University of California–Los Angeles, 1977), 93.

3. Two articles were helpful in constructing this historical background: "SCIC'S First President: Delmar J. Nejo," Twenty-Eighth Annual Pow-wow Program (Garden Grove, Calif.: SCIC, Inc., 1996; reprinted in part from the *Orange County Register*, 20 February, 1968); and "History of SCIC," Thirtieth Annual Pow-wow Program (Garden Grove, Calif.: SCIC, Inc., 1998), 10.

4. Bureau of the Census, "Table 28: Characteristics of the Population, For Counties: 1960," *Characteristics of the Population, Part 6 California*, 1960 Census of Population (Washington, D.C.: Government Printing Office, May 1963), 6, 196–97.

5. Bureau of the Census, "Table 5: Race and Hispanic Origin: 1990," *General Population Characteristics, California, Section 1 of 3,* 1990 Census of Population (Washington, D.C.: Government Printing Office, July 1992), 28–29.

6. In December 1998 John Castillo left SCIC to complete his doctoral dissertation research. In January 1999 the SCIC board of directors selected Paula Starr to be its executive director. At this writing (November 1999), she continues to serve her community in this capacity. Ruth Ann Abrams (Seneca) assumed the title of associate executive director with Ms. Starr's promotion.

7. The quotation marks here indicate that this word is jargon used by the community of social service providers and the public and private contracting and granting institutions with which the SCIC administrators interact.

8. Quotation marks are used here to indicate that the phrases represent the actual words of John Castillo and Paula Starr.

9. See Bureau of the Census "Table 50: General Characteristics for Selected Racial Groups for Counties: 1980," *Characteristics of the Population, General Population Characteristics, pc80-1-B6 California,* 1980 Census of Population (Washington, D.C.: Government Printing Office, November, 1983), 6-678, 6-681. For the 1990 census count of Native Americans in Los Angeles and Orange Counties see Bureau of the Census 1992, 28–29.

10. In chapter 4 of this volume Lobo also notes "increased economic and class diversity in the San Francisco Bay Area's Native American community."

11. The phrase in quotation marks was the slogan of the Native American Special Task Force on the Census and appeared on its community outreach materials prior to and during the 1990 census-taking period.

12. The words in quotation marks reference the book *Surviving in Two Worlds: Contemporary Native American Voices,* edited by Lois Crozier-Hogle and Darryl Babe Wilson (University of Texas Press, 1997).

13. See A. F. C. Wallace's *The Death and Rebirth of the Seneca* (New York: Random House, 1972); Alexander Moore's *Cultural Anthropology: The Field Study of Human Beings* (San Diego: Collegiate Press, 1992), 303–9; and E. Adamson Hoebel's *The Cheyennes: Indians of the Great Plains,* 2nd ed. (Fort Worth: Harcourt Brace Jovanovich, 1977).

14. Words that either paraphrase or complete a sentence when the speaker's answer was overly convoluted, ambiguous, or incomplete are bracketed so that the reader will know that these are not the exact words of the speakers.

15. The term *organized anarchy* was introduced by Michael D. Cohen and James G. March in "Leadership in an Organized Anarchy," (385–99). Thomas J. Peters and Robert H. Waterman coined the phrase *loose-tight properties* in their chapter entitled "In Search of Excellence: Simultaneous Loose-Tight Properties," (508–12). Shoshana Zuboff used the term *informated organizations* in a chapter entitled "In the Age of the Smart Machine: The Limits of Hierarchy in an Informated Organization," (547–60). Finally David Osborne and Ted Gaebler discuss the "bankruptcy of bureaucracy" in "Reinventing Government: Introduction" (529). All four references are found in *Classics of Organization Theory,* 4th ed., ed. Shafritz and Ott (Fort Worth: Harcourt Brace College Publishers, 1996).

16. Elliot Jaques, "In Praise of Hierarchy," in *Classics of Organization Theory,* ed. Shafritz and Ott, 245.

17. As Straus and Valentino note in chapter 5 regarding Chicago, most of the college educated administrators and staff members of the urban Native American organizations in Southern California have also come from among the ranks of the "second-generation urban residents, individuals who had been raised and even born in the city, although they had reservation experience as well." In chapter 4 Lobo underscores the widening range of educational experience of the San Francisco Native American population.

18. In 1977 the SCIC financial comptroller and Indian Child Welfare coordinator were the two non-Indians among a staff of thirty-five full-time and seven part-time employees.

19. Peter F. Drucker, *Managing the Non-Profit Organization* (New York: Harper Collins, 1990), 7.

20. See the articles in the 1996 and 1998 SCIC annual pow-wow programs cited in n.3.

21. *Native Americans in the Twentieth Century* by James S. Olson and Raymond Wilson (Urbana: University of Illinois Press, 1984) still offers some of the most colorful descriptions and incisive analyses of the Native American militant movement and activities of the 1960s and 1970s.

22. See especially Arndt's discussion of the Chicago group's "determination to control their own urban organizations" in "Contrary to Our Way of Thinking," 121.

23. By November 1999 this number had grown to five hundred.

24. See Osborne and Gaebler, "Reinventing Government," 532–34.

25. A second meeting with the SCIC executive directors was held on November 15, 1999. At that time the participants included executive director Paula Starr, associate executive director Ruth Ann Abrams (Seneca), and board members Starr Robideau (Cheyenne/Chippewa) and Eugene Herrod (Creek).

26. Paula Starr, in the November 1999 meeting, however, pointed to three recent and promising breaches of this urban/rural Indian political divide. Native Americans throughout California saw the Proposition 5 issue as a political rallying point (either pro or con) in the 1998 elections, and an example that Native Americans can make the national political system work to their advantage. Secondly, the first Annual Southern California Intertribal Music Festival took place on the opening day of SCIC's Thirty-First Annual Powwow (July 30, 1998). Sponsors of and financial contributors to this event included the Sycuan, Barona, and Viejas Bands of rural Southern California as well as the tourism department of the Navajo Nation. Finally, the Barona Band has expressed an interest in becoming involved in SCIC's emerging urban Indian housing project.

27. Although Ms. Starr did not cite her source during our November 1999 conversation, I feel sure that her assertions are based on the populations figures reported in "Table 5: Race and Hispanic Origin: 1990" of the *1990 Census of Population, General Population Characteristics, California*, section I (Washington, D.C.: Government Printing Office, November, 1992): 28–29.

Cities

CARTER REVARD/NOMPEWATHE

are a way of keeping grass
from growing under feet

of spreading oil upon
the troubled earth

of squaring heaven, setting
pillars of fire, pillars of smoke

around a hi-fi voicebox that
speaks but cannot answer—

have crumbs for winged beings
who decorate its leaders' heads,

are inside-out cathedrals
brightest at night, staining

their darkness visible
with green gold and scarlet

—they make sure pale faces pass,
signing them onto exit-ramps,

put space-probes into Venus,
fingers of doubting a Thomists—

know how we must be saved:
BE NUMBER, OR YOU PERISH!

nothing we plant in one
is food or medicine; feeds

the eye or banks into
a sharp-eyed pocket:

where flowers know their place
illuminating margins,

where wild things paw the trash
around white reservations

that darken spread and flake
like ringworm in green hair.

Continuing Identity
Laguna Pueblo Railroaders in Richmond, California

7

KURT M. PETERS

A CONVENIENT ROUTE to California, water for steam locomotives, and resources for construction to the Pacific dictated late–nineteenth-century United States railroad expansion west through New Mexico Territory.[1] Land tenure conflicts in New Mexico plagued the Native American people of Laguna Pueblo and by the 1880s their economy was shifting away from its traditional agrarian base. There is substantial evidence that declining agricultural success forced the people to look outside their traditional structure for subsistence. The arrival of railroading provided a needed outlet for internal economic pressures on the tribe.[2] Appearance of the steam locomotive in the Southwest offered alternative employment. Railroads led directly to the departure of many Laguna people to distant regions as wage laborers.

After years of warring with tribes that plundered their villages, resisting Spanish, Mexican, and Anglo-American invaders, and accommodating squatters of all types, the Laguna Pueblo people came under a new pressure: railroads would now vie for use of their land. In 1866 the Atlantic & Pacific received a federal grant of more than thirteen million acres for a rail line between Albuquerque and the Arizona–California border at the Colorado River.[3] Laguna territory lay squarely in the path of railroad surveys favoring a route from Colorado through New Mexico to California along the thirty-fifth parallel.[4]

The Atlantic & Pacific entered New Mexico in 1880 and began laying track south of Albuquerque and west of Isleta Pueblo, toward Laguna. The Lagunas took the arrival of the railroad's construction crew as an opportunity to set a precedent: according to modern narratives, Jimmy Hiuwec, secretary of the Tribal Council, halted the crews preparing to lay track across Laguna land. In stopping this extension of the rail line, Hiuwec set in motion a visit from eastern railroad authorities, resulting in another accommodation of outsiders. The Lagunas and the railroad negotiated a peculiar innovation. They agreed the railroad could pass through the Laguna territory unmolested, with one stipulation: the railroad would forever employ as many of the Lagunas to help build and maintain the system as wished to work, so long as the governor of their pueblo granted the workers his approval.

117

This oral agreement in 1880 guaranteed the Laguna people jobs and the railroad an assurance of unhindered right-of-way. A handshake sealed the bargain, referred to in the narratives as "The Gentlemen's Agreement of Friendship."[5] Every year thereafter, the Lagunas and the late–nineteenth-century purchaser of the Atlantic & Pacific lines—the Atchison, Topeka, and Santa Fe—met to reaffirm the contractual terms. Laguna people call this annual contract renewal "watering the flower."[6] There is a lack of documentation regarding whether a written contract between the railroad and the Lagunas exists to corroborate these remembrances. While no document is extant, descendants of the Lagunas involved believe that a valid oral contract continues in force.[7]

In 1880 Laguna men began work building track. Some eventually became section maintainers on the portion of the rail line passing through the 125,225 acres of Laguna land.[8] Others accepted Atchison, Topeka, and Santa Fe work at Albuquerque, Gallup, and other locations along the rail line outside the area. Throughout the era from 1880 and into the first quarter of the next century, the Lagunas provided loyal adherence to their agreement with the railroad. Just following the end of World War I this loyalty would undergo a trial, however.

Emergency wage increases granted during World War I contributed to railroad and government animosity toward labor unions. This antagonism erupted during a series of railroad strikes as management tried to roll back those gains. One such confrontation, the Shopmen's Strike of 1922, strangled the operations of the railroads nationally. Service disruptions were commonplace. In one instance, striking Atchison, Topeka, and Santa Fe workers loyal to the unions put over three hundred passengers off the train, leaving them in the summer heat at Needles, California. A request from company management for assistance tested the strength of the Laguna Pueblo agreement. The Laguna governor responded. More than a hundred men moved from the pueblo in New Mexico to the Atchison, Topeka, and Santa Fe terminal at Richmond, California, to replace striking workers. Coach cars transported the Lagunas from their home through the picket lines. Once in the rail yards at Richmond, they bunked and ate for the duration of the strike in the assembly hall, one of the several maintenance buildings at the terminal.[9]

As the strike continued, some railroads signed a compact known as the Baltimore Agreement, which essentially put control of terms of rehiring strikers in management hands. The Atchison, Topeka, and Santa Fe continued to hold out and did not initially sign on to the negotiations. Instead management injected the diminished labor force with nonunion workers, including the Lagunas. The role of these Native Americans during the 1922 strike was the dangerous one of "scab."

The Shopmen's Strike was settled in September 1923.[10] According to Laguna narratives, some of the men remained at the Richmond terminal, or at least remained with track crews using the facility as their base. Many Lagunas transferred to Atchison, Topeka, and Santa Fe centers at Barstow, Winslow, Calwa, and Needles, while others returned home.[11]

Settlement of the strike was an ignominious defeat for the unions and initiated a sharp decline in membership.[12] Lagunas were well aware of the significance of their role in the Shopmen's Strike; they saw participation as the proper action under their agreement with the railroad and as the proper Laguna response to direction from their governor in New Mexico. The Laguna governor asked the Acoma Pueblo to send men to Richmond in order to buttress the insufficient supply of Laguna replacements, and so Acoma Pueblo also became involved with the growing "Indian Village" at Richmond. Lagunas interviewed insist, however, that they do not consider the Acomas included under the 1880 contract.[13]

As a result of general unionization, the railroad brotherhoods drew the Native American workers into their ranks during the 1940s. Laguna recollections are not clear as to exactly when they voted to organize the Richmond shops.[14] The post-unionization attitude of the Laguna laborers remained loyal to the spirit of the agreement made in 1880. They made annual visits to the Atchison, Topeka, and Santa Fe regional office in Los Angeles to "water the flower."[15] Laguna workers, however, also honored the principles of their union membership. One Laguna said later that "after the union come in, you join us or you're out."[16]

Before 1940, the Richmond area, described by historian James Gregory as a "dull industrial suburb," encompassed a population of about twenty-four thousand residents.[17] During the late 1930s, a second group of Native Americans came from New Mexico to live in the terminal yards, but the Atchison, Topeka, and Santa Fe and the city of Richmond were about to feel the pressures of World War II. The opening of the Kaiser Shipyards alongside the existing railroad shops, the Standard Oil Refinery, and the Ford Assembly Plant made Richmond the "quintessential war boom town." Its population exceeded a hundred thousand after three years of rapid growth.[18]

By World War II there were several settlements along the Atchison, Topeka, and Santa Fe lines between Albuquerque and Richmond, in addition to the six Laguna villages on the reservation. Major villages of workers developed at Gallup, Winslow, Barstow, Richmond, and Los Angeles. The communities at Gallup, Winslow, Barstow, and Richmond applied to the Laguna governor at home for formal recognition as "Colonies of the Laguna Pueblo in New Mexico," and received this status. With this recognition came a more formalized community structure. The village at Richmond was thereafter headed by an annually elected governor. Village men were required to attend meetings to vote on matters involving the home pueblo during which only their native language was spoken. Decisions were then transmitted to New Mexico by official correspondence from the village administration. Representatives from the village government often traveled home by train to attend important functions. The Atchison, Topeka, and Santa Fe Railroad eventually adopted the same "colony" designation for the village at Richmond.[19]

During the early war years at Richmond the men bunked in the railroad's firehouse. When wives and families from New Mexico began arriving, the company

Santiago "Sandy" Sarracino (Laguna), at work in the Atchison, Topeka, and Santa Fe railroad yards, Richmond, CA., circa 1940. (Photo courtesy of the Sarracino family)

provided more permanent rows of boxcar housing set on sidings. The company joined the boxcar homes in sets of two, and two families were assigned to each unit. Finally, the company installed a shower and commode in each duplex, one set per family. Former residents remember the boxcar living quarters as "cozy."[20] The clustering of boxcar homes grew out of the wartime need to accommodate the men's spouses and families indefinitely. As Laguna men joined the military ranks away from the Richmond yards, the women filled their jobs.

The Atchison, Topeka, and Santa Fe employed two thousand women in 1925, and thirty-five hundred by World War II, an increase that included many Lagunas.[21] Sharply growing demands on labor pools during wartime found women filling such diverse railroading jobs as signal tower operators, agents, freight handlers, turntable operators, yard clerks, track sweepers, drill press operators, sheet metal workers, engine wipers, fire builders, and timekeepers.[22] Among the Laguna families retired from the Richmond yards are many women who began their first off-reservation employment during World War II.[23] One woman from the village recalls "doing everything" on the job formerly done by the men, including changing the wheels on the locomotives. When asked about the rate of pay, she laughed and replied, "We wouldn't *let* them pay us less than the men."[24]

The village developed a reputation as a focal point for entertaining returning Native American military men passing through the San Francisco Bay area. Sometimes the Natives brought along their friends—"you know, white boys," recalled a former worker—to enjoy "Indian food" prepared by the village Ladies' Club.[25] An active leader at the village remembered taking his accordion to entertain at the Atchison, Topeka and Santa Fe auditorium every Saturday during the war. He recalled other Native Americans there as having saxophone, guitar, drums, and banjo, and playing "pretty good" in his "orchestra" at the village. As the servicemen left military service, "they stop over there and I put up a dance for them . . . all different tribes," he said. Asked if the band ever went on tour, he replied that it was "just for the village" and played so that a "nice time" greeted the returning military men. He did acknowledge appearing personally in local talent shows and playing for senior citizens' groups. This retiree exclaimed, "those old folks, they sure like it," and added that the melodies were "old Spanish music" he had learned without any formal musical training.[26] Another Laguna family spoke of participating in community activities when they arrived during the early 1940s. One person reported that "everyone" went to the Four Winds Club, a Native family social organization in Oakland. Several non-Native Americans, including a "former mayor of Oakland and his wife," participated in the club activities.[27] Although the club's activities never brought it to Richmond, "folks from the village" enjoyed Thanksgiving dinners and Christmas parties at the Four Winds in downtown Oakland. Local news media covered club events, recalled one Laguna. The Four Winds, which met at the Oakland Women's Club in the YMCA/YWCA building, was a common ground for Native people migrating from the reservation and rural homelands during the late 1940s and early 1950s. The wife of a former village governor remembered Native American employees of the Atchison, Topeka, and Santa Fe "were there before the federal government started to relocate the Indians from different reservations."[28]

Asked about village relations with the surrounding community, she replied, "We had our own recreation hall [a converted boxcar] where our own Indian people put up dances that could not be seen by the white people." They were able, she said, to maintain their "own ways" in the train yards. This woman's daughter remembered "deer dinners," tribal meetings, church Confirmation parties, and a teen club all taking place in the boxcar meeting hall. The teen club used an eight-foot by ten-foot room for gatherings. One Laguna kept several home movies of traditional dances at the village, including the butterfly dance with ritual costumes. Another woman explained that Lagunas held "closed" sacred dances as well as "feast" and social dances open to visitors. Residents celebrated the annual "Grab Day" by throwing candies and gifts to the village children from boxcar roofs.[29] These and other events re-created the traditions of the home pueblo in New Mexico. They maintained strong cultural ties both within the train yards and with their home pueblo during their Richmond sojourn.

Additions to the railroad system after 1940 resulted in major concentrations of Native American labor at the growing junctures of urban populations and the railroad. The Atchison, Topeka, and Santa Fe shops at Richmond employed an increasingly high percentage of the railroad's laborers. The work force expanded as trackage increased and the land in New Mexico, Arizona, and California became more settled. During 1955, an Indian center formed in Oakland. Some of the same village residents acted as organizers and active members of the center.[30]

Natives in the village remember using an "electric train" to cross the San Francisco Bay Bridge. Also, a "barge with cars and even a little restaurant" traveled between Point Richmond and San Rafael across San Pablo Bay. The well-known Playland at the beach in San Francisco was another favorite destination for Laguna laborers and their families. One mother who spent many hours there remembered the now-razed Playland as a "nice place" where many Lagunas liked to spend their days off.[31]

The Native American community in the Atchison, Topeka, and Santa Fe terminal enjoyed a peaceful and fruitful life. Lagunas relied on many rituals, including the annual "watering the flower," in the maintenance of identity. The ability to make excursions into the surrounding community and return to the familiarity of their replicated home pueblo in the train yards added to their sense of leading a rich, full life. A Laguna woman born at the pueblo in New Mexico and nurtured in the village who continues to live near her old Atchison, Topeka, and Santa Fe home site summed up her experience in the Richmond train yards this way: "We had everything!"[32]

Atchison, Topeka, and Santa Fe records are not extant from the years of annual meetings to "water the flower," and there are no indications of the company name for the meetings. According to a company public relations representative, one of two known record sets disappeared during two moves of the Coast Lines offices in Los Angeles. Records were discarded in 1979 and again in 1989. The second set disintegrated in flooding at a company storage location.[33] In contrast to the feelings of the Lagunas themselves, in August 6, 1982, the first page of the Contra Costa Independent newspaper stated dourly:

> There is little information available about the Indian Village. Throughout the years the families who lived there insisted upon their privacy in their daily lives as well as ritual events, meetings and social functions, and were supported in this desire by Santa Fe. The Indians maintained their cultural identity and political allegiance with their New Mexican pueblos; the village was regarded as the place to live while the Indians worked for the railroad, not as a permanent home. When the worker retired the family would return.[34]

The company moved three modular homes into the village about 1970. All the new houses were claimed by Acoma families. For Lagunas familiar with the agreement of 1880, the Acomas are viewed as not having the same employment and housing rights. Their intervention and claiming of the new houses continues as a source of irritation to some Lagunas.[35] A ten-year plan to accommodate the technological changes in railroading did not include the Indian Village at Richmond. Physical change after World War II, both at the home pueblo and in the train yards, moved slowly to an inexorable end. Only the persistent sense of Laguna identity survived, changed forever by the amalgamation with the Atchison, Topeka, and Santa Fe railroading experience. "Today the Santa Fe Indian Village has been torn apart [and] the last two families, one from the Acoma Pueblo and the other from the Laguna Pueblo, have moved," *The Contra Costa Independent* quoted an Atchison, Topeka, and Santa Fe official as saying. "One of the two remaining families had been given a cash settlement and was moving to El Sobrante [California]."[36] The other resident bought a Richmond city lot to receive their duplex and the "boxcars will be removed from the property altogether," the official said, explaining that "Santa Fe needs the property for the continued development of its twelve-million dollar intermodal facility."[37]

"We hated to go over there," said a Richmond terminal supervisor in 1993. "Those last two boxcars just wouldn't give up, the wood kept splintering, and we broke our hammers." When asked what the wrecking crew finally did, he said, "We dug a hole and buried them." He pointed to the center of a broad expanse of train yard asphalt, and said, "Right over there!"[38]

One elderly African-American Richmond resident claimed there was "another part" of the village, the St. Johns Apartments, or former Mexican Village. She said, "That had really been an Indian Village at one time, but it belonged to Santa Fe." When the apartments were built, she said, "a lot of people got upset about it because they said that they had graves over there, and they built on top of that." She concluded,

"I imagine that if they were to start excavating they would find Indian relics down there."[39] One of the last village residents, a Laguna, speculated about the demise of her home. "Do you think," she asked, "those scientists [archaeologists] will dig my boxcar up someday?" Then she said, "Will they know it was an Indian house?"[40]

Waves of migrant Laguna laborers, augmented by members of the neighboring Acoma Pueblo, left New Mexico, passing in and out of the boxcar houses at the Richmond terminal from 1922 through the mid-1980s, when the Indian Village disbanded. They adapted themselves selectively to surrounding non-Native American functions, yet clung to tradition, returning often to their pueblos for nurturing celebrations and rituals. Employment by the Atchison, Topeka, and Santa Fe aided that nurturing process with steady work and an affirmed community life in the train yards. Still, the Lagunas steadfastly remained Laguna first, and railroaders second.

Historian Michael McGerr posits that, while structurally relevant to the economy, corporations had limited influence on Americans' attitudes and behavior as individuals. A paradox results: "For all their scope, corporations and other bureaucracies have failed to remake their own workers, let alone American culture." To explain this phenomenon, McGerr says, "We need to go beyond our faith in the power of organizations to transform people and culture." He concludes that "our nation may well be exceptional not for the power of organization, but for the persisting sense of human agency."[41]

One reason for this contradiction may lie in the fact that as creations of the state, corporations are also agencies thereof. For Native American societies, such as that at Laguna Pueblo and the village at Richmond, the unity of state and community structures was traditionally taken for granted. These amalgams in the twentieth century, however, always remained just slightly at the margins of the larger, state-bound social and economic systems. That marginality was sometimes self-imposed and maintained as an act of resistance against real and imagined hardships. The immediacy of these hardships, when filtered through history's lens, effects change in strategies for tribal survival and maintenance of identity. Edward Spicer wrote that "an identity system . . . develops independently of those processes by which a total culture pattern, a set of particular customs and beliefs constituting a way of life, is maintained." He maintained, "The *continuity* [italics added] of a people is a phenomenon distinct from the persistence of a particular set of culture traits."[42]

During the workers' employment at Richmond, the village functioned as a de facto satellite of the distant Laguna Pueblo. Sociologically and psychologically the village remained inextricably a part of the home pueblo, as if situated along the railroad right-of-way, west of the Rio Grande River in New Mexico. The shared experience of the laborers who occupied the village was a tribute to the cultural persistence of those who "watered the flower" of the Atchison, Topeka, and Santa Fe contract. In the process, the participants extended the continuity of their communities and expanded their own cultural tradition.

Notes

1. Various railroad expeditionary surveys were conducted in 1853 and subsequent years to determine the most economically advantageous southern route through New Mexico, linking California to Colorado and Kansas. For the considerations that eventually weighted a decision in favor of the so-called thirty-fifth parallel route, see land survey reports, Santa Fe Collection (Topeka: Kansas State Historical Society).

2. Edward H. Spicer commented on pueblo economics at the time of the railroad's arrival in New Mexico Territory:

> With occasional loss of crops due to floods, the necessity arose, especially after the 1880s, for finding additional means of support from time to time. Work on the railroad which was built through the Pueblo country in the 1880s became available as the Anglo cities increased in population and as various kinds of jobs became available in Albuquerque, Santa Fe, Bernalillo, and the many new towns. In addition, the population of every village was slowly but steadily increasing, and there was less and less possibility of new families taking up the land, as a result of the Mexican and Anglo population expansion through the whole Pueblo area. Outside employment was more and more relied on as a way of making at least a portion of one's living. New skills were acquired and a closer acquaintance with Anglo-American culture steadily developed.

Edward H. Spicer, *Cycles of Conquest: The Impact of Spain, Mexico, and the United States on the Indians of the Southwest, 1533–1960* (Tucson: University of Arizona Press, 1962), 176.

3. Merle Armitage, *Operations Santa Fe: Atchison, Topeka & Santa Fe Railway System* (New York: Duell, Sloan, and Pearce, 1948), 204.

4. See land surveys by Atlantic & Pacific for the thirty-fifth parallel route. Santa Fe Collection (Topeka: Kansas State Historical Society).

5. Personal interviews with community members from Richmond, California, and Laguna Pueblo, New Mexico, who were employed by the Atchison, Topeka, and Santa Fe Railroad at various times between 1922 and 1982. All interviews indicated here were conducted by the author at the University of California, Berkeley, and Laguna Pueblo between 1991 and 1993. Due to requested anonymity by those interviewed, they are hereafter referred to as "personal interviews." Interview notes, audio recordings, and relevant transcripts are in the author's collection.

6. Personal interviews.

7. For an example, see letters requesting copies of a documented contract written by the Sacramento Agency, Bureau of Indian Affairs, on behalf of Acoma residents at the Richmond Village. Record group 75/BIA, subgroup Sacramento Area Office, Coded Central Files 1910–1958, Box 7, folder 039 Acoma Pueblo (National Archives, Pacific-Sierra Region, San Bruno, California).

8. Frederick Webb Hodge, ed., *Handbook of North American Indians North of Mexico, Part 1*, Smithsonian Institution, Bureau of American Ethnology, Bulletin 30 (Washington: Government Printing Office, 1907), 752. The 1993 acreage under Laguna tribal control is figured at 458,933. Marlita A. Reddy, ed., *Statistical Record of Native North Americans* (Detroit: Gale Research, 1993), 1036.

9. Personal interviews.

10. James Quigel, *Labor Conflict in the United States: An Encyclopedia*, ed. Ronald L. Fillippelli (New York: Garland Publishing, 1990), 435–36.

11. Personal interviews.

12. Quigel, *Labor Conflict in the United States*, 435–36.

13. Personal interviews.

14. Two Lagunas interviewed recalled the year as being 1943. It is also possible, however, given the arrival of large numbers of workers at Richmond just before World War II, that the vote to organize was made during the period between President Truman's seizure of the railroads in 1946 and the work rule disputes of 1950. See Bryant, *History of the Atchison, Topeka & Santa Fe Railway*, 324.

15. Personal interviews.

16. Personal interviews.

17. James N. Gregory, *American Exodus: The Dust Bowl Migration and Okie Culture in California* (New York: Oxford University Press, 1989), 176.

18. Gregory, *American Exodus.*

19. Copies of Atchison, Topeka, and Santa Fe documents, loaned by former employees, bear the designation of "colony" as applied to the Richmond village.

20. Personal interviews.

21. Bryant, *History of the Atchison, Topeka & Santa Fe Railway*, 322; L. L. Waters, *Steel Trails to Santa Fe* (Lawrence: University of Kansas Press, 1950), 327.

22. Waters, *Steel Trails to Santa Fe*, 327.

23. Personal interviews.

24. Personal interviews.

25. Personal interviews.

26. Personal interviews.

27. Personal interviews.

28. Personal interviews.

29. Personal interviews.

30. "Fact Sheet" for the Intertribal Friendship House, Community History Project (Oakland, Calif.: Intertribal Friendship House).

31. Personal interviews.

32. Personal interviews.

33. Personal interviews.

34. "The End of the Indian Village," *Contra Costa Independent*, 6 August 1982.

35. Personal interviews.

36. "The End of the Indian Village."

37. Ibid.

38. Personal interviews.

39. Judith K. Dunning, *Harry and Marguerite Williams: Reflections of a Longtime Black Family in Richmond*, Regional Oral History Office, Bancroft Library (Berkeley: University of California, 1985), 117.

40. Personal interviews.

41. Michael McGerr, "The Persistence of Individualism," *Chronicle of Higher Education*, 10 February 1993.

42. Edward H. Spicer, "Persistent Cultural Systems: A Comparative Study of Identity Systems That Can Adapt to Contrasting Environments," *Science* 174 (November 1971), 798.

Feminists or Reformers?
American Indian Women and Community in Phoenix, 1965–1980

8

PÄIVI HOIKKALA

> Coming to the city here in Arizona is still a culture shock. . . .
> It's such a fast pace and [Indian people] have such a family-
> oriented idea about life. Their family comes first, so even if
> they live here during the week, every weekend they're home [on
> the reservation]. . . . You have to know where you've been, so
> you know where you're going.
>
> —PATRICIA HELTON (SHOSHONI/PAIUTE)

PATRICIA HELTON'S WORDS summarize the experience of many Native Americans in the Valley of the Sun—Phoenix, Arizona. The city is an alien place for those who move there from close-knit reservation communities. For those born in the city, connections to the tribal past become blurred and sometimes are lost altogether. When Helton moved to Phoenix in 1976, she recognized this dilemma, especially among Indian youth. She worked for the school district for ten years, developing retention programs for Indian high school students that raised their self-esteem through knowledge of their cultures and pasts. She then moved on to work for the Phoenix Indian Center (PIC) as an employment specialist. For Helton, the future of Indian people in urban areas holds promise: "I feel that they are realizing that they can get an education, that they can succeed. And they can still know their culture and still do the same things they did on the reservation. They can have a balance in both worlds."[1]

Finding this balance constitutes a major theme in the history of Indian Phoenix. According to the 1990 census, approximately thirty-eight thousand Native Americans called the city home. Phoenix thus ranks among the largest urban Indian centers in the nation, although Indians count for less than two percent of the total population.[2] Other than the Yaqui settlement of Guadalupe in South Phoenix, the city has also lacked a clearly identifiable Indian neighborhood, although Native Americans have tended to settle in the areas close to the Phoenix Indian School and the Indian Health Service (IHS). Despite these small numbers, Phoenix is clearly an "Indian city." There

127

are four reservations in the vicinity of Phoenix, adding to the Indian presence: Salt River, Fort McDowell, Gila River, and Ak Chin. Phoenix has also developed into a major administrative center for Indian affairs. Besides the Bureau of Indian Affairs (BIA) and the Indian Health Service, Phoenix houses the offices of several statewide Native American organizations. These agencies draw reservation residents to town on tribal business and provide employment opportunities in the city. The Phoenix Indian High School contributed to the city's profile until it closed in 1990. Other educational facilities in the metropolitan area continue to bring Indian youth into the urban environment. Finally, Phoenix is a major center of southwestern Native culture. Throughout the year, the nearby reservations and local Indian groups organize pow-wows and other cultural events in the metropolitan area. The Heard Museum and the Pueblo Grande Museum not only promote Native arts and history, but they sponsor annual Indian markets, attracting artists and craftsmen from around the country. These institutions thus serve an important function as cultural centers for Native people as well as cultural brokers between Indian and non-Indian populations.

Although the city of Phoenix has vigorously utilized Native cultures in its promotional campaigns since the late nineteenth century, Indian people themselves remained marginal in these efforts until the 1960s, when the situation changed dramatically. Attracted by economic and educational opportunities, the Native American population of Phoenix increased by nearly 60 percent from 1950 figures.[3] This growth intensified in the following decade, bringing to the forefront the many issues that reservation residents faced in the urban environment. Finding the balance proved difficult. At the same time, the federal government, under the auspices of Lyndon B. Johnson's Great Society, devoted attention and monies to poor and disadvantaged urban communities. American Indians in Phoenix used this opportunity to lobby for a variety of services in the city. By 1980 the Indian community had matured and developed a structure that warranted an unprecedented role for Native Americans as an interest group in Phoenix. This chapter focuses on these formative years of the Phoenix Indian community.

Interviews with activists reveal that women played a significant role in this process of building community. They served as volunteers in church organizations, helped to create child care and other services, worked as professionals in the Phoenix Indian Center, and attempted to organize Native people as a political force in the city. By engaging in cultural, educational, and political activities, women often drew on tribal notions of womanhood, family, and community—notions shared by many Indian people who came to Phoenix. Women's lives are thus intricately intertwined with the life of the community. The history of the community is the history of their involvement. As activists, women gained experience with the public sphere and awareness of the unequal power relationships that limited their choices as Indians *and* as women. This multilayered perspective on discrimination shaped their activism. Women understood that the history of Indian–white relations affected all members of their families—

male and female—as well as the entire Indian community. Women's issues thus inter-twined with community issues, further implicating race and class. Arizona Indian women also organized as *women*, identifying issues in terms of gender and displaying attitudes and opinions reflective of feminism. Yet, interviews with these women offer a very different perspective from feminism and feminist interpretations of such ac-tivism regarding their motivation and their relationship to feminism. Are they femi-nists or reformers? This chapter allows Indian women to answer.

On October 20, 1870, the 240 Anglo residents of the Salt River Valley approved a new town site and its name, Phoenix, thus marking the birth of the future capital of Arizona. Phoenix assumed a character as an Anglo city where minority groups formed an underclass that promoters used to realize their goals to build an Anglo city in the desert. Similarly, Phoenicians had little tolerance for the Indians who came into town to sell their handicrafts and firewood, to deliver grains to the local mills, and to ac-quire supplies on which they had come to depend. Contemporary newspaper com-ments suggest the irritation that local residents felt over Indians in public places; es-pecially offensive were the scant clothing and the occasional intoxication of these frequent visitors. In 1881 the city began to pass a series of ordinances to regulate the visits and behavior of Native Americans in town. This first restrictive piece of legis-lation required that they wear "proper" clothing and leave town before sundown. Vi-olators were subject to fines, even hard labor.[4]

Such ordinances did not keep Indians from coming to Phoenix to conduct busi-ness. Instead, they quickly adapted to the restrictions and came up with ways to get around them, exhibiting great ingenuity and most likely laughing at their white brethren. In her autobiography, Anna Moore Shaw, a Pima from the Gila River reser-vation, tells the story of how her people got around the ordinances:

> Then a young brave had a bright idea. "I know! Let's buy one or two overalls. Then we'll take turns wearing them into town!" A basket was passed around and each person threw in his few coins. . . . It so hap-pened that there was a mesquite thicket nearby [the city]. . . and it was just the right spot for the Indians to change their clothes. . . . When it was evening and all [men] had bought their groceries, they rolled up their overalls and safely hid them in the thorny branches of the mesquite. Then they mounted their ponies and rode home.[5]

The opening of the Phoenix Indian School in 1891 marked a change in the rela-tionship between Native Americans and Anglos. When two leading citizens of Phoenix suggested that the BIA establish a school in Phoenix, they had more than the edification of Indian youngsters in mind. The Anglo promoters of the school saw it as an economic asset; it would inject federal dollars into the economy and thus boost the growth of the city *and* it would provide local businesses with a cheap labor force.

By the early twentieth century the Indian school became part of the city's campaign to promote tourism. Parades, carnivals, and fairs began to incorporate Native elements. "The [Indian School's] boys' and girls' battalions always had a place on the fair's Indian Day program," reminisces Shaw, and "the loud clapping by the non-Indian spectators rewarded us for our efforts."[6]

Not only did the school bring money, tourists, and Indian youngsters into town, but it signaled the beginning of Phoenix as a center of Indian administration. The establishment of a sanatorium next to the school in 1909 provided the next step in this process, and by the 1940s the two institutions had become focal points for all Native Americans in the state. Furthermore, the Indian school encouraged the students to establish homes and look for employment in the city after graduation. The outing program served the same goal of assimilation by sending Indian girls to work as domestics in Phoenix families while the boys worked in menial tasks at local business enterprises.[7]

Although most school children returned to their home reservations, a small number made the city their home, including Anna Moore Shaw. In 1920 she married her school sweetheart Ross Shaw, a Pima from Salt River, and, according to Pima tradition, the couple returned to live with the husband's parents on the reservation. In her autobiography, Shaw poignantly illustrates the difficulties they experienced returning to reservation life after their education that "had prepared us to bring in money from the white man's world; it would be wrong to waste all those years of schooling on a life of primitive farming." The Shaws decided to move back to Phoenix. Ross Shaw got a job at the American Railway Express Company loading trains, eventually advancing to the position of supervisor of drivers. Anna Moore Shaw tended to the family household in a multiracial neighborhood of mainly Mexican Americans, Indians, and blacks.[8]

Anna Moore Shaw became a major focus for her family in the city. She provided continuity with tradition as she assumed a role as caretaker and housekeeper, tasks reflective of women's roles in traditional Pima society. Another important factor in finding balance was the frequent visits to the Salt River reservation. These visits reinforced the identities of the Shaw family members as Pimas, speaking to the pivotal role of traditional support networks in adjustment to the city. The family's outside interests centered on the Central Presbyterian Church. Organized in 1915, the church quickly assumed a character as the "Indian church" in the city, as much of its membership consisted of Native people. Central Presbyterian also served an important mediating function in the community. Worship services and social activities brought together people from different tribal groups and from different walks of life. Residents from nearby reservation communities also participated in church services and other events. Finally, the congregation included non-Indian members. The church thus offered a cultural mediating ground between different tribal cultures, between the reservation and the city, and between Indians and non-Indians. Central Presbyterian became the "one place [where Indians] mix with white men but still control things."[9]

World War II marked an important watershed in the history of Central Presbyterian, echoing the changes in Indian communities brought about by the war experience. As the city attracted more Native Americans in search of employment opportunities, church membership diversified. In 1949, Central Presbyterian also received its own building—an event of great symbolic meaning. As a tangible manifestation of the presence of Indians in the city, the building also gave them legitimacy as part of the larger American Indian community in Arizona. Furthermore, the church increasingly took on the role as the nexus for Phoenix's urban support structure.[10]

Many of the new arrivals in Phoenix were not as lucky as the Shaws in their proximity to their home reservation; moving to the city meant a leap away from reservation family networks into the urban unknown. In this context, the church congregation replaced the family. Women active in the church assumed roles as community mothers in this extended urban Indian family. Much of what they did as community mothers, indeed, fell within the confines of the female sphere. The Women's Missionary Society provided food and refreshments at church events; women engaged in charity and fundraising activities; they sang in the church choir. However, these duties also brought women into prominence as leaders. In 1956 the society sent two of its members to leadership training in California, signaling a change toward official visibility for women in the church organization. The ordination of the first female elder, Anna Moore Shaw, in 1958 solidified women's leadership authority.[11] Shaw thus exemplifies women's work in the community during these years of growth. In addition to her commitment to the church, Shaw extended her involvement to the larger community through PTA meetings and by joining the United Church Women as its only Native American member in the early 1940s. Shaw notes that "my determination to conquer prejudice by proving that the American Indian is an asset to our nation" served as a strong motive for her to become active in these non-Indian organizations.[12]

Shaw and her contemporaries pioneered women's community work in Phoenix. Brought up in an era that emphasized assimilation, their motives were strongly based on Christianity and a desire to prove that American Indians were worthy members of society. They acted in the context of their experiences as mothers and wives, relying on tribal notions of womanhood as well as those of mainstream America, and asking for the inclusion of Native Americans in the national community. Much in the tradition of women reformers of the turn of the century, they helped extend the boundaries of womanhood to include official leadership roles in the Indian community. Yet there is very little evidence in these women's narratives that they defined issues in terms of gender. They did believe that motherhood gave them the authority to act, but they did not question their roles as mothers and wives nor did they experience injustice in power relationships between men and women. The injustice, in their minds, existed in the relationship between Indian people and Anglos.[13]

The next generation of community activists built on the accomplishments of these pioneering women. Instead of asking for the inclusion of Indian people in the larger community, they focused on services for urban Indians as a distinct group. Central Presbyterian formed the link between the two approaches. Not only did it provide a meeting ground for people of different ages, but it strongly encouraged leadership development among its youth. In 1956 a group of young church members formed a chapter of the Westminster Youth Fellowship that came to reflect a growing awareness of local community issues as well as the national debate over racial equality in the Civil Rights era. Most important, the fellowship allowed young people in the community to establish friendships. Many future community activists and leaders participated in its functions and formed lasting relationships that later helped them recruit people to work in community projects.[14]

Federal funding through Great Society programs made it possible for the Central Presbyterian Church to realize its commitment to providing for more than just the spiritual needs of urban Indians. In 1965 the preschool board applied for funding from the Office of Economic Opportunity (OEO) to underwrite a community action program that would include both preschool and daycare services. By the following summer, the church operated a Head Start program for approximately thirty children. This program filled a dire need for child-care services, but it also provided women with an unprecedented opportunity to become involved in the community. Head Start allowed women, who were mothers and educators in their own families, to employ these skills in the context of the community. For example, between May 1968 and March 1969 only one of Head Start's fifteen staff members was male. Women also volunteered their services to the program and participated in the various school events and parent-teacher meetings.[15]

Women's experiences as staff members and volunteers served as a boost to their overall involvement in the community. Cecelia Miller (Tohono O'odham) noted that "some of [the activism] came out of Head Start, . . . parents wanting more funding and more things for their children."[16] Miller herself exemplifies this activism. She came to Phoenix to attend high school, dropped out in 1956 to get married, and had five children between 1957 and 1965. After her marriage ended in divorce, Miller found work at Head Start and became active in the Central Presbyterian Church. Contacts with women like Anna Moore Shaw undoubtedly influenced Miller and provided a model for her involvement. As in the case of these older women, Miller's motivation derived from her concerns as a mother of five children—but, as a single mother, economic issues featured more prominently in her activism. Miller emphasized the role of Head Start in acquainting her with issues of concern to Indian people in the city. These concerns often had a direct correlation with the poverty of Native American families. Her efforts to improve community life through Head Start and her church work established her reputation as an activist and a "trustworthy" member of the community. The community came to expect her participation, and Miller reciprocated.[17]

Other women shared Miller's experience in Head Start. Working with children and their parents, they learned about problem areas in the community. Staff members benefited from the training they received through the city's poverty agency and at the nearby Arizona State University. They gained experience in dealing with various agencies that before might have seemed overwhelmingly unfamiliar. They learned about funding sources available for programs and the process of applying for those funds. Most importantly, they gained self-esteem and the knowledge that they *could* change things. The Head Start program also appears to have encouraged community cohesion as people realized that they had power over their own affairs. An indication of this cohesion is the high percentage of Indian children in the program, although it was open to children of all ethnic backgrounds. By 1968, 60 percent of the children came from Native American families. The governing body of the Central Presbyterian Church also noted that "Indian people are moving to this area due to the program," creating an identifiable Native American community around the church.[18]

This newly found community cohesion resulted in an acute awareness of the lack of Native American representation in the city structures. In December 1968, a group of Head Start parents went to the city's poverty agency in an effort to establish a neighborhood council and to list the needs of the Indians in the community. They received funding to establish such a council to serve a twenty-block radius of Central Presbyterian, and in June 1969 the Central Community Council, known as the Tri-C, became one of the seven community councils in Phoenix under its poverty agency.[19] The organization of the Tri-C signaled an important watershed in the history of the relationship between the city of Phoenix and its Indian residents. For the first time, Native Americans as a community had official representation in the poverty programs and could benefit directly from the funding available through this agency.

Women's concern for families and children continued to drive community efforts. Despite Head Start, the lack of daycare facilities remained a major problem. Of special concern were the children of single mothers who had no traditional daycare alternatives such as extended family available to them. In 1970, 16.3 percent of the Native American households in Phoenix were headed by women; of these households, 20.4 percent had children under six years of age.[20] To alleviate the situation, women at the Central Presbyterian Church—including Cecelia Miller—took action and started a cooperative daycare center in 1971. With staff help from another daycare facility in the area and funding from various metropolitan area churches, this effort culminated in the incorporation of the Kee N' Bah Child Development Center in October 1971.[21]

The significance of Head Start and Kee N' Bah lies not only in providing desperately needed low-cost services to Indian families in Phoenix, but in the role they played as vehicles of empowerment for those women and men who helped initiate and operate the programs. Kee N' Bah in particular proved to be much more than just a daycare facility. From its very beginning, it sought to develop community leadership, responsibility, and concern by involving the parents. Parents of enrolled children made up two-thirds of the board of directors and acquired experience in community affairs.

Mothers were especially active in the operation of the center, and as volunteers they gained knowledge of child care and other related matters. The center also offered employment opportunities for mothers with little education. The skills they acquired and the confidence they gained in Kee N' Bah helped them advance to other jobs; many returned to school to complete their educations. Finally, Kee N' Bah helped families by informing parents of work and educational programs and available social services. Miller acknowledged the program's impact on her personally, on all the women who worked in Kee N' Bah, and on the community as a whole. She said, "It gave me a lot more self-confidence in terms of what I could do . . . [and] I feel like it was really able to help a lot of parents. Some of the women I see today and some of the jobs they have, I think, . . . were helped by their working for Kee N' Bah."[22]

Kee N' Bah represents a transitional phase in women's involvement as they moved from volunteer to professional community work. At the same time, the Phoenix Indian Center (PIC) replaced the church as the focus of activism. Founded in 1947, the center served as a point of contact for local Indians and those new to the city. Lack of funding limited the center's activities to social gatherings and initial assistance to newly arrived Indians in finding housing and employment. In the mid-1960s, developments both at the national and local level changed the relationship between the PIC and the City of Phoenix. Nationally, the War on Poverty focused attention on the problems of the inner city and the necessity of involving the poor in the planning of services. The City of Phoenix responded by creating the LEAP commission, or Leadership for the Advancement and Education of Phoenix, in 1964 as the city's poverty agency. The first Indian representative on the commission, Kent Ware, Sr., drew attention to the conditions of poverty and the invisibility of Native Americans in Phoenix. Simultaneously, the PIC contacted people who worked in the city's poverty programs. City officials responded in 1969 by funding a study of the needs of Indians in Phoenix; the grant also included a demonstration project to provide services for Indians through the PIC. In 1969 the Tri-C was also included in LEAP as one of its community councils.[23]

Recognition by the city did not solve the PIC's financial difficulties as the need for Indian-oriented programs increased with the growing number of migrants. The answer to these financial needs lay in the monies available from a variety of federal programs designed to address the problems of impoverished urban groups. The Central Presbyterian Head Start undoubtedly served as an example for the PIC to apply for funding from the Office of Economic Opportunity. At the same time, the national rise in Indian activism drew attention to Native Americans, specifically in urban areas. The first OEO grant came in 1970, designed to "develop more comprehensive programs, such as social services, recreational services, and professional information and referral services for the urban Indian population."[24]

Part of this grant went to hiring new staff members, and in September 1970 the center increased its staff from six to twenty employees. Among the new hires was

Karen Thorne (Pima). Her background and career exemplify the new generation of women involved in community work as professionals, funded by federal monies. Many of these women were born in Phoenix. Thorne was raised by her mother, who worked as a domestic for a wealthy Phoenix family. She recalls growing up almost as a member of this family and attending a local North Phoenix elementary school. After her mother remarried, they moved to the inner city, "into a more culturally diverse neighborhood. And that in itself was another kind of learning experience in my life."[25] Although the family returned to the mother's home reservation of Gila River for visits, Thorne's identification as a Native person remained minimal. Moving to central Phoenix contributed to her growing awareness of her identity and of other Indian people in the city. Thorne's contacts with the Indian community came mostly through Central Presbyterian where she participated in the Westminster Youth Fellowship activities. She was also a member of the Indian Club at Phoenix College, which she attended after graduation from high school in 1965. After two years, she transferred to Arizona State University with financial assistance from the tribe in Sacaton, Arizona. Thorne commented on how the social activism of the times and the availability of funding contributed to her decision to work for the Indian community in Phoenix:

> It was an exciting time, being in college or university, because of all the social issues and things that were happening. And I think a lot of minority people, particularly Indian people, [were] getting help with [their] education costs from [their] tribe. I think a lot of the tribes looked at it: "Well, once you get your education, your training, then you can come back and help your people." And I think a lot of us bought into it. . . . But then the reality of the fact was that I had really no close ties! I had not lived down there so how was I gonna help "my people"? And so probably that . . . explains why I ended up here at Phoenix Indian Center, in terms of working with Indian people.[26]

Another influence on Thorne's career choice came in the summer of 1968 when she attended an Indian studies workshop in Eau Claire, Wisconsin, with two of her friends. This workshop brought together Indian youth from both urban and reservation backgrounds, offering classes in cultural history, contemporary issues, and the role of the BIA in the lives of Indian people. Thorne reflected back on the summer as "sort of an eye-opener in terms of part of my [Indian] background." It also exposed her to people and experiences from different parts of the country and introduced her to the concepts of pan-Indianism and Indian activism: "So here we all came back, these militant young women! And I guess . . . each one of us had begun to look at what we could do, you know, what kind of an impact we could make."[27]

After the summer institute, Thorne became active in the Indian Club at the university. However, she dropped out of school because of medical problems and family matters. She also grew tired of the routine, wanting to accomplish more in life. The position as social worker at the Indian Center gave her that opportunity. The PIC was transforming from a small neighborhood center into a professional community organization. The staff was small and the atmosphere casual. Furthermore, most of the new jobs were in traditionally female areas: clerical work, social and educational programs. Many staff members, like Thorne, had some professional education but had not finished their degrees. At the same time, Thorne's experience reflects the instability of the center's footing in the community at this transitional stage. After less than a year, she was abruptly laid off together with a number of other employees.

Thorne suspects that these layoffs were related to the controversy between the PIC board of directors and the Indian community.[28] As the PIC began to offer more programs, community members grew more interested in its operation. The closed nature of the center's governing body drew criticism focusing on the failure of PIC to meet the social and economic needs of the community despite continued funding from the OEO. Personal disputes also entered the conflict. At the same time, the Indian community underwent a transformation as more young people attended colleges and universities and assertively pursued their goals. Like Thorne, they acted in campus organizations, influenced by national Indian activism and events like Alcatraz. What ensued were several years of discord over the governance and representativeness of the PIC. This conflict divided the community, but it also became the rallying point for various grassroots organizations. Their activism reflected the rising community consciousness among Phoenix Indians and helped secure services that they desperately needed.[29]

The coordination of this discontent fell to a newcomer among Indian organizational efforts, the Southwest Indian Development (SID). This organization emerged in 1969 as an advocacy group on the Navajo reservation, but it soon assumed a broader perspective on Indian affairs. In the early 1970s, SID organizers shifted their interest to the metropolitan Phoenix area, which they saw as a focal point for Native American activities in the Southwest. They expressed concern over the factionalism and conflict in the Indian community while citywide and neighborhood problems remained unresolved. Because the public bureaucracy had failed to respond to the city's Indian community, SID organizers believed it critical to increase Native American involvement in the decision-making process. Accordingly, SID sought to unite Indian groups in the city and to create a self-sustaining Indian community structure based on grassroots involvement. They thus helped develop local leadership by actively searching out and educating potential leaders. In sum, SID attempted to enhance the sense of an Indian community and its values in Phoenix.[30]

John Lewis (Pima/Mohave/Tohono O'odham) assumed an instrumental role in SID. Son of the first American Indian pastor at Central Presbyterian, Lewis grew up in Phoenix and was active in the church, including the Westminster Youth Fellowship. During these years, he formed friendships and connections with other Indian youth that he later used to recruit people for SID and other activist organizations. His own activism took shape in the context of the social reform in the 1960s. He attended Phoenix College, Arizona State University, and the University of Oklahoma, where he graduated in 1965 with a major in history and anthropology. During his college years Lewis became acquainted with Indian activists and after graduation he worked on the Colorado River reservation in community action. After receiving a master's degree from Arizona State in 1970, he shifted his focus toward Phoenix.[31]

Diane Daychild (Pima) was one of Lewis's early recruits. She got involved in 1972 because "John knew me because of my family, and he knew that I had lived here all my life. He knew that I knew the community pretty well."[32] Daychild participated in SID's grassroots organizing efforts, chairing the steering committee that addressed the PIC issue. Her background—like that of Lewis and Thorne—sheds light on Indian leadership in Phoenix at the time: young, with at least some college education, aware of social reform and activism of the times, and concerned with both reservation and urban experiences, although not immersed in reservation culture. Daychild grew up in Phoenix, living with her aunt and uncle and attending public schools. Her contacts with Pima culture and language remained minimal, and she did not start exploring her identity as an Indian person until college, where she met reservation youth and participated in the Indian Club. Daychild's awareness of her background culminated when she attended an Indian summer institute in 1967, and again the following summer together with Thorne. As in Thorne's case, this experience launched Daychild into community work. She explained, "that was the turning point, as far as my own involvement with tribal people and concerns and understanding why Indian people have these overriding problems regarding identity and socialization."[33] And, like Thorne, Daychild dropped out of the sociology program at Arizona State University and went to work for the PIC. She resigned in June 1971, together with five other PIC employees, in protest to the management policies of the chairman of the board of directors. Daychild thus positioned herself for political activism in SID.[34]

In addition to the PIC issue, SID focused on creating awareness of the needs of the Indian community among Phoenicians and the city government. The city responded to the pressure in May 1973 by forming a permanent Urban Indian Advisory Committee (UIAC). The city manager's office also helped sponsor a citywide Indian conference in June 1973 to discuss issues of health, education, and inclusion of Native Americans in city politics. This conference elected the Indian representatives to the UIAC, thus formalizing the relationship between the city structure and the Indian residents of Phoenix that had begun to take shape in 1969. The conference also provided the occasion for the creation of a pressure group separate from the city government: the Metropolitan Phoenix Indian Coalition (MPIC). The MPIC merged a number of various groups and activities under one umbrella organization. John Lewis defined its task as that of "a moving committee to focus on the issues." In the summer of 1973, this attention centered on the PIC controversy, and the MPIC's role at the head of this discontent launched the organization into community leadership. Furthermore, the publicity around the controversy attracted new segments of the urban Indian population to become active in community affairs. The representative base of the organizational efforts in the city thus widened to include a cross-section of its Native American residents.[35]

Mildred Marshall (Blackfoot/Chippewa/Cree) got involved in community activism because of the PIC issue. She came to Phoenix in 1962 to work for the BIA, after her husband had left her and their four children. Until the PIC controversy, Marshall had very little contact with other Native Americans in the city. Instead, she recalls her skepticism of and disillusionment with Indian people. Her first response to the PIC issue reflects these feelings: "[I saw] a bunch of Indians standing at the corner [of the PIC]. I drove by and stopped and asked them, 'Are you guys waiting around for the government to come down and give you hand-outs?' They answered that they were demonstrating [against] the PIC policies. [I felt that] Indian Center should be for all Indians, [and said], 'I'll just stop with you here.'"[36] Marshall then "got sucked into other things. We decided that standing around wasn't going to do anything." The issue of an organized pressure group came up in discussions among community activists, resulting in the establishment of the MPIC. Marshall co-chaired the committee with Floyd Bringing Good from Oklahoma.[37]

In examining the involvement of Thorne, Daychild, and Marshall, it is clear that their motivation derived not from a sense of maternal responsibility but from the political realities facing Indian people in urban areas. Influenced by the Civil Rights Movement and national Indian activism, they realized the inequality of the power relationships in Phoenix. As participants in the youth group at Central Presbyterian, Thorne and Daychild had formed connections with the community that they used in their efforts to improve the quality of life in the city. Marshall came in as an "outsider," but found a niche in the community as an Indian person. All three women participated in community development first and foremost as members of the "Indian" community. Their goal was the inclusion of all Indian people in city governance and the establishment of services for all Native Americans in the city. Gender inequality played a minimal role in their involvement despite their awareness of the women's movement. These women encountered few obstacles to their leadership in the Indian community because of their gender.

During the summer and fall of 1973, resolving the issue of PIC leadership dominated the MPIC efforts. Besides appeals through the political establishment, the MPIC employed such activist tactics as picketing and mass protests. Under these mounting pressures, the conflict came to an end in the spring of 1974. The board of directors elected five new members in an open meeting and reorganized the PIC's management structure. Syd Beane, a South Dakota Sioux, was elected executive director of the PIC in August, launching a period of extensive growth in its programs and constituency.[38] Under his leadership, the center developed into a comprehensive community service agency responsive to the Indian population in the Phoenix metropolitan area. Phyllis Bigpond (Yuchi), who followed Beane as executive director in 1978, agreed with this contention: "[The PIC] experienced a major growth and new resources coming in—and more of [Indian] control. [It was] under the control of Indian people more than it had been previously."[39]

Expanded services translated into an increase in employment opportunities at the center. These new employees tended to be young, educated—and female. Phyllis Bigpond held a master's degree in social work when she started working for the center in 1975 in its new mental health program. She already had experience working in the community as supervisor of a project to place Phoenix Indian High School students in jobs in the city and elsewhere. In addition, Bigpond had taken an interest in community affairs, serving as president of MPIC and sitting on the PIC board of directors.[40] The center also rehired former employees, including Karen Thorne, who returned to work in the employment services department in the mid-1970s. After being dismissed from the center in 1971, Thorne had worked as a consultant for Southwest Indian Development. She commented on the positive changes in PIC services during her years of absence, agreeing that the programs were "more productive than ever." The center now constantly reviewed and improved its services, and the "level and commitment of the staff was better."[41]

By 1980, the Phoenix Indian Center had evolved from a small neighborhood gathering place into a professional community work agency, offering services ranging from employment assistance to education to alcoholism programs. The employees reflected this metamorphosis: they held professional degrees more often than in the early 1970s, and those without degrees could get additional training and education while at the center. Because many of the new jobs were in fields within the traditional female sphere, women became a prominent group in the center. At the same time, the PIC's role in the community changed, and its importance as the nexus of activity subsided. Phyllis Bigpond reflected on these changes during her eleven years as director of PIC. She pointed to the emergence of other community organizations as one reason for the diminishing role of the PIC. The abundance of organizations also meant competition for resources while funding began to dwindle in the 1980s. Furthermore, Bigpond commented that organizing activity decreased significantly in all sectors after services were in place; organizations seemed to lack a rallying point, and enthusiasm died down. Finally, the focus of activism shifted from exclusively Indian organizations to involvement in the broader community to advocate Native American issues.[42]

Women's extensive involvement in these formative events resulted in the emergence of a strong female support network. Like Bigpond, many activists served the community in more than one capacity and came to rely on each other for advice and support. As they worked in close proximity with the community, they also came to see some issues in terms of gender. Brenda Young (Cherokee) worked at the PIC on a child-care project. She commented on her realization of problems specific to Indian women:

> I dealt with so many families where it was a one-parent family, almost always a woman, almost always working as a clerk or typist or secretary, raising one or two children on her own. And you get to see the inequities of the system, how difficult it is for these people! . . . Woman [*sic*] having such a difficult time, because, women's lib or no women's lib, women wind up with the children![43]

Other women recognized similar patterns and began to discuss their concerns as *women*, undoubtedly influenced by the increased visibility of the women's movement and women's concerns in society. In September 1975 several women from the metropolitan area attended the Southwest Indian Women's Conference in Window Rock, Arizona. Annie Wauneka (Navajo) had initiated this conference as part of the International Women's Year to address issues of concern to Native American women. The following January, Indian women in the Phoenix area held a follow-up meeting where they discussed their involvement in family, education, politics, and employment. They resolved that "Indian women have always been a guiding influence for Indian people," and to continue this guiding role, they agreed to hold a statewide conference of Arizona Indian women.[44]

When the Arizona Indian Women's Conference met in Phoenix in October of 1976, approximately four hundred women attended and participated in its eight workshops and other events. The conference theme, "Indian Women's Rights: Revolution or Return to Tradition?" reflected the role of women in tribal societies "with full rights and responsibilities," stressing the need "to reaffirm this tradition, rather than revolutionize [women's] current situation."[45] Keynote speaker Veronica Murdock, vice chair of the Colorado River Indian Tribes, emphasized women's knowledge as a valuable resource and urged conference participants to get involved in all aspects of community life and to share their expertise. Murdock especially encouraged women's political participation as an essential element in self-determination: "You talk about self-determination. That's an individual type of undertaking that the tribes have to take. It didn't take that law [Indian Self-Determination and Education Act of 1975] to tell us to be self-determining. We ourselves must be self-determining. That is the only way we can move forward," she said.[46]

The workshops at the conference addressed a variety of issues affecting the lives of American Indian women. They included employment, changing occupational roles, education, service resources, the status of elderly women, and legal rights. By far the most popular workshop addressed abuse and violence in Indian communities. In the discussion, women clearly identified some violent behavior as primarily a women's concern. The discussants also pointed to male bias as a reason for the lack of support for rape and abuse victims. On the other hand, these gender-specific issues became community issues as women recognized that cultural changes, resulting from the history of Indian-white relations, often were at the root of Indian men's problems:

> We talked about the historical reasons for spousal abuse, and it was brought out that it is related to the fact that Indian men historically have been the pampered people in the family. . . . As the Indian people were settled on the reservations, these kinds of cultural props were broken down and were no longer existent. The women did not have their cultural props taken away. They were there to a limited degree, and the women could still function.[47]

An examination of statements at the conference as well as interviews with participants supports the conclusion that, although Indian women recognized gender as a differentiating factor in their lives, the larger context of the community informed their involvement and activism. The conference emphasized that women use their traditional roles in tribal societies as a starting point for their community involvement. In other words, they should first act as mothers, educating their children of their heritage and their choices. Once they had determined what kind of mothers they were going to be, they could move on to other endeavors in their community so their children would have the strong base of both family and tradition to guide them.

Activist women in Phoenix had followed this guideline, each generation building on the experience of those before them. As the community became established and firmly footed in the urban environment, women also gained an awareness of power relationships that limited their choices not only as Native people, but as women. Like Brenda Young, who saw single mothers struggling for family livelihood, other women recognized inequities in the system. Their own work in the community and within the bureaucracy gave them the knowledge necessary to identify these inequities and to take on the injustice. In the process, they grew even closer together as women.

Although Indian women's discussions certainly reflect feminist concerns, including issues such as sexual abuse and job inequity, feminist rhetoric and ideology do not seem to have played a significant role in their organizing efforts. Instead of jumping on the feminist bandwagon, Native American women felt ambivalent about feminism as a concept and ideology. This ambivalence in part reflected uncertainty about the meaning of the word. Joy Hanley (Navajo) accepts the term as part of Navajo vocabulary, interpreting feminism as women's strong presence in community life and assertiveness in pursuing their goals: "Navajo women invented the term [chuckle]! Navajo women are really very, very strong—very, very, very aggressive."[48] But even if they accepted women's assertiveness as the basic premise of feminism, most felt uncomfortable with the strict boundaries that identifying as a feminist seemed to set on them as members of their tribal and urban communities, as well as individual women. Brenda Young expressed this viewpoint poignantly in her comments about feminism as an elitist movement:

> I think that a lot of Indian women feel very uncomfortable with an organization like NOW [National Organization for Women], or [the] kind of group of people that are involved in women's issues. . . . Feminism is like a subculture, like a club, that feeds itself. They just don't know enough about Indian cultures. . . . It always makes me nervous. Like the question you asked me, "What do Indian women want?" Wow, there *are a lot* of Indian women out there, a whole bunch of different tribes! And for me to speak for them, I don't really feel comfortable.[49]

The primary identification of activist Indian women in Phoenix was thus with the identity "Indian." They acted out of a communal consciousness that was based on solidarity between women and men of the same group. This feeling of unity combined with an awareness of women's traditional roles in tribal communities. Women thus accepted the tasks assigned to them in the gender systems of their societies but, by the same token, they demanded the rights that their obligations entailed. In their questioning of gender relationships, these women displayed attitudes and opinions reflective of feminism; yet they felt uncomfortable about identifying with feminism as it seemed to constrain them as members of Indian communities. Feminists or reformers? The women overwhelmingly reply, "Reformers!" To return to Patricia Helton's words, these women very clearly know where they have been and have a clear sense of where they are going—as women and as Indian people.

Acknowledgment

This article relies on interviews conducted with activists in the Phoenix Indian community in 1993 and 1994. Most of them continue their work for the community in different capacities. I would like to express my gratitude to all of them for sharing with me their experiences and insights.

Notes

1. Patricia Helton (Shoshoni/Paiute), interview with author, Phoenix, Arizona, 5 November 1993.

2. Bureau of the Census, *General Population Characteristics: Arizona, 1990* (Washington, D.C.: Government Printing Office, 1992), 7. The figures include people identifying themselves as Eskimo or Aleut.

3. Edward Liebow, "A Sense of Place: Urban Indians and the History of Pan-Tribal Institutions in Phoenix, Arizona" (Ph.D. diss., Arizona State University, 1986), 84; Paul Stuart, *Nations Within a Nation: Historical Statistics of the American Indians* (New York: Greenwood Press, 1987), 85.

4. Robert A. Trennert, "Phoenix and the Indians: 1867–1930," in *Phoenix in the Twentieth Century: Essays in Community History*, ed. G. Wesley Johnson, Jr. (Norman: University of Oklahoma Press, 1993), 53–55; Bradford Luckingham, *Phoenix: The History of a Southwestern Metropolis* (Tucson: University of Arizona Press, 1989), 12–16, 33; Ibid., *Minorities in Phoenix: A Profile of Mexican American, Chinese American, and African American Communities, 1860–1992* (Tucson: University of Arizona Press, 1994), 14–17.

5. Anna Moore Shaw, *A Pima Past* (Tucson: University of Arizona Press, 1974), 113–14.

6. Ibid., 133–34; Luckingham, *Phoenix*, 57; Chapter 2, "An Oasis in the Desert," of Robert A. Trennert's *The Phoenix Indian School: Forced Assimilation in Arizona, 1891–1935* (Norman: University of Oklahoma Press, 1988), 12–32, provides an overview of the establishment of the school. Trennert's article "Educating Indian Girls at Nonreservation Boarding Schools, 1878–1920," in *Unequal Sisters: A Multicultural Reader in U.S. Women's History*, ed. Ellen Carol DuBois and Vicki Ruiz (New York: Routledge, 1990), discusses the female experience in the boarding school system, using Phoenix as a case study.

7. Trennert, "Phoenix and the Indians," 64; Liebow, "A Sense of Place," 84, 122–23, 135.

8. Shaw, *A Pima Past*, 150–54; quote on page 150.

9. Reverend Joed Miller, quoted in James E. Cook, "The Urban Red Man," *Arizona Republic*, 17 May 1970; Central Presbyterian Church, *Seventy-Fifth Anniversary, March 3–4, 1970*, anniversary publication, Miscellaneous Files, Central Presbyterian Church, Phoenix, Arizona.

10. *Seventy-Fifth Anniversary*, 3–4.

11. Minutes of the Annual Congregational Meeting, 19 January 1955, 18 January 1956, 16 January 1957, 26 January 1958, and 17 January 1960, Church Register, Central Presbyterian Church, Phoenix, Arizona.

12. Shaw, *A Pima Past*, 189–93, quote on page 189.

13. In addition to Shaw's autobiography, these conclusions rely on the following interviews: Florence Seely [pseudonym](Pima), interview with author, 13 January 1993, Salt River Pima-Maricopa Indian Community; Alma Lewis [pseudonym](Pima), interview with author, Salt River Pima-Maricopa Indian Community, 13 January 1993; Margaret Sedongei [pseudonym](Tohono O'odham), interview with author, Phoenix, Arizona, 6 April 1994; Sallie Lewis (Pima), interview with Linda Salmon, 23 October 1981; and Elsie James (Hopi), Oral History Collection, Arizona Historical Society, Tempe, Arizona, 21 April 1977.

14. Minutes of the Annual Congregational Meeting, 16 January 1957 and 26 January 1958, Church Register, Central Presbyterian Church, Phoenix, Arizona; John Lewis (Pima/Mohave/Tohono O'odham), interview with author, Phoenix, Arizona, 8 December 1993; Karen Thorne (Pima), interview with author, Phoenix, Arizona, 16 November 1993.

15. Minutes of the Regular Session Meeting, 11 May 1965 and 20 June 1996, and Minutes of the Annual Congregational Meeting, 22 January 1967, Church Register, Central Presbyterian Church, Phoenix, Arizona; Head Start Director Tania Potter in a letter to the parents, 30 April 1969, Miscellaneous Files, Central Presbyterian Church, Phoenix, Arizona.

16. Cecelia Miller (Tohono O'odham), interview with author, Phoenix, Arizona, 3 November 1993.

17. Ibid.

18. Annual Congregational Meeting, 22 January 1967, Church Register, Central Presbyterian Church, Phoenix, Arizona.

19. Minutes of the Regular Session Meeting, 9 December 1968, Church Register, Central Presbyterian Church, Phoenix, Arizona.

20. Jim Red Corn, *Subject Report: American Indians of the United States by Place* (Oklahoma City: American Indian Census and Statistical Data Project, n.d.), 11.

21. Pastor's Report, Minutes of the Annual Congregational Meeting, 13 February 1972, Church Register, Central Presbyterian Church, Phoenix, Arizona; minutes of the Regular Session Meeting, 13 September 1971 and 18 November 1971, Church register, Central Presbyterian Church, Phoenix, Arizona; Kee N' Bah Child Development Center, "Articles of Incorporation," October 1971, Arizona Department of Library, Archives, and Public Records, Arizona Corporate Commission, Incorporation Division, Phoenix, Arizona.

22. Ibid; Miller interview.

23. Liebow, "A Sense of Place," 201; Sister Mary Rose Christy, "American Urban Indians: A Political Enigma. A Case Study: The Relationship Between Phoenix Urban Indians and Phoenix City Government," (master's thesis, Arizona State University, 1979), 168–77; Helen Drake, "Chronological History of the Human Resources Department, Operation LEAP" (Human Resources Department, Phoenix, Arizona); Don Wilkerson, "The American Indian in Metropolitan Phoenix," draft for a paper for the Governors' Conference at Lake Tahoe, Nevada, August 1969 (Governor's Office, Governor Williams, 1967–69, Box 504, Arizona Department of Library, Archives, and Public Records, Archival Division, Phoenix, Arizona).

24. Phoenix Indian Center agency profile in a grant application to the Arizona Department of Health Services, 31 January 1975 (Governor's Office, Governor Castro, 1974–75, Box 26, Folder 3, Arizona Department of Library, Archives, and Public Records, Archival Division, Phoenix, Arizona), 2.

25. *Arizona Republic*, 20 August 1970; Thorne interview.

26. Ibid.

27. Ibid.

28. Ibid.

29. Christy, "American Urban Indians," 179–81; Edward B. Liebow, "Urban Indian Institutions in Phoenix: Transformation from Headquarters City to Community," *Journal of Ethnic Studies* 4 (Winter 1991), 7.

30. Christy, "American Urban Indians," 182–84; Joyotpaul Chaudhuri, *Urban Indians of Arizona: Phoenix, Tucson, and Flagstaff* (Tucson: University of Arizona Press, 1974), 29–30; Luckingham, *Phoenix*, 219; Lewis interview.

31. Lewis interview.

32. Diane Daychild (Pima), interview with author, Phoenix, Arizona, 10 November 1993.

33. Ibid.

34. Ibid.; *Arizona Republic*, 17 June 1971.

35. Lewis interview; Christy, "American Urban Indians," 185–88; City of Phoenix, "Operation LEAP Manual," Policy Document no. 3-20, Urban Indian Advisory Committee, Department of Economic Security, HEW Grants, 1971–1976, Box 11 (Arizona Department of Library, Archives, and Public Records, Archival Division, Phoenix, Arizona) 1–9; *Arizona Republic*, 18 May 1973, 23 June 1973, and 24 June 1973.

36. Mildred Marshall [pseudonym] (Blackfoot/Chippewa/Cree), interview with author, Phoenix, Arizona, 5 April 1994.

37. Ibid.

38. Ibid.

39. Phyllis Bigpond (Yuchi), interview with author, 4 April 1994, Phoenix, Arizona.

40. Ibid.

41. Thorne interview.

42. Bigpond interview.

43. Brenda Young (Cherokee), interview with author, 7 December 1993, Phoenix, Arizona.

44. Arizona Indian Women's Conference, "Indian Women's Rights: Revolution or Return to Tradition?" conference report (Phoenix, Arizona: 1976), 33.

45. Ibid.

46. Veronica Murdock, Vice Chairperson of the Colorado River Indian tribes, keynote address, Arizona Indian Women's Conference, "Indian Women's Rights," 3.

47. Ibid., 6–10; quote on page 10.

48. Joy Hanley (Navajo), interview with author, Phoenix, Arizona, 4 November 1993.

49. Young interview.

"Metropolitan Indian Series #1," © Hulleah J. Tsinhnahjinnie

The Cid

9

JULIAN LANG

N OTE: A BIASED VIEW EXISTS. So we must first scuttle the idea that insinuates that the only valid indigenous cultural expression emanates from the remote Indian reservations, communities, and villages of this country. This being done, it is now possible to explore the subject of Indians living in the city without feeling self-conscious.

Popular culture, media, and the American educational system have engrained into us so many fallacies about Native cultures and Native Peoples that we should probably sue them. And, perhaps we will. Today all of us have been miseducated to perceive Native Peoples and cultures as mere petrified remnants left over from the 1800s. The book you hold in your hands reveals a current experience: Native Peoples born and living in the cities of America that challenge this view.

Certain attitude adjustments are in order to maneuver successfully through the four generations of history during which Native peoples have been living in cities. The old urban American folkloric perception that people from the country are bumpkins and city dwellers are by nature wiser, more worldly, and sophisticated is reversed when the story is told in remote Native communities. Until recently, Native traditionalists, close to the land, noted that the sophisticated "sidewalk Indian," the city slicker, more often than not was ill prepared to function in the traditional, spiritual, and natural worlds back home on the rez. In the last twenty years the reversed bumpkin-versus-slicker condition has reversed again. A tide of urban Indian youth has been returning home to the rez specifically to learn and practice their traditional ways. Today many urban Indians return home to the rez for years at a time, questing for their tribal roots and spiritual destiny. Some return to the city (bringing their visions), some don't.

There is a bias expressed by many Indian leaders that urban Indians are less important to their culture than those who remain at home on the land. The belief is that urban Indians have lost their connection with the land and have become divorced from tradition and cultural vision. A look at the advancements for Native Peoples since 1900 in education, health, land claims, and other struggles reveals that urban Indians have always been significant contributors to Native causes. Often urban Indians were the first to advocate to the non-Indian population the important political campaigns and calls

9

for much-needed positive change in Indian Country. We need only recall the occupation of Alcatraz Island, the founding of D.-Q. University, Wounded Knee, and the Longest Walk. Each of these historic events, and many more like them, were strongly supported by Indian people and their friends living in cities. Ultimately the beneficiaries of this support and effort have most often been Indian people living back home on the rez.

In whatever way we might perceive the urban Indian, we can honestly say that Native peoples have known cities for as long as they have existed on this land. We were living here long before they started spotting the hemisphere, for God's sake.

The city experience, like all life experiences, is only as good as you make it. For most indigenous people, or better yet, indigenous belief(s), the city is an abstraction: an eco-balanced reality gone unbelievably out of control. This is especially true for those who have never left their traditional worlds, that is, their aboriginal homelands. For many of them the city is a place "outside." It's a part of the *other* Earth, the *other* way of life that exists beyond the boundary of their traditional homelands and outside the relationship many of them still maintain with the Earth.

I am of the Karuk people. We live in the remote mountains of northwestern California. Our word for city is "down below," usually meaning the San Francisco Bay Area. All during my childhood years, I remember the old people telling stories about those who lived "down below." As I have found, there is a long history binding my people to the Bay Area, along with many other California and non-California peoples.

There is a story about Captain John, a Hupa headman (from one of our neighboring tribes), who was taken to San Francisco during the late 1850s by the U.S. military. The government's agents intended to prove to him just how futile it was for his people to continue fighting with the American soldiers. As the ship neared the Golden Gate, Captain John saw the city's first skyline. He asked his white escorts, "For how many generations has this town been here to be this big?" He was told that the San Francisco he was looking at was a mere ten years old.

Samfasiskûu (Karukacized English for San Francisco) has figured into some of the oldest Karuk songs, some of which are still sung today. For instance, there are a couple of men's love songs that tell how a sweetheart was taken away from home and carted off to Samfasiskûu. (Rural California was one of the last holdouts refusing to institute Abe Lincoln's Emancipation Proclamation to abolish slavery in this country.) Many young Indian women were kidnapped by white men well into the 1870s under the legal pretext that they were available as indentured servants. The love songs of that era reveal the heartaches that the white man's strange law forced many of our men and women to endure. A dream song, composed a few years before the turn of the century, predicted the San Francisco earthquake of 1906. Clearly we have known San Francisco for a long time.

The subject of this book is Indians living in the city. I know the San Francisco Bay Area and have lived there. I continue to travel to these cities and others across the country in the course of my work. I have traveled throughout Indian Country as well.

Invariably, I run into another Indian person who tells me something like, "I lived in Oakland for five years." Inevitably we discover that we know many of the same people. Then we're able to laugh about the same silly things, since we know the same places and many of the same people. We call this "life in the Big Cid." Never mind that our discussion is taking place just below Black Butte on the San Ildefonso Pueblo in New Mexico. The same incident is as likely to happen upon meeting a Seneca, Anishinabe, Dené, Puliklah, Tohono O'odham, Tongva, Lakota, Yaqui, or Tsalagi in their own home country, thousands of miles from San Francisco.

In spite of the ongoing, five-hundred-year-old political, social, economic, and spiritual campaigns against our ways of life, at least one member of every indigenous group that has survived the holocaust into the current year can be found in the city today. Recently I was in New York City and met one of the last remaining eighteen members of the people indigenous to Tierra del Fuego at the tip of South America. Native Hawaiian, Haida, Seminole, Micmac, you name it, one of their people lives in the city. There's a certain magical quality in knowing that so many tribal groups have persisted into the twenty-first century. And it's inspiring to meet someone from these nations.

If you know where Indian people congregate in the Bay Area, you can go there and find them: La Boheme Coffee Shop, where the AIMster artists hang, the Hilltop, where you're liable to see anyone, the Klub Kommotion, a performance space, the American Indian Contemporary Arts gallery, or the Intertribal Friendship House, the most long-lived community house for Native peoples in the Bay Area. These are the obvious places to rub elbows with Indian people. There are many more. You never know who you might see at the International Indian Treaty Council offices (Rigoberta Menchu, for example), or at the News from Native California offices. I make it a habit to stop in and see Ruth Hopper at the UC Berkeley Native American Studies office. I go to these places to hear what's really happening in the Cid. I'm both checking in *and* checking it out.

One of the beautiful things about Native life is that wherever one goes, be it to the sacred High Country, down to the Mission district, over to the Fruitvale district, to the Rez, or even the beaches of Hawaii, we find our own people. And we're reminded that we share a history that has remained essentially positive and happy, in spite of often dire socioeconomic conditions. Wherever we go, we discover someone we know. The Ikxaréeyav, the Great Spirit, has created an interesting time for his people these days. He makes it possible for us to recognize, as if we could ever forget, that this land is *our* home, that we alone originate from this place.

It's true, you know, that enough can't be said about how destructive the city has been to Native peoples over the generations. However, I for one have left behind many fond memories, friends, and loves in the city. When I return there I see the same beautiful smiles and I get scolded for not writing or phoning more often. And I realize that going back to the city is a lot like returning home to the family.

May we all live to be a long time.

"Derek and Peter Discuss the Pro's and Con's of City Life" © 1991 L. Frank Manriquez

An Urban Platform for Advocating Justice   10
Protecting the Menominee Forest

DAVID R. M. BECK

I N LATE 1969, when Menominee Indians living in Chicago and Milwaukee first
began to meet at Jim Washinawatok's house on North Kimball Avenue in
Chicago to discuss ways to halt the destruction wrought by the termination of
their status as a federally recognized tribe in their forested Wisconsin homeland,
they were following long-standing traditions of advocacy within both Menominee
cultural history and Chicago American Indian community history. In fact,
Menominees have actively lobbied for protection of their forest from the early
treaty years, and American Indians in Chicago have attempted to use their broader
urban connections to remedy problems throughout Indian country since Carlos
Montezuma lived here at the dawn of the twentieth century. These traditions have
intertwined to permit Menominees to effectively use Chicago as a place from
which to strengthen or renew protection of their forest on more than one occasion,
most notably in the successful fight for restoration of their relationship with the
federal government in the early 1970s.

The Menominee homeland once encompassed eight to ten million acres of
Wisconsin and Michigan northwoods, a rich forest environment providing the
land- and water-based resources that the tribe's numerous small bands needed for
survival. In a series of treaties of cession negotiated between 1831 and 1856, this
homeland was diminished to the present 234,000-acre (ten-township) site on both
sides of the Wolf River north of Shawano Lake.[1] Even previous to the signing of
these treaties, the Menominee began a process of advocacy for their forest resources when Oshkosh and other leaders traveled to Madison to report theft of
their timber to the governor, who also served as superintendent of Indian affairs
in the Wisconsin Territory.

In 1871 when Menominees began cutting timber on a small-scale basis, in
1890 when they began to harvest twenty million board feet of timber on an annual basis, in 1905 in response to a major blow-down of timber, and in 1908 with
the establishment of a sawmill in Neopit, Menominee leaders effectively pushed
U.S. federal policy toward utilization of this resource for tribal needs. In fact, the
1908 LaFollette law not only established a sawmill, but required the federal

government to manage the Menominee forest so that it would provide for the tribe in perpetuity and to train Menominees to do the requisite jobs. When the U.S. failed at both of these objectives, the Menominee sued over the former and learned forestry skills on their own to remedy the latter. The Menominee finally won the lawsuit in the 1950s, but Senator Arthur Watkins of Utah used the disbursement of the money from that, along with a variety of other underhanded subterfuges, to bribe and trick the tribe into accepting termination of federal supervision, the greatest modern disaster to befall the Menominee.[2]

Meanwhile, before the rapid growth of the community in the 1940s and 1950s, Chicago supported a small but active American Indian population. From the beginning it was diverse. Some of the Indians living in the Chicago area were professionals who had been educated in government-run boarding schools and so hailed from a variety of tribes from across the United States. Others came from nearby reservations and Indian lands in the Great Lakes region, or came to Chicago from farther away by rail and worked either as entertainers or laborers. Carlos Montezuma, a renowned stomach surgeon, was known as a one-man social service provider for Indian people passing through Chicago. Toward the end of his life, Indian organizations began to take on this role.[3]

The first of these organizations, though short lived, was founded in 1919, the same year that the state passed a law recognizing the fourth Friday of every September as American Indian Day. The Indian Fellowship League consisted of non-Indians together with Indian members of thirty-five different tribes. In the early 1920s, the Fellowship League cosponsored the annual celebrations of American Indian Day, which included encampments in Chicago-area forest preserves, as well as forums in which well-known Indian speakers shared their views with the larger public.[4]

One such speaker at the 1920 celebration was Reginald Oshkosh, a Menominee forester educated at Carlisle Boarding School, the son of Neopit Oshkosh and the grandson of Chief Oshkosh. The Fellowship League hoped his appearance would break down misconceptions about Indians. According to a newspaper report, it succeeded. A *Chicago Tribune* reporter wrote,

> Surely "How!" and the traditional grunt was the utmost in the way of illumination one could expect from Oshkosh.
>
> After Oshkosh in the first half dozen sentences he uttered had softly and precisely pulled such words as "auxiliary" and "inadequate" and "sanitary," and had flattered ignorance by saying, "As you know, the tenure of land is based upon discovery, conquest, and peaceable purchase," then you were prompted swiftly to readjust your method of approach to the untutored child of the forest—so untutored that he speaks the English language with more precision and more respect for it than you or I do.

The significance of the impression Oshkosh made on non-Indians in the crowd cannot be overstated. During this time, Indians, who were not yet citizens of the United States, were still viewed as the last remnants of a dying race, and it was under these conditions that the Menominee were attempting to gain some control of their forest resource, as required by federal law but ignored by federal officials. Oshkosh went on to discuss the basis of Menominee claims to this forest resource, saying, "And we Menominees maintain that we hold our lands in Wisconsin by right of all three of the principles of land tenure. We discovered it, we conquered it, and, after the Black Hawk War of 1832 we came into peaceable possession of it through trades," by which he means treaties. At the end of Oshkosh's speech, he held an in-depth discussion on forest management with Ransom Kennicott, Cook County's chief forester, and with Bill Johnson, the Forest Preserve's chief nurseryman.[5] Recognition of Oshkosh's professionalism by these officials and the *Chicago Tribune* could only help the tribe in its public relations efforts.

During these years the Menominee Forest was under threat of allotment, a nationally enacted federal policy to individualize land holdings and a congressional effort to turn a majority of the reservation into a national park. The tribe successfully fought off both these attacks as it had fought off previous attempts to sell the forest from beneath them, in part through efforts like those of Reginald Oshkosh in Chicago.[6] In 1924 and in 1928 William Kershaw, a Menominee attorney from Milwaukee who would later become assistant attorney general for Wisconsin, spoke at the annual Indian Day celebrations. He emphasized social conditions among Indians and the fact that Indians were "eager to build up their people on the same standards set by the white race," in the words of a newspaper reporter.[7]

Such was the role that urban Indians would play when they wished to help their home reservation communities: they not only sent aid in whatever form they could, they also advocated to the larger public on their people's behalf. Some four decades later, this would be the dual function of Determination of Rights and Unity for Menominee Shareholders, or DRUMS, as it was called—an urban organization of Menominee activists who played a key role in the Menominees' monumental attempts to reverse the effects of the federal policy of termination on their homelands.[8]

By then, Chicago's Native American population had increased dramatically. The federal attempts of the 1950s to "get out of the Indian business" included not only the termination programs applied to Menominees and many other Indian nations, but also a relocation program that paid young able-bodied men and their families to abandon their reservation homelands for America's cities. Chicago was one of the key target cities for this program. At the same time, in the wake of the post–World War II economic boom, Chicago, long known as the "city that works," also attracted a large number of American Indians who came to the city on their own, without federal program aid. While it is probable that less than a thousand American Indians lived in Chicago in 1940, the number has been estimated at somewhere between sixteen and twenty thousand some thirty years later, as the re-location program began to wind down.

Chicago's Indian population became a dynamic and fluid one. As it long had, it retained its broad diversity. The All-Tribes American Indian Center, now known simply as the American Indian Center, founded in 1953 and arguably the oldest such urban Indian Center in the country, reflected that diversity in its very name, as well as in the clientele it served. The organizations, families, and individuals that moved to the city continued the long-standing practice of advocating on behalf of Indians both in Chicago and back home on the reservations.[9] Even today, many in Chicago's Indian community view Chicago as only a temporary place to stay, not really home, although they end up staying for twenty or thirty or forty years. Many plan to, and do, retire "back home." This includes people born in Chicago who did not even grow up "back home."

One such family, the Washinawatoks, moved to Chicago in 1956 and stayed for nearly twenty years. Jim and Gwen Washinawatok, like many Menominees, were angry about termination, and that anger was catalyzed to action by the sale of Menominee land to non-Indians.[10] The termination had vested decision-making authority over tribal resources in the Menominee Enterprises, Inc. (MEI), a corporation with a majority of voting members who were not Menominee. Though Menominee tribal members owned voting certificates that could be used in decision-making at annual meetings, the First Wisconsin Trust Company held and voted all shares of minors and those deemed incompetent. With low voter turnout among Menominees deemed competent, the First Wisconsin Trust voted 80–93 percent of the annual vote.[11]

A "disputed advisory vote of the corporation's stockholders" on September 23, 1967, gave MEI the wedge it needed to begin development of tourist property for sale to non-Menominees. A series of small lakes were flooded to create one large lake, called Legend Lake or Lake of the Menominees, and in July 1968 sale of individual lots to non-Menominees began. Within three years, thirteen hundred lots were sold.[12]

Jim Washinawatok later recalled the early meetings that brought together the core group that established DRUMS. Menominees from Chicago and Milwaukee would meet at his house on the north side of Chicago. "We would just sit around and talk about things that were happening up on the reservation," he said.

> We were all concerned about the destruction that was going on, and the development of what they called Legend Lake, or Lake of the Menomi-nees. . . . And we would come up here [to the reservation] and visit our par-ents and they would take us out to the area where this was being developed and we would see the bulldozers out there knocking down trees, and scrap-ing and digging up . . . our old springs, which our old people considered sacred. . . . And we were especially disturbed by [the developer's] motto, which said, "Another improvement on nature." . . . And they kept referring

to this land as substandard and of marginal value, that it was nothing but scrub oak growing out there, and the land was of little value. And to us, that disturbed us, because all our land was valuable to us, it was land that our ancestors . . . had fought very, very hard for, and sacrificed many years of their lives. So that, when you'd go to these old council meetings, you would always hear these people get up and say that they . . . had to think of their grandchildren and their great-grandchildren of future years and have a place where they could always call home. . . . And that's why we used to sit down in Chicago and Milwaukee and talk about these things and wondered what we could do about it.[13]

Every member of that group lacked political sophistication, savvy, or know-how, however. Although they felt overwhelmed at first, they began two courses of action that would become the foundations of their movement: they began to visit the reservation and organize protest meetings there and they sought the help of outside groups and individuals with long experience at community organizing and action. These outsiders included Wisconsin Judicaire, which provided legal advice, Saul Alinsky's Industrial Areas Foundation, the musician Buffy Sainte-Marie, LaDonna Harris's Americans for Indian Opportunity (AIO), and the Center for Community Change. The Center for Community Change provided funding for transportation to Washington, D.C., in early efforts to lobby Congress. AIO provided the connections to enable that to be successful. Harris and her husband, Senator Fred Harris, opened their home, their offices, and their services to Menominee tribal members—first Jim Washinawatok and, later, Ada Deer—and provided a base for the Menominee lobbying effort.[14]

But the most important work focused on the reservation and the state of Wisconsin. Many of the state's newspapers reported that the Menominee were eager to sell their land. Washinawatok described the organization's goals in relation to public sentiment within Wisconsin:

> The Milwaukee Journal, and The Milwaukee Sentinel, and The Green Bay Press-Gazette were producing propaganda . . . to the state of Wisconsin public that we wanted to sell this land. And that . . . all these big organizations were doing this to help the poor Menominees survive Termination, you know. And that was the picture that was being presented to the public in the state of Wisconsin. And we wanted the state of Wisconsin to know that this was not true, that we did not want to sell our land.[15]

DRUMS members had little help from tribal members on the reservation at first. Established leaders told them the land sales simply could not be stopped, and termination could not be reversed. Potential allies back home would have to jeopardize their jobs working for MEI or the tribe, and thus their own families' welfare, if they protested against the lakes project. The first times DRUMS members traveled home they were unable to secure meeting rooms, but nonetheless they began demonstrating at the site of the new development. Washinawatok recalled,

> My family and I drove up every weekend. If we missed a weekend it was so insignificant I can't even remember it now. . . . And it was through those demonstrations alone, you know, that we were able to stop the Legend Lake project. . . . I told our people in the organization many times, if we quit and we do not follow up on what we're doing, I said the Menominees will never ever recover from that. So I said once we commit ourselves to doing this we've got to fight it right out to the end. And no matter what happens if we do our best and fight it out to the end and not give up we'll stop the sale of land. And we did that through our demonstrations. And we were consistent, we never missed unless it was an emergency, and we'd come up here every weekend and we'd demonstrate out at the project to let these people know we didn't want to sell our land. And eventually . . . it affected the land sales and the project. We had them dissolve the partnership between Menominee Enterprises Incorporated and the land developer, and the project was dissolved.[16]

This was done with the legal help of Wisconsin Judicaire and with increasing support of tribal members. In October 1972, tribal members staged a ten-day march from the reservation in Keshena to the state capitol in Madison, stopping to demonstrate in the hometown of the lakes project developer along the way. This march culminated on Columbus Day and garnered support from non-Indians throughout the state. The success at ending the land sales spurred DRUMS members and other tribal members to begin to push for a restoration of tribal rights through a congressional overturn of termination. This too was a slow, difficult process in which tribal members and the numerous allies of the tribe worked together in a remarkable effort that has been credited with playing a significant role in reversing federal policy, and moving federal Indian policy in the direction of self-determination.

Throughout these efforts, the Washinawatok family remained based in Chicago, while the core of the DRUMS group was based in both Chicago and Milwaukee. The important work they did carried on long-standing Menominee traditions and long-standing customs within the Chicago Indian community as well. These activities provide a valuable historical picture of cooperation between urban and reservation communities and the too-often ignored connections between tribal members who have left home and those who have stayed. The Menominee restoration effort could not have occurred without significant contributions from both groups of people.

Notes

This work is based on a paper presented September 19, 1998, at "Crossing Borders: American Indians and Encounters with Diversity," The Newberry Library, Chicago. The author is indebted to the Washinawatok family and the Menominee Tribal Historic Preservation Department.

1. The Menominee treaty-making era lasted from 1817 through 1856. The first treaty was a treaty of peace, and those signed in 1820–1822 were never ratified, though they caused the tribe many problems. In 1827 the United States claimed land based on a treaty negotiated at Butte des Morts, but it was not until 1831 that Menominees consider that they had ceded land to the United States.

2. For detailed discussion of the Menominee forest, see Brian C. Hosmer, *American Indians in the Marketplace: Persistence and Innovation among the Menominees and Metlekatlans, 1870–1920* (Lawrence: University Press of Kansas, 1999); Thomas C. Davis, *Sustaining the Forest, the People, and the Spirit* (Albany: State University of New York Press, 2000); and David R. M. Beck, *Siege and Survival: Menominee Responses to an Encroaching World* (Ph.D. diss., University of Illinois at Chicago, 1994), Chapter 7. For detailed discussion of the Menominee Termination see Stephen J. Herzberg, "The Menominee Indians: From Treaty to Termination," *Wisconsin Magazine of History* 60, no. 4 (Summer 1977), 267–329.

3. An overview of Chicago American Indian Community history can be found in David R. M. Beck, "The Chicago American Indian Community, an 'Invisible Minority,'" in Maxine S. Seller and Lois Weis, eds., *Beyond Black and White: New Voices, New Faces in United States Schools* (Albany: State University of New York Press, 1997), 45–60.

4. Detailed discussion of the Indian Fellowship League can be found in Rosalyn R. LaPier, "'We Are Not Savages, But a Civilized Race': American Indian Activism and the Development of Chicago's First American Indian Organizations, 1919–1934," (M.A. thesis, DePaul University, 2000).

5. Eyewitness, "These Indians Can Give White Man Pointers, 1,760 Own and Prosper on Big Forest Tract." *Chicago Sunday Tribune*, 26 September 1920, 3.

6. Discussion of these successful efforts can be found in Beck, *Siege and Survival*, chapters 3 and 7. The Menominee League of Women's Voters, under the leadership of Lillian Oshkosh, played a significant role in averting allotment. See 235–36.

7. "Honor Indians at Exercises Tonight, Fellowship Committee Meets in Evanston," *Evanston News-Index*, 26 September 1924, 1; "Plan Program for Bettering Indian Tribes, Evanston Conference Results in Decision to Work for Reforms," *Evanston News-Index*, 27 September 1924, 1; "Indians' Descendants Help to Observe Indian Day," *Chicago Daily Tribune*, 29 September 1928, 10; "Indian Day" press release, A Century of Progress Publicity Division, 5 September, 1934 (University of Illinois at Chicago Manuscript Collections).

8. Detailed discussion of DRUMS's role in the restoration process can be found in Nicolas C. Peroff, *Menominee Drums: Tribal Termination and Restoration, 1954–1974* (Norman: University of Oklahoma Press, 1982). This book provides a policy theory based analysis of the movement. DRUMS also published its own newsletter and its own book, edited by Deborah Shames, entitled *Freedom with Reservation: The Menominee Struggle to Save Their Land and People* (Madison: The Committee to Save the Menominee People and Forests, 1972).

9. See David R. M. Beck, "How Chicago American Indian Organizations Display Traditional Leadership Characteristics," paper presented at American Society for Ethnohistory Conference, Bloomington, Indiana. November 5, 1993.

10. Interview of James Washinawatok, October 4, 1993. Menominee Tribal Historic Preservation Department, Oral History Program, Phase II Interviews. Interview conducted by Carol Dodge, recorded on videotape. Transcription by the author, July, 1998.

11. Peroff, 140–42.
12. Peroff, 148–52.
13. Interview of James Washinawatok.
14. Interview of James Washinawatok.
15. Interview of James Washinawatok.
16. Interview of James Washinawatok.

INDIVIDUALS AND FAMILIES IN URBAN CONTEXTS   III

Introduction

SUSAN LOBO

THIS SECTION MOVES from a focus on urban communities as a whole to looking at and hearing from families and individuals about their urban experiences. There are two principal emphases here: the interplay between Indian identity and urban life, and maintaining well-being in the face of the strains
and pressures of city life.

Gonzales begins the section in a thorough discussion of American Indian identity
issues. This chapter outlines the historical role played by the federal government in establishing "official" criteria for racial identification and how these criteria have in turn
influenced and reinforced stereotypes among the general population regarding American Indians. She, along with myself and others, notes the distinctive ways that identity is formulated in urban areas in contrast to more rural tribal areas. Pena Bonita's
photographs "Ironworker" and "Ironworker II," Luna's "Half Indian/Half Mexican,"
and Hulleah's "Metropolitan Indian Series #1" assert clearly that identity may not be
a simple concept—but that it is ours to define.

How is identity defined and maintained over the generations in urban areas? This
is the question that Jackson addresses, particularly in the struggle of individuals to
construct their personal identities in the face of a lack of intergenerational sharing of
cultural information. Likewise, Lowery brings to light a series of life histories and ex-
plores social, relational, and cultural identities.

Hand in hand with defining identity are the still-lingering sets of questions related
to settling into city life. Jackson and Lowery's chapters don't deny the presence of alcohol and life on the streets, the hardships and loneliness that city life can bring, or the
shadow of racism that hovers nearby. These are also a part of the urban picture described in a gentle and personal way by Bomberry. Here too are the classic photographs
taken by John Collier Jr. in the homes of relocated families during the early 1960s, expressing the hint of loneliness and alienation alongside hope of life in the city. Belin's
poem "Ruby Roast" sizzles with urban pain and street sense, while Edgar Jackson's poem
epitomizes the longing for home from the inside, looking out of an urban jail cell.

Julca's work focusing on economic strategies of Andean (Quechua and Aymara)
immigrants from Peru to New York does not deny the poverty and hardship either, but

emphasizes instead the determination of the people to find a way to create individual and family economic security and well being. Ramirez describes seeking wellness in a different way, through an exhibit and series of events in the San Jose urban Indian community that sought to actively and consciously create community healing of the psychological and social scars remaining from the history of the Indian holocaust.

Earlier in the book, Trujillo describes the role of education for the Yaqui people in creating stability. There are still other voices, younger voices, asserting city-born-and-raised Indian pride—the rap music of WOR (WithOut Rezervation) in "Red, White, and Blue," and Mike Rodriguez standing next to his just-installed wall art. These are all ways of being urban and being Indian.

But, hey! What's that in the midst of this urban struggle, longing, and hardship . . . what is Kokopeli doing gigging in the city? What is Abel Silvas doing being threatened by a grizzly bear while doing mime, and what's that you say, Charlie Hill? As Price won't let us forget in his chapter on Indian stand-up comedians, Indian humor was not left behind on the rez, but flourishes in its own way in all sorts of unexpected nooks and crannies in the city. Even the whimsy of Pena Bonita's photograph of the "Youngest Trapper on 7th Street" brings out the smiles.

Telling the story of city life does not end here but continues to unfold. As Butler implies, movement is life, as much as breathing itself. Even Mattie sits in the back seat of her family's car, ready to "go traveling."

Ruby Roast

ESTHER BELIN

Snapping grease
sizzling flesh
on L.A. streets

Over the years
slow baking
at 250 degrees

Red turning smog yellow-brown
haze ugly-deep

Yellow-born tender
bloody-rare
obstructs the heart
blinds the eyes
vision of confusion
tunneling digestion
through skin

Urban Indian
already eaten

Urban (Trans)Formations
Changes in the Meaning
and Use of American Indian Identity

ANGELA A. GONZALES

O N A RECENT RETURN to my alma mater for homecoming weekend, I ran into a former classmate and his wife. Since we hadn't seen each other in nearly ten years, he asked the usual battery of questions about my professional and personal life. Just as I began with the ritual reciprocation of questions about his life, his wife cut me off and exclaimed, "I'm part Indian, you know!" Well, no, I didn't know, but I groaned deeply within my soul because I had heard that line so many times before and I knew right away where it was leading. Having made that awesome pronouncement, she awaited my reaction (something like, "Wow! No kidding? Way to go!"). So, like a puzzled dog, I tilted my head to one side, stared at her, and ventured the opinion, "I'll bet you're part Cherokee." Her response: "Angela! How did you know?" Obviously I couldn't say, "What else could you be, Zuni?" Instead I said something like, "Your cheekbones tell the whole story." There she was, Ethnic Identity Incarnate, telling me, "I'm 1/32nd Cherokee"—just enough to cultivate her deep fascination with dream catchers, but just little enough that she didn't have to give her Indianness a second thought.

Such tentative or partial assertions of Indian identity are made in a variety of ways and for many different reasons. Having once been identified as Indian, who among us hasn't encountered at least one descendant of that legendary Cherokee Princess? This popular hobby of tracing one's roots to a mythical Indian ancestor may reflect a longing some people feel for the loss of connection to place, people, or a way of life. For others, however, identification may be more instrumental— a way to gain advantage or access to resources earmarked for American Indians. Among some American Indians, the term *ethnic fraud* has been used to describe many of these "new Indians" who are seen as deliberately falsifying or changing their ethnic identities for personal advantage or gain.[1] Perceptions of ethnic fraud, whether real or imagined, have fanned the flames of an ongoing debate among American Indians as to what constitutes "legitimate" identity.[2]

According to sociologists, we now live in a world where individuals are supposed to be able to decide—in some active sense—who they are, and even once-irrevocable personal characteristics such as ethnic identity are now imbued with an element of choice. Nowhere is this more evident than in census data collected on American Indi-ans. Since 1960, when the U.S. Bureau of the Census changed its enumeration proce-dures from ascription to self-identification, the American Indian population has grown nearly three-fold. Unable to attribute the population growth to usual factors (i.e., improved enumeration procedures, immigration, increased birth to death ratios), sociologists have concluded that much of the increase results from "ethnic switching" by individuals changing their racial self-identification to American Indian.[3]

The complexity of identity is even more pronounced among urban Indians. To-day, more than half of all American Indians live in cities and, unlike earlier genera-tions of Indians who migrated from rural reservation communities, many are now sec-ond- and third-generation urban Indians whose identity is more firmly grounded in pan-Indian activities and multitribal urban communities.[4] Moreover, as interracial marriages become the norm rather than the exception, ethnic boundaries once taken for granted have become increasingly ambiguous and difficult to define.[5] Particularly among urban Indians, intertribal marriages add another layer of complexity for indi-viduals of multiracial and multitribal background. Complicating this still further are individuals such as my friend's wife who, by virtue of being able to recall an Indian ancestor, are now identifying as American Indian.

American Indian identity is a social construct shaped and crafted by the tra-jectories of history, science, culture, and politics, emerging and reified through so-cial interaction between and within groups. To understand the use and meaning of identity for American Indians today, this chapter will examine the relationships among three different levels of meaning: (1) the individual level of what people think and believe; (2) the interaction level of social relations; and (3) the institu-tional level of bureaucracy and public policy. In so doing, my purpose is not to an-swer the oft-asked question, "Who is American Indian?" but to provide a founda-tion from which we might better understand how our ethnic self-understanding has been shaped by others' definitions of us and how 'American Indian/Native Amer-ican' as an embodied category has transformed over time.

One More Time: Who Is American Indian?

From Race to Ethnicity

In recent years, the trend among social scientists and government officials has been to subsume race under ethnicity. This shift was stimulated more by politics than by piety but, despite having been discredited, the concept of race continues to be expressed in public policy and persists as a powerful force in the way Americans identify themselves and others based on skin color and other physical and cultural characteristics. As a means of political contention, the concept of race and the use of racial categories re-flect particular political positions, social relations, and social values embedded within a specific historical context.[6]

During the nineteenth century, the concept of race was founded in biology, and at the time, blood was believed to be the carrier of physical and behavioral characteristics. Thus, the amount of blood that an individual possessed of a particular race would determine the degree to which that individual would resemble and behave like persons of similar racial background. Ascribed at birth and strictly immutable thereafter, the classification and categorization of people by race presumed that they shared inherent, intrinsic, and unalterable characteristics.

Unlike race, ethnicity has strong cultural elements transmitted through the process of socialization, not DNA. Ethnicity can be understood as the extrinsic characteristics usually marked by a person's style of dress, speech/language, and culturally patterned behaviors and customs. Although ethnicity is often used in relation to a group's assumed racial identity, strictly racial attributes are not necessarily a feature of all ethnic groups. A slippery and imprecise term, ethnicity often gives rise to conceptual confusion. For example, the U.S. census uses the term *ancestry* for its operational definition of ethnicity.

Ethnic Groups and Ethnic Categories

Within sociology, ethnic groups are commonly understood as a self-conscious group of people sharing an identity that arises from a collective sense of shared origin, common history, culture, language, beliefs, and traditions. Typically assumed to be transgenerational and endogamous, ethnic groups should be distinguished from social classes, since membership crosscuts the socioeconomic stratification within society. Within the urban context, members of Indian communities share a similar sense of "groupness" and identity as that usually attributed to reservation Indian communities. As described by Lobo in chapter 4, urban Indian communities are a deeply intertwined "network of relatedness," linking individuals to the larger Indian community in a shifting network of social relations. Created through a process of retribalization, the invention of community within urban settings should not be interpreted to mean that such inventions are any less meaningful to its members who share a common sense of culture and identity—a feature inherent in all ethnic groups.

Unlike ethnic groups, ethnic categories are to be understood as aggregates of people categorized and classified into groups based on the presence of "objective" ethnic criteria (i.e., ancestry, religion, language, nationality, etc.) believed by either themselves or others to characterize the group. In most cases, ethnic categories are externally defined and independent of ways in which those categorized may identify themselves. Arbitrarily defined, ethnic categories do not reflect natural divisions within society, but are social constructs designed to serve administrative and bureaucratic needs. For example, in their collection of data on "race," the U.S. census asks individuals to identify their race from among a list of racial categories, only one of which may be selected. Census documents emphasize that "race" does not "denote any clear-cut scientific definition of biology stock," but reflects patterns of racial self-identification.

The choices include: White, Black/Negro, Hispanic, Japanese, Chinese, Filipino, Vietnamese, Asian Indian, Hawaiian, Guamanian, Samoan, Eskimo, Aleut, Indian (American), and a catch-all category labeled "other."

Ethnic Identity

During the past decade there has been an increasing body of literature pertaining to ethnic identity. As a concept, identity (ethnic and otherwise) has been used widely and loosely in reference to one's sense of self and one's feelings and ideas about oneself. Ethnic identity, as understood by early anthropologists, was held to be primordial, ascribed at birth, and associated with kinship, group solidarity, and common culture.

Criticizing these earlier studies for emphasizing an overly static and naturalistic view of ethnic identity, recent theory has shifted the focus from the culture-population-group frame of reference towards one that emphasizes a cognitive-behavioral-strategic framework for describing ethnic identity. The concept of ethnic switching, used to explain increases in the American Indian population, is consistent with this view. With ethnicity no longer ascribed at birth and immutable thereafter, individuals can and do change their ethnic identity in response to changing situations and personal needs, as in the case of my friend's wife. Identification as American Indian, for many of those changing their self-identity, may be a matter of pride and personal volition, having little to do with his or her daily life and social relations.

At the individual level of what people think and believe, we know who we are because of what others tell us. Internalized during early childhood, an individual's sense of ethnic identity develops during early socialization. An interaction between self-identification and social categorization, ethnic identity as a matter of personal choice runs the risk of emphasizing agency over structure, obfuscating how identity continues to be ascribed to both groups and individuals.

Ethnic Boundaries

Closely associated with the terms described above is the concept of boundaries. By definition, a boundary is "something that indicates a border or limit."[7] Boundaries can be physical, social, ideological, symbolic, permeable and flexible, or rigid and impenetrable. Fredrik Barth, in his seminal work *Ethnic Groups and Boundaries*, critically addresses the historical dynamism of ethnic group boundaries. He argues that in order to understand the social organization of ethnic groups, examination should focus on the boundaries that differentiate and keep groups distinct rather than their culture content.[8] Offered as a corrective to anthropology's conventional wisdom of ethnic groups as static, rigidly bounded cultural systems, Barth emphasizes the social processes that produce, reproduce, and organize boundaries of identification and differentiation. For him, ethnic groups are not the "sum of 'objective' differences, but only those which the actors themselves regard as significant."[9] In contrast to rigid, geopolitical, and culturally circumscribed boundaries that define tribal communities, boundaries that define urban Indian communities are far less absolute, continually (re)negotiated and (re)defined though social interaction between members.

Ethnic boundaries can be external, differentiating between groups, or internal, marking differences within an ethnic population and differentiating among members of the same ethnic group. Internal boundaries can mirror criteria imposed from outside or can be concepts that members hold of what constitutes legitimate identity.

At the interaction level between individuals and groups, many urban Indians identify themselves as members of the "Indian community." The problem with this identification, however, is that it presupposes a self-conscious community whose members share a common recognition of the group and its boundaries. This problem, of course, is compounded when questions of identity hinge on whether an individual is "recognized by the Indian community"—a criteria difficult to satisfy and nearly impossible to prove.

Ethnicity and the State
In the U.S., the choice and efficacy of certain ethnic identities results from state policies that employ ethnic categories as the basis for certain rights, entitlements, and benefits. Not only do these official categories enhance ethnic identification by designating certain groups as legitimate, but they encourage identification "consistent with official boundaries rather than with more traditional or culturally relevant units."[10] In the U.S., official ethnic categories and meanings are generally political. As the State has become the dominant institution in society, policies that define ethnic identity increasingly shape ethnic boundaries and influence patterns of identification.

Like other ethnic groups in the U.S., American Indians are designated as a racial group with minority status. However, unlike other racial and ethnic groups, American Indians are also aggregated into tribes, not all of which are recognized by the federal government as distinct political entities. As quasi-sovereign nations, Native peoples' political status derives from treaties signed between the U.S. government and Indian tribes. To the extent that treaties involved the cession of land, they also acknowledged Indian tribes on the aggregate as political entities with a sovereign status similar to that of other foreign nations with which the United States has dealt. However, in dealing with a people who did not share the same notions of nationhood, Indian tribes were sometimes "created" by the federal government by consolidating several ethnologically distinct groups into a single tribe for political, legal, and administrative purposes.[11]

Who Is American Indian?
A Cacophony of Voices and Perspectives
Questions of individual identity and ethnic "authenticity" become particularly contentious when individuals are seen accruing benefits earmarked for American

Indians. "These are people who have no business soaking up jobs and grants, people who have made no claim to being Indian up to their early adulthood, and then when there is something to be gained they're opportunists of the rankest stripe, of the worst order. . . . We resent these people who just come in and when the going's good and skim the riches off the surface."[12]

Following the passage of Civil Rights legislation and the War on Poverty, a plethora of federal aid programs emerged targeting American Indians and other minority groups. According to some, the set-aside programs aimed at helping the truly disadvantaged proved a boon to individuals able to locate an Indian ancestor in their family tree: "It was in the 1970s that people claiming to be Indian began to take jobs intended for Indians and to write books claiming to be authorities on Indians. These instant 'wannabes' did us far more harm than good. Not only did they often give out misleading information about Indians, but they also took jobs that left many qualified genuine Native Americans out in the cold."[13]

Among American Indians, debate over what constitutes legitimate identity has spawned a vocabulary of terms to describe those of dubious identity. *Wannabe* is used to label individuals who publicly avow themselves to be Indian or attempt to pass themselves off as Indian through conspicuous style of dress or use of other symbols associated with American Indians. Similarly, *pretender* describes an individual who claims to have some vast knowledge of Indian culture or spirituality. Recent popular interest in American Indian spirituality has spawned a buyer's market of "Plastic Medicine Men" (both Indian and non-Indian) offering their services to the unsuspecting consumer willing to pay for what they believe to be an "authentic" American Indian ceremony, sweat, or vision quest.

A number of terms have been used to describe those who claim to be "more Indian" by virtue of certain personal characteristics. *Regionalists* describe those who believe their particular tribe or region to be the source or last refuge of 'traditional' Indian culture. Likewise, *reservationists* describe Indians who insist that one must be from a reservation in order to be a 'real' Indian. The term *urban Indian* is sometimes used to imply that those raised in urban communities are somehow less Indian or not authentically Indian, usually in contrast to oneself.

Individuals may also label themselves if such identification will confer to them a greater sense of self-import or authority. Adjectives commonly applied to oneself are "elder" and "traditionalist." Among many American Indians, however, such self-aggrandizing labels, whether used to establish authority and greater degree or Indianness, are not to be claimed for oneself, but bestowed upon one by virtue of personal characteristics and behavior recognized by others. As a positive self-portrayal, the value of self-labeling is in its ability to confer to an individual a greater sense of self-importance.

Identity disputes among American Indians quickly digress into arguments over ethnic authenticity and legitimacy so polarized that they collude to make discussion nearly impossible. Public debate, while limited, has tended to be among those who have realized both the substantive and symbolic value of being American Indian—politicians, scholars, writers, artists, and activists—many of whom have used their place within the dominant society to establish their personal authority and to promote their political agenda.[14]

A mythology of American Indians, embedded in the American imagination since contact, has been aided by the influence of mass media, popular culture, and technology. Today, stereotypes of American Indians range from the bronze, muscular, raven black-haired Indian warrior gracing the covers of countless popular romance novels with little more than a breechcloth and feathered headband, to Disney's buxom, doe-eyed, "Indian Princess" Pocahontas. Appropriated and commodified to fulfill individual and political agendas, these same stereotypes have irrevocably influenced American Indian self-understanding and identity. For many Indians and non-Indians, identity can be reduced to a few critical characteristics that are believed to express the essential qualities of Indianness. As a litmus test for identity, the extent to which an individual meets these criteria is used as a measure of their Indianness.

The Essential Indian:

- Residence (current or previous) on an Indian reservation.
- Enrolled member of a federally recognized Indian tribe.
- Documented Indian blood quantum—the higher the percentage, the greater one's Indianness.
- Stereotypically identifiable Indian features or style of dress—long, straight black hair, dark eyes, brown skin, "chiefly looks" or "doe-eyed, comely beauty," leather moccasins, ribbon shirt, beaded, silver, or turquoise jewelry.
- Ability to speak a tribal language or demonstrable use of Indian colloquialism, i.e. "mother earth," "the great spirit," "the two-legged, the four-legged, the winged," "a-ho," etc.
- Publicly practice what is believed to be American Indian spirituality—powwow dancing, drumming, "sweating," or burning cedar, sage, or sweetgrass.

A reflection of internalized stereotypes, the above list idealizes how "real" Indians are supposed to look, act, talk, and dress. The significance of a particular criterion will, of course, vary according to context, relative to one's own identity and ethnic attributes. For example, among urban Indians, the importance of tribal-specific knowledge or cultural practices might be devalued in favor of pan-Indian ones, such as the powwow.[15] For those without tribal membership, recognition might instead be vested in the "Indian community." Others, lacking stereotypically identifiable Indian features, might instead assert their identity through conspicuous style of dress or other forms of ethnic ornamentation. Ethnic boundary markers, in creating areas of inclusion and exclusion, are used by some to establish their personal power and authority in all matters relating to American Indians.

Who or what is an American Indian? This is a question that scientists, anthropologists, historians, and government officials have debated for many years, and with very little resolution. In so far as we have internalized the government's taxonomy that defines us according to biological, cultural, political, and administrative conventions, the terms we use to describe ourselves and others reveal the dichotomy between inclusion and exclusion—*reservation/urban, traditional/assimilated, enrolled/non-enrolled,* and *"authentic"/"wannabe."* If we are to answer for ourselves the oft-asked question, Who is an American Indian? we must begin by asking, Who perceives these differences as significant? What circumstances render these differences important? How are these differences defined and by what criteria?

Self-Identification

Largely a self-explanatory convention, self-identification suggests that Indians are those who say they are—as indeed an increasing number of people are doing. Self-identification, however, requires little more than an awareness (real or imagined) of American Indian ancestry. According to Snipp, self-identification runs the risk of creating a completely nominal category with a population too heterogeneous to be of much analytic value.[16] Nowhere is this more evident than in the enumeration and collection of census data for American Indians.

Since 1960, when the U.S. Bureau of the Census changed its enumeration procedure from ascription to self-identification, the American Indian population has grown nearly three-fold (see table 11.1). As discussed earlier, researchers concluded that a substantial portion of the increase results from "ethnic switching" by individuals changing their racial self-identification to American Indian. As one census bureau official flatly stated: "Apparently, people who did not call themselves Indian in an earlier census are now doing so."[17] However, for the many American Indians who have heard countless stories about someone's Cherokee great-great-grandmother, such declarations are usually met with suspicion and doubt.

**Table 11.1.   Comparative Census Enumeration:
American Indians and Total U.S. Population, 1950–1990**

	American Indian		Total United States	
Date	Population	Percentage Change	Population	Percentage Change
1950	357,499		151,325,798	
1960	523,591	+46.5	179,323,175	+18.5
1970	792,730	+51.4	203,302,031	+13.4
1980	1,366,676	+72.4	226,545,805	+11.4
1990	1,959,234	+43.3	246,750,639	+ 8.9

Sources for the census data from 1950–1980 were found in Russell Thornton, *American Indian Holocaust and Survival: A Population History Since 1492* (Norman: University of Oklahoma Press, 1987), 160. Census data for 1990 was taken from Bureau of Census, database, C90STF1C (1996).

Using 1980 census data, the first in which respondents were asked questions on both race and ancestry, Snipp identified three distinct subcategories within the self-identifying American Indian population: *American Indians, American Indians of multiple ancestry,* and *Americans of Indian descent.* Included in the category *American Indians* were persons who had exclusively self-identified their race and ancestry as American Indian, most of whom conformed to common perceptions of Indians as culturally distinct and economically disadvantaged.[18] The subcategory *American Indians of multiple ancestry* included those persons who racially self-identified as American Indian but listed other non-Indian ancestry and who, like many Indians living in urban areas, do not easily conform to American Indian stereotypes.[19] Lastly, *Americans of Indian descent* included those persons who did not racially self-identify as American Indian but did include it as part of their ancestry, 93 percent of whom racially self-identified as white. Scoring higher on most measures of socio-economic status (education, earnings, employment) than American Indians and American Indians of multiple ancestry, Americans of Indian descent differ from other segments of white mainstream American society "mainly by virtue of recollecting an Indian ancestor in their family tree."[20] The degree to which individuals in the latter two categories are socially recognized as Indian or are actively involved in urban Indian community organizations is difficult to assess. While many American Indians see those newly identifying as threats to economic resources and cultural integrity and object to self-identification, Thornton argues that

> American Indians have always had tremendous variation among themselves, and the variations in many ways have been increased, not reduced, by the events of history, demographic and other. Allowing self-definition and the differences it encompasses is simply to allow American Indians to be American Indian, something done all too infrequently in the short history of the United States.[21]

Cultural Definitions

While self-identification renders American Indian identity a matter of personal choice, cultural definitions make use of behavioral markers that are recognized as emblematic of American Indian culture. Influenced by the early work of anthropologists, much of our understanding about American Indians comes from the study of Indian tribes as static, rigidly bound entities, marked by a group's style of dress, language, religion, material culture, and culturally patterned behaviors. Cultural markers of identity for both urban Indian individuals and communities are often invisible to non-Indians more familiar with stereotypical representations of Indians. In most urban Indian communities, a form of pan-Indian culture and identity has developed that cuts across tribal lines. As both an identity and a culture, pan-Indianism draws heavily from popular images and traditions of Plains Indians, namely the Lakota (Sioux). Such ethnic markers are normative, ahistorical, and often based on stereotypes.

Cultural definitions subsume individual and group difference under a homogenized group image, ignoring the historical process of change and marginalizing those who do not conform. Pointing to this internalization of stereotypes, Deloria argues, "Everyone doesn't have to do everything that the old Indians did in order to have a modern Indian identity . . . yet both Indians and whites are horrified when they learn that an Indian is not following the rigid forms and styles of the old days."[22] To do otherwise is to ignore that tribal cultures—like all cultures—have changed, and will continue to do so over time.

Cultural criteria are frequently conflated with other markers of ethnic identity. For example, during a meeting of American Indian faculty at an urban West Coast university, a member of the faculty publicly avowed that he would only support the hiring of "darker skinned" Indians. Conflating skin color with culture, he argued that only they possessed "experiential knowledge" and were able to "practice their heritage with pride and confidence," whereas "lighter skinned" Indians were "more assimilated."[23] This example reflects the uncritical acceptance of the concept of race that renders divisible that which is indivisible.

Definitions based on static and essentialist notion of culture, moreover, penalize those who have suffered most as a result of governmental policies and campaigns involving missionization, education, forced relocation, and other strategies aimed at destroying Indian culture. Is it reasonable, then, to declare that a person of Indian descent for whom these policies succeeded the most to be an "ethnic fraud" or "wannabe"? As a determinant of Indian identity, cultural definitions are vulnerable to inappropriate standards of evaluation and raise the question of which or whose set of cultural patterns will be used to determine ethnic legitimacy.

Biological Definitions: Blood Quantum

Intended to hasten the process of assimilation by dissolving collectively held tribal lands into individual land allotments, Congress passed the General Allotment Act of 1887 (more popularly known as the Dawes Act). The criteria used to determine allotment eligibility was based on individual Indian "blood quantum."[24] Determining blood quantum, however, required a benchmark, so shortly after passage of the act, federal enumerators began canvassing Indian lands, counting Indian households, recording the number of adults and children and the blood quantum of each. For the most part, enumerators had to rely on their subjective judgment, individual self-report, and information supplied by neighbors, friends, and relatives. Compiled into what became known as the Dawes Rolls, these records continue to be used in tribal enrollment decisions and eligibility for special programs and services provided by the federal government for American Indians.

Inferred from the racial background of the parents, if both parents were of 100 percent Indian blood, their offspring would also be 100 percent and quantified at four-fourths Indian blood quantum. Children of mixed parentage—for instance, if the father was white and the mother was Indian—would possess one-half Indian blood quantum. This fractionalization of Indian identity gave rise to such deriding terms as "full-blood," "half-breed," or "breed" and demonstrates how, by simple arithmetical division, one's Indianness may be diluted.

This "fractionalization" of one's identity into ethnic "parts" is the subject of American Indian performance artist James Luna's piece, *Half Indian/Half Mexican*. The product of a Mexican father and a Luiseno Indian mother, Luna challenges the government's taxonomy of Indian identity according to percentage of "Indian blood." The three images, mounted side-by-side, capture the duality of his identity as it forces both Indians and non-Indians to confront our uncritical acceptance of blood quantum and its associated stereotypes. In the photo on the left, Luna appears in profile as the Indian. His opposite, "the Mexican," is the photo on the far right. Situated between those "opposites" is a frontal close-up of Luna's face comically divided in half.

According to biological conventions, full-blooded Indians are the "most" Indian, while others of lesser blood quantum are Indian in diminishing degrees. Those who possess higher amounts of Indian blood quantum frequently make subtle (as well as pointed) reference to others' lesser degree of blood quantum, questionable motivations for identifying as Indian, and supposed lack of Indian culture. For some individuals, however, the presence of any "Indian blood," regardless of how remote or unconnected, provides the basis for their identification as American Indian.

Among urban Indians, however, blood quantum is less important than participation in Indian community organizations and activities. Free from the structural constraints imposed by the federal government on Indian tribes, membership in an urban Indian community is far less formal, permitting individuals the opportunity to determine their level of participation and involvement. In multitribal urban

"Half Indian/Half Mexican" © 1990 by James Luna

Indian communities, one's network of social relations is a more important determinant of identity than one's percentage of Indian blood. Non-Indian spouses and
others without documented Indian ancestry may be accepted as members of the
urban Indian community if they participate in community activities and contribute
in ways that demonstrate their commitment and sincerity. Similar to the ways Indian people traditionally identified and defined their members, membership in an
urban Indian community is constituted by a network of social relations that link
the individual to the larger group.

Legal Definitions

Of all the definitions used to define American Indians, the most rigid and narrow are
legal definitions, which are promulgated by the federal government and unrelated to
ways that American Indians traditionally defined themselves. As Cohen explains:

> The term "Indian" may be used in an ethnological or in a legal sense. If a
> person is three-fourths Caucasian and one-fourth Indian, that person
> would ordinarily not be considered as Indian for ethnological purposes. Yet
> legally such a person may be an Indian. Racial composition is not always
> despotive in determining who are Indians for the purposes of Indian law.
> In dealing with Indians, the federal government is dealing with members or
> descendants of political entities, that is, Indian tribes, not with persons of
> a particular race. Tribal membership as determined by the Indian tribe or
> community itself is often an essential element. In fact, a person of com-
> plete Indian ancestry who has never had relations with any Indian tribe may
> be considered a non-Indian for some legal purposes.[25]

Unlike cultural and biological definitions predicated on the "race" and behavioral
characteristics of the individual, legal definition are based on the political status of
"Indian tribes" that confer to tribal members a status like that of citizenship.[26] Tribal
citizenship (commonly referred to as membership) does not, as Cohen has noted, necessarily denote interaction with other tribal members or participation in cultural or
community activities.

While tribal membership requirements vary, there are three basic types of members: base enrollees, automatic enrollees, and adoptees. Base enrollees are those persons
who were living on the reservation in the year that the base roll was established and, in
most cases, did not have to meet any other requirement for enrollment. Automatic enrollment is determined primarily by birth—where you were born, who your parents are,
and your Indian blood quantum, usually distinguishing between "general Indian blood"
and "tribal Indian blood." Lastly, adoption is similar to naturalization of a foreigner
into U.S. citizenship. Criteria might include marriage to a tribal member, residency on
the reservation, and/or approval by a majority of tribal members or tribal council.

As a boundary marker, legal definitions have the virtue that they are clear, absolute, and exclusive. Their appeal is in their ability to render questions of identity a simple matter of documentation. However, claiming that legal definitions "trump" all other forms of identity replaces relational ties—those linking the individual to the tribe or community as a whole—with ties based solely on political status. Moreover, the clarity that ideally characterizes legal definitions dissolves upon closer inspection, particularly if one considers the process by which such definitions come to be established. While some critics argue that the entire system of regulating Indian identity through tribal enrollment should be abolished, most Indians recognize that any strategy aimed at abolishing its use could erode the basis of tribal sovereignty.[27]

Conclusion

The variation, vicissitude, and contradiction in criteria used to define American Indians was reported by the American Indian Policy Review Commission in their 1977 annual report to Congress:

> The Federal government, State governments and the Census Bureau all have different criteria for defining "Indians" for statistical purposes, and even the Federal criteria are not consistent among Federal agencies. For example, a State desiring financial aid to assist Indian education receives the aid only for the number of people with one quarter or more Indian blood. For preference in hiring, enrollment records from a Federally recognized tribe are required. Under regulations for law and order, anyone of 'Indian descent' is counted as an Indian. If the Federal criteria are inconsistent, State guidelines are even more chaotic. In the course of preparing this report, the Commission contacted several States with large Indian populations to determine their criteria. Two states accept the individual's own determination. Four accept individuals as Indian if they were 'recognized in the community' as Native American. Five use residence on a reservation as criteria. One requires one-quarter blood, and still another uses the Census Bureau definition that Indians are who they say they are.[28]

Promulgated by the federal government and unrelated to ways that Indians have traditionally defined themselves, these sociolegal definitions were referential and strategic to U.S. policy and society. Treaties recognized Indians on the aggregate as tribes, blood quantum made Indian identity a matter of degree, and tribal status made both individual and tribal identity a matter of political recognition. To equate Indian blood or tribal enrollment with ethnic authenticity reifies these constructs—which have been shaped and crafted by the trajectories of history, science, and politics—replacing and devaluing relational ties based on kinship, clan, and other patterns of social interaction. The bureaucratic efficiency of legal definitions, moreover, is compromised by the fact that neither state nor federal agencies agree on a single definition.

The efficacy of ethnic identity is a result of state policies that use race and ethnicity to classify groups and individuals for allocation of certain economic and social resources. Official classifications legitimate groups and influence patterns of identification, but the convenience with which official classifications group individuals as "Asian American," "Hispanic/Latino," or "Native American" belies the difficulty faced by individuals of mixed heritage, for whom no single category applies.

Today, individuals are considered members of the ethnic groups to which they self-identify, but as the census data indicates, the ability to racially self-identify has resulted in a substantial number of individuals changing their racial identity to American Indian. If we consider this in relationship to the blood quantum projections in table 11.2, by the year 2080 the American Indian population will have grown to 15.8 million—a nearly twelve-fold increase.

Table 11.2.   Population Projections by Blood Quantum, 1980–2080 (Percentage of Population in Parentheses)

Year	Percentage Blood Quantum			
	50%–100%	25%–49.9%	Less than 25%	Total
1980	1,125,746	123,068	46,636	1,295,450
	(86.9%)	(9.5%)	(3.6%)	(100%)
2000	1,722,116	345,309	146,092	2,213,517
	(77.8%)	(15.6%)	(6.6%)	(100%)
2040	2,188,193	2,418,528	1,454,754	6,061,475
	(36.1%)	(39.9%)	(24.0%)	(100%)
2060	1,866,738	3,971,782	4,090,935	9,929,455
	(18.8%)	(40.3%)	(41.2%)	(100%)
2080	1,292,911	5,187,411	9,286,884	15,767,206
	(8.2%)	(32.9%)	(58.9%)	(100%)

U.S. Office of Technology Assessment, *Indian Health Care* (Washington: U.S. Government Printing Office, 1986), as taken from Snipp, *American Indians*, 167.

Among those who racially self-identified as American Indian in the 1980 census, 49 percent of Indian men and 41.6 percent of Indian women are married to non-Indians.[29] These percentages are misleading in that they reflect the population average. For American Indians residing on reservations (particularly in the Southwest), racial endogamy is the norm—nearly 99 percent of Indians marry other Indians. Among urban Indians, however, a far greater percentage are married to non-Indians. In California, for example, which has a large percentage of urban Indians, 77 percent of all married American Indians have non-Indian spouses.[30] Given the relative size of the Indian population in relation to other groups in urban areas, the overwhelming percentage of potential marriage partners are non-Indian. However, this too may be misleading because of severe census undercounts of American Indians in urban areas.

Contrary to how sociologists conceptualize ethnic identity, the debate among American Indians over what constitutes legitimate identity remains more than an academic or personal matter. Directly affected by the recognition of "legitimate" identity are issues of political and criminal jurisdiction, child custody rights, health benefits, land claims, and a myriad of other legal and financial matters. While many of those newly identifying as American Indian may do so based on an awareness (real or imagined) of Indian ancestry, their identification differs from that of others whose education and earnings, rates of unemployment, and standard of living are circumscribed by their identity as American Indian.[31] For many of those newly identifying as American Indian, such identification may be more a matter of personal choice and entirely devoid of tribal affiliation, cultural traditions, or community relations that are so vital to the Indian identity of others. During the next century, while the American Indian population will increasingly be made up of mixed-blood Indians (less than 25 percent Indian blood quantum), reservation communities will most likely continue to show high rates of racial endogamy. For American Indians in urban areas, however, high rates of intermarriage will reduce the percentage of Indian blood in successive generations, requiring a rethinking of how both tribal and individual identity are defined.

Notes

1. For several examples specific to American Indians see Crystal Cage, "Claims of American-Indian Heritage Become Issue for Colleges Seeking to Diversify Enrollments," *Chronicle of Higher Education*, 29 April 1992, A29; Joe Nelson, "University Must Protect Against Ethnic Fraud," *Daily Bruin Online*, 20 February 1996; Michelle Quinn, "Ethnic Litmus Test a Problem for American Indian Artists," *Los Angeles Times*, 18 June 1992, FI; Jerry Reynolds, "Indian Writers: Real or Imagined," *Indian Country Today*, 8 September 1993, AI; Page St. John, "American Indians Hurt by College Admission Abuses," *Detroit News*, 12 April 1992, PI.

2. Unlike the practice to use the terms *American Indian* and *Native American* interchangeably, I limit my use to *American Indian* and *Indian* when referring to the descendants of the aboriginal inhabitants of North America resident in the United States. I use the term *Native American* only when referring to policies or sources that make use of the term.

3. Karl Eschbach, "Changing Identification among American Indians and Alaskan Natives," *Demography* 30, no. 4 (1993): 635–52; Joane Nagel, "American Indian Ethnic Renewal: Politics and the Resurgence of Identity," *American Sociological Review* 60 (1995): 947–65; Ibid., *American Indian Ethnic Renewal: Red Power and the Resurgence of Identity and Culture* (New York: Oxford University Press, 1996); Jeffery Passel, "Provisional Evaluation of the 1970 Census Count of American Indians," *Demography* 13 (1976):397–409; Matthew C. Snipp, *American Indians, The First of This Land* (New York: Russell Sage Foundation, 1989); Russell Thornton, *American Indian Holocaust and Survival: A Population History Since 1492* (Norman: University of Oklahoma Press, 1987),

4. In 1990, the U.S. census indicated that 56.2 percent of American Indians live in urban areas. Bureau of the Census, *Census of the Population: General Population Characteristics, American Indian and Alaskan Native Areas, 1990* (Washington: U.S. Government Printing Office, 1992).

5. Among the growing literature on mixed race, several excellent collections include Maria P. Root, ed., *Racially Mixed People in America* (Newbury Park, Calif.: Sage, 1992); Naomi Zack, ed., *Race and Mixed Race* (Philadelphia: Temple University Press, 1993); Ibid., ed., *American Mixed Race: The Culture of Microdiversity* (Washington: Smithsonian Institutional Press, 1995). For a discussion of mixed race and the problems associated with American Indian racial boundaries, see Matthew C. Snipp, "Some Observations About Racial Boundaries and the Experiences of American Indians," *Ethnic and Racial Studies* 20, no. 4 (1997): 667–89.

6. Michael Omi and Howard Winant, *Racial Formation in the United States: From the 1960s to the 1990s* (New York: Routledge, 1994).

7. *American Heritage Dictionary*, 1985, s.v. "boundary."

8. Fredrick Barth, Introduction, *Ethnic Groups and Boundaries: The Social Organization of Cultural Difference* (Oslo: Norwegian University Press, 1969).

9. Ibid., 14.

10. Nathan Glazer and Daniel P. Moynihan, eds., *Ethnicity: Theory and Experience* (Cambridge: Harvard University Press, 1975), 10; Joane Nagel, "Constructing Ethnicity: Creating and Recreating Ethnic Identity and Culture," *Social Problems* 41, no. 1 (1994): 154.

11. Felix S. Cohen, *Handbook of Federal Indian Law* (New York: AMS [reprint] 1942), 5–6.

12. Alfonso Ortiz as quoted in Reynolds, "Indian Writers," A3.

13. Tim Giago, "Big Increases in 1990 Census Not Necessarily Good for Tribes," *Lakota Times*, 12 March 1991, 4.

14. For a few examples, see Sandra D. Atchinson, "Who is an Indian, and Why Are They Asking?" *Business Week*, 26 December 1988, 71; Ward Churchill, "Nobody's Pet Poodle," in *Indians Are Us: Culture and Genocide in Native North America* (Monroe, Maine: Common Courage Press, 1994), 89–113; Candelora Versace, "What is Real Indian Art? Does It Matter?" *Indian Artist* (Winter 1996); 58.

15. Long-ingrained in the American imagination, these images gained renewed popularity following the movie *Dances with Wolves* and its lesser acclaimed spin-offs, *Last of the Dogmen, Thunderheart*, and *Incident at Oglala*. For a historical analysis of the roots of pan-Indian identity, see Hazel Hertzberg, *The Search for an Indian Identity: Modern Pan-Indian Movements* (New York: Syracuse University Press, 1971). For a detailed examination of these images, their historical basis, and influence on non-Indian perception and attitudes towards American Indians, see Robert F. Berkhofer, *The White Man's Indian: Images of the American Indian from Columbus to the Present* (New York: Knopf, 1989); Roy Harvey Pearce, *Savagism and Civilization: A Study of the Indian in the American Mind* (Berkeley: University of California Press, 1988).

16. Snipp, *American Indians*, 251.

17. Dirk Johnson, "Census Finds Many Claiming New Identity: Indian," *New York Times*, 5 March 1991, A1.

18. Snipp, *American Indians*, 53–6.

19. Ibid., 57.

20. Ibid., 57.

21. Thornton, *American Indian Holocaust*, 224.

22. Deloria quoted in Robert A. Warrior, *Tribal Secrets: Recovering American Indian Intellectual Traditions* (Minneapolis: University of Minnesota Press, 1995), 93–94.

23. Correspondence from Duane Big Eagle to Jacob Perea, Chair of American Indian Studies at San Francisco State University, 12 February 1996. In a department faculty meeting, the author distributed copies of this letter to all those present, including the author.

24. See Snipp, *American Indians*, 32–35. For a general discussion of racial theories and their application to American Indians, see Robert. E. Bieder, *Science Encounters the Indian, 1820–1880* (Norman: University of Oklahoma Press, 1986).

25. Cohen, *Handbook of Federal Indian Law*, 19.

26. The legal status of Indian tribes was assured with the passage in 1934 of the Wheeler-Howard Act, more popularly known as the Indian Reorganization Act (IRA), which, among other things, stopped allotment, made provisions for the return of Indian lands, provided money for reservation economic development, and encouraged tribes to formally organize themselves into tribal governments.

27. M. Annette Jaimes, "Federal Indian Identification Policy: A Usurpation of Indigenous Sovereignty in North America," in *The State of Native America: Genocide, Colonization and Resistance*, ed. M. Annette Jaimes (Boston: Southend Press, 1992), 123–138; Sharon O'Brien, "Tribes and Indians: With Whom Does the United States Maintain a Relationship?" *Notre Dame Law Review* 66 (1991): 1461–92; Lenore A. Stiffarm and Phil Lane Jr., "The Demography of Native North America: A Question of American Indian Survival," in *The State of Native America: Genocide, Colonization and Resistance*, ed. M. Annette Jaimes (Boston: Southend Press, 1992), 23–53.

28. American Indian Policy Review Commission, *Final Report* (Washington: U.S. Government Printing Office, 1977), 12.

29. Snipp, *American Indians*, 158.

30. Eschbach, "The Enduring and Vanishing American Indian," 95.

31. Snipp, *American Indians*, 53–6.

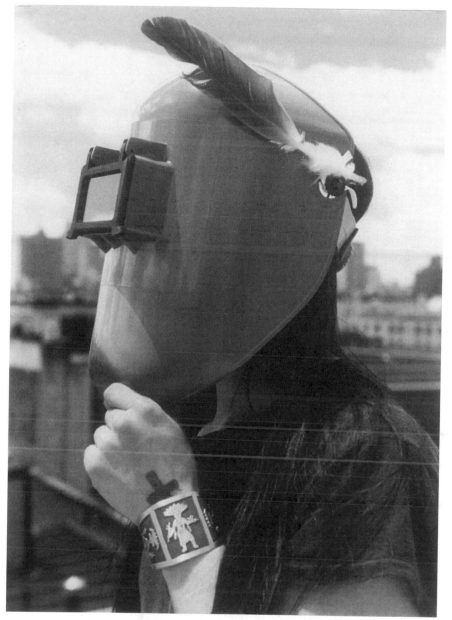

"Ironworker I" © Pena Bonita

"Ironworker II" © Pena Bonita

"This Hole in Our Heart"
The Urban-Raised Generation and the Legacy of Silence

12

DEBORAH DAVIS JACKSON

> The majority of us [city-raised Indian people] walk around with this hole in our heart. We know we're different, that there's a piece of our life that is missing.
>
> —MICHELLE DUNCAN[1]

SINCE THE MIDDLE of the twentieth century, when large numbers of American Indian people began migrating from reservations to cities in search of work and a better life, the "urban Indian" phenomenon has attracted only narrow—and usually negative—types of scholarly attention. While a few ethnographic or ethnohistorical works have appeared recently that seek to describe entire urban Indian communities in all their complexity, the great majority of urban Indian studies done to date focus on some aspect of the circumstances, problems, and adjustment strategies of those who grew up on reservations and then moved to a city, or those who move back and forth between the two sites.[2] This emphasis, while valuable, neglects an increasingly important segment of urban Indian communities—those whose parents grew up on reservations, but who themselves have grown up in the city. In this chapter, I focus on this first generation of urban-raised Indian people.

Based on over two years of fieldwork (September 1993 through December 1995) in the American Indian community of a Great Lakes–area city I will call Riverton, my analysis relies heavily on life-historical interview material. I consider the role of silence as it emerges in the narratives of urban-raised Indian people—not the silence of the interviewees themselves, but rather their childhood experience of their parents' silence on certain topics. In the discourse of these interviewees, silence does not manifest merely as the absence of speech; instead, it looms as a salient presence in the process of ethnic identity construction for this first generation of city-raised Native American people. The significance of these silences in the life-historical narratives of urban-raised American Indians will be explored below; first, however, a brief introduction to Riverton's American Indian community will prove useful.

Urban Riverton

Riverton is the major city in a county I will call Birmingham, an area that had traditionally been home to the Great Lakes area's indigenous Chippewa (Ojibwa) people,
but from which most Native people had been "removed" (in accordance with the U.S.
government's Indian policy) by the end of the nineteenth century. It was only at mid-
century, starting during the Second World War, that Indian people began returning to
the area in large numbers from reservations and off-reservation rural communities
around the Great Lakes (as well as from more distant regions). This was due both to
the "push" of poverty and lack of job opportunities on reservations, combined with
the threat of termination of Indian tribes by the federal government, and the "pull"
of relatively good wages and job security to be found, even for unskilled, uneducated
people, in Riverton's auto factories, which were then booming.[3]

While some came only for a short time to earn quick money before returning to
their home communities, many Indian people stayed on in Riverton, married, and
raised their families there. The result was a growth in the American Indian population
from the 1940s through the 1970s, culminating in a Native American population of
almost four thousand (out of a total population of 450 thousand) for Birmingham
County in 1980. As is the case with urban Indians in many cities (see Lobo, this volume), Native American migrants to Riverton did not settle into geographically
bounded neighborhoods, but rather tended to scatter throughout low-income neighborhoods, interspersed with Mexican Americans, African Americans, and other poor
minorities. But a genuine sense of community developed early on among those Native
Americans who kept in touch with other Indian people through social connections
such as potluck dinners, a bowling league, and work parties to help one another with
home improvements projects. In the late 1960s and early 1970s, a number of institutions were formed to address the needs of the Indian people of Riverton, such as the
Birmingham County Indian Association, which established an Indian Center in downtown Riverton in 1971. Though now somewhat diminished in size from its peak in
1980 (the 1990 census shows a Native American population of about three thousand
for Birmingham County), the American Indian community in the Riverton area has
remained vigorous. Its institutions, both formal and informal, have remained intact and
continue to play a meaningful role in the lives of many of Riverton's Indian people.

While Riverton's American Indian community comprises people from many
different tribal backgrounds, including Cherokee, Iroquois, Lakota, Apache, Dine
(Navajo), Hopi, and others, the majority are from the tribes indigenous to the Great
Lakes region, the Native-language term for whom is *Anishinaabe*: Chippewa, Ottawa,
and Potawatomi. Furthermore, the staff, board members, and volunteers in the official institutions are most often Anishinaabe people now in their thirties and forties
who are the first generation to have grown up in the city. They are the children of people who grew up on reservations or in rural Indian communities or small towns
around the Great Lakes area, who then moved to Riverton as young adults. Members

of this generation are generally proud of their Native American heritage and express their Indian identity openly. These urban-raised Indian people tend to be verbal and vocal about their Native American heritage; they *talk* about being Indian in public settings, among themselves, and with their children.

However, in the discourse of life-historical interviews with me, descriptions of their own childhood experiences have a very different tone. In that context, many in the second-generation Anishinaabe talk about an elusive American Indian heritage that hovered around the margins of their childhood, not quite present, yet never completely absent. Furthermore, it is in descriptions of the past that their complex and difficult feelings come to the fore, as they express the pain, confusion, and shame that seem to have constituted an all-too-salient aspect of their "American Indian heritage" during their childhood years. It is to these narratives that I now turn.

Recollections, Revisions, and Reassessments

From as far back as he can remember, Jake Benson knew there was something wrong on his father's side of the family—that "somebody had done something they were real ashamed of."[4] Jake grew up in Riverton, and although two of his father's brothers also lived in Riverton with their families, and Jake occasionally saw these relatives, he never really got to know them. Furthermore, Jake recalls how, on a trip to northern Wisconsin when he was about ten, as the family was driving through the father's home town, he saw a large group of people out on the front porch of a house they were passing. He knew it was his father's family—he recognized some of his aunts and uncles—and could see that they were having a family reunion. But Jake's father just drove on by; he said he wanted nothing to do with that "Benson trash."

This is how Jake describes the way he grew up—knowing there was something unspeakable about his father's side of the family and haunted by questions of what it might be. Finally, in 1991, at age 45, Jake learned the answer: the Bensons were Chippewa Indians. Thus, explicit confirmation of his American Indian heritage came late to Jake. However, certain experiences and interactions with his father earlier in his life, especially during his childhood, had left Jake feeling that he both knew he was Indian and did not know. Some further background on Jake and his family will help make sense of this seeming contradiction.

Jake recounts that his father came to Riverton around 1940, just after having graduated from high school in the small northern Wisconsin town where he had grown up, to take a job at a Buick plant. Then, much later, when he was in his mid-thirties, he married a younger woman (who was not Native American), and they started a family. Jake was the second of three children and the only boy. He reports memories from a very early age of his father commenting on his coloring in relation to that of one of his sisters, who was considerably lighter. One comment that made a strong impression on Jake was his father saying, "Jake's so dark, he always looks dirty." Furthermore, according to Jake, his father openly favored the sister who was light haired and fair skinned. Jake did not know what to make of this and only became further confused when he started school.

It was a Catholic school, and the other students were either Mexican or white. Jake remembers thinking he should belong to one group or the other: his coloring was too dark for him to fit in with the white kids, so he tended to socialize more with the Mexicans, but he knew he was not Mexican either. So Jake experienced confusion as a child about "what he was" in terms of racial/ethnic identity, but he could get nothing from his father except reinforcement that he was "too dark" and somehow "dirty."

Jake also recalls his father once warning him about "Indians" when the two of them were alone: "He told me that if I ever got in a fight with one, to bite him, kick him, scratch him—never let him up. Do anything I could to hurt and humiliate him—make sure he'd never come back and try me again. . . . And there was an absolute hatred in his voice for them." So Jake knew that there was some shameful secret about his father's side of the family, that he and his father both had dark coloring and there was something wrong with dark coloring, and that his father feared and hated Indians. Certainly there were hints at the connection between these factors, but Jake's father maintained a resolute silence as to what that connection might be. Jake could only guess and wonder.

Jake Benson's account is no doubt extreme in that it portrays a father so seemingly unequivocal in his renunciation of family, and thus his denial of his Native American ancestry. But if extreme in degree, Jake's story is nonetheless similar in kind to that of many of the sons and daughters of American Indian people who left reservations and off-reservation rural Indian communities to migrate to Riverton (and other Midwestern cities) during the manufacturing boom years of the mid-twentieth century. Most people in this first city-born generation had more contact with their American Indian extended families during childhood than Jake did, and some even recall some fairly explicit acknowledgments (examples to be given below) on the part of their parents that they were Native American. But a theme that emerges, in one form or another, in the narratives of all of the second-generation urban Indian people I interviewed, is that of their confusion and frustration at their parents' reluctance, unwillingness, or inability to really speak about being Indian.[5]

Michelle Duncan, in her forties at the time of the interview, moved to Riverton with her family when she was five and her father got a job at a Ford Motor plant in the area. Her mother was white, and Michelle subsequently learned that her father was Ottawa, but that Native American heritage was not readily apparent to Michelle during her childhood. Her father did keep in touch with his extended family who still lived in their home Ottawa community in southern Ontario. But while he admitted that these people were Native, he would not admit that they were family. Michelle recalls her father saying, "We're going to see some Indians," and then they would travel to his home community and visit people that she now knows were her father's first cousins—but this relationship was never explicitly acknowledged. Similarly, Michelle has childhood memories of her family going to visit other families around the River-ton area and hearing her father and some of the other adults "talk in a funny lan-guage." She now knows that language to have been her father's native Ottawa, but this was never explained to her at the time.

There were other ways in which Michelle's father hinted at his—and therefore Michelle's—Native ancestry without actually telling her the family background. For example, Michelle tells of her father's response when she was in elementary school and was upset because an older boy from the junior high school next door had said to her, "You're nothing but a dirty little squaw, and the only thing you're good for is to throw down on your back." Michelle went home crying and told her father, who said, "You're going to run across that. . . . All you can do is just hold your head up high, be proud of who you are." And her response, thinking back on this today and giving voice to what she could not bring herself to express at the time, is to say, "But wait a minute, Dad. I don't *know* who I am. What *am* I? Am I white, or *am* I that dirty little squaw?" Michelle continued to be confused about this question for many years.

A similar theme of silence and evasion emerges in the narrative of another inter-viewee, Tom Richards.[6] Tom's childhood family situation differs from that of Jake and Michelle in that, in Tom's case, it was his mother who was American Indian (Chippewa), and his father who was white.[7] His parents had met in a predominantly rural area in a county that borders the north side of Birmingham County where both had grown up. After they were married in 1940, they moved to Riverton where Tom's father got a factory job and his mother stayed home to raise the children. Tom was well aware that his mother was Indian because she maintained close ties with her rel-atives from her home community—a predominantly white town I'll call Whitfield—where her family had moved when Tom's mother was a young child in the mid-1920s. Prior to that, the family had lived in an area known to local whites as Indian Town—a rural Chippewa community that existed near Whitfield until the 1940s, when all the land was bought, much of it under rather suspicious circumstances, by local white farmers. Some Indian Town families then moved to cities, while others, including many of Tom's mother's relatives, moved into Whitfield.

When Tom was a child during the 1940s, his mother would take him and his sib-lings to visit the Whitfield relatives. Similarly, relatives from his mother's extended family would sometimes come and stay with Tom and his family in Riverton. Tom de-scribes these contacts as follows:

> We would go socializing with my mom's relatives almost every single week-end. [The relatives] didn't have telephones, yet they all managed to meet about the same time on Saturday afternoon in Whitfield. . . . There were a lot of social activities, dinners. . . . I remember when everyone got together at our house to help put up a stone and cement retaining wall terrace in front of the house. All my [maternal] relatives showed up.[8]

Overall, then, Tom describes considerably more contact with his American Indian relatives than does Michelle, whose father's family lived much further away than Tom's mother's family. And he certainly describes far more interaction than does Jake, who hardly ever visited with his father's brother's families, even though they lived right there in Riverton.

This contact did give Tom some sense of his Chippewa heritage. For example, in discussing his maternal grandfather's extended visits to their home in Riverton, Tom says: "As far as the Indian heritage itself, he talked an awful lot about his dad making ax handles and making baskets. Some of my earliest memories are . . . we had Indian baskets all over the house—my mom's laundry basket was a large, probably two-bushel basket that was all handmade of black ash."[9] However, it is important to keep in mind that this is Tom talking *now* about his childhood memories. At the time, these were not "Indian baskets" that were all over the house—they were just baskets. And while Tom now knows that making ax handles was a skill typically practiced by the Chippewa people of the area up into the early twentieth century, he did not realize when his grandfather was telling him about the ax handles that he was learning about his "Indian heritage." Tom reports that at the time, when he was a child, his mother and other relatives did not talk much about "Indians" at all, especially with regard to their own family. Furthermore, in addition to the silence that surrounded the family's American Indian heritage, Tom reports being witness more than once to his mother's outright denial of being Indian. He remembers occasions in his childhood when the subject of his Native American heritage came up with outsiders (for example, at school), and hearing his mother insist that that was because Tom's *father*, not she, was Indian. Thus, even Tom, with his close ties to an extended Chippewa family that lived nearby, reports a childhood filled with silences about certain aspects of his Indian ancestry and outright denials by his mother of her own ancestry.

These silences on the part of the elder generation of rural-raised Anishinaabe relatives were interpreted by their (now grown) children as having a number of different causes or motivations. However, one theme that emerged more than any other was shame. These interviewees clearly perceived their parents as being ashamed of being Indian. A story told by another woman, Doris Rider, also focuses on shame as a powerful force in perpetuating silence—not only her American Indian father's own silence, but that of a member of *his* elder generation, as well.

Doris, in her late thirties at the time of the interview, tells of having just discovered recently that her father, who had worked all his adult life in a Riverton auto factory, was a full-blooded Potawatomi. She could not recall a single time he had ever spoken of this heritage. Doris has very dark coloring—dark eyes, brown skin and black hair—like her father (her mother was white), and had always wondered why this was. Like Jake, Doris explains that as a child, she knew she was not Mexican; she also knew she was not African-American, although she had sometimes been called "nigger" by her classmates in school. But this topic was never discussed in the family. So upon finding out about her Potawatomi heritage while looking through some old documents from her father's side of the family after his death, she wanted to learn more. Consequently, she took the opportunity, during a visit to her father's aunt, to ask, "Is it true we're Indian?" Although the two of them were alone in the house, Doris's great-aunt looked around hurriedly as if to make certain no one could overhear. Then she whispered fiercely: "*Shhhh!* Don't *ever* speak of that!" She added, as if to explain the importance of maintaining this silence, "Indians are *dirty!*"[10]

This act of silencing—Doris's great-aunt's reaction to a (seemingly) benign question—is shocking in its strength and intensity. Her "*Shhh!*" has a brute force which no doubt found its source during her earlier years, in the brutality of countless experiences that served, time and time again, to shock her into her deep conviction that "being Indian" must never be spoken of—that Indians are "dirty." The partial answers, omissions, ambiguities, and outright denials described in others' narratives may be less dramatic than Doris's great-aunt's fierce insistence on complete silence. Yet they, too, appear as brute forces, pushing against the childhood awareness of young people just beginning to wonder who they were, abruptly precluding questions that could not even be fully formulated, let alone given voice.

As adults, first-generation urban-raised Anishinaabe people not only have learned how to formulate those questions—they have also become tenacious in seeking their answers in the knowledge and practices of the cultural heritage they have come to feel is their birthright. They seek to, in the words of Michelle Duncan, "fill the holes in their hearts." In the full passage from which the shorter quote at the beginning of this chapter is excerpted, she explains:

> The majority of us [city-raised Indian people] walk around with this hole in our heart. We know we're different, that there's a piece of our life that is missing. And once we can [find out] what's missing, and fill that hole ourselves, then we see a whole person emerge. We start asking questions, and we become these enormous sponges, and we just want to absorb, absorb, absorb. And it fills that hole.

This "absorption" is evident to one degree or another in the current life choices of virtually all the members of this generation whom I have spoken with or interviewed, including those profiled here.

All four of these interviewees (and many other first-generation urban-raised Anishinaabeg I came to know in Riverton, as well) present themselves as now having a strong sense of Native American identity and a commitment to Riverton's various urban Indian organizations. Michelle has served for a number of years on the board of the Birmingham County Indian Association (BCIA); Tom, who went to college and later earned an MBA, uses his business knowledge to assist Native American groups and individuals in the Riverton area who want to start their own businesses; Jake has become active on the committee that organizes and operates the BCIA's annual summer pow-wow; and Doris volunteers her time at Riverton's Indian Center, helping to develop programs and activities for American Indian children in the community. All four attend at least some of the various Native American functions and events that occur in the Riverton area throughout the year. Finally, all four have become involved in attempts to recover in their personal lives something of the heritage they feel was lost to them.

Michelle, in addition to having collected documentation on her father's family (birth certificates, school records, marriage licenses, etc.), has been seeking out older Indian people around the area over the past several years, learning all she can about traditional spiritual beliefs and practices. Jake has become an amateur genealogist, tracing his father's side of the family several generations back, and learning a great deal in the process about large-scale movements of Native people around the Great Lakes area, back into the early nineteenth century. Doris has been involved in helping document the ancestry of members of her father's Michigan Potawatomi tribe, which has recently received federal recognition. Finally, Tom has become a family oral historian of sorts, seeking out older relatives on his mother's side of the family and conducting tape-recorded interviews with them about Chippewa culture and language so he can document their knowledge before they die and take their memories with them. These efforts to reclaim a positive Native American identity have played a significant role in the lives of Jake, Doris, Michelle, and Tom. Yet each reports a negative consequence as well—that such overt interest in and public displays of American Indian heritage have caused problems with the parents who struggled so hard not to be known as Indians.

Jake, of course, had the most difficulty in this regard. His genealogical work, as well as his involvement in Native American activities, which include pow-wow dancing in full regalia, resulted in total estrangement between him and his father. At the time of Jake's father's death in 1993, he and Jake had not spoken in five years. Still, Jake did what he could to make peace with the father with whom he had experienced such difficulties by means of the heritage his father had renounced so violently: "I went back up [to northern Wisconsin] and scattered his ashes in the woods. And I used smudge and did the Indian ceremony over him, because he wasn't buried Catholic. So I figured that was the least I could do. Even though I don't fully understand the traditional ways." Jake says he now feels "resolved" about his relationship with his father.

Michelle's story starts out sounding very much like Jake's, but finds a happier resolution. She reports that when she first started to get involved with Riverton's Indian Association, her father "threw an absolute fit. He did not talk to me for almost a year. Because I was acknowledging the fact that I was Native American." But, she goes on, "He's accepted it now. He's accepted it, once he realized that it was okay—it was okay to be Indian." Similarly, Tom's mother, who no longer denies her Chippewa heritage, now occasionally accompanies Tom to pow-wows and other American Indian events around the area and shows interest in the work he does in advising American Indian entrepreneurs. (Doris has no such experiences to report; her father died before she started becoming involved in the Native American community.)

All of those profiled in this chapter, and many other first-generation urban-raised Anishinaabe as well, are struggling to "fill the holes in their hearts"—to make sense of the American Indian heritage that lurked in the shadows of their childhood experience, and to bring that heritage out into the light of day. For this generation, Riverton's official American Indian institutions provide a much-needed community that makes information on traditional Native practices and beliefs available, encourages political activism on behalf of Native American causes, and provides opportunities for socializing with others of American Indian ancestry. Most importantly, these institutions create an atmosphere in which it is not only "*okay* to be Indian," but where American Indian heritage is respected, valued, even *celebrated*. Furthermore, while many in the parent generation have only a marginal connection, if any, to the official institutions, most of these elder, rural-raised Anishinaabeg are gradually coming to terms with the choices their grown children are making. They are recognizing that a new climate in the dominant culture—manifested in the recent proliferation of positive images of Native Americans and a general openness to "cultural diversity"—renders these choices "harmless" in a way that similar choices could not have been in the past.

Even the urban-raised generation, growing up in Riverton in the 1950s and 1960s, had to endure, as we have seen, social ostracism, racist slurs, and at times, physical attacks. The childhood experiences of the elder, rural-raised generation were even more fraught with such difficulties, which were further intensified by the extreme poverty that plagued most Indian communities throughout the first half of the twentieth century. In their search to understand their own childhood experiences, many urban-raised Anishinaabeg are now reinterpreting their parents' contradictory statements, denials, and silences with a new understanding and sympathy, based on their growing knowledge of the very different social and political climate that prevailed at mid-century and earlier, when their parents were young.

This more sympathetic perspective often takes the form of recognizing their parents as workers in the dominant society. While regretting and perhaps resenting their parents' (seeming) assimilation, they have come to respect the successes of these parents in adjusting to urban life, to sympathize with the hardships inherent in that transformation, and to understand the coping strategies their parents had to develop to survive. First-generation urban-raised Anishinaabe people have come to appreciate—in both senses of the word—the obstacles their parents had to overcome and the sacrifices they had to make in order to achieve success in an alien environment, thereby giving their children advantages and opportunities that they, the parents, had never had.

Both Jake and Michelle portray their fathers as having suffered prejudice and bigotry in the factories where they worked, commonly referred to as "the shop."

Their fathers spoke very little about the problems they faced on the job, but a brief comment here or there gave glimpses into the abuse they endured. For example, Jake reports that his father was called "Indian Joe" in the shop (his name was not "Joe") because he "looked like a pure blood." He expresses his general sense that his father felt ridiculed and humiliated at work. Also, it is clear from the way Jake talks about his father's drinking that he sees it as tied to the shame his father experienced, in the shop and elsewhere, about his Native American ancestry—the primary source of the "demons" Jake mentions below. After discussing his father's shortcomings as a parent, Jake goes on to say, "I understand that in a lot of ways, he was a good dad. And he had his own demons. . . . He didn't want to be identified [as Indian]. . . . He would never admit to being Indian." Jake has gained this sympathetic perspective only in his adult years, as he has struggled with his own "demons" (including alcoholism, from which he is recovering) about his past and his identity.

Michelle talks about these same kinds of issues with regard to her father, but she makes a more explicit connection between her father's anger, his drinking, and his situation at work:

> My father was an alcoholic. A very sad man. Even though he tried not to be. And I understand now that it was because he was denying who he was. He was denying who his children were. And there was a lot of anger that he suppressed over the years. And to get rid of that anger, he drank. And my father got in many fights [with co-workers], because they would call him "Chief," or they would make derogatory comments. . . . And he has a lot of scars from his battles.

This denial of "who he was" and "who his children were" was primarily caused, according to Michelle, by her father's experience at an Indian boarding school, where he was beaten for speaking his Native language—"that was the beginning of his humiliation, of his punishment for being who he was." Therefore, "he said that his children would not suffer that discrimination—to the point that he even listed us as white on our birth certificates."

Michelle sees her father's drinking as the result of shame and anger that was deeply rooted in childhood experience and was then exacerbated by abuse he suffered on the job. Yet, despite this extreme hardship Michelle sees her father as having endured, she also sees a positive side to his work experience. After depicting her father's life in the shop as quoted above, Michelle continues, "And it's sad because, well . . . [but] it's *not* sad! I'm really, really proud of my father, because the more discrimination that he suffered, the harder he tried. And when he retired, he was one of the top two electricians for his entire division of the Ford Motor Company!" This theme—that despite the racial prejudice suffered in the shop, or perhaps in some way because of it, the worker role came to be of central importance as a means of achieving admiration—is echoed by Jake as well. He explains how he sees this kind of dynamic operating in his own father's life:

> His whole life revolved around the job. . . . I guess he wanted to be a "normal white person" somehow—that was very important to him. And he had to show that he was smarter than everybody else. And better at his job. . . . My mother and him worked at the same factory, and they'd talk about the shop all night long. They'd sit and drink, and I'd just hear about "Buick, Buick, Buick."

So the factory, and the role of worker, take a central position in Jake and Michelle's fathers' lives as constructed in their narratives. Unlike the American Indian heritage that was only hinted at, the worker identity that Jake's and Michelle's fathers struggled so hard to develop was quite openly discussed within the family.

Tom's situation is somewhat different, since, in his case, it was his mother who was the American Indian. While in many cases Native women worked outside the home, whether in professional or (far more often) working-class jobs, Tom's mother was able to stay home and care for her five children, since Tom's non-Native father's factory job provided enough income for the family to get by on. Therefore, Tom does not have any stories about his mother trying to fit into the world of work outside the home. However, he does talk about how she worked, during the years Tom and his siblings were growing up, to practice the habits and skills of a "homemaker" that were valued by the dominant society. After describing his mother's efforts to maintain a clean and well-ordered home, along with her shunning of "Indian ways" even within the home, Tom offers the following sympathetic explanation for his mother's choices:

> It was hard for my mother, because she was the youngest, but she was the only one who finished high school and they had by that time moved into Whitfield [which was nearly all white], and so I think she tried then to be a different person, unfortunately. Which happens a lot. She tried to leave it all behind her, and pretend it never happened.[11]

The "it" in the last sentence of this quote refers to life in the Indian Town where Tom's mother had spent her early childhood years and all the hardships and prejudice her family faced there.

To convey a sense of what might have been behind his mother's need to "leave it all behind her," Tom gives an example of the ill treatment his mother's family had suffered in Indian Town:

> My Great-Aunt Grace talked constantly about how my uncle (mother's brother) would be arrested. The local police would just come up and say "Oh, we think you've been poaching" and they would throw him in jail. . . .

> [She also told of a time when] he had been doing work for [a white farmer] cutting wood, and [the farmer] said he could have the wood that was on the ground. So [my uncle] hauled the wood away. Then the farmer next door came along and they started fighting. So the policeman threw [my uncle] in jail and *then* he asked the white farmer [for whom the uncle had been working] what had happened. . . . So there were some pretty strong memories there.[12]

He adds that this type of prejudice followed his mother even to Riverton, because "the Ku Klux Klan was very strong in this area," and the house that his parents bought in Riverton in 1940 "had a deed restriction against selling it to American Indians. It was, of course, legal at that time. They could have taken [my parents'] home away from them in court because she was Indian. So she apparently had a lot of contact with the law that was very bad."[13]

Thus, recognizing the hardships and difficulties that his mother had faced and the choices she made as a result seems to be helpful to Tom as he struggles to understand why his mother had always been so reluctant to discuss or even acknowledge her Chippewa heritage. Even something as seemingly positive as her own mother's impressive success as a traditional Chippewa healer, for both Natives and whites around Whitfield, was a source of great conflict for Tom's mother. As Tom found when he did some oral historical research into his mother's family background, his maternal grandmother had used indigenous spiritual practices as well as medicinal remedies. But when Tom tried to discuss this with his mother, already in her seventies at the time, he found that

> she has a real problem because she wants to identify as being a Christian, and so she still has problems talking about [her mother's Native spiritual beliefs and practices]. So it has been very difficult for her. And none of the other family members have spoken about [her]. . . . none of my mother's brothers and sisters ever mentioned their mom.[14]

Tom reports that he has been at least partially successful more recently in getting his mother to discuss her mother's healing practices and other matters of traditional spirituality, but it has not been easy—he has really had to "drag it out of her."

Tom's recollections of his mother during his childhood years depict her as resolute in her determination to be a Christian and a Euro-American-style homemaker and mother, and to have nothing to do with the "Indian ways" her own mother and other relatives had practiced. Despite the interest Tom has developed as an adult in his Chippewa heritage, and therefore the sense of loss he feels at having not been "raised Indian" in a more overt manner, he concedes that his childhood was no doubt eased by having a mother who was more or less like those of his (non-Native) friends.

Thus, Michelle, Jake, and Tom (and Doris, as well) each recognize, looking back, the benefits they reaped as a result of their Native parents' efforts to be like "normal white people," thus giving their children, insofar as was possible, the chance to live the lives of "normal white people." This first-generation of urban-raised American Indians had a level of financial security while growing up that had been entirely unavailable to their parents during their own childhood years. This financial stability led to opportunities in adult life for this generation, as well. While Jake chose to follow in his parents' footsteps, working for twenty-five years at the same Buick plant where they worked (and that they talked about incessantly while he was growing up—"Sometimes I think they loved the shop more than they loved me"), the other three all obtained college degrees. Michelle now has a professional career as a substance abuse counselor, Doris works as an accountant for a large corporation, and, as mentioned previously, Tom went on to earn an MBA and has become a successful businessman.

These first-generation of urban-raised Anishinaabeg profiled here (as well as many others with whom I talked) are well aware that their lives are considerably better in material terms than their (Indian) parents' lives have been, in large part due to the hard work and sacrifices of those parents. That is, urban-raised Indian people such as Jake, Michelle, and Doris see the *worker* identity their fathers developed (or, in Tom's case, his mother's choice to devote herself to being a homemaker, thus providing a "good home" for her children) as a key factor in allowing them to enjoy the benefits they did. But they see their parents' worker identity as having come at the price of their Indian identity. Becoming "like a normal white person" at work (in the shop and in the home)—the means of succeeding and providing a good life for their children—also meant "putting away" (in the phrase of one interviewee) the American Indian ways they had acquired growing up in their rural Anishinaabe home communities.[15] Of course, this was the assimilation and the entry of American Indians into the lowest tier of the labor force that the federal government had deliberately fostered with its termination and job relocation policies (as discussed in a number of the chapters in the present volume). Despite the considerable constraints on the Indian identity of their parents, however, each of the first-generation city-raised people being profiled here also includes in his or her narrative at least some shred of a "positive identity" about being Native American that was conveyed by their Indian parent when they were growing up.

One such instance has already been quoted—I refer to Michelle's father's having told her to "hold [her] head up high" and "be proud" of who she was. Although her father did not actually *tell* her on that occasion "who she was," Michelle did pick up enough hints from these and other incidents to have some sense that she was somehow "Indian." So, on another occasion during her childhood, after having seen Indian people on television portrayed as "blood-thirsty savages," she remembers asking her father straight out, "Are we Indian?" His response, Michelle reports, was to say, "Yes, we are. But not like they show on TV." Michelle adds that then "he just let it go at that"—that the topic was not "open for discussion." Yet Michelle at least was able to get confirmation that they were Indian, and reassurance that that did *not* mean they were like the "Indians" portrayed so negatively on television.

Tom reports that despite his mother's reluctance to talk about the *spiritual* (and therefore "non-Christian") aspects of her mother's healing practices, she was very proud of her mother's ability to effect cures for *physical* ailments and illnesses and to deliver babies using traditional Chippewa herbal remedies and techniques. He says, "I recall many times when my mother talked about her mom, because of her mom going around healing people." Tom explains that the fact that his grandmother healed by traditional Indian means was very important to his mother, because many of the grandmother's patients were white people who either could not get a white doctor to come to their small town, or who had tried a conventional (non-Native) medical treatment that had failed. He reports that his mother was quick to point out, with pride, that her mother had a very high success rate with these patients, using the *Indian* ways.

Finally, even Jake's father had some positive things to say about Indians (although he still never admitted to *being* one). Jake describes how his father would "express admiration for things Indian. He would talk about the way an Indian would do something in the woods, or . . . about hunting game. Things like that. Or he would talk about the way they lived . . . in the old days." Furthermore, Jake reports that his father would talk about how someday, "our society as a whole" was going to collapse, and then "the people up north will be strong again." Jake explains that this was an old Chippewa belief—that the Indian people would have to teach the Whiteman how to live. Though Jake's father "never acknowledged that it was an Indian belief," he nevertheless did express in veiled form (substituting "the people up north" for "Indians") his admiration for the traditional ways of his Chippewa ancestors.

I did not directly elicit these examples that my interviewees gave of times during childhood when their parents showed pride in their American Indian heritage, exhorted their children to have pride, or simply expressed positive attitudes about Indian people and culture. Rather, as we talked, these statements seemed to arise unbidden as a sort of counterpoint to the predominant themes of confusion and frustration that pervaded the narratives. Clearly, as part of their need to "fill the holes in their hearts," these urban-raised Anishinaabe people need to find some hint of positive identity in their childhood experience, however oblique or fleeting. This no doubt allows them some sense of continuity between a past characterized most strongly by its lack of a "positive Indian identity," and a present in which such an identity has come to have central importance.

The Legacy of Silence

All of the people considered here—Jake, Michelle, Tom, and Doris—speak readily, easily, and proudly about their Native American heritage, and seek ways to express that heritage in the context of Riverton's Indian community. And yet they also speak—sometimes with resentment and bitterness, sometimes with compassion and understanding—of their parents' and other older relatives' failure to acknowledge openly the American Indian heritage that has now become a source of such pride. Their narratives of these parents portray a poignant image: one of American Indian people who sought a better life for their families and struggled in the often hostile environment of mid-century Riverton to develop a new identity—that of an intelligent, competent, Christian worker and member of mainstream society. But their children also tell the story of how their parents' Indianness could not be completely eradicated. These are *not* the grown children of "assimilated Indians" who had succeeded in becoming "normal white people"—who really did "leave it all behind." They describe childhood memories freighted with clues, hints, and traces of an Indian heritage that was not discussed. They speak of the dark coloring and Indian features of their parent (and in some cases, of themselves, as well); trips to "see some Indians" in a faraway community, and other visits closer to home where a "funny language" was spoken; admonitions to stay away from Indians as well as exhortations to "be proud"; cryptic denials of being Indian and equally cryptic acknowledgments that they were Indian.[16]

None of the people profiled here, and few of the dozens of other first-generation urban-raised Indian people I talked with, ever learned about their heritage in a straightforward way from their Indian parent or other older relatives. The elder generation conveyed a reticence on this topic that was readily perceived by the children—this was not a subject to be pursued. This was a topic on which they must remain *silent*, as their parents remained silent. And yet, these adult children of American Indians who migrated to Riverton now convey, in their present-day narratives, a strong sense of the confusion and ambivalence that characterized their childhood experience of their ethnic and racial heritage. The absences that the city-raised people now perceive as having made "holes in their hearts" are also presences. That is, far from being unconditionally "empty" or "silent," these absences are filled with a cacophony of competing messages—a mix of shame and pride, rejection and acceptance, whispering of something "lost" but not saying what it was. So now, in their adult lives, these men and women speak of their efforts to determine what it is they lost and to reclaim it—of how they seek to replace that legacy of silence from their childhood experience with the powerful voice of a strong, positive American Indian identity.

Acknowledgments

This chapter first appeared, in slightly different form and under a slightly different title, as an article in a special "American Indians and the Urban Experience" issue of the *American Indian Culture and Research Journal*. I thank the *Journal* for permission to republish it here, as well as all those (named in the acknowledgments of that article) who took the time to read and comment on that, or an earlier, version.

The research on which both are based was part of a larger dissertation project that was funded by the Horace H. Rackham School of Graduate Studies of the University of Michigan, the Wallenberg Fellowship Committee of the University of Michigan, and the Phillips Fund for Native American Studies of the American Philosophical Society. I am grateful for their support, as well as for the National Institute on Aging's NIA Grant T32-AG0017, under which the final preparation of the journal article for publication took place.

Additionally, I appreciate the helpful editorial suggestions made by Jennifer Collier of AltaMira Press for revising that article into this chapter. Finally, I want to extend deepest gratitude to Susan Lobo and Kurt Peters, who labored long hours to make first the special issue of the *AIC&RJ*, and then this volume, a reality.

Notes

1. Michelle Duncan (not her real name) is one of those profiled in this chapter. I have changed the names of all persons quoted and referred to herein (as well as the name of the city and county where they live, and other potentially identifying information) in order to protect the anonymity I promised those who participated in my study. This particular quote comes from the transcript of an interview I conducted on March 28, 1995. All subsequent quotes attributed to Michelle Duncan come from this same interview.

2. Notable examples of recent ethnographic or ethnohistorical works that seek to describe entire urban Indian communities are: Joan Weibel-Orlando, *Indian Country, L.A.: Maintaining Ethnic Community in Complex Society* (Urbana: University of Illinois Press, 1991); and Edmund Danziger, *Survival and Regeneration: Detroit's American Indian Community* (Detroit: Wayne State University Press, 1991). Examples of works examining problems related to the move from reservation to city or vice versa include: Joan Ablon, "Relocated American Indians in the San Francisco Bay Area: Social Interactions and Indian Identity," *Human Organization* 23 (1964): 296–304; James N. Kerri, "'Push' and 'Pull' Factors: Reasons for Migrations as a Factor in American Indian Urban Adjustment," *Human Organization* 35 (1976): 215–90; Alan Sorkin, *The Urban American Indian* (Lexington, Mass.: D.C. Heath and Company, 1978); Jack O. Waddell and O. Michael Watson, eds., *The American Indian in Urban Society* (Boston: Little, Brown, 1971).

3. Like that of many Midwestern cities, Riverton's main industry during this time was the manufacture of automobiles and auto-related parts.

4. This quote is from the transcript of an interview I conducted on September 25, 1995, as part of my ethnographic field research. All subsequent quotes attributed to Jake Benson are from this same interview.

5. I conducted tape-recorded interviews with approximately twenty first-generation city-raised Anishinaabe people in the Riverton area and conversed informally with many more. In this chapter I am drawing on only four cases in order to convey the experience of my interviewees as richly and vividly as possible.

6. Tom Richards is a member of the Riverton Indian community and was one of my interviewees. But he also participated in an "Intergenerational Family Interview Oral History Project" sponsored by a Chippewa tribe located in the general part of the state where Riverton

(and more to the point, Tom's family's home community) is located. This oral history was carried out during 1995–1996, and I served as director of the project and primary interviewer. Since there was some overlap between my interviewees in the Riverton area and tribal members who participated in the project, I donated some of the interviews I had collected during my dissertation research to the tribe for use in the project—with full permission of the interviewees, of course. In quoting from these transcripts, I have used the same pseudonyms assigned in the Oral History Project and indicate the origin of such quotes by referencing them as "Kellogg" in the endnote, followed by the page number on which the quoted material appears in the edited collection of transcripts.

7. The reader will no doubt have noticed that all three interviewees that have been introduced so far have only one Native American parent, with the other being non-Native/white. This is also the case with the fourth person profiled in this chapter, to be introduced below. This raises the question: Are the people I focus on in this chapter "representative" of first-generation of Anishinaabe people raised in Riverton? My response is as follows. First, it is important to understand that the great majority of people who identify as American Indian and who grew up in Riverton are of mixed heritage. (I got this impression during my fieldwork, and it is supported by census reports and other demographic surveys. Also, see Gonzalez's comments [chapter 11 of present volume] regarding the significantly higher rate of interracial marriages among off-reservation Indian people as compared with those living on reservations.) Thus, those profiled in this chapter *are* "representative" of the first generation to grow up in Riverton with regard to heritage. Furthermore, to the extent that I was able to get to know, and in some cases interview, first-generation urban-raised Indian people whose parents were both of Native American heritage, I found many of the same themes that are discussed in this chapter echoing throughout their conversations and life-historical narratives as well.

8. Kellogg, 688.

9. Ibid., 689.

10. This quote, which is actually Doris's quote of her great-aunt's words, comes from my fieldnotes on a conversation I had with Doris and several others on April 15, 1994, in which Doris told this story.

11. Ibid., 691.

12. Ibid.

13. Ibid., 692.

14. Ibid., 690.

15. For an example of a "proletarianized" American Indian community that was able to succeed to a large extent in retaining its Native traditions, see Peters, this volume.

16. In emphasizing the lack of overt "culture content" in the messages conveyed, I do not mean to imply that no positive Native cultural values and practices were passed down from parent to child. It is true that among these particular interviewees (and most other first-generation urban-raised Anishinaabe people in Riverton with whom I spoke) there was virtually no overt instruction with regard to traditional Anishinaabe culture; but positive values, perspectives and interaction styles were nevertheless conveyed. That is, each time a family got together with other Anishinaabe people, the urban-raised children were witness to a certain kind and level of Anishinaabe culture. The elder, rural-raised generation engaged in patterns of style and practice that, though not readily perceived by the younger generation as "Indian," had been formed by

the elder generation during their own childhood years, growing up on reservations and in off-reservation rural Indian communities. At some level, the interaction and behavior patterns of the rural-raised elder generation no doubt registered on the awareness of their urban-raised children, thus giving them a connection to an American Indian heritage that, though subtle and seldom fully recognized, was nonetheless present and apparent. For a full description of such Anishinaabe behaviors and styles, see chapter 6 of my forthcoming book, *"Our Elders Lived It"*: *An Exploration of Urban American Indian Identity* (DeKalb: Northern Illinois University Press).

"Living Room of an Indian Family in the San Francisco Bay Area: Mantelpiece" © 1962 by John Collier Jr.

"Girl Watching T.V." © 1962 by John Collier Jr.

Quiet Desperation

FLOYD RED CROW WESTERMAN and JIMMY CURTISS

My soul is in the mountains
My heart is in the land
But I'm lost here in the city
There's so much I don't understand
And this quiet desperation—coming over me
Coming over me.

I've gotta leave; I can't stay another day
There's an emptiness inside of me
I can't bear the loneliness out here
There's another place I gotta be—
Another place I gotta be.

I've gotta leave; I can't stay another day
There's an emptiness inside of me
I can't bear the loneliness out here
There's another place I gotta be—
Another place I gotta be.

I long for you Dakota
Smell the sweetgrass on the plain
I've seen too much meanness
I feel too much pain
And this quiet desperation coming over me
Coming over me.

I've gotta leave, I can't stay another day
There's an emptiness inside of me
I can't bear the loneliness out here
There's another place I gotta be—
Another place I gotta be.

Weaving Andean Networks in Unstable Labor Markets

13

ALEX JULCA

F IRST-GENERATION MIGRANTS left highland villages and small towns in the Peruvian Andes—often with minimal formal education and urban skills—for the promise of progress that Lima represented for them and their children (second-generation migrants). In an interesting twist, since the late 1960s first- and second-generation Andean migrants have taken the baton by developing long-distance international networks. Today there are about eighty thousand Peruvians in New York City, of whom about sixty-four thousand are legal residents.[1]

Do networks of help and reciprocity serve indigenous-descendant Andean immigrants to cope with unsteady labor markets? By analyzing the case of Peruvian-Andean immigration to New York City through participant observation, census data, and interviews with sixty-five people living in Queens and Brooklyn,[2] this chapter sheds light on the dynamics of kin and *paisano* networks in contemporary labor markets. While industrialization in Lima opened up possibilities for upward mobility to primarily Andean parents—many of them Quechua speakers—from the 1930s to the 1960s, increasing urban stratification caused their endeavors to fall short. Their children often looked outside the country to continue this upwardly mobile thrust.

The structure of relations—inter- and intra-kin and *paisanos*—has defined the structure of reciprocity and negotiation as well as the limitations and conflicts inside Peruvian-Andean immigrant networks. Furthermore, unstable immigrant links to labor markets have led to greater reliance on interpersonal economic networks and also other network structures. Network membership is in itself an asset with short-term costs balanced against short- and long-term insurance for a wide variety of risks, some of them quite unknown at the time of investment. This argument is an extension of Murra's argument about the Andean archipelago, where communities own lands at various altitudes in order to diversify their production and decrease harvest risks, while sharing and exchanging resources with other communities.[3] At the transnational level, first- and second-generation Andean-Peruvian immigrants recreate those ways of confronting adversity and uncertainty by developing a long-range web of links connecting distant countries—with money, information, and other resources exchanged.

Characteristics of the New York City
Labor Market

The employment picture for Peruvians in New York City (1970–1996) appears strikingly similar to that they left behind in Lima. Peruvian immigrants in New York City are currently facing a similar period of economic change unaccompanied by creation of enough steady jobs. Unlike late–nineteenth-century immigration to the U.S., the market commodity dynamism and massive social mobility brought about by Peruvian modernization from the 1940s on was not accompanied by a similar boost in the demand for steady labor.[4] As has been widely discussed in the migration literature, there have been two general shifts in the U.S. labor market over the past twenty-five years: the evolution from an industrial to a service-based economy and the decline in job security associated with deregulation.[5] Accordingly, the tendency for new immigrant communities to fill menial jobs has persisted.

Job security is defined by the market characteristics of the activity itself (seasonality, growth), underlying inequalities, the degree of deregulation, the strength of the relationship of the worker with management inside the workplace, and the market niche that the employing firm has. Recent statistics indicate that a large proportion of Peruvians are working in occupations that are likely to offer insecure employment and low wages. This trend has persuaded Peruvian immigrants in New York City to work at one and a half or two jobs to meet their personal and social responsibilities. Table 13.1 on New York employment broadly illuminates class, gender, and race inequalities by depicting the types of jobs in which Peruvians have found regular employment (minimum eight-hour days), compared to their Hispanic and U.S. American counterparts.

The overwhelming majority of Peruvian immigrants are not unionized, and, as noted above, construction work is heavily seasonal. Interviews indicate that the workload in garment factories also tends to vary with the fashion seasons, and contrary to

Table 13.1.   **Percentage of Employed Peruvians, Hispanics, and Total NY State by Occupational Group, 1990**

	Peruvians*		Hispanics		Total	
	Total	Female	Total	Female	Total	Female
Manag. & Professional	13.8	5.9	15.8	8.0	30.0	10.0
Tech., Sales & Admin.	23.6	13.3	29.3	17.1	33.1	20.5
Services	28.4	13.3	23.1	10.0	14.4	7.4
Precision Prod. & Craft	13.1	1.1	10.1	1.3	9.4	0.8
Operators & Laborers	20.5	6.4	20.9	6.9	12.0	3.0
Farming & Fishing	0.6	0.1	0.8	0.1	1.1	0.2
	100.0	40.1	100.0	43.4	100.0	41.9

Source: Based on the Bureau of the Census, *Social and Economic Characteristics*, (Washington: Government Printing Office, 1993). Employed persons sixteen years and over.
*Includes U.S. born Peruvians. Peruvians make up about 5 percent of all Hispanics.

stereotypes, both men and women are employed in these establishments. As is also clear from table 13.1, the occupational group most strongly correlated with job security, "managerial and professional" workers, is the category in which Peruvians are under-represented: 13.8 percent of all Peruvians hold such jobs compared to 15.8 percent of all Hispanics and 30 percent of the total population. The tendency toward insecure employment is also captured in official unemployment figures for Peruvian immigrants in New York City: 8.7 percent for Peruvians over sixteen years old, 11.3 percent for Peruvian women.[6] The latter include Peruvians working informally whose earnings are paid under the table, often without social security.

Peruvian immigrants in New York are on average thirty years old, and, as noted before, are often sons and daughters of previous Andean migrants to Lima. One reason their parents made the move to Lima was to guarantee their children a high school education. In fact, Peruvians in New York State are highly likely to have a high school diploma: 82.4 percent of Peruvian men and 83.2 percent of Peruvian women in New York State between twenty-five and thirty-four years old are at least high school grad-uates, and 13 percent of legal Peruvian immigrants over twenty-five have completed college studies.[7] Thus it is ironic that, given the simple skills described in the occupa-tional structure above, most Peruvians in New York City have higher qualifications than what the market demands.

Lack of command of English does not prevent an immigrant from finding a job, but it greatly reduces promotion potential and the possibilities of switching from tem-porary to permanent employment. Furthermore, English skills qualify an immigrant for cleaner and less physically stressful jobs such as secretarial and sales positions. In New York City only 42 percent of Peruvians have strong English proficiency, which is lower than the Hispanic average of 56 percent, which is itself lower than the non-Hispanic White average of 90 percent.[8]

Command of English links the immigrant to wider job networks and also in-creases his or her desirability to an employer, since the employing firm also wants to access wider networks. For instance, Pepe, who lives in Brighton Beach (Brooklyn), in 1989 was not able to be promoted to foreman in a private construction firm in Man-hattan because his English was poor, but he knew that learning English would have improved his abilities to deal with Manhattan resident customers and prospects of mobility in the construction sector.

Frequently Peruvians learn English on the job, first learning basic words and phrases used colloquially, then increasing their vocabulary if they are exposed to cir-cles of other English speakers such as non-Latino bosses, bilingual Puerto Ricans, apartment tenants, landlords, telephone operators at public utilities, grocery store owners, and co-workers. "My husband decided to learn ten new English words a day [twenty years ago], and that is how he improved," Luisa, Víctor's wife, commented. Yet Víctor's English abilities were also stimulated by his work as a doorman in a building in midtown Manhattan, where most of the residents did not speak Spanish. Víctor and Luisa live in Jackson Heights, Queens. While time constraints work against the immigrants' desire to overcome lack of English proficiency, Peruvian parents readily register their children at English or bilingual schools. Sophia, who lives in Flushing, intends to raise a child who will offset her own educational shortcomings. "When we look for an apartment or need to call AT&T, Luisito reads the newspaper or talks on the phone," Sophia praised her ten-year-old child.

First-generation Andean migrants in New York City—mostly older than fifty— have fewer chances to learn English, although their command of Quechua and Spanish languages helps preserve their families' heritage and keep connected with traditional customs and celebrations. Peruvians, particularly the second-generation migrants, quickly learn that language limitations reduce informational resources to Spanish newspapers, Spanish TV channels, and communication with other Latinos.

State intervention in the labor market leaves clear marks on immigrant mobility patterns, to which immigrants respond by gathering substantial economic and informational resources from the network. Because there is no more powerful barrier to immigrant settlement and social mobility than the condition of being undocumented, Peruvian community networks are structured around the distinction between "legals" and "illegals." "How did you come?" (undocumented through Mexico or with legal visa) would be the first question—right after exchanging names—that an "old" Peruvian resident would ask of a recent immigrant to New York City. According to the answer, many "old" Peruvians (documented and undocumented) will measure the degree of risk and trust involved in entering into social and economic commitments with undocumented fellows.

The need to legalize immigration status to better access the labor market makes obtaining residency the highest priority for undocumented Peruvian immigrants. Legal immigrants can more easily use formal channels for their job searches (such as newspaper want ads, employment agencies, and New York City government offices), and can therefore more easily reach labor demand at shops, factories, subcontractor and service establishments than their illegal counterparts, to whom these avenues are generally closed. In the case of construction work, legalization opens the possibility of finding employment with a firm that can sponsor union membership, and thus the possibility of more steady work and social benefits. Obtaining a "green card" plus a job with social benefits also opens the avenue to deeper roots of incorporation into U.S. society, including active citizenship. Yet even with legalization, access to non-manual, better-renumerated jobs, will still require further language and professional qualifications and the right contacts. Nonetheless, a legalized immigrant experiences less psychological pressure than the undocumented immigrant who leads a fugitive life, for whom every day is pregnant with risk-filled events.

For the legalization process, Peruvian immigrants use illegal as well as legal strategies. For example, some U.S. residents can be paid off to enter into spurious marriages. A *sotto voce* motto among members of the Peruvian community is, "To marry a legal resident [or get the "green card"] is like winning "the Lotto" or even better. Puerto Ricans and other legal residents know this. That's why they charge from twenty-five hundred to thirty-five hundred dollars to arrange marriages. They need the money anyway . . . many of them live on welfare." Although some immigrants obtain false "green cards" and social security numbers to access certain jobs, they are never certain that these false documents will be accepted at another job. Lack of permission to work can also prevent immigrants from obtaining other documents, such as driver's licenses or bank cards, which in turn close the avenue to other jobs and credit opportunities.

Friends, Kin, and *Paisanos*

Having outlined the characteristics of the labor market and of the Peruvian immigrants, the question arises as to how immigrants contact the labor market. Peruvians' knowledge of the wide New York City labor market is constrained to what their contacts inform them. For a new immigrant, particularly if undocumented, the network of information for jobs is basically kin, close family friends, and telephone numbers of contacts given by friends in Lima. Family and/or friends' help in finding jobs is expected to be paid back through similar actions in the future (given the uncertainty of the job market) or sharing the new income and getting involved in other social commitments such as savings and reciprocal loans. "I am going to visit a Peruvian friend in New Jersey. I asked him on the phone about a job and he wanted me to come to his house to talk about it," said Luis, who arrived in New York City six months before. His friend has lived in New Jersey for about twenty years, and currently works as a doorman at a three-star hotel. Before leaving Peru, Luis compiled addresses of a list of people that he could contact in the New York area, some of them collected when these people returned to Peru to visit. Luis brought this list even though his mother and sisters, already living in Queens for about three years, offered to host him and put him in contact with his new employer.

Just as immigrants are restricted to using their contacts, so, on the other hand, employers increasingly facilitate the use of network contacts by welcoming network hiring. Employers are at ease with this strategy because "network hiring, in which current employees bring their friends and relatives to fill vacant jobs, eliminates many costs of recruitment and training while providing high quality employees, since co-workers are only likely to bring into the workplace new workers who will be dependable."[9]

The use of kin and *paisano* networks by Peruvian immigrants to find jobs is rooted in the social fabric of negotiated help and reciprocity, inculcated since childhood. For Peruvians, as for some other immigrant communities, the purpose of immigration is to improve the social and economic welfare of the family, not just that of the individual immigrant. To make this feasible, indigenous Peruvian immigrants share what might be called a culture of savings, in striking contrast to the culture of consumption prevalent in the U.S. Although investment in social relations is strongly stimulated by long-term benefits, in the short term there are concrete expected rights and obligations. If in the short term there are no signs of reciprocity, the tie has a strong possibility of breaking or of developing only weakly (particularly if lack of reciprocity is a trend).

Peruvian migrants on the move know that their situation is particularly risky, so their strategy tends to be to tie to one another, exchange resources, and assign different roles, as well as to punish those who "misbehave." Examples of reciprocity include: help in pursuing studies repaid with household work, a place to stay repaid with a "voluntary" contribution from the weekly wage, an uncle praises a nephew's accomplishments in exchange for advice to his child, a reduced rent is granted in exchange for babysitting "voluntarily" a few hours a week. Networks, ultimately, become a special and crucial kind of asset, with expected short- and long-term social and economic returns. Thus, their power is greater than a purely economic investment.

There are three basic circles of relations tying Peruvian immigrants together: nuclear family, extended family, and *paisanos*.[10] Of all the kin to whom an immigrant is related, the closest ties are to *nuclear family*. Siblings are particularly important in the migration endeavor because they have been brought up to support each other as well as their parents. Moreover, older children have the responsibility to help raise their younger brothers and sisters giving advice and support even into adulthood. In New York City, brothers and sisters are the first to be called upon to mobilize the community to find a job for the newly immigrating younger sibling. The reciprocal sense of obligation between siblings is so strong that monetary advances may be returned in the form of nonmonetary favors (such as house construction, chores, babysitting, job search, and information sharing), making the means for meeting obligations more flexible. However, for the same reason and due to the density of reciprocal ties, conflicts between siblings might have a disturbing effect on network dynamics, that is, breakage or transformation of the tie.

Extended family may provide the same type of information or financial assistance as nuclear family but is less obligated to do so. If an immigrant is the first person in his or her nuclear family to immigrate to New York City, he or she will try to find out if any extended family live in the area. Yet the less flexible relationship of rights and obligations may persuade immigrants to concentrate their energies on developing stronger ties with *paisanos* and friends.

Whereas in Peru *paisanos* are related by descent from the same geographic space (often from the Andes), in New York City *paisanos* include all Peruvians, and the term might even be extended to other Latino immigrants. Dario says, "I am more *paisano* with somebody from Cuzco in the Andes, but I am also *paisano* with any Peruvian. Maybe the Dominican lady from the video store is like a *paisana*, too, because she speaks Spanish." If a person is the first in the family to immigrate, he or she might build a *paisano* network by asking neighbors, colleagues, or schoolmates in Lima for contacts in New York City and, once in New York City, by seeking out other Peruvians.

Most Peruvian immigrants try to reach out beyond their kin to *paisanos* by participating in church, soccer, school, and party activities. They will be vehicles for information and contacts for better jobs, second part-time jobs, and immigrant legalization endeavors. However, the predominantly reciprocal relationship in the nuclear family may have as a counterpart a more negotiated relationship among *paisanos*. Conflicts may occur because values, relations, and money involved are not homogeneous.[11] If ties between *paisanos* are not strong, Peruvians will not loan money without charging "loan shark" rates of interest, because for some families money made by lending is fundamental for their financial security. The high rate of interest is also due to the higher possibility that the borrower will default on the loan if there is neither a formal enforcing mechanism nor as strong a sense of moral obligation as between family members.

While these are the basic divisions in Peruvian network ties, the migration process itself (first from the Andes to Lima, then from Lima to New York City) has also transformed kin structure and introduced new relationships. Long-range networks of support for the nuclear family have often weakened links with other relatives as well as *paisanos*. Sometimes they reencounter each other in New York City after a period of little communication in Lima. For example, during the first generation's migration from Quechua villages to towns and cities from 1940 to the late 1960s, some kin members developed a separate integration into Lima's society. Even when they maintained contact with members of the extended family, life in Lima encouraged them to develop new network branches on the job and in the neighborhood. As a result, migrants' children developed even weaker ties with their extended families. However, the migration of this second generation to New York City added a new tone to kinship ties. They have sometimes relinked with extended family, or relied on strong ties with ex-coworkers, friends, or neighbors from Lima, especially in the initial period of the late 1960s and early 1970s, when kin, and especially nuclear family, were not necessarily present in New York City.[12]

Although nuclear family is the basic resource for help and reciprocity, Peruvian networks in New York City are hardly neatly divided into the two categories: kin and *paisanos*. It is each migrant's particular history that creates the actual possibility for using the potential link between two points—nuclear family, extended family, or *paisanos*—in the network. Peruvian migrants keep in mind each feasible useful tie, new or old, developing some while abandoning others.

The opportunity for economic and social improvement opened to the family by immigration cannot occur without draining the resources available to the kin network (in both the Lima and New York City branches). The immigrant, therefore, assumes the responsibility to reciprocate by complying with commitments to family and *paisanos*. Three such social commitments are repaying debts, sending remittances, and helping other members of the family to immigrate. However, the ability for the new immigrant to comply with these social responsibilities will depend on the job(s) he or she finds in New York City and on his or her ability to save.

Repaying Debts

Pressure to repay debts affects the job in three ways: first, the immigrant must perform well on the job, or even overperform, in order to keep it; second, the immigrant attempts to become skilled as soon as possible; and third, he or she is likely to take a second job or additional shifts. New immigrants very likely arrive in New York City with debts and/or social commitments, whether they arrive legally or illegally, whether or not they have family in New York City. This is partly because the average income in Peru is about $120 per month, while the cost of airfare to New York City is $1,200, and if the immigrant is undocumented, the costs may rise to around $5,000. These costs demand the participation of kin, *paisanos*, and friends, who sometimes will be lending their life savings. The immigrant turns to close family first, but if the immediate family does not have the resources, the immigrant will then turn to extended family or to close friends and *paisanos*. Well-cultivated relations with some of these individuals will help achieve a good result. Of course, if the immigrant has contacts already earning dollars in New York City, it may be easier to raise funds for immigrating.[13] The probability that the New York City contact may advance money for the immigration expenditures is higher the closer the family relationship.

Would-be immigrants do not only call upon the network for financial resources. The immigrant leaving Lima may ask for assistance taking care of children while he or she is away, or with cooking if the mother is immigrating. More to the point, it is understood that brothers and sisters of a wife whose husband is immigrating will look out for her while he is away, and vice versa. Outside the family, would-be immigrants ask friends and *paisanos* in Peru to put them in contact with any relatives they may have in New York City. Once the immigrant settles in New York City, he or she then reciprocates, again sometimes using informational or labor resources rather than money—for example, by passing on to Peru information about job opportunities in New York City, sending gifts, or sending back goods requested from the U.S. for family or *paisano* businesses based in Peru.

In the case of women with young children in New York City, nonfinancial assistance is particularly important, since, even if a job is available, they must find a person to baby-sit in order to work. Having parents or other kin at home could ease this problem, but if that is not the case, childcare will involve more stringent time coordination, even requiring assistance from close friends or neighbors outside the home. When childcare cannot be arranged, jobs or promotions are simply not taken. Elsa is a dramatic case, since she works the nightshift as a data-entry operator at the U.S. Post Office, and her cousin Perico takes care of her child at night. Even with this assistance, she expresses the extreme stress to which she is subject by saying, "Sometimes I only get two hours of sleep."

If the immigrant was able to borrow from family, social processes may temper the repayment obligation. For example, maybe the immigrant can find a job someday for the son of the sister who lent him the money. However, the extended family tends to be less flexible than the nuclear family when lending money because something the immigrant does for the nuclear family won't necessarily help the extended family financially: if married, the extended family member is supporting a separate nuclear household. The extended family usually expects repayment as soon as they learn that the immigrant has obtained a steady job in New York City.

Remittances

Remittances are a second social responsibility that immigrants using the family network assume. When a person immigrates, social improvement for the family is only potential. The immediate effect is to cut physical contact, particularly difficult in the case of nuclear family. The immigrant needs to send remittances to Peru as soon as possible as a sign that the immigration process is worth the effort and will improve the family's well-being.

There are different kinds of remittance obligations, all of which must be met out of the immigrant's current wages. Obligations to *spouse and children* back in Peru are strongest, and remittances to them should be larger and especially stable. The spouse and children need funds for housing, food, and school. Even if the spouse works in Lima or has already immigrated to New York, the immigrant is obligated to send remittances to children. Although varying in degree, this is a permanent and nearly unbreakable commitment.

Immigrants also tend to help *parents* by remittances, in the case that they are still in Peru. Although few Peruvian parents receive a decent pension, parents probably don't depend for their entire income on the immigrant's remittance because the immigrant's brothers and sisters help support the parents, each according to his possibilities. Remittances to parents may take the form of goods or currency for living, for health care, or for birthday and Christmas gifts. "*Hoy voy a enviar la encomienda para mi mamá, pobrecita, debe estar necesitando*" [Today I will send the remittance in kind to my mother, poor woman, she will be needing it], La Cholita would say, on one of the occasions on which she sent remittances to her family. Even grandparents, who often had helped parents to raise the kids, are subject to Peruvian immigrants' attention, by sending remittances when not sponsoring them to come to "*los Estados Unidos.*" On the other hand, sometimes parents use their skills to help their children, even when they are grown.

Immigrants with some years of settlement in New York City also send remittances to the family for buying land (in the countryside or the city), for buying material to construct a house, or for opening or improving a small store. The house would either be for the parents or for the immigrant himself or herself—in the latter case, the dream house for returning to Peru at some future date. In either case, the siblings might live in the house in return for taking care of parents or preparing for the immigrant's return, but the house would not be permanently destined for brothers or sisters. Whereas with parents the immigrant has an obligation to give without expecting to receive anything in return, with *siblings* there is an ongoing back-and-forth relationship of benefit and obligation. However, the immigrant would also expect that the sibling would use part of the income to support the parents.

Helping Family Members Immigrate

There is a cycle to the remittance process: a better way to help your family than sending remittances is to bring a family member to New York City.[14] This isn't something that can happen immediately. First the immigrant must establish himself or herself for at least two or three years. After this period, the immigrant might have become a legal resident, found a stable job, or accumulated some buffer savings.

One way Peruvian networks facilitate accumulating the savings necessary to meet social obligations such as debt repayment, remittances, or funding new immigrants is through the organization of *juntas*. This financial mechanism is the Peruvian immigrant version of the "rotating credit association" studied by Geertz and Granovetter.[15] A *junta* is a saving/credit system organized by a group of six to ten immigrants, documented or undocumented. Mutual trust among the members of the *junta* is the key to its success. Group members are often related by kinship, *paisano*, and job-ties, and are not necessarily only Peruvians. They often include Colombians, Puerto Ricans, Dominicans, and Ecuadorans. Each member deposits a certain amount of money weekly, and one member has the right to use the total money gathered. "We deposit a hundred dollars each week. For example, next week it's my turn, so I will receive a thousand dollars because we are ten members. This money I will use to buy a video camera and to send money for Christmas to my relatives in Peru," Jenny explained to me. She added, "In this way one can 'see' the money, because if we don't do this, money disappears like magic. Do you want to take part in this *junta*, Alex?" The person who organizes and administers the *junta* benefits by receiving the first week's "pot," but in return for this right assumes the obligation to cover any member's default or delay in the weekly quota.

The enforcement of the social commitment is based partly on the immigrant's own shared belief in family care and reciprocity, and partly on the immigrant's thirst for prestige and power through control over resources. However, the immigrant may not be able to pay back the debt as quickly as the creditor desires, or the immigrant may find a conflict between debt repayment and remittance obligations. The network has social enforcement mechanisms to promote repayment despite such conflicts, through the flow of information between its New York and Lima branches. For example, the people the immigrant is staying with in New York City are often related to the creditor in Lima. Through them, it is not difficult for the creditor in Lima to learn the level of the immigrant's success in New York City. Furthermore, the immigrant still has family in Lima that wants to maintain good relationships with the benefactor who granted the loan.

A humble way to gain prestige is to meet one's social obligations. Thus the immigrant who pays his or her debts on time, sends remittances to Peru, or makes it possible to bring a new immigrant to New York City also forges prestige among family and close friends in both Lima and New York City. To be able to fulfill all these commitments often means that the immigrant has a secure job, so very likely could serve as a liaison with other Peruvians or family members for job recommendations and various kinds of contacts. The person who administers successful *juntas* also gains a reputation as trustworthy and reliable, so it will be easier for him or her to organize new ventures.

As part of the moral punishment for not complying with the network's moral code, Duly, a New York City resident for two years, would inform her friends about her "ungrateful" brother, "Esteban is a bad son because he never sends his mother a penny." As noted earlier, conflicts based on perceived breakdowns in reciprocity between brothers and sisters can generate transformations in the network itself, possibly manifested in less dense or tight ties between them. Another example of the network's disapproval concerns Camilo, an Afro-Peruvian who worked as a stevedore in Lima before immigrating to New York City. He could not repay on time the expenses incurred by the Peruvian garment factory owner who funded his immigration through Mexico. He had to tolerate the teasing of his friends and harassment in the street by his creditor. On the other hand, according to his friends, he might not have put enough effort into complying with his debt. As a result, he does not enjoy the trust of the Peruvian neighborhood in Brighton Beach. Thus, even though he has been in New York City for several years, his job and housing situation remains fragile.

The ultimate punishment that the network can impose on a defaulting member is *de facto* ostracism, temporary or permanent. This is vividly illustrated by Fausto's case. He is a legal resident in the US, speaks English, and has regular employment. He invested sixty thousand dollars in a fourteen-wheel tractor-trailer for a business in Peru hauling freight across the Andes. He financed the purchase through a combination of personal savings, bank loans, and a personal loan from his aunt in Lima. The collateral for the bank loan was his aunt's house. After several months of operation, the tractor-trailer suffered a serious breakdown that Fausto could not afford to fix, and the business suffered. His aunt demanded that Fausto return to Peru or pay the overdue debt, but he could do neither, leaving the aunt in the position of repaying the debt herself or losing her home. In attempting to control the situation, Fausto wound up accumulating additional debts in New York. Finally, he fled to a Peruvian friend in Ohio to escape the moral censure of his family network.

Dynamic Social Networks and Fluctuating Markets

Now that the nature and structure of Peruvian networks have been discussed, the question remains of the dynamic interaction between these networks and the unsteady labor market in New York City. Unsteadiness in the labor market has four visible effects on the workings of Peruvian networks: first, it increases the new immigrant's dependence on the host network; second, it adds flexibility to the length and location of the work day, which affects the role of members of the household; third, it increases reliance on network contacts beyond kin; and fourth, it increases the importance of bringing additional family members to New York City.

In the first place, unsteadiness in the New York City labor market increases the dependence of the new immigrant on the host network during the first period of adaptation. Since obligations are more elastic between nuclear family members, an unreliable job situation makes it more important for the new immigrant to be hosted by nuclear family. The advantage of relying on nuclear family rather than extended family or *paisano*, in terms of favors or money loans, is that the time frame and nonmonetary form for meeting the respective obligation tends to be longer and more flexible respectively. Nuclear family is likely to be more diligent about locating a job for the new immigrant. In terms of housing, the nuclear family is more likely to endure overcrowding and delayed payment of the rent. For example, the absence of family members in New York City made Dario's situation more precarious. When hosted by his *paisano*, Pepe, he had to make rent and utility payments immediately. Close kin would probably have been more flexible in the first months while Dario found work.

Second, unsteadiness in the labor market also increases the flexibility in length and location of the workday. Immigrants take on two different jobs, work overtime at their first job, or take piecework home. When bringing work home, it could be for their own employment or that of other household members. For example, sewing and jewelry making are activities subject to household (often kin) involvement. Although this kin strategy brings work stress home, it does not necessarily decrease time shared with family. Rather, it changes the roles that family members play while at home. The net benefit is the higher likelihood of accumulating savings to comply with social commitments, in addition to coping with basic economic needs.

Third, insecurity on the job increases reliance on contacts with *paisanos* and friends. The unsteady labor market pushes immigrants to make contacts beyond kin networks—among *paisanos* and relatives of friends, friends of relatives, friends of friends, old friends and neighbors from Peru, and new neighbors and coworkers in New York City. In the case of undocumented Peruvians, this drive to build ties beyond kin is also stimulated by the need to make contact with people who can assist in getting the legal identification necessary to get a job (a social security card or a sponsor for a work permit). Strong ties among *paisanos* are fostered, for example, at the soccer gatherings that take place on almost a daily basis in various public parks in Brooklyn and Queens, among men on weekdays and with family participation on weekends. These are propitious occasions for exchanging information about jobs, wages, and legalization—as well as for getting updates on various social issues in the Peruvian community such as parties, gossip, soap operas, boyfriends, girlfriends, and news from Peru. Other gatherings

A group of Peruvians, including the author, in Manhattan celebrating "Señor de los Milagros" on October 18, 1998. © 1998 by A. Julca

On the day of "Señor de los Milagros" Doña Margarita sells Peruvian food on a corner in Manhattan. Doña Margarita owns a Peruvian restaurant in New Jersey. © 1998 by A. Julca

include different kinds of weekend family parties (for baptisms, birthdays, welcoming new arrivals, and celebrating holidays), and informal conversations at the workplace. In general, other Latino friends (Ecuadorans, Puerto Ricans, Colombians, and Dominicans) and intermarried couples are invited to Peruvian parties. Sometimes as many as half of the guests are other Latinos and nonfamily members who, together with Peruvians, dance *merengue* for most of the party. The *huayno*, the most celebrated Andean music in Peru, is only danced at the end of family parties or social events.

The fourth effect of the unsteady labor market is to increase the importance of bringing additional family members to New York City. An unreliable job means unreliable income, so the probability that any one person can send remittances on a stable basis to Peru is lower. However, if the family sends additional members of the same nuclear household to New York City, there will be two positive effects. First, it decreases the probability of fluctuating remittance flows, even if the paychecks for each person continue to be unsteady. The second advantage of bringing another family member to New York City is that there will be fewer dependents in Peru relying on the remittances.

This is illustrated by the last five years of Alicia's family history of immigration. In 1991, two adult siblings in New York City were supporting two dependents in New York (Alicia and grandson) and assisting two households in Lima, of four and five members respectively. Today, there are five heads of household in New York City (three daughters and a son/wife couple), and the only person remaining in Lima is self-supporting. Actually, Alicia's family history illustrates the first two points raised as well: despite the unsteady nature of her three daughters' employment in the garment industry, their strong family ties have enabled them to be hosted in one small apartment, even expanding temporarily to include a *paisana* with her child. This friend, a skilled jewelry worker, then reciprocated by finding one of Alicia's daughters a job with more promotion potential than sewing in a sweatshop, which illustrates the importance of network contacts beyond kin for maneuvering through the vagaries of the New York City labor market.

This chapter has attempted to show that Peruvian kin and *paisano* ties, rooted in indigenous Andean values and practices, have enabled and constrained the attainment of upward mobility in the unsteady New York City labor market over the last thirty years. The harsh, thoughtful, strategic, and risky decision-making of Peruvian immigrants reflects the uncertain political economy in which they operate, as well as their determined defiance of it. However, whereas the New York City labor market puts downward pressure on the improvement of Peruvians' livelihood, kin and *paisano* transnational networks of help and reciprocity create the space for contending formal limits to upward mobility, striving to control and use available economic and informational resources.

More specifically, controlling for job insecurity and wage levels, Peruvians' possibilities for economic and social growth are assured by the existence of their savings. These are generated through two mechanisms: first, by households earning multiple incomes, and second, by nonmonetary social arrangements to share undertakings and resources. On the other hand, allowing for diminishing job security and a downward trend in real wages, this process has not occurred without tight economic constraints and risks of defaulting on commitments. And yet, without disregarding the conflicts among kin and *paisanos* carried along the way, social undertakings such as remittances, loans for airfare, helping kin construct a home, *juntas*, and job search assistance have reinforced community-based support as well as transformed the customary ways that Peruvians bond with one another. As a Peruvian immigrant told me on the subway one weekday at 6 A.M., while he was on his way to his construction job, "We have to help each other, that is the only way."

Notes

1. This figure is based on census data and interview material on the estimated number of undocumented immigrants, Bureau of the Census, *1990 Census of Population: Persons of Hispanic Origin in the U.S.* (Washington: U.S. Government Printing Office, 1993).

2. These are the population concentration centers of Peruvians in the New York area.

3. John V. Murra, ed., *Visita de la Provincia de León de Huanuco en 1562*, vols. 1 and 2 (Huánuco, Perú: Universidad Nacional Hermilio Valdizán, 1967); Iñigo Ortiz de Zúñiga, *Visita de las Cuatro Waranqa de los Chupachu*, vol. 1–2 (Huánuco, Perú: Universidad Nacional Hermilio Valdizán, 1967).

4. Jurgen Golte and Norma Adams, *Los Caballos de Troya de los Invasores: Estrategias Campesinas en la Conquista de la Gran Lima* (Instituto de Estudios Peruanos, 1986).

5. Saskia Sassen, *The Mobility of Labor and Capital* (New York: Cambridge University Press, 1988); and Saskia Sassen, *The Global City* (New Jersey: Princeton University Press, 1991).

6. Bureau of the Census, *1990 Census of Population: Social and Economic Characteristics* (Washington: U.S. Government Printing Office, 1993), 313.

7. Ibid., 309.

8. Ibid., 244, 309; Orlando Rodríguez, *Nuestra America en Nueva York: The New Immigrant Hispanic Population in New York City, 1980–1990* (New York: Institute for Puerto Rican Policy, Hesperian Research Center, Fordham University, 1995).

9. *Migration News*, no. 10 (October 1995), 2.

10. For the case of migration from the Andes to Lima, Susan Lobo, *A House of My Own: Social Organization in the Squatter Settlements of Lima, Peru* (Tucson: University of Arizona Press, 1982) provides a detailed description and analysis of the social structures of two Andean settlements in El Callao, Lima founded in the 1960s, Dulanto and Ciudadela Chalaca.

11. Viviana A. Zelizer, *The Social Meaning of Money* (New York: Basic Books, 1993).

12. See also Lobo, *A House of My Own* (1992 edition) for Peruvian strategies of adaptation to the U.S. milieu.

13. Massey and García, 1987.

14. Alejandro Portes, ed., *By-Passing and Trespassing: Explorations in Boundaries and Change* (Baltimore: University of Maryland Urban Studies and Planning Program, 1995a), 137–42; and Portes, ed., *The Economic Sociology of Immigration: Essays on Networks, Ethnicity, and Entrepreneurship* (New York: Russell Sage Foundation, 1955).

15. Granovetter, M. S., "The Strength of Weak Ties," *American Journal of Sociology* 78(6): 360–80.

A Poem Maybe for Tina Deschenie

MICHAEL THOMPSON

There will be a time months from now, maybe years,
probably when I'm driving in some heavy LA traffic
with some crashing music on the radio
and spouts of fire from the Wilmington oil refineries
erupting alongside the freeway,
when my stomach will grow tight like a fist,

and I will want to remember
that there is a beautiful Navajo woman living in New Mexico
with her family close about her,
who helps keep all our lives in balance
and fills the blue sky with her beauty

I will recall the snapshot of the woman in the red dress smiling

and I will be thankful for women like Tina Deschenie
who is a woman made of beautiful words
who is a woman made of beautiful words
who is a woman made of beautiful words

I will be watching Disney's *Pocahontas* with my grandchild one day
and I will turn off the VCR and say,
Hoka Hey, little one, let me tell you a story about a real Indian woman
so beautiful she would make Pocahontas hang her head
want to chop off all her hair and go back to England
with her blond aerobics-lookin' husband

I will remember that she would have this way of tilting her head to answer
like a pinion tree with full dark branches who, thinking its reply so gently,
the little canyon wind would have time to brush lightly through her beautiful hair and that she would incline her neck so slightly toward earth so
that her eyes would be peering up behind her dark lashes with curiosity
and regard for the beauty around her—around her in all directions—the

beauty that moves outward from her Diné eyes always shining forever and
speaking with a voice as soft as sage smoke or the little wind whirring always
just above the desert floor

I will recall the snapshot of the woman and her child
standing beside the big truck which had the tires with the heavy mud-grip tread
She looks small but meaning business, boy
You better damn believe it—and I think
maybe she's the reason, the real reason, they started
giving all those jeeps and trucks those Indian names—
Some guy in Detroit musta seen something like that picture, huh

There will be another memory I have of her too,
like a dream of Marilyn Monroe,
but with thick brown hair and a crooked Navajo smile
pulling her mouth upward to one side—
that smile dragging my eyes along like a just-roped calf

I still remember her sitting on the floor of her Chicago hotel room,
there for a seminar on Native American Lit,
her books in stacks around her
her books in stacks around her
her books in stacks around her
her books in stacks around her
her pose relaxed, her small feet tucked under her long soft skirt
drinking some good ice-cold beer out of the bottle,
having her own mini-vacation from all the rest of us,
taking off her jewelry piece by piece and rubbing the little
lobes of her ears between her fingers,
a book open in her lap and her eyes blessing the pages

And you know I'm probably thinking, if I was twenty years younger
and not married more than once or twice yet,
I'd be sure trying hard to snag that Tina Deschenie

"Kokopeli Gigging in the City" © 1999 by Larry Rodriguez Sr.

Red Wit in the City
Urban Indian Comedy

14

DARBY LI PO PRICE

U RBAN INDIAN COMEDY is antithetical to dominant images of Indians as humorless and rural. Living and performing primarily in cities, urban Indian comedians have been overlooked in books on Indian humor, which have focused on rural, tribal, or literary forms of humor.[1] Emphasizing intersections between comedians' experiences, comic worldviews, humor, and the contexts from which their laughter arises, this essay examines comic expression and identities among Indian standup comedians in urban contexts.

Character Development

Individual character or persona is the medium through which standup comedians express their message or worldview.[2] Comedian Al Hans explains, "You want to establish your personality and character so your way of seeing things or point of view opens up to them."[3] Standups are expected to address how distinguishing physical features such as ethnicity, race, gender, or body type shape their experiences and perspectives. Establishing character helps open audiences to their way of seeing things. In turn, making jokes about themselves or their own ethnic groups ingratiates themselves with their audiences and increases their ability to make fun of the dominant group. Otherwise, disparaging the dominant group would be too antagonistic.[4]

Indian identities may serve as central, secondary, or even minor aspects of routines, and may be conveyed in numerous humorous ways. While some Indian comedians grew up with strong Indian identities and ties to communities prior to becoming performers, others have found performance to be a catalyst for expressing their Indianness.[5] This appears to occur more frequently among comedians who grew up in cities, apart from reservations or large Indian communities.

Margo Boesch is a Chippewa-Irish-Italian comedian who has been featured on *Entertainment Tonight*, *Evening at the Improv*, and national comedy tours.[6] She establishes her persona through the incongruities in life she experienced as an Indian who was adopted by whites and grew up in Newark.

> Once when I was five, my mother found me in front of our apartment
> building with my ear pressed against the concrete . . . listening. I explained

that Indians could tell when their relatives were coming by listening to the earth. She laughed, dusted me off, and suggested I use the phone instead. I knew she didn't get it . . . I did. I was Indian and that's how we did things, I had just seen it in a movie. In the 1950s in Newark, New Jersey, movies were the only way a "split feather" could learn about family.

Having grown up surrounded by non-Indians provides Boesch with plenty of material for observational humor and critique of other ethnicities. "Growing up in an Italian neighborhood had its drawbacks. These people were pleased that Columbus had made it. I, on the other hand, would have preferred it if Ol' Chris had made a left and fell off the edge like those other guys." While Columbus is equated with "discovery" among many non-Indians, for Boesch "being discovered" meant "getting lost," and the beginning of a long journey to discover her fragmented heritage and childhood fantasies.[7]

She recalls trying as a child to establish herself as an Indian. Like many adoptees, Boesch didn't know which tribe she was from. "So when I was asked, I said Sioux (thank God for Saturday matinees)." Boesch then discusses her quest to find acceptance as "a Chippewa raised in an Italian and Greek family where half the relatives were Jewish. So I know from tribes, lost or otherwise." Growing up before the ethnic pride movements of the 1960s as "the only Chippewa on the block in Newark, New Jersey, was not easy job. Back in the fifties anyone I met who claimed Indian blood was related to Pocahontas." By age sixteen, she "had chalked up 187 of Pocahontas's great, great, sorta-kinda, maybe relatives" and "a hundred fourteen Cherokee Princesses," and "one Kiowa Queen, my friend's uncle, but I don't want to talk about him tonight." She jokes about "subtle signs that I was Indian. Like every Columbus Day . . . I would go down to Port Newark, and as the ships were coming in I'd yell, 'Take a left, take a left!'" She jokes about choosing an Indian name: "Big problem, cause I wanted my name to truly reflect the adopted kid raised by Greeks and Italians and half the family was Jewish . . . so I chose Tonto Shaloom. Good choice—every time I dance it rains money."

Surviving three adoptions, two divorces, a double mastectomy, and many expensive therapy sessions, Boesch jokes, "I paid $800 for a workshop to learn that what I want is not what I need, and what I need is not what I want . . . and what I get is always inconvenient and inadequate. . . . Heck, I could have stayed late at a pow-wow and learned that for nothing." "I know who I am, I know where I am going, and I'm my own best friend . . . and I don't have a dime to take me out." She helps others heal themselves in humor/wellness workshops she conducts under the auspices of the Public Health Advocacy Institute in Phoenix, where she currently lives.[8] Boesch compares her standup and her social work: "I am often asked if there's a difference between standup and social work. . . . Not really—at my day gig, I sit down and the audience is in a circle." Some whites still expect her to wear "traditional" clothes. "I had a woman book me for a speech, and she asked if I could wear my 'cos . . . cos . . . cos . . .' 'Do you mean my traditional dress? I don't have one.' 'Could you borrow one?' 'For you, sure.

How many feathers would you like? . . . And by the way, on the podium can I stand next to the Dutch guy with the wooden shoes?'"[9]

Abel Silvas, of Ajachamen and Spanish–Mexican American descent, grew up in San Diego vaguely aware of his Native American ancestry. When he initially began standup, his Native heritage was primarily conveyed in one-liners. Walking on stage in T-shirt and jeans with a beer in his hand, he would (appear to) twist the bottle top in his eye socket and exclaim, "That's my opener. . . . What's wrong? Isn't that how you do it? Or maybe you prefer to do it like this [bends over and twists bottle in his rear]." Then, challenging stereotypes of Indians as humorless: "My great great-uncle was the first comedian, Rodney Danger Bear. He'd make jokes like, 'Hear the one about the deer with diarrhea? Yeah, it's all over town.'"[10]

As a student at the University of Michigan, Silvas became inspired to develop longer performances based on his Native heritage when he studied under the master mime Marcel Marceau. Silvas recalls Marceau saying, "'You're Native American, right?' 'Yeah.' 'Well, you should go back to your people because your people always communicated in mime.'" Silvas wrote to the Bureau of Indian Affairs and found out he was Juaneño. His tribe, the Ajachamen (pronounced "Ahashamem"), had been en-slaved by Spanish missionaries at the Mission San Juan Capistrano and given the name Juaneño. He learned California Indians in particular used mime as a medium to com-municate across the many different California language groups.[11]

Drawing from conversations with relatives, elders, and historical accounts, Silvas replaced his white grease paint with characters that reflect his California Indian her-itage. In the character of Running Grunion, Silvas incorporates rabbit furs, shells, mime, storytelling, and comedy to enact how his people lived in precolonial, Spanish, Mexican, and American eras.[12] His success with Running Grunion led Silvas to start a children's mime troupe on the Viejas Indian Reservation. The troupe performs for other schools and local cultural celebrations such as San Diego's annual Grunion Fes-tival, which Silvas founded to acknowledge California Native traditions.

Ed Perez (a.k.a. Beecher Sykes) is of Otomi and Mexican descent, and has spent most of his life in the Palo Alto, San Jose, San Francisco, and surrounding Bay Area. Perez initially began doing standup as a Mexican *cholo* character with a black leather jacket, black pants, black gloves, black sunglasses, hair slicked back, a boom box radio, and a high voice. He established a Mexican persona with jokes such as, "I'm Mexican, which you may not believe since I'm six foot tall and don't have a mustache." "I can tell you're surprised to see me on stage, not in the kitchen. . . . A lot of people say Mexicans are lazy. That's not true, you try smoking a big doob and see if you feel like working." Perez says he was just trying to say that Mexicans are just like everyone else. Recalling his *cholo* garb, Perez reflects, "I think the *cholo* character was a disguise I was hiding behind." He also recalls how some people didn't like his *cholo* character, even though others had laughed. One club owner asked him, "Could you be a little less Mexican so people could have some-

"The bears were too big, so he let them go." From "The Legend of Running Grunion" © Abel Silvas. Photo © Laura Aragon, Santa Barbara Natural History Museum.

thing to relate to?" Another manager told him he was afraid of Mexicans.[13] To avoid being identified, Perez hid behind the stage name Beecher Sykes for several years until he became more comfortable performing as himself.

The general acceptance of and positive feedback on his Indian identity over his Mexican persona led Perez to change his stage persona entirely to an Indian. According to Perez, a lot of people feel threatened by Mexicans, whom they see as illegal immigrants taking their jobs. He believes they have more empathy for Indians because they think of Indians as existing in the past or far away rural areas rather than in urban areas. He jokes about showing his mother a history book with an old picture of an Otomi woman captioned, "The sophisticated Otomi girl wearing a hat and shawl." "I'm like, 'Mom, what are you doing in this picture?' since it looks like her." Perez gets away with saying critical things about whites when he performs as an Indian much more than as a Mexican: "People empathize with Indians. Blacks will come to me afterwards and say, 'I can really relate to the hardships of your people' and whites will apologize and I'll tell them, 'Well you didn't do it.'"

Perez jokes, "A lot of people think this comedy boom has only been in the past ten or twenty years. But that's not true, you see Indians used to do standup way back before there even was a United States of America. The history books tell you that Indians were a bunch of wandering nomads following the buffalo. But actually what they were doing was going from village to village putting on comedy shows." To "reenact a Native American comedy show," Perez turns his back to the audience, loosens his

Ed Perez, a.k.a. Beecher Sykes
(© Ed Perez)

ponytail, and turns to the audience with long hair covering half his face. In a markedly lower and exaggerated stereotypically "Indian" tone of voice he begins:

> How (pause) is everybody doing tonight? It's good to see everybody at the Club Minnehaha. Last time I was here, I really massacred the place. This place is really packed tonight. You must have made reservations. My name is Wind in His Drawers. Let me tell you about myself . . ."[14]

After a series of impersonations of an Indian character from the rural past, he switches his persona to a contemporary urban Indian. Emphasizing that Wind in His Drawers is an impersonation, Perez laughs about a woman who mistook Wind in Drawers for a "real" Indian: "True story—this woman comes up to me after a show in Sacramento and says 'Wind,' like she knows me, 'do Native Americans find white people as hard to understand as white people find Native Americans?' I said, 'What do you mean?'"[15]

For some comedians ethnicity may play a secondary role to other aspects of their identity they emphasize in their routines. This is often true for female comedians. Rebecca Ward is of Cherokee descent on her father's side. She has lived in Louisville, Kentucky, Santa Monica, California, Nabb, Indiana, Branton, Missouri, and San Francisco, where she has done standup for ten years. Although she has a few Indian jokes,

Rebecca Ward
(© Rebecca Ward)

most of her routines involve issues she deals with as a woman, such as insecurities over body image and clothes, dating men, or life as a mother of two kids.[16] Ward says she bases her Indian jokes primarily on what she thinks non-Indians stereotypically think of Indians. She introduces her Indian heritage with "I should tell you a little about myself. I'm part Indian. Part Cherokee. My dad's half Indian and half Irish, so it's kind of a family tradition that every St. Patrick's Day we go out and scalp concert tickets." "Dad was kind of cheap, half the time he'd pay our allowance in beads and trinkets." "I'm part Indian but my husband isn't. So every time we play monopoly he likes to get me drunk and steal my properties a little bit at a time." The concept of this joke is never far from the surface of Indian humor about whites.[17]

Al Hans, of Bella Coola descent, lived on the Bella Coola reserve in Canada then moved with his family to Vancouver. He began standup in Toronto in his twenties and currently lives in Los Angeles. Hans says at comedy clubs "urban audiences have few Indians. The mystique and curiosity about Natives is high so I play with them because they are nerdy and naive. For example, I'll tell them I can't eat hot dogs or go to a place because it's sacred. Then let them know I'm just kidding."[18]

He prefers to be thought of as "Al" rather than as a "Native American." Believing that being identified according to ethnicity has a "provincializing effect," Hans asserts, "I'm individualistic, almost anti-collective. If I can get people to not look at me as Native American, but as Al, then it goes against preconceived notions of what I am." To establish himself as Al instead of "the Native guy," he tries not to give away his Native identity right away. He likes to joke about current events before introducing his Indian heritage. He then jokes about his Indian background: "I'm Bella Coola. We're fish Indians. We have nine names for salmon and twenty-nine names for beer, so when we run out of salmon we have to drink beer." Hans says he has received criticism for doing this joke because the tragedy of Indian alcoholism is still too present in the minds of many people. Hans notes that despite intentionally limiting the amount of Native material in his routine, it seems to be the part that people remember him for. "It's a catch-22. Ideally I would have preferred to figure this out in Canada and come to L.A. as Al. . . . I thought I came as Al, but people thought I came as the Native Canadian."

Charlie Hill is the most prominent Native American comedian. An Oneida/Mohawk/Cree raised in Detroit and the Oneida reservation in Wisconsin, for the past twenty years Hill has been living in New York City, Seattle, and Los Angeles, where he is a regular at The Comedy Store. His comedy career has included televised appearances with Richard Pryor, Johnny Carson, David Letterman, Jay Leno, and Rosanne. Establishing himself as an Indian who lives in the city but retains reservation ties, Hill typically walks on stage in T-shirt and jeans, sometimes singing funny songs (accompanied with harmonica) about urban life: "I got them reservation blues. . . . I left my family back on the rez, big city lights, I miss my family and kids, been gone so long, I don't know who I is."[19]

Hill is known for doing humor expressing the underrepresentation of Indians: "I was at UCLA last week: University of Caucasians Lost Among Asians."[20] Community ties inform Charlie's attitudes about his comedy, "I try to get people to laugh with us instead of at us. If I put on a headdress and acted stupid I could be a millionaire in Vegas. But people who do that don't have to answer because they don't belong to Indian communities. Real Indian humor is grass roots stuff, it's about things in the community." According to Hill, "I let my work talk for itself. . . . I think whether an Indian writes a letter or brushes his teeth, in America that is a political act. It seems like everything we do is called political."[21]

Urban Contrasts

> I have spent years denying it, ignoring the evidence, pretending it wasn't true, but I just can't do it anymore. I have reached a point of personal awareness in my life where I must face certain unavoidable realities, no matter how painful. After sixteen years living in Canada's largest city, I have finally admitted to myself that . . . I . . . am . . . an . . . Urban Indian!
>
> —DREW HAYDEN TAYLOR, *FUNNY YOU DON'T LOOK LIKE ONE*

Taylor's and other Indians' dislike of the term *urban Indian* is a response to reservation Indians' derision of urban Indians as not being "real" Indians. In his book, *Funny You Don't Look Like One*, Taylor describes reserve relatives who laughed at him for trying to run away from mosquitoes and told him, "You've been in the city too long." This makes him finally acknowledge he is an urban Indian. "Not that I have anything against Urban Indians. Some of my best friends are Urban Indians. But I just never thought I would ever be one." He says the perks of urban life have made him soft. "In just two more years I'll have spent exactly half my life in the big city, drinking cafe au laits, eating in Thai restaurants (it's hard to find good lemon grass soup on the reserve), riding the subways (also notoriously difficult to locate on the reserve), and having pizza delivered to my door, etc. I've grown soft."[22] Discussing how city living is different than reserve life, Taylor jokes, "A long time ago I heard an Elder wisely say to a group of young people, 'We must go from being hunters in the forest to being hunters in the city.' I now hunt for a good dry cleaner" (90).

A writer by trade, Taylor notes the irony of living in the city and writing about rural life. "In the past I used this simple fact to tell myself that though my body lived in an apartment near Bathurst and St. Clair, my spirit somehow was fishing in an unspoiled, unpolluted lake, nestled in the bosom of Mother Earth, somewhere up near Peterborough, Ontario." Addressing how city life has changed him, he says, "Instead of the easy, 'I'll get there when I get there,' saunter so many of my 'Rez' brothers and sisters have, I now have my own 'I have to get there in the next five minutes or life as I know it will end,' hustle. Somehow it loses something in the translation," (90). "I've traded roving the back roads in pickup trucks for weaving in and out of traffic on my bicycle. Instead of blockading roads to defy authority, I refuse to wear a safety helmet. Where once I camped on deserted islands, I now get a thrill out of ordering room service in a hotel" (90).

Some reserve Indians believe real Natives only live on reserves. Taylor responds, "Now, there are many people who live on reserves who feel you aren't a proper Native person unless you're born, live, and die on that little piece of land put aside by the Government to contain Indians. How quickly they forget most Aboriginal nations were nomadic in nature. So when I tell these people, 'Take a hike,' I mean it in the most Aboriginal context" (90).

Taylor ponders returning to the reserve. "If the gods permit, I could return to the community that spawned me and reintegrate myself into the heart and soul of the reserve." He believes this is an option that "weighs heavily" on his mind as well as upon the minds of other "Urban Dwellers of Aboriginal Descent (UDADS)." However, he enjoys the comforts and autonomy of city life. "As my mother says, I know home will always be there. So will the mosquitoes and the gossip and relatives who still treat you like you are twelve years old . . . and those who walk in my moccasins know the rest." Such thoughts leave Taylor content with his current status as an urban Indian: "Until then, if there is a then, I shall be content to acknowledge my current civic status. To celebrate, I think I shall go out this morning into this urban landscape, partake of some brunch and perhaps peruse a newspaper or two. I may be an Urban Indian, but I'm also an Urbane Indian" (91).

Contrasting urban and rural Indian life, Rebecca Ward explains that her grandfather lived on a reservation in Oklahoma. Recalling how their local radio stations only played country music, she says,

> There's actually a country song called "You're the Reason God Made Oklahoma." Is that supposed to be a compliment?! Isn't that kinda' like saying, "You're the reason God made Bakersfield or Fresno" . . . We used to visit my grandfather on the reservation in Oklahoma. People sometimes ask me what Oklahoma is like in the winter. Imagine a meat locker but it's a little colder and a lot less interesting. . . . Our high school dances were never successful since it was mostly an Indian population. We'd get rained out every time we started dancing.[23]

According to Hill, differences between urban and rural Indians are less than they were a generation ago due to greater ability to travel between cities and reservations. However, dominant portrayals of Indians in the rural past still lead some people to consider urban to be antithetical to Indian.

> I met another tourist one time, he said, "Like, you know, like, my dad is Indian, man." This really threw me because they always talk about their grandmother or something. I said, "That means you're Indian then, man, be proud of who you are, damn it." He said, "Oh no, man, I just, like, live out here in L.A. and I don't practice it." How do you practice being an Indian? "Yeah, uh, I've got Indian practice tonight."

Contrasting urban with nonurban life, Hill bemoans third graders bringing guns to school and exclaims, "There's so much crime in Los Angeles, the women, this is how they rock a baby to sleep at night—[makes siren sound]."[24]

Drew LaCapa, an Apache, Hopi, and Tewa comedian in his late thirties, has lived all his life at the Fort Apache reservation in Arizona (except for eighteen months in Oakland and a year in San Diego) and provides a contrast to urban Indians. One thing that is unique about him as a standup is his dress. He does part of his show in an Apache woman's work dress made of cloth with a string. He explains that people from Fort Apache laugh when they see him wearing the dress because they know his dress is just a costume. However, he recalls overhearing kids in Oakland arguing over whether he was a transvestite. He says urban kids usually don't know much about rural or traditional life.

LaCapa explains his dress to urban audiences as a way to teach them about traditional culture. During a performance in Oklahoma City a woman yelled at him for twenty minutes for wearing a dress. He took that as an opportunity to explain that he wears a dress because in the Hopi tradition the dress shows respect for matriarchy. He told the woman, "As a man you shouldn't be afraid to wear a dress. I have three kids and have been married for ten years and as soon as you get out of your Levi jeans, I'll get out of the dress." LaCapa says, "In the Hopi way, when clowns are made, it is a way of serving penance, so the more outrageous, the more the return will be. Many people in the city have no inkling of what a clown does."[25]

Demonstrating a rural point of view, LaCapa jokes, "The city is too fast for me, I like kicking back and walking through the woods. I'd rather be chased by bears than people with guns. . . . Oakland is a funny place because of all the Plexiglas. You go to Circle K and have to ask for potato chips through six inches of Plexiglas." Observing differences in material wealth, he jokes, "People in Marin are so rich, they even got chastity belts for their dogs to restrain them when they're in heat!"

Despite some differences between his work and that of urban Indian standups, LaCapa says there are even more similarities. For one, the comedy tours bring rural comedians to urban audiences. LaCapa finds most urban Indians can relate to similar issues such as drugs, alcohol, and violence. He says the main difference is generational: "People from forty years old in an urban setting will understand rez jokes about no hot water, washing clothes by hand, washing ourselves in the river. Younger urban kids will understand drugs, gangs, violence, rap, MTV, and view reservations as a secondary experience." He believes rural kids understand jokes about animals better. For example, "The only thing like a mangy dog is John Wayne—he walks sideways." LaCapa says urban kids don't get this joke but rez kids do because they've all seen sick dogs. According to LaCapa, urban Indians are universally aware of pow-wows, snagging, relationships, Indian love, how people laugh, people from the reservation. Finding common ground with other peoples he muses, "There's a lot of wannabes and a lot that have to be—Mexicans, Filipinos, they love Spam and fry bread too."

Reflections

Poking fun at social beliefs, norms, and values, comedians often serve the role of cultural critics. Given the mainstream society's marginalization of Native Americans, it is not surprising that much of Indian humor is targeted towards revealing the shortcomings, errors, and contradictions of the dominant culture. Indian comedians often play jokes on white audiences to reveal their lack of knowledge about Native peoples. Silvas demonstrates how he can play on audiences' misconceptions about the meaning of "Native" in the following exchange:

> Silvas: So where's all the Native Californians? (cheers)
>
> Silvas: From what tribe dude?
>
> Audience member: Cherokee.
>
> Silvas: That's not Californian, man, I'm saying I'm Native Californian Indian![26]

Perez challenges the dominant practice of equating "American" with the United States or white.

> It's very complicated being who I am. People look at me and ask, "Are you Indian?" to which I reply, "Yup." Are You Mexican? "Si." "Are you Spanish?" "Uh huh . . ." When people just ask, "What are you?" I say, "American," which really seems to confuse them. They seem to forget that America is a continent not a country. . . . When I'm being really pissy and someone asks me what I am, I say, "Californian."

He explains that many of the names of states and cities across the country—Oklahoma, Minnesota, Wichita, Kansas, Winnebego, Massachusetts, Ohio, Wyoming, Utah, Tennessee, Tacoma, Manhattan, Napa, Sonoma, et cetera—are Native names rather than English names and reflect their prior existence as Indian lands. "When the 'settlers' were migrating across the country they would meet the people that were already there and, being lost, one of the first things they'd ask is 'Where are we?' or 'What do you call this place?' To which you might get the reply, 'Arkansas' or 'Idaho.'"[27]

Making fun of New Agers, Hill jokes, "You get this a lot in the Bay Area: 'I was an Indian in a previous life.' But not now, so get out of my driveway!" Hill tells New Agers to quit appropriating Native cultures:

> And all the New Agers stop pimpin' our religions and our ceremonies. You can pray with us in our circles but you need to figure out who you are. This Lynn Andrews bullshit, or this guy Swift Deer—we call him Fast Buck. Anytime you see a medicine man with a 900-number run. We talk to our ancestors with our ceremonies. White people can't talk to their ancestors with our ceremonies. It's impossible because they're the ones who killed them. So relax, find out who you are. Then we can all get healed together.[28]

After joking about white tourists who flock to reservations and ask dumb questions such as, "What Indian tribe was the fiercest?" or "Can I take your picture?" Hill exclaims, "We Indians ought to be tourists in the suburbs in a white neighborhood and see how they like it: 'Are you really white people? Goddamn! Can I take your picture? How do you survive in these suburbs? My God!'"

Taking a crack at mainstream political orientations, Hill gibes, "Last week I did a show for the American Indian Republican Party. Three of the nicest gentlemen I ever met in my life." Putting liberals in perspective, he quips, "Liberals aren't quite sure about Indians: 'Oh, we love the Indians.' Then give us back our land! 'Okay, we're not that liberal.'" Hill jokes about people who are offended by his humor: "I had a heckler last night. I know I shouldn't judge a man by the color of his neck or anything like that, but he said, 'I don't want to hear any of that crap, I'm an American god damn it, why don't you go back to where you came from?' So I camped in his yard."

Taylor finds plenty of material for comedy from his experiences writing for television and theater. Critical of the barriers imposed upon Native writers by whites who think they are the best judges of how Indians should be portrayed, Taylor describes producers telling Indian writers to make their characters "more Indian" in his book *Funny You Don't Look Like One.*

> I guess as a Native person, I don't know how real "Indians" talk. Bummer. . . . For a story to be "Native enough" must there be a birch bark or buckskin quota? Perhaps there is supposed to be vast roaming herds of moose flowing past the screen. Oh geez, I guess I'm not Native enough. I momentarily forgot, moose don't herd, they just hang out with flying squirrels that have their own cartoon show. (57)

Taylor's experiences as the artistic director of the Native Earth Performing Arts Theater Company in Toronto are another source for humor. He recounts phone calls with absurd questions such as,

> "I'm trying to find Sam Ke-something or other. I really don't know how to pronounce his last name. Do you know where I can find him?" "I'm trying to locate a Bob Whitecloud of the Sioux tribe in the States. I heard he might be in Canada. Can you tell me how to get in touch with him?" "I'm with a casting company for a movie. I'm looking for a Native man, tall and lean with long dark hair and a presence. Preferably he should be in his early thirties. And yes, he has to look very striking." Yeah, most of the women in my office are looking for him too. What do you want me to do about it? The line starts behind them. And, "I'm Herman ——— from Germany. I'm looking for people of the Bear clan. My last name means bear in German. Do you know any or can you help me find the Bear clan?" Sorry, we have yet to update our database and cross-reference our membership, actors, directors, stage managers, and others by clan affiliation. We're waiting for the software to come out for Windows. (59–61)

Native Earth Performing Arts is regularly called by students or professors doing research on Native theater. "And each time I put the phone down I shudder. I can't help but wonder—what wonderful images are they getting from our work?" Taylor goes on,

> When is a door not a door? When it's ajar. When is a symbolic metaphor describing the Native individual's relationship with the Earth, or Turtle Island as they call it, and the spiritual and physical sustenance that it provides, as well as the water being an allusion to the blood of said Turtle Island, or perhaps in this reference, the term Mother Earth would be more accurate, not a symbolic metaphor? . . . Sometimes you just wanna yell, "He's just fishing, for Christ's sake!" (86)

Taylor thinks it is a strange preoccupation of academics to spend their lives constantly studying and analyzing other people's writings and works, but seldom attempt the same work themselves. "It's sort of like people who watch pornographic movies but never have sex" (86).

Common Ground

Many Indians in California and the Southwest have close ties to people of Mexican descent. Despite their Native American roots and the prior existence of California, Texas, Colorado, Arizona, and New Mexico as part of Mexico, people of Mexican descent have historically been treated as unwanted "non-American" immigrants by many white Americans.[29]

Silvas applies the premise of multiethnic jokes to an opener about being a Mission Indian. "I'm California Indian. I'm a Mission Indian from the Ajachamen tribe—can you say it? [audience repeats 'Ahashamen'] Bless you! [blank looks] That's a Mission joke." Playing upon the audiences assumption that Mission Indians must be doubly serious as Christianized Indians, Silvas breaks the tension by revealing that the joke is on the audiences' seriousness. This opens the way for Silvas to explain that Ajachamen (or Juaneños) are Indians who were enslaved at the Mission, where members of his family still live. "I'm a California Indian. Actually I'm half California Indian on my dad's side and my mom's side is Mexican, so that makes me 'rust.'" Emphasizing how Mexicans are viewed as illegal aliens, Silvas jokes about his childhood. "We used to play Cowboys and Indians and Mexicans. I used to play the Mexican—'*Aqui viene la migra!*' [mimics running] which means, 'Here comes the border patrol!'"[30]

Through the character of Running Grunion, Silvas explains that when the Spaniards came the Natives welcomed them, but after time, differences grew and borders were drawn that split people apart. Donning a red headband and plaid shirt, he impersonates Mexicans running to the sound of the "La Bamba" song. He mimics climbing over a fence and being blinded by spotlights; he raises his hands, then has them cuffed behind him. This border skit enacts how the border violates people's rights. "Since we were here before the border, we didn't cross the border—we were crossed by the border." He emphasizes that the border is the problem, not the border-crossers. Moreover, his tribe was there before San Diego existed: "We didn't move to the city—the city moved to us." Urbanization for his tribe was a process of encroachment rather than migration (see chapters by Trujillo and Lobo for further discussions of urbanization as an encroachment process).

Silvas is trying to include Indian and Spanish peoples in San Diego's public Old Town history. As a board member of Protectors of Historic Sites, he is challenging the California State Park's plan to build an American-style visitor's center in Old Town over the remains of historic Spanish and Indian home sites. Silvas jokes about being the "underground tour guide" for a group of state officials who "seemed disappointed because there was nothing to see" since the historic sites are all buried:

> I'm the underground tour guide for the Protectors of Historic Sites. We
> located old Spanish and Native American historical sites beneath San
> Diego's Old Town Historic State Park. But we're having a hard time get-
> ting the state to recognize the sites. I gave these officials a tour but I
> think they were disappointed because they couldn't see anything because
> it's all buried. I'm standing with this map and pointing, "Buried over
> there is an adobe house built by my great grandfather Silvas in the
> 1820s, and over there is a site that was occupied for several thousand
> years by Kumeyaay Indians."[31]

Silvas challenges the "official" Anglo-American history that minimizes the prior existence of Native and Mexican peoples in the area. He notes that the Euro-American marginalization of Indians has led to many "Hispanics" denying their Indian ancestries, sometimes even despite their having Indian relatives with the same last names.

Addressing global issues or placing local concerns in global contexts is a common feature of Native American humor.[32] Multiethnic jokes often serve as a bridge to jokes that emphasize commonalities shared by different groups. Shared indigenous heritage among different groups can serve as a premise for such jokes. Hill asks if there are any Latinos in the audience and jokes, "The Latinos, that's our first cousins. We've been here since before the white people in Europe were trying to figure out if they were monkeys. The Spanish came here in 1500 and the Mexicans came nine months later." Embracing Latinos/Mexicans in terms of shared indigenous roots, Hill then emphasizes shared history: "Since there's Latinos here tonight I need to thank them for kicking Davy Crockett's ass!" Inverting the image of Davy Crockett as a heroic figure, Hill jokes, "They always say, 'Oh, Davy Crockett he was a famous Indian fighter.' That means, oh, he murdered people—in fact, he was a terrorist."[33]

Hill emphasizes common ground between American Indians and Native Hawaiians. At a Native American benefit in which Hawaiian musicians participated, Hill bonds with Hawaiians by saying. "Aloha to the Hawaiians, and I love the Hawaiian people. They're the same as us. The only difference between the Hawaiians and the Indians here is the ocean, and that's the only thing, that's it, the same thing." Hill makes comparisons: "They have their medicine people and we have our medicine people. They have their tragedies like us. We have Wayne Newton. They've got Don Ho." "The Hawaiians, when they say hello they say Aloha, when they leave and when they come. The government has messed them up so much they don't know if they're comin' or goin'!"

Urban Indian comics imaginatively disrupt dominant preconceptions, undermine limiting inventions, and dispel fantasies of Indians as solely rural and humorless. Lucy Lippard writes,

> Irony, humor, and subversion are the most common guises and disguises of those artists leaping out of the melting pot into the fire. They hold mirrors up to the dominant culture, slyly infiltrating mainstream art with alternative experiences—inverse, reverse, perverse. These strategies are forms of tricksterism, or *"Ni Go Tlunh A Doh Ka"*—Cherokee for "We Are Always Turning Around . . . On Purpose" . . . subverting and "making light of" the ponderous mechanisms to "keep them in their place."[34]

Always cracking jokes on purpose, urban Indian comedians are intercultural mediators who expand their audiences' conceptions of Indians through their wit.

Notes

1. Darby Li Po Price, "Laughing Without Reservation: Indian Standup Comedians," in *The American Indian Culture and Research Journal* 22, no. 4 (1998): 255–71. For a study of rural literary humor, see Kenneth Lincoln, *Indi'n Humor: Bicultural Play in Native America* (New York: Oxford University Press, 1993). For a study of humor in a Western Apache community, see Keith Basso, *Portraits of the Whiteman: Linguistic Play and Cultural Symbols among the Western Apache* (Cambridge: Cambridge University Press, 1979).

2. Dave Schwensen, *How to be a Working Comic: An Insider's Guide to a Career in Standup Comedy* (New York: Back Stage Books, 1998).

3. Al Hans, interview by author, Berkeley, Calif., July 10, 1996.

4. See Christie Davies, "Ethnic Jokes, Moral Values, and Social Borderlines," *British Journal of Sociology* 33 (1982), 383–403.

5. For a discussion of performance as a means of searching for and securing self-identity, see Glen D. Wilson, *Psychology for Performing Artists* (London: Jessica Kingsley Publishers, 1994).

6. Margo Boesch, personal telephone interview, November 2, 1999.

7. Unpublished comedy scripts sent by Boesch to author, 1999.

8. Boesch created a comedy program and instruction book for children that was adapted by the AmeriCorp Training program in Pensacola, Florida.

9. Boesch unpublished comedy scripts.

10. Video of Abel Silvas's performances in San Diego from 1989–92.

11. Interviews by the author in San Diego California, November 1996.

12. Abel Silvas, "Running Grunion: Southern California Native Storyteller," KPBS, San Diego, 1992.

13. Interview by author, Oakland, October 2, 1993.

14. Performance at the Ohanna Cultural Center's "Color of Funny Comedy Competition," Oakland, August 29, 1993.

15. Ibid.

16. Ward believes it is difficult for women to become successful standups, especially if they have kids, because it's harder for them to "hang out with the guys"—the mostly male comedians, managers, and club owners—and being a mother makes it difficult to cater to the late schedules of comedy clubs. Interviews by author, Berkeley, August 12, 1993.

17. Rebecca Ward, performance August 8, 1993, "Color of Funny Competition," Ohanna Cultural Center, Oakland, August 8, 1993.

18. Interview by author, Berkeley, August 10, 1995.

19. Charlie Hill, performance at the University of California–Berkeley, December 4, 1997.

20. Ibid.

21. In Wishelle Banks, "Comedian Charlie Hill," *Cowboys and Indians* 21 (November 1997): 166–69.

22. Drew Hayden Taylor, *Funny, You Don't Look Like One* (Penticton, Canada: Theytus Books, 1996), 90.

23. Rebecca Ward performance, Oakland, August 12, 1993.

24. Charlie Hill performance, San Francisco, October 14, 1996.

25. Drew LaCapa, telephone interview by the author, Berkeley, December 2, 1996.

26. Abel Silvas, performance video, San Diego, 1991.

27. Ed Perez, letters to author, February 7 and 17, 1997.

28. Charlie Hill performance, October 14, 1996.

29. See Rudolfo Anaya and Francisco Lomeli, *Aztlan: Essays on the Chicano Homeland* (Albuquerque: University of New Mexico Press, 1989).

30. Abel Silvas, performance video, San Diego, 1992.

31. Abel Silvas, telephone interview with author, Berkeley, November 12, 1999.

32. Allan Ryan "Postmodern Parody: A Political Strategy in Contemporary Canadian Native Art" *Art Journal* 51, no. 33 (Fall 1992): 59–65.

33. Charlie Hill performance, San Francisco, October 14, 1996.

34. Lucy R. Lippard, *Mixed Blessings: New Art in a Multicultural America* (New York: Pantheon, 1990), 199.

"Indian Pride," © 1999 by Mike Rodriguez. "This plywood is currently hanging up (bolted) on Twenty-first and L Streets on an abandoned campaign headquaters building. On the middle of the ply are the letters I. P. (for Indigenous Pride or Indian Power). They are designed in what is called 'wildstyle' so that cops cannot read it!"

Healing through Grief 15
Urban Indians Reimagining Culture and Community

RENYA RAMIREZ

> This exhibit is very informative. Our Native peoples, "federally" recognized and unrecognized, full-blood and mixed-blood, from North, South, and Central America, need to unite and free our minds from the colonial borders and governments imposed on our hemisphere.
>
> —AN EXHIBIT-GOER REACTION, MAY 1996

T HE AMERICAN INDIAN HOLOCAUST EXHIBIT is a project organized by the American Indian Alliance (AIA), a group of urban Indians, who first came together in 1993.[1] Tensions and rifts within the San Jose Indian community encouraged Laverne Morrissey, a very strong, soft-spoken Paiute woman, to form this group.[2] Al Cross, a Mandan-Hidatsa man, and Roberto Ramirez, an Indio/ Chicano, organized this exhibit, which was open for a week or so each year from 1995 until 1997. Exhibit organizers used images, drawn by the colonizer, Xeroxed from books and then enlarged.

In 1995, the exhibit concentrated on the first fifty years of the invasion of Central and South America. In 1996, it focused on the European assault in the southeastern part of the United States. In 1997, it included more images concentrating on the Northeast of the United States. Even though the exhibit has not gone on display since 1997, organizers hope one day to focus on all the different areas of the Western Hemisphere.

The purpose of this chapter is to examine this group's vision of community healing. Al and Roberto argued that the historical trauma resulting from the scattering, the death, the torture, and the rape of the American Indian Holocaust experience could be healed through images, grieving, Indian-oriented history, and ceremony.[3] Part of their vision was to create an exhibit that not only decolonized knowledge, but also reconnected relationships. The social imaginary of the Western Hemisphere, for example, became a unifying principle, bringing together Indian groups that had been separated by colonization.[4] In this chapter, I will show how these activists challenge much of the past academic literature, which has portrayed urban Indian culture and community as separated by geography. They also dispute how social scientists have placed urban Indians into fixed categories on a continuum between the traditional and the modern. In contrast, they reimagine culture and community to help us all heal from the historical trauma caused by the American Indian Holocaust. I will also provide the reader with my own analysis of the images in the exhibit, then switch from the position of the observer within the exhibit space to that of an observer of the reactions and analysis of Indians and others who participated in this event.

Getting Involved

Prusch Park is situated right next to Story and King Avenues in the middle of the east side of San Jose, California. A large banner with the words, "American Indian Alliance," was strung over the entrance to a grayish building. As I passed through the entrance, the outstretched arms of my niece, Chandra, greeted me. Seated at three or four tables were Indian people I had met at previous meetings. At one table was a group of Indian community activists interested in organizing a public exhibit about the American Indian Holocaust.

I had been coming to these meetings as part of my doctoral fieldwork trying to understand more about urban Indian identity and issues of community healing. My own mixed background, as Winnebago, Chippewa, and white, raised in a town a little north of San Jose, made my entrance into the lives of Indians living in an urban area easy and hard at the same time. I had experienced the deep honor of meeting people who had known my mother when she was active in this community in the early 1970s during one of the first American Indian Alliance meetings. The easy part was feeling good connecting with other Indian people. The hard part was trying to figure out how to do research about Indian people and write about it in a sensitive as well as scholarly fashion.[5] These thoughts came to my mind as I crossed the room and proceeded to sit at the table with those interested in organizing an exhibit.

Al sat to my right. His tall body swallowed up the small, black folding chair. He leaned back slightly and quietly spoke: "Indians need to heal. Indians have not had a chance to deal with the pain. We (as Indian people) need to begin to deal with our own painful history." His voice was melodious and calming. Al helps Laverne Morrissey, the leader of the American Indian Alliance, in her mission to heal the tensions within the Indian community.

Roberto sat across from Al. These two men had worked together for many years as social workers until Al retired. Since Roberto became an Aztec dancer in the 1970s, he has felt a strong connection to his Indian brothers in the north. He wore a white T-shirt with a picture of Columbus landing. Indians were standing on the shores looking at the first explorer. Across the bottom of his shirt was the proclamation, "Columbus did not discover America. He invaded it—1492–1992." Roberto sat forward in his chair, glanced around the table and responded, "The holocaust affected all of the indigenous people from the north and the south. I keep thinking about the Taino people. There must be pictures of the killing. Researchers, teachers, and students need to pull together. We need to develop a professional, well-done exhibit."

Al traced his fingers across the smooth beige surface of the table that separated him from Roberto. He looked attentively at him and explained, "When they put us on reservations, there was genocide. Mothers had babies who were weak. The food supply was limited. Their whole way of life was taken away. Indians died from European diseases. The connotation was that Indians were inferior." His voice had a tinge of sadness.

Roberto sat up straight and pressed his spine against the molded plastic folding chair. His arms were folded across his chest. He leaned forward and spoke in an adamant tone:

> Genocide comes in many different forms. There is living and dying on the reservations. What is going on in the Americas today? In Chiapas they are taking the land away from the Indian. We need to respect the land. We need to respect the creator. I see a picture of genocide and I cry for my people. Millions of Indians died. This exhibit will help us deal with our feelings. We have to deal with our grief. This kind of exhibit has never been done before.

Al shifted in his chair. He slowly picked up a stack of papers and then set them down. His eyes focused on Roberto and he carefully began to speak.

> We have to figure out the first step. Maybe we can show the exhibit at the Indian Center, maybe here at Prusch Park. Drinking and then people getting in car accidents, those behaviors come from this historical situation. The exhibit can address this. It is just like grief. You go crazy for awhile. There is so much pain. Indians used to cut their fingers to deal with grief. We don't have any time to deal with our feelings. People need to sit back and get a shock. This exhibit is going to arouse a lot of emotions. In our schools, we need to be taught what was omitted. First, we heal the Indian community. The larger community will benefit. We will not leave out the Southern Hemisphere. We don't want to perpetuate any stereotypes.[6]

This conversation made me sit back in my chair. Hearing about the need to face the death of our Indian ancestors, to grieve and thereby heal, made my throat tighten and my heart ache. As I sat with these community activists, I remembered my own experience with grieving—the shock, the anger, the denial, and the gradual acceptance. I thought about the policeman who had stood at my doorstep two years before with a small yellowish scrap of paper in his hand with my mother's name scrawled on the wrinkled edge, asking me whether I knew the name he so coldly pointed to. This uni-formed messenger standing without emotion announced the end of her life to me. The deep, wracking pain and surreal quality of that moment of my own personal grief sent a shiver of recognition down my spine as I listened to the conversation about collective genocide. I thought about how Indian people have had to go through the continual erasure of our presence, our names, and our histories by the dominant so-ciety. My mom's beauty, knowledge, history, her connection to all of her relations as a Winnebago/Chippewa woman seemed to have no meaning or importance to this po-lice officer. The searing pain of loss that pierced my chest had been intensified by the dehumanization of my mom's beautiful name, Woesha Cloud North.

I felt a sense of connection to these community activists who were talking about a deep collective wounding that spanned the centuries of suffering for Indians and Chicanos/as in the Americas. The all-encompassing nature of this kind of grief made me sit up with interest and wonder. I thought about some American Indian psychol-ogists and Indian community members who had named this suffering resulting from physical and cultural genocide *soul wound*.[7] They argue that the core of American In-dian awareness, the soul where dreams, mythology, and culture emerge, is wounded from the holocaust experienced throughout the Americas. The manifestations of this collective soul wound include Indian peoples' suffering from high rates of suicide, al-coholism, and dropping out from school.[8] During these initial planning sessions, Al, Roberto, and others conceptualized an exhibit that would be a strategy to begin heal-ing from the long history of genocidal trauma that the term *soul wound* describes.

Holocaust and Fragmentation

This exhibit as a strategy to create a sense of unity across differences is critical in a world that has systematically tried to fragment and create divisions within and be-tween Indian and other groups. For example, the Spanish created the concepts of the *mestizo, coyote, lobo, cholo, pardo, color quebrado*, and many other categories to separate Indian people from themselves and from each other. These classification schemes integral to the development of racism favored European descent and light skin. The Spanish gave privileges to people who were mixed with European ancestry. They were allowed to wear European clothing and move about more freely than *indios*. As a result, this sys-tem caused conflict between Indian people, as each classified group wanted to gain privileges at the expense of the others.[9]

By the turn of the twentieth century, many different factions and conflicts had been created by contact with Euro-American society. Religious controversies arose between traditionalists and Christian Indians. There were tensions between Indians who wanted to remain separate and those who wanted to interact with white society as well as be-tween "mixed-bloods" and "full-bloods."[10] Many tribes agreed to live together on the same reservation when they signed the same treaty. Other reservations were set up for remnants of tribes that had almost vanished because of the federal policies of extermination and relocation, and the virulent impact of diseases. In California, there were thousands of landless, "unrecognized" Indians, resulting from eighteen unratified treaties.[11] In the 1840s, by the Treaty of Guadalupe Hidalgo, the United States acquired from Mexico the regions of California, Nevada, most of Arizona and New Mexico, and parts of Colorado and Wyoming.[12] This new border crossed Indian tribes, splitting up groups like the Tohono O'odham. Governments have created further borders between groups of Indian people by narrowing the construction of Indian identity, such as between the acknowledged and the nonacknowledged individuals and tribes.[13]

The American Indian Holocaust experience has largely gone unnoticed or disregarded.[14] Activists use the word *holocaust* to encourage the public to open their eyes and face the terror, torture, and death of Indian people throughout the Americas. They hoped that this powerful word would create a linkage between the Jewish and the American Indian holocaust experiences. Al and Roberto wanted the public to become aware of Indians' genocidal trauma.[15] The following description is an excerpt from my field journal concerning one of the first holocaust meetings that took place in 1994.

American Indian Holocaust II

When I stepped inside the exhibit, a cool pocket of air, saturated with the sweet aroma of sage, rushed toward me and enveloped my body. Small globes of yellow light illuminating enlarged images of genocide in the otherwise darkened room of the community center also met my eye. I looked to my left and saw the words "Invasion of the Americas by Britain, France, Portugal, and Spain" typed on a large map of the Western Hemisphere. The names of the explorers, DeSoto, Ponce de Leon, and Columbus, were also typed on this black and white map next to the sites and dates of their invasion of Indian lands. I glanced in front of me and saw a small table with a guest book, opened up for people to sign. Above this table was a large white cardboard sheet where Al Cross had written the multifaceted purposes of the exhibit, which were: to bring out the "other story" erased from the historical record; to debunk the European myth of discovery; to disrupt the romantic and nostalgic stereotypes constructing Indian people as "remnants of the past"; and to provide a space for the descendants of the American Indian Holocaust to grieve the loss of millions of lives.

Fifty or so prints included dogs hunting down Indian people, Indians being hung and burned alive, Indians getting their hands and noses cut off by the Europeans, and Indians resisting the Europeans with spears. A corner of the room was devoted to honoring the plants important to Indian people from the U.S. Southeast. Potted green plants, mounds of brown dirt, and drawings of cornfields dominated this part of the exhibit. Sepia-toned pictures of Cherokee and Seminole women covered another wall. Drawings of weapons used by the Europeans hung opposite these pictures of Indian women. On another wall, draped from the floor to the ceiling, was another huge map of the Americas. Next were numerous maps of the United States. One map chronicled De Soto's Trail of Destruction. Another showed the removal of Indian nations to Oklahoma. Another portrayed the sites of the worst epidemic outbreaks for Indian people. A final map presented the gradual depletion of Indian lands and the location of present Indian reservations. A wall dominated by a large drawing of a twenty-dollar bill documented the Trail of Tears. One half of the face on the dollar bill was Andrew Jackson; the other half was Hernando Cortes. At the end were three-by-five cards, tacked to the wall with pushpins, where the public had written their comments.[16]

Healing

As part of their healing vision, the holocaust group used the colonizer's own images and then inserted indigenous perspectives in order to undermine dominant representations of Indian people. In this way, the organizers were attempting to decolonize knowledge. In the following, I will provide examples of how the holocaust group recoded words and images originally recorded from a Eurocentric point of view in order to assert an Indian perspective.

The organizers went through books and pulled out the history that the Europeans had recorded using woodcuts. They then blew up the images, changing the perspective from a Eurocentric to an indigenous one.[17] Al explained that in these woodcuts the colonizer drew Indian bodies to look like European bodies.[18] Indian people were drawn to appear weak. The conquerors were drawn to look masterful. Indian men's bodies were feminized, and Indian women were sexualized. Both groups were drawn to look submissive to communicate European control. However, by enlarging these images, and placing them next to words printed on white sheets of paper, Al, Roberto, and others inverted their original purpose. Now these images exposed what the colonizer had done.

The words of a Spaniard who traveled with Christopher Columbus, Michele de Cuneo, were placed on the walls of the community center: "I captured a very beautiful Carib woman who the admiral [Christopher Columbus] gave to me. . . . I wanted to put my desire into execution. . . . She did not want it and treated me with her fingernails. . . . I took a rope and thrashed her well. She raised such unheard screams."[19] After reading this, I knew that these words were not about sex, but about violence, power, and control of Indian women as well as the land. The "empty" lands were believed to be "virgin" territory as yet to be explored.[20] The "virgin" lands, symbolized as female, were to be penetrated and raped by male explorers. In these traveler accounts, Indian women were described as extremely beautiful, their sexuality open and unashamed, unburdened by European guilt. This "very beautiful" Carib woman is, like the landscape, imprisoned within de Cuneo's sexual fantasy and imagination. He describes beating her without shame and is somehow surprised by her screams. She is not a human being, capable of feelings and pain, but becomes an object to help him put his "desire into execution." The exhibit organizers made visible this rape of an Indian woman—in the process humanizing her, decolonizing knowledge, and disrupting patriarchy.

Suzanne Smith, a white nineteen-year-old college student, displayed an oil painting done by Alfred Jacob Miller in 1845 as part of the exhibit on Indian women.[21] In this image, an Indian maiden is wearing a knee-length white buckskin dress. Her hair is neatly brushed and cascades down the back of her dress. In the background, there is a bare-chested, dark-skinned Indian woman with tousled hair and a red blanket wrapped around her waist. She is crouched on the ground, leaning away from the center of the painting. The Indian maiden's hand is highlighted, passively holding the hand of the trapper. The other woman seems to be fearful, wanting to stay away from the spectacle taking place between the Indian maiden and the trapper. The unkempt, messy, disorganized, cowering woman represents the savage squaw. The other, who is beautiful, clean, and submissive, represents the Indian maiden or princess. An Indian warrior in the background holds a pipe in his outstretched hand, waiting to give it to the settler.

Suzanne recoded this painting by telling the public in printed captions that it projects the common misperception that Indian women had romantic relationships with white men. Showing the distorted representation next to a quote about history, she encouraged people to become conscious of their negative assumptions about Indian women. Further, the juxtaposition was meant to make visible Indian women's lives and experiences that have been left out of the historical record.[22] Suzanne explained that by placing modern-day images on the walls of the community center, she wanted to counter the common assumption that Indians have been exterminated. Her fear made sense, since the dehumanizing logic of racism is hinged upon images of Indian people as stuck in the distant past, completely exterminated, or caught in damaging stereotypes of the present such as "dirty Indians," alcoholics, stupid squaws, Indian maidens, or as some kind of New Age shamans.[23]

In conducting her research, Suzanne found out that very little had been written about Indian women.[24] She also discovered that Indian women had multiple leadership roles. They were midwives, artists, basket weavers, horticulturists as well as mothers and bearers of tradition within tribal communities. She honored these roles by describing them on rectangular pieces of paper and placing them on the exhibit wall. For Suzanne, it felt cleansing to bring Indian women's knowledge and experience into the public eye. She felt a deep respect for "who they were and what they had done." Suzanne described an increased sense of well-being making Indian women's lives visible, showing that inserting Indian peoples' lives back into history and back into public life can be a healing experience for *all* people.

College students Evonne Wilson, a Navajo, and Shelby Corey, both from San Jose State University, also worked to decolonize history. They opened up the border between U.S. and Mexico through the use of a double-faced image. On one wall of the community center there was a huge twenty-dollar bill. Etched on the back was President Andrew Jackson. Hernando Cortes covered half of his face. In the 1500s, Cortes conquered the Aztec empire and seized Mexico for the Spanish crown, savagely exterminating Indian people along the way. Three hundred years later, President Jackson forcibly removed the Cherokees, making thousands walk the Trail of Tears from the Southeast to Oklahoma.[25]

For me, this image linked the brutality of the conquest of Mexico and the U.S. policy to drive Indians from their homelands onto tiny pieces of reservation land. Placing these two histories together made me, an Indian from the North, feel a sense of solidarity with Indians from the South. This double-faced image points to the holocaust project's hemispheric approach. The students were not allowing national borders to interfere with their portrayal of colonial history.

Ceremony

For spirituality, another aspect of the exhibit organizers' healing vision, a sacred space supporting the creation of positive visions for the future was carved out. Each evening spiritual people would offer a blessing before scholars, poets, or community members gave presentations about the American Indian Holocaust. One evening an Apache spiritual leader, Mary Hyatt, stood up and held an abalone shell with wafts of smoke and the aroma of sage spilling over the shell's edges. She walked into the center of the exhibit hall and stood in the middle of a group of Indians, Chicanos/as, and whites, offering a blessing to the four directions. She pointed the abalone shell in each direction, praying for each woman nation. Her voice got taunt and tears began to flow down her cheeks as she prayed for women to be able to heal from all the violence that they have suffered through. Mary reminded the audience how each woman has a special place inside, pointing to her womb. She prayed that women could heal and protect this special place.[26]

The aroma and smoke from the sage blessed the people to encourage healing and transformation. Mary's prayer caused people in the audience to cry, in part because this historical violence against Indian women is rarely acknowledged. Mary provided everyone with the opportunity to grieve and release some of the emotion pent up inside. The womb has been portrayed as the site of injury resulting from male settlers exploring and penetrating Indian women's bodies and the land. Mary pointed to her womb and prayed that this trauma could be healed.

Mary prayed for all of the women nations, the four races of people, represented by the colors red, yellow, black, and white. This prayer reminded everyone of the importance of healing the human family—because women of all colors have suffered from a history of violence. Mary and her husband, Jack Hyatt (Cherokee/African-American), have participated in sundances for a number of years. Mary brought native spirituality into the exhibit, which in this case supported envisioning interconnection between all of the women of the world.

Healing through Grief

Grief was also used to encourage healing. Al and Roberto explained that Native people must grieve so that they can live the rest of their lives in a sacred manner. Roberto urged the descendants of the holocaust experience, Indians as well as Chicanos/as, to call up and face the genocide in order to begin to trust each other and begin to work together.[27] Al discussed how this exhibit could provide a place for people to start the grieving process, providing them a space to deal with their emotions.[28] Al argued that after facing the "truth," Indians and others could finally begin to respect one another and become full human beings.[29]

Consequently, the holocaust exhibit is a place for Indians, Chicanos/as, and others to reconnect with the memories that the dominant world has denied them. Facing and going through emotions and memories that have been submerged by the dominant society entails a re-enactment of these forgotten moments in history.[30] This group's decision to face death as part of its strategy to heal challenges how death is usually viewed in American society. Death is seen as scary, to be hidden in our sterile, florescent-lit morgues and the dark shadows of our funeral parlors. For many, deceased bodies are presented for short hours of visitation and funerals last just a morning or an afternoon.[31]

This fear of death is in sharp contrast to the Winnebago-style wakes I attended as a child, when my relatives' bodies were brought back into the home and ceremonies were performed to help their spirits pass over to the other side. These wakes lasted for four days and four nights. Death was seen as a part of life's cycle, and this four-day vigil was as much for the souls of the dead as it was for the living. I remembered when my beautiful sister Trynka was brought back into her home, gracefully lying in a large wooden casket wearing her Winnebago powwow outfit, its brilliant colors celebrating her Winnebago soul. She had died tragically of breast cancer at the young age of thirty-eight, the age I have just turned as I sit at this computer, trying to write about healing through grief. Her male relatives carried the heavy casket across the threshold of her home with the rest of her family watching, and my breath stopped, wondering if I could handle seeing her beautiful body without movement or breath. The funeral director hesitated before leaving and told us how unusual it was to bring a body home to be honored for an all-night wake. I thought of this as I sat listening to the conversation between Al and Roberto. I remembered that death was seen as a natural course to be experienced through the deep healing rituals and ceremonies passed down from the ancestors. These ceremonies have helped me face the shock of my own loved ones' deaths and helped me heal through the grieving process. Based on my own experience with death and dying, the organizers' plan to help Indian people grieve through the use of pictures of Indian peoples' suffering and death as they offered blessing, ceremonies, and prayer, made sense.[32] Death is not to be hidden in the shadows; proper ceremonies need to be performed for the spirits of the ancestors to be able to rest in peace, so the bereaved can once again move on with their lives. Blessings were invoked during the exhibit to help the souls of the ancestors, who were violently tortured and killed, to cross over to the spirit world and be at peace.[33]

Mixed Identity and the Holocaust

The holocaust group also used the reality of mixed identity to bring together groups of people. During one evening, Paul Rubio, a Chicano/Yaqui artist, brought into a public forum an issue that has plagued Indian communities for a long time. He began, "Mixed-bloods and pure-bloods, we have a division within Native American society. I am hoping for a healing along these lines."[34] Paul then discussed how both sides of his family tree were represented, the Spanish and the Indian, on the images on the walls of the community center.[35] Paul urged others to connect to "the culture that took care of this mother earth rather than the one that tried to destroy other peoples and destroy the earth." In this way, he encouraged the audience to develop a consciousness that reimagines culture to live in harmony with the earth. Thus, the earth became a unifying category to develop an awareness to create a respectful world.

During an interview Paul discussed the importance of honoring all parts of himself, the Indian, the Chicano, and the Spanish. He argued that much pain results from people wanting to label and pull out one piece to represent their entire sense of identity. He explained, "I think the labels create some of the hurt. They allow people to narrow their identity down to something that is at odds with something else."[36] Paul celebrates difference within himself, letting go of the teachings of Western culture dependent on static categories in the construction of otherness. His strategy during the exhibit for cross-cultural communication was to emphasize his own experience of mixed identity.

Through his presentation, Paul provided a means to avoid the replication of the binary categories that Europe imposed on the colonized throughout the world, causing conflict between groups of people. Paul acknowledged the difficulties living as a descendant of these different experiences, but rather than rejecting one or another, he used their synthesis to move towards the creation of a qualitatively new social order.[37] This new social order is grounded within a world infused with indigenous knowledge, spirituality, and philosophy. Using the earth as a unifying symbol, the holocaust group created a space that conceptualized belonging from indigenous perspectives.

In addition, Paul's presentation provided an alternate framework for understanding urban Indian culture and identity to those of the past academic literature. Urban Indian researchers have often relied on static notions; Indians are placed in fixed categories, representing boxes filled with different kinds of culture.[38] These homogeneous wholes are assumed to be situated within bounded geographical communities. Urban Indians, according to acculturation theory, have been placed on a continuum between the traditional and the modern. Problems in urban adjustment are understood to result from the inability of individuals to progress through this continuum smoothly. As a result, urban Indians are said to suffer from "culture conflict," are "caught between two worlds," or are viewed as "marginal," a disappearing and a "dying breed."

This reliance on static models has exacerbated tensions between the "traditional" and the "modern," the "full-blood" and the "mixed-blood," as well as between Indians and other groups. Within this framework, there is no room for Indians to intermingle and mix and still remain who they are. There is no possibility for Indians to belong to more than one identity. It also leaves white people trapped within a position of power and privilege, unable to learn, mix, and mingle with marginalized members of the rest of society. Urban researchers who create a binary between Indians and whites ignore the presence of other groups of color. In contrast, in his presentation Paul opened up the boundary between Indians and whites, as well as between "mixed-bloods" and "full-bloods." In this exhibit, mixture was not something to be feared, but became as a means to encourage communication and understanding across groups.

Laverne also described her understanding of urban Indian culture and community, which does not just include the activities within the San Jose city limits, but the urban area is the center of a hub.[39] This hub includes Indians living in the urban area and also reaches each person's tribal community. The city is an information center where Indians from all the different tribes can share and then send this information back home. Thus, Laverne argues that the city can act as a hub of Indian peoples' ideas, culture, community, and imagination that can be transported back home and can impact thousands of people across the country.

Within Laverne's framework, the holocaust exhibit serves as a collecting center for peoples' ideas, culture, and knowledge not only from the different tribes, but also from different ethnicities. Within this vision, cultural and physical boundaries are not seen as obstacles, but instead become openings between different groups of people. This connection can support the creation of a sense of unity across differences, strengthening Indian peoples' collective voice and ability to mobilize for social change. This common identity, however, must not be confused with prior anthropological notions of pan-Indian culture, which assume that there will be a continuing loss of differences and a cultural convergence among Indian groups.[40] In contrast, the sharing among cultures in Laverne's model supports intermingling without cultural loss.

Therefore, Laverne's hub challenges acculturation theory. Placing urban Indians on a continuum between the traditional and the modern does not make sense using her framework. Indian culture is fluid, and flexible, and can be renewed as Indians travel and communicate back and forth from the urban to the reservation areas. Indians are not necessarily "traditional" or "moderns" depending on where they live. Indians can support their sense of tradition, culture, and identity in the hubs or gathering spaces in the urban areas. This is another example of how these activists, like other authors in this volume such as Lobo, Peters, and Strauss and Valentino, challenge classic anthropological theory.

Furthermore, the imagery of the hub explodes the dichotomy anthropologists have made been the urban and the reservation, since it includes the urban and the reservation as a network of culture and relations. Laverne sees the possibilities of communication networks that flow out from the urban centers and include the reservation area. The exhibit as a hub is a center of a communication network that encompasses the entire Western Hemisphere. Borders between nations, peoples, and cultures are blurred to bring together a community that had been separated through colonization.

In this exhibit, urban Indians also challenge the classic anthropological assumption that they are people without culture.[41] In contrast, they revision[42] culture to create a world that Leslie Marmon Silko foretells in *Almanac of the Dead*.[43] Silko tells us that mother earth will eventually purify herself from all the wounding from Eurocentrism that has ripped open her flesh and confused her children. This wounding has scattered people, created conflict, and numbed people from feeling love for each other and the land. She also tells us that loving relationships with the land and each other will support a renewal of community that will reclaim the Americas. Similarly, the holocaust group reimagines a world that includes all human beings who can respect each other and the mother earth.

These teachings are contained within the indigenous prophecies that guide *Almanac of the Dead*. Prophecy also guides the actions of Laverne and Roberto. Laverne envisions the day when the community will heal and there will be a Coming Together Time of all of the races. Roberto, an Aztec dancer, feels a responsibility to work with Indian people from the North as he follows the old Zuni prophecy that people from the South will bring the scattered back together again.

Some Reactions to the Exhibit

Pushpins held up small cards on the wall at the end of the exhibit. Many people had written their reactions to the exhibit in pen as well as in pencil. Here are three examples:

> As a white man I am tempted to say that I am sorry. But instead I'll say it not as a white man, but as a man. I'm sorry for all the horrors man inflicts on men. I didn't do these things but I am sorry others did, as others do. I guess I'm just ashamed sometimes to be a human being.

> This exhibit is very informative, our Native peoples, "federally" recognized and unrecognized, full-blood and mixed-blood, from North, South, and Central America, need to unite and free our minds from the colonial borders and governments imposed on our hemisphere.

> "Mexican" is simply a term given by non-Indians to conveniently divide the Indians, north and south of the false border. *Mexicanos*, accept what you really are![44]

These reactions as well as others point to the exhibit fulfilling its purpose to heal for some who attended. The national borders and narratives—causing divisions between Indians, Chicanos/as, whites and others—were opened up, supporting the creation of an imagined community infused with an indigenous consciousness that spanned the Americas. For the non-Indian, some could face looking at Indian history with both eyes and hear the cries of pain across the generations, echoing throughout the darkened hall of the exhibit. On the exhibit wall, the message written by "a white man" apologized for the horrors of history. He focused on his own sense of humanity to bridge the racial categories that have separated us, pointing to a strategy to heal from the holocaust. Denying the reality of the holocaust experience is harmful to non-Indians, as they are living a lie. Opening and facing this lie is a healing experience.

Tacked on the wall, the second reaction to the exhibit seemed to verbalize the exhibit's essential purpose, to help Indian people reimagine a hemispheric and inclusive sense of Indian community that crosses "colonial borders." Thus the healing space of the exhibit hall supported the lifting of boundaries between groups divided by nationalist projects.

The third reaction points to how the exhibit opened up the border between United States and Mexico. By respecting the Indian part of the Mexican identity, there is the potential to build bridges of unity across populations that have been divided by the creation of the dominant version of the mestizo. The writer argues against Spain's method of incorporating the huge Indian population in Mexico. From a dominant perspective, this is a whitening process, an attempt to pull Mexicans from their Indian origins. By not respecting their Indian origins, mestizos often view Indians as inferior, uncivilized, at the bottom of society. The writer demands that *"Mexicanos"* accept the Indian aspect of their identity and learn to connect with their Indian relations across national borders. The writer is urging people to reconnect with the Indian, the aspect of *Mexicano/a* identity that has been relegated as the premodern.[45] In this exhibit, an indigenous consciousness was asserted and became a site of healing, supporting connections between Indians, Chicanos/as, and others. This exhibit, therefore, seemed to realize its goals for healing as evidenced by some of the reactions that were placed on the wall.

Thus the exhibit as a "journey through the Americas" supports a mobile, fluid sense of community, culture, and identity that rebuilds a sense of connection in the midst of distrust and dislocation. Utilizing Indian-oriented history, experiences of mixed identity, grieving, art, and ceremony, the holocaust group worked to heal themselves and others from the five-hundred-year-long holocaust. Al, Roberto, Mary, Paul, Laverne, and others are living by a consciousness that connects back to the mother earth to guide their actions. Roberto explained, "The mother earth is suffering and it is going to take all of us to come together to heal her. We cannot do it by ourselves. The four colors must come together as one and deal with the truth and begin the healing."[46]

Notes

1. The term *urban Indian* is problematic, since it supports the assumption that Indians living in urban areas form their sense of community bound to the geographical region of the city. This is not true. Indians form their senses of community across geographical boundaries, including their reservations, and, in this article, the entire hemisphere. Thus I use this term with caution.

2. "Sacred Circle: Laverne Morrissey Heals Community Rifts," *Metro*, 14–20 July 1994.

3. Field notes, 13 October 1994.

4. Victoria Bomberry, a Muscogee/Lenape/Choctaw/Chickasaw scholar, has named this reimagining *western hemispheric consciousness*. Her forthcoming dissertation, "Indigenous Memory and Imagination: Thinking Beyond the Nation" (Stanford University) discusses this reimagining of Indian community as part of indigenous knowledges that interrupt the negative constructions of Indian peoples throughout the Western Hemisphere.

5. There has been much discussion in Indian communities about researchers taking knowledge from Indian communities without proper approval. See Devon Mihesuah, "Suggested Guidelines for Institutions with Scholars who Conduct Research on American Indians," *American Indian Culture and Research Journal* 17 (1993): 131–40.

6. Field notes, 13 October 1994.

7. Eduardo and Bonnie Duran, *Native American Postcolonial Psychology* (Albany: State University of New York Press, 1995), 24–25.

8. Ibid., 45.

9. Jack Forbes, *Aztecas Del Norte: The Chicanos of Aztlan* (Davis: University of California Press, 1973), 189.

10. Vine Deloria, Jr., *The Nations Within: The Past and Future of American Indian Sovereignty* (New York: Pantheon Books, 1984), 187.

11. Allogan Slagle, "Unfinished Justice: Completing the Restoration and Acknowledgment of California Indian Tribes," *American Indian Quarterly* 13 (1989), 325–46.

12. Wayne Moquin, ed., A *Documentary History of the Mexican Americans* (New York: Praeger Publishers, 1971).

13. See, for example, Annette Jaimes Guererro, "Federal Indian Identification Policy," *The State of Native America* (Boston: South End Press, 1992); Teresa O'Nell, *Disciplined Hearts: History, Identity, and Depression in an American Indian Community* (Berkeley: University of California Press 1996).

14. Field notes, 13 October 1994.

15. Ibid.

16. Field notes, 22 May 1995.

17. Ibid.

18. "Indian Holocaust: History Seen through Natives' Eyes," *San Jose Mercury News*, 23 May 1996, Peninsula section.

19. Field notes, 22 May 1995.

20. Anne McClintock, *Imperial Leather: Race, Gender, and Sexuality in the Colonial Conquest* (New York: Routledge, 1995), 3.

21. This interviewee's name has been changed in order to protect her privacy.

22. Ibid.

23. Robert E. Berkhofer Jr., *White Man's Indian: Images of the American Indian from Columbus to the Present* (New York: Alfred A. Knopf, 1978), 86–91.

24. Ibid.

25. Field notes, 22 May 1996; "Indian Holocaust," *San Jose Mercury News.*

26. Field notes, 21 May 1996.

27. Roberto Ramirez, interview by author, San Jose, California, 15 December 1994.

28. Field notes, 13 October 1994.

29. This group's healing practice attempts to change our future, which is so closely linked to breaking through social amnesia and confronting and reclaiming the violent history of our past. See Howard Winant in *Racial Conditions: Politics, Theory, Comparisons* (Minneapolis: University of California Press, 1984).

30. See Francisco Alarcon, "Reclaiming Ourselves, Reclaiming America," in *Without Discovery: A Native Response to Columbus*, ed. Ray Gonzalez (Seattle: Broken Moon Press, 1992). He writes, "In order to understand history and be able to exorcise the past, we need to relive in flesh and spirit this history. We need to re-enact all the misunderstandings, confrontations and contradictions, all the suffering and havoc brought about by the so-called discovery of this continent" (32). The holocaust exhibit is part of this re-enactment.

31. See Ruth Behar, *The Vulnerable Observer: Anthropology That Breaks Your Heart* (Boston: Beacon Press, 1996). She argues that grief is hidden in Western society so as not to interfere with capitalism and the need for people to work. Grieving is seen as interfering with capitalist production.

32. See Michelle Rosaldo, "Toward an Anthropology of Self and Feeling," in *Culture Theory: Essays on Mind, Self, and Emotion*, ed. R. A. Shweder and R. A. Levine (Cambridge: Cambridge University Press, 1984). She argues that experiences of emotion are inherently cultural rather than psychobiological.

33. Roberto Ramirez, interview by author, San Jose, California, 15 December 1994.

34. Field notes, 29 May 1996.

35. Ibid.

36. Paul Rubio, interview by author, San Jose, California, 28 May 1996.

37. See Gloria Anzaldua, *Borderlands/La Frontera: The New Mestiza* (San Francisco: Spinsters/ Aunt Lute Book Company, 1987), 79, 80.

38. See, for example, Joan Weibel-Orlando, *Indian Country, L.A.: Maintaining Ethnic Community in Complex Society* (Urbana: University of Illinois Press, 1991). Weibel-Orlando categorizes Indian people as "progressive," "traditional," "full blood," and "mixed blood." These static categories fit within acculturation and Eurocentric models of blood quantum. She does not problematize the history of the designations of mixed-blood and full-blood as devices used by the European to divide and conquer Indian people. The Europeans categorized Indian people, coming up with these static terms to encourage conflict among Indian people throughout the Americas. This exhibit attempts to break down these static categories and valorizes Indian peoples' experience of mixed identity.

39. Laverne Morrissey, interview by author, Los Altos, California, 29 February 1993.

40. See, for example, John Price, "U.S. and Canadian Indian Urban Indian Ethnic Institutions," *Urban Anthropology* 4, no. 1 (1975).

41. See, for example, Mark Nagler, *Indians in the City: A Study of Urbanization of Indians in Toronto* (Ottawa: Canadian Research Center for Anthropology, Saint Paul University, 1970).

42. Mary Pratt uses the term *revision* in "Daring to Dream: Revisioning Culture and Citizenship." Renato Rosaldo also uses the term *revision* in "Cultural Citizenship, Inequality, and Multiculturalism" in *Latino Cultural Citizenship: Claiming Identity, Space, and Rights*, ed. Bill Flores and Rina Benmayor (Boston: Beacon Press, 1997). I use *reimagine* and *revision* interchangeably.

43. Leslie Marmon Silko, *Almanac of the Dead: A Novel* (New York: Simon and Schuster, 1996).

44. Field notes, 22 May 1996.

45. This claiming of a space by Chicanas/os within the exhibit is not to take away rights that are set aside for American Indians in the U.S. Rather, it acts as a site to decolonize categories created by Europeans that have caused divisions between groups of people. I want to thank Paula Moya for a conversation regarding this issue during the 1998 Chicana/o Colloquium, March 10, 1998, at Stanford University. For further discussion on this issue see Ines Hernandez-Avila, "An Open Letter to Chicanas: On the Power and Politics of Origin" in *Reinventing the Enemy's Language: Contemporary Native Women's Writing in North America*, eds. Joy Harjo and Gloria Bird (New York: W.W. Norton, 1997).

46. Roberto Ramirez, phone interview by author, 13 February 1996.

Red White & Blue

CHRIS LAMARR
from the rap group WithOut Rezervation (WOR)

Red White and Blue, let me tell you
who's the fool and who is true!
I got the gat, ready to blast!
I got the lines, ready to rhyme,
cuz now it's the time for me
to get mine! hold me back
and I'll attack and you don't want that!
cuz when I rap it's about the truth,
so how about you? do you want the facts?
a heart attack, how about a payback?
anyway I'll have my say, cuz I'm here
to stay and when I'm through, you could
say you knew about the
TRUE red, white and blue

Blood shed red, a bullet to the head.
"better off dead," that's what they said!
but that was their plan to get our land,
won't you understand?
Annihilation of my nation!
my people died. they tried to hide
all the lies but realize, that the red
in the flag is blood rag! a body bag!
it makes me sad, what we had
compared to what we have.
but I ain't trippin' cuz they're slippin
and we're coming back strong
back to where we belong!

Man is white, thinks he's right
but that I'll fight, cuz I'm M.C. Hiddesse!

cuz I know better, soon they'll be deader
better change their ways cuz we're here to stay
better deal cuz this sh** is real!
I saw LA, so whatcha gotta say?
better stop dissin', take time to listen
if you refuse, we're all gonna lose!
been this way for 500 years.
we'll shed no tears,
instead put 'em in fear
but that's today, the American way—
where might makes right,
so America, prepare to fight

White man in blue beating on you,
what's the clue?
blue on black, blue on red,
blue on brown, keeping us down!
they got a gat, a license to cap
and a power trip, how about that?

they beat Rodney King, didn't do a thing
caught it on tape, a judicial rape! a white cop free!
but if that were me, where I'd be? the penitentiary!
but that's the system set up to miss 'em
so if you're white in blue, you'll never lose
here's some advice: you'd better think twice!
you're rolling the dice if you call the vice.
so end of story, kinda gory
it's the red white and blue straight from WOR to you!

"Youngest Trapper on 7th Street" © *Pena Bonita*

My Uncle

TAWEAH GARCIA
(Mono/Pit River) Grade 5

He is a Chippewa Indian.
He is old.
He is nice.
He has no daughters of his own.
He loves me more than anybody.

His wife's name is Bobbie.
They live in Sacramento.
When he misses his family
he visits Minnesota.
While he was young
he was playing with guns.
Then he lost his arm.
My uncle loves me.
He brought me a Chippewa basket
filled with wild rice.

Downtown Oklahoma City—1952 16

VICTORIA BOMBERRY

O NE OF MY EARLIEST MEMORIES is like a well-worn black and white snapshot. It is the view from our front yard on what was then the outer southwestern edge of Oklahoma City. I would stand barefoot in the grass in my thin white panties, gazing at the skyscrapers that rose like fierce monoliths out of the prairie. Mesmerized, I tried to invent words to match their grandeur. It frustrated me to the point of anger that my tongue would not or could not capture what I saw. It seemed that I would make unintelligible word sounds forever. I had no way of knowing that it was just practice that I needed to make the sounds of the words that I wanted to say.

I learned the magical names of the three tallest buildings even though I could not say them correctly: The Hilton and The Biltmore Hotels, and finally the third and grandest, the First National Bank. It was the most exciting because it had a long, thin, needlelike tower that pierced the sky. The gleaming glass, smooth pale concrete, and cool, shimmering steel of the tall buildings fueled my young imagination. To me, the simple skyline was a fairytale city rising out of the dry, dusty landscape. Even during the daylight hours their silhouettes seemed to glow, and at night the red light at the tip of the tower throbbed expectantly. The pulsing light seemed to be a thousand miles away from the working-class neighborhoods that sprang out of sandstone and clay on Oklahoma City's South Side after World War II.

It must have been 1952 and I was three years old. Bob Poole had a grocery store at the corner of 44th and May. A new shopping center catty corner from Bob Poole's had the most modern incarnation of the five- and ten-cent store of the day that we said as if it were one word, *Teegeenwhy* (TG&Y). Lee Roy, the teenage boy next door, worked at the soda fountain that was part of any drugstore worth visiting. Next to the shopping center was a pale red brick church that had what I thought had to be the steepest and whitest wooden steeple in the Bible Belt.

Our neighborhood was racially mixed. There were white Americans like Flossie, her husband, and their sons. Flossie's husband was a phantom of sorts. He seemed to be at work all the time, and his first name was never used around the house. I did see a long row of workpants—neatly fitted on metal frames to evenly crease and stretch them so Flo didn't have to do heavy ironing—hanging on the clothesline in the back of their house. Flo had a husky voice from the Chesterfields she always held in her tobacco-stained fingers. She often invited my mother to her house for coffee. When my mother sat with her at her kitchen table Flossie seemed to have the lowdown on everything. Hers was the graveled voice of city wisdom.

The Villareal and Esquivius families were across the road, while the Muñoz family lived next to Lee Roy's house. They spoke Spanish among themselves but knew English too. All of them had come up from Mexico to work in the slaughterhouses and meat packing companies near the fairgrounds. They looked like us and cooked beans and corn like we did. When I looked at them I just saw Indians. The Ezequiel brothers were hardworking too, but friendly. They always greeted all the children in the neighborhood.

The unmarried brother was the taller of the two. He combed his hair in a high, shiny pompadour and kept his mustache well trimmed. He performed magic tricks and, like all good magicians, never gave away his secrets. There were disappearing nickels, quarters that appeared in surprised ears, pencils that miraculously turned into useless floppy rubber. We were delighted and always asked him to perform magic tricks. With a magician's gleam in his eye, he kept us begging for more.

The Smith kids lived next to the Villareals with their mother and stepfather. He was a mechanic who parked his shiny black, chrome-trimmed motorcycle close to the kitchen door right against the house. Around the corner a family welding business operated out of a makeshift garage. The neighborhood kids loved to go past the garage so we could sneak a dangerous peek at the sparks that rained off the red-hot metal under the welding wand. We liked tempting fate since we had been warned that without a protective mask you could go blind if you looked.

Our family had hard-boiled eggs and toast every Sunday before my mother sent me to Sunday school promptly by eight o'clock. It didn't start until eight-thirty, so there was no chance of being late. She was always conscious of time and what people would say if we edged in the door, even with a minute or two to spare. Although we lived in a neighborhood where brown and white coexisted, she knew how tentative the world really was. The boundaries between people were stretched in new ways, and our place in the city was never really secure because of the muttering complaints of white folks who were always on the look-out for a misstep. Those complaints could interpret and condemn us within the structure of the racial stereotypes of the day. Mama would say, with a laugh that hinted of defiant resignation, "When in Rome, do as the Romans do!" Of course, our Romans did not have to get up as early as we did, nor work as hard as Mama and Daddy. Indian time was early at Grandma's country home and at our home in the city.

I really do not recall my first trip downtown, but what I do remember is that my mother would always say don't forget to put on your shoes. I vividly recall when, in the excitement of the moment, I forgot; I did not give my gleaming white sandals a single thought in my hurry to get out of the door. My tough little feet walked easily across concrete and nudged the occasional pebble out of my way. I happily jumped over the cracks in the sidewalks. Each hop caused my hair to pull at my temples, since it was tightly and neatly braided for the occasion. I smiled at strangers and felt sorry for them when they didn't smile back, imagining some deep heartbreak was the cause of their furrowed brows and unsmiling faces.

Just as we were getting ready to go into Montgomery Ward's, my mother noticed. She was so embarrassed and ashamed when she looked down at my sun-browned feet. She must have felt that they gave us away instantly. No matter that her hair was perfectly curled and her flowered skirt draped her slim but shapely hips just so. Or that her white blouse made of cool cotton ironed smooth by her expert hands was fresh with sun, clean air and the slight touch of starch. It didn't matter that her carefully plucked brows looked natural and classy at the same time and that the shape of her lips was accented by luscious red lipstick. It didn't matter that her daughter was dressed to the nines in a pretty little summer dress. Or that she had all the family bills in her purse with the money to pay them. All her care, self-confidence, and competence were stripped away because I had no shoes. No shoes and the brownest of brown feet, and of course, by that time the bottoms were blackened with the dirt and soot of downtown city streets.

I looked in my mother's face and felt her distress and shame. It burned my cheeks deep red. I looked down at my feet and realized that the unsmiling faces of strangers carried a different meaning from what I had thought. I imagined I heard them whisper through clenched teeth—dirty Indians, look at the dirty Indians. Instead of feeling sorry for them, I felt the sting of their rejection and something that I didn't know at the time was their hate. In my young mind, I blamed myself for being a thoughtless disgrace who publicly shamed my mother. I was angry with myself for hurting her. I was angry with her for caring about what strangers thought. Anger was like a small, hard hickory nut stuck in the middle of my throat. I wanted my mama to protect me from their hard stares—maybe stand up even straighter and proclaim her pride in strong brown feet that didn't need shoes to protect their tender bottoms or straps to confine them.

What I did not understand then that I do understand now is that my mother was just as wounded by the looks. It didn't matter that my mother was an educated, intelligent, hardworking woman and looked it. Mother and daughter were judged and found lacking before anyone ever saw my feet. They were just an excuse to treat us with disdain. Maybe Mama wanted to protect me when she laughed, but I heard a different kind of laugh from one that signaled that it was all right. It was a laugh that covered embarrassment turning to shame.

I rode the escalator that day without my usual joy at safely jumping over the teeth at the tops and bottoms of the disappearing stairs. My delight in escaping their bite was gone. I wanted to go home to the sounds of Muscogee, Spanish, and gravelly English.

Letter Home

EDGAR JACKSON/ANAWROK
(INUPIAT)
FAIRBANKS CORRECTIONAL CENTER
MAY 30, 1982

Slowly the night comes to life
in the corner of my bed
The picture of you smiles at me—
I do not know if you are thinking of me

I can hear music in the background
My heart grows sad as laughter fills the air
I cannot tell whether the laughter is real

I gather my body and walk to the window
As the darkness awakens memories
everything around me ceases to exist
There is only your face
your smile
your voice
the silence that talks to me—

Rejection and Belonging in Addiction and Recovery
Four Urban Indian Men in Milwaukee

17

CHRISTINE T. LOWERY

S CHOLARLY ATTENTION may underrepresent urban experiences of Native Americans, but if a dominant stereotype of urban Indians has emerged, it is dominated by images of destitute alcoholics and lonely addicts. Contesting these stereotypes, the stories in this chapter depict the lives of four Indian men in urban Milwaukee, who speak of the broader context of their addictions to alcohol and drugs and of their recoveries. The chronology stretches from memories of childhood from 1944 through the 1970s, problems with addiction in the 1980s, and recovery processes in the early 1990s. This study focuses on a sample of Indian men (ages thirty-five to fifty-three) who are Wisconsin natives, share Oneida or Chippewa ancestry, are second-generation urban dwellers, and see themselves as Indian men. All have lived in Milwaukee, "A Gathering of the Waters" on Lake Michigan, for at least twenty-five years. These men qualify as embodiments of Vizenor's crossbloods, with "postmodern tribal blood-line[s]" including Chippewa, Irish, Oneida, Mexican, and Serbian-Croatian. The cross-blood encounters are communal rather than tragic, and these stories are "splendid considerations of survivance."[1] It is the communal that I want to emphasize in this telling.

The subjects' revelations form a common pattern, ranging from emotional and physical neglect to abandonment and rejection. The men constructed "belonging" in their addiction and continued this cognitive and emotional work in their recovery. These stories are as much about addiction as they are about recovery, as much about not belonging as constructing fit, and as much about who the men are as about who they are becoming.

Background

Potawatomi Bingo and its recently expanded casino are located in the industrial part of the city, just across the Milwaukee River from downtown. Potawatomi Bingo is one of the primary sponsors for September's Indian Summerfest, one of several ethnic celebrations on the lakefront that makes Milwaukee a city of festivals. The Milwaukee Indian Community School (MICS), grades one through eight, has served the community since 1969. MICS is housed in the former Concordia College buildings on West Kilbourn Avenue, and the "Migizi Express," the school newsletter, serves as a

277

community newsletter as well. The Indian Health Board, financially rocky, last served the Indian community in South Milwaukee off Mitchell on Eleventh. Tribes sponsor social services, such as Oneida Social Services. Organized church services are sponsored by United Methodist Native American Ministry, Catholic Congregation of the Great Spirit, and the Siggenauk Interfaith Spiritual Center.

In 1980, the overall count of American Indians in Wisconsin was just under 29,500—less than 1 percent of the state's total population.[2] The 1980 census indicated 30.1 percent of the American Indian population in Wisconsin resided in fourteen designated central city areas, 32 percent lived on reservations, and 37.2 percent lived in rural areas and small towns. Almost five thousand Indians were counted in Milwaukee, with thirteen hundred Indians counted in Green Bay. The 1990 census data counted 1,733 Indian households in Milwaukee, with a base population of 5,650. Females headed a third of these households and almost half of this group lived below poverty levels. Just over a third included married couples. A third had no high school education, just under a third were high school graduates, and almost a third had some college or an associated degree, with just under 6 percent with a bachelor's degree or more college.[3]

The men's stories were part of a research study (1993–1995) on addiction and recovery processes with American Indian women and men experiencing at least two years of recovery from alcohol addiction. Mike, age fifty-five, was born in the county hospital in Waukesha, west of Milwaukee. Mike is one-quarter Oneida, one-sixteenth Ojibwe, and eleven-sixteenths Serbian-Croatian. Bill is full-blood Oneida, born in Green Bay at the juncture of Wisconsin's peninsula, a slender finger pointing north across Lake Michigan to the Hiawatha National Park in Michigan's Upper Peninsula. He was raised in foster care on the Oneida reservation southwest of Green Bay until he left for the military in Texas at eighteen. Gus, age forty, and Fred, age thirty-five, share connection to Odanah where northern Wisconsin's Chequamegon Point reaches out for the Apostle Islands in Lake Superior. Gus, three-quarters Irish and one-quarter Chippewa, was born in Ashland, nestled in Chequamegon Bay and west of Odanah, and lived with his maternal grandparents for four years while his mother and his Oneida stepfather migrated to Milwaukee. Fred, half Chippewa and half Mexican, lived in Odanah for "two or three years" as a child.

The men started drinking when they were fifteen or sixteen and quit drinking within two years of each other, between 1989 and 1991. Mike reports a drinking history with cocaine and heroin use of thirty years; Bill claims twenty-five years of drinking; Fred reports ten years; and Gus describes a drinking period of thirteen years along with a marijuana-use history of eighteen years. The men were serially interviewed from mid-1995 to mid-1996. Mike, Bill, and Fred each participated in six interviews; Gus had four. Each man was interviewed over a two-month period. Each interview lasted an hour and a half and all interviewees were paid. The analysis of the data is limited to thematic description. Rejection and belonging are two themes that are explored because of their consistency across the four men's lives.

The "Growing Up" Stories

Two connected themes emerge from childhood—felt emotional abandonment by a parent or foster parent and an environment that supported drinking behavior. Mike had an environment filled with male relatives and a strong Croatian grandmother, but the emotional environment was characterized by loneliness. Bill completed high school as expected, but he was a foster child, isolated in a family environment of which he is not a part. Fred dropped out school in the ninth grade when his mother left home. And Gus took care of his brothers and sisters while his parents and aunts and uncles worked.

Mike: "Walking around with a chip on my shoulder"

Mike has early memories of his paternal grandmother's house in West Allis, now on the southwestern periphery of Milwaukee proper, but home to a compound of small farms in 1944. His "life began" at age five when his father was given custody of the small boy after the divorce from his mother—part Ojibwe, part Oneida—who struggled with schizophrenia and alcoholism. His father brought the boy from the southside Milwaukee home of his Indian mother and her parents to a Croatian household steeped in a legacy of politics, hard work, heavy drinking, and even moonshine production at one point in the family history. His Croatian grandmother was the "cornerstone" of the family and the dominant figure in his early life, hard at work cooking, making sausage, canning, gardening, and butchering farm animals. As an adult, Mike felt he knew his grandfather, a "practicing alcoholic," better than most people. He admired his grandfather's commitment to the communist party and his humanitarian spirit beneath a stern exterior. In 1944, Mike's father left for the Air Force to "fight the fascists." Mike was caught up in the family tradition of politics at a time when the boundaries were clear: "You were either for the people, a socialist-thinking or -minded person, or you were a fascist or a Nazi."

He was a child with "no parents," "treated like a little prince" by his grandparents for two years and resented by his uncles who straddled adolescence and early manhood. Still, Mike remembers feelings of loneliness and a desire for affection and closeness.

> I think that there were a lot of people coming up in that era, people came up through hard times. . . I know it was very difficult; they were people of the land, peasant people. So I guess they really didn't know how to show their feelings. I remember one of my dad's last days at the Veteran's Hospital [he was dying of cancer]. He had been reading a book . . . something to do with expressing love. I guess that was something he had come to recognize.

His relationship with his father was "never as close" as he wanted it to be. When his father was discharged from the military, the five-year-old Mike saw him coming down the road, and his grandmother encouraged the excited child to greet his father with a big hug.

> And I remember he stuck out his hand to shake hands. I felt like I had been hit with a stick. I think of rejection as something I was keenly aware of. I still am trying to overcome that. For most of my life I was walking around with a chip on my shoulder. And when I was being sent to the children's home, I feel that my grandmother loved me dearly, but I still took that as a form of rejection. And that was kind of traumatic for me, being dumped off, a hundred miles from home.

Sending Mike to a boarding school in Des Plains, Illinois, at age seven was to make a Croatian boy out of him, to teach him the language, to play a musical instrument, and to learn the dances. Somehow, none of that happened. He came back home at age nine when his father remarried. He started school with neighborhood friends, spent time with his grandparents, and had infrequent visits with his mother. "What nationality are you?" was a frequent question. In junior high, he would drink a can of cold beer under a hot sun while working with the male members of his family. His first experience with being stumbling drunk "opened doors for me, or I thought that it did." Interaction with others became easy and he "didn't know anyone could feel that good." Still he never dated in high school; the fear of rejection was too great.

Bill: "I was just a worker"

Bill was born in late summer of 1949 in Green Bay, the largest town near the Oneida reservation and the current site of the Oneida tribe's casino and hotel. Bill was six in 1956 when his mother died of tuberculosis in a sanatorium in Wisconsin. He, his brother, and sister were removed from their maternal grandmother's home and placed in the Oneida community. Charlotte, a long-time friend of his mother, asked that Bill be placed with her, her husband, and her grandchildren. Except for interactions at school, Bill was somewhat isolated from other Indian children at that point. Charlotte shopped in Seymour "because her husband was white" instead of the Indian town of Oneida, and Bill did not have contact with his relatives. But his Indian foster mother was active in the politics of her tribe, and he would accompany her to meetings.

Bill understood early that his place in this family group was primarily economic. "I was just there to help her," Bill remembers. She needed someone to clean house, to help cook, and in the summertime to report what happened on daytime soap operas. However, after a dishonorable discharge from the Air Force, he tried to return "home" at age twenty. He was permitted to stay for a week. "We're not getting paid for you anymore," he was told. "This is not your home. You have to go live with your relatives." Bill noted, "They won both ways. They got a free worker and they got paid for it. . . . It was a family environment, but I wasn't part of it. I was just a worker."

Still, he credits his Oneida foster mother for teaching him to work. Working became the life theme he used to separate himself from "the rest of the drunks and the homeless." She also taught him to make sure he was clean, had a haircut, and to tell people the truth "because it's going to come right back on you anyway." His foster father was an avid hunter and this freed Bill in a way. "I enjoyed a free life, hunting, and fishing. . . . We had access to firearms at all times." Later, he understood the relationship between working and being free in a different way—the more he worked, the more he could drink.

Fred: "Keeping to myself"

Fred was born in Odanah, Wisconsin, in 1960. His mother was Chippewa and his father was Spanish-Mexican from Arizona. He grew up on the near north side of Milwaukee around Thirty-eighth and Galena in a mixed neighborhood with Indians, whites, blacks, and Puerto Ricans. Pabst Blue Ribbon was the "big thing in them days" and the closing of the Pabst Brewery in 1996 is testament to the change in the economic structure of the Milwaukee brewing industry. Fred remembers, "The neighborhood wasn't bad. There were lots of fights. You used to be able to walk down the block and everybody would be sitting on their porch. By the time you got two blocks away, you would be all drunk and high. You would have to turn around and go back home. Everybody was partying on their porches."

Fred spends little time thinking about the past because "it seems like there was really nothing there." He dropped out of school in the ninth grade, the year his mother and father divorced. His mother left home when he was fourteen, and he and his older sister were alone. His father owned a bar and worked in a foundry and was still there after thirty years. Fred's father was just as consistent in his emotional absence and was his mother.

> [My father] would get up and go to work at six-thirty in the morning and worked until three-thirty, come home, eat something and go to sleep until six-thirty at night, then go to the bar till the bar closed. Then when the bar closed, he would come home and go to sleep and get up and go to work. He used to just leave and say, "Here's some money, get something to eat," and that was it.

When the family physically separated, Fred stayed with a friend and his family who lived a couple houses down the street. The first few months, he waited until the family was "done eating" before he would eat. After that, "It was just like I was their kid. My mother didn't like it, but what can you do? I had to do something. . . . Fourteen is an awful age to be out there on your own." Fred's older sister was eighteen and went to live with her boyfriend. A year later, when she returned home, she brought her first baby and a welfare check. By this time, Fred's father found a girlfriend and moved in with her. "I don't know what you guys are going to do, but this is what I'm doing, goodbye." Fred and his sister both lived off welfare supplemented by Fred's growing ability to play pool and win.

Fred says he grew up in a bar. His experiences in his father's bar started with mopping the floors at twelve, learning how to play pool from the Mexican men who frequented the bar at fourteen, and graduating to playing pool for money by the time he was sixteen. For three years, he roamed the near north side and south side looking for a good pool game, having become "one of the top ten pool players" in the city. Fred combined stealing cars and bikes, income from playing pool, and a knack for car maintenance to support himself in his late teens. Steak knives, nail files, and even forks were pruned to open doors and start cars. Fred remembers his adolescent prowess: "I ain't braggin' or nothing, but at fifteen there wasn't a car made that I couldn't take. We would take them on Second and Mitchell [Milwaukee's south side], strip them down there. They use to give up to fifty dollars for a Cadillac. . . . Then [1975] those were the best cars you could get."

In his late teens, Fred started a pattern of finding girlfriends with apartments, living with them until he was kicked out for never being home, and bouncing back to his sister's place. By the time he was nineteen, he had a broken marriage and young son and he stopped stealing. In the first two years his mother was gone, Fred had intermittent contact with her. She'd stop by every few months with money for food or he'd run into her in bars.

Gus: "We were still with the family"

"My dad was not an Indian man and nobody wanted to talk about it. . . . Once in a while when [my aunts and uncles] would be drinking too much, they'll say something, but who pays attention to people that drink? . . . I'm going on the assumption it was a one night stand."

Gus's mother was nineteen when he was born, and for awhile, it was the two of them. When his mother married and moved to Milwaukee, he lived with his maternal grandparents for three years on the Bad River Reservation in northern Wisconsin. Then, he moved in with his Oneida stepfather's mother for a couple of years. By the time he was in grade school, he was in Milwaukee. He had nosebleeds that would not stop and a heart condition that prevented activity in gym classes. This demanded his mother's attention for at least half of each year as they sought treatment from the clinic to the children's hospital and back again. Being a "sickly kid" intermittently released him from the omnipotent structure of a Catholic school, but not from the drinking lifestyle of his extended family.

> When I was growing up, [the cousins] were pretty much shoved together . . . because the aunts and the uncles would go out hitting the bars on Fridays and Saturdays and Sundays, and so we all had to watch out for each

other. We were pretty much on our own . . . I would say from five to thirteen. And we took that as being the norm. A lot of Indian people we knew were doing the same things, so we just thought that's the way things were done. We were still with the family, so how do you know that that's not the way it's suppose to be?

As a thirteen year old, Gus was influenced by protest-style music, Vietnam, rock and roll. That year he became "fiercely Indian." He responded to a writing assignment by blaming the Catholic Church for everything that happened to the American Indian in a fledgling protest song. He and his mother were called into the principal's office for suspected plagiarism because his academic background did not predict the quality of the writing. His mother made him proud. "It was the first time I ever seen a nun cringe. My mom says, 'Goddammit! I seen him sit down and write this shit!' . . . I decided right about eighth grade to become a writer."

At the same time, he was pulling his parents out of bars, stopping fights between them, and lifting money from his stepfather's wallet to feed his brothers and sisters. He found company with other kids who were taking care of their siblings, black and white youths whose "houses smelled like stale beer" and who shared his rejection and pain. The only time he saw other Indians was when he visited his cousins on the west side, in the Concordia Park neighborhood, Milwaukee "Indian Country" in the 1960s and 1970s. In Concordia Park, west from Water Street to Sherman around Thirty-fifth on the east, from Lisbon on the north to I-94 on the south, he and his cousins could "go from one block to another and either meet somebody that was related to us or was from the same reservation."

In the early 1970s, Wilbur Wright middle school on Eighty-fourth and Burleigh was busing students. This forced a "war" between black kids and white kids, with about three Indian kids caught in the middle, Gus recalls. The only joining they did was to smoke joints with kids in their neighborhood. The transition to Marshall High School, on Sixty-fourth and Fiebrantz just off Capitol, was "totally" different. It was no longer blacks and whites, but "freaks" and "greasers," and marijuana was plentiful. Gus was a "'freak' with patchy blue jeans, long hair, military coats with upside down patches." Here he found similar drinking patterns and problems among kids who came from "really nice houses" in "really nice neighborhoods." Money gave you choices, he decided. "Our parents could afford Blatz beer and Pabst Blue Ribbon and these people drank Schlitz . . . mai tais, gin and tonics."

Gus was going to be a rock and roll star. He could play a decent guitar and with black and white friends he formed the "ultimate basement band." The group did their best work—Yes, Captain Beyond, Hot Tuna, "bluesy rock," obscure Credence, or new Santana, "aggressive music [that demanded] technical proficiency"—in the basement of the Catholic Church starting on Friday nights and plunging into the next daylight. They managed to make a disaster of their performance work, plagued with technical problems and the short-fused tempers of insecure adolescents on pot. Acid was an experimental drug, pot and speed were used regularly, and sex was hot and heavy, just skirting the edge of paternity. Writing "angry young teenage boy type crap" in English class kept him in high school until he felt "they couldn't teach me anymore." Gus was kicked out.

Constructing Belonging

The theme that is common throughout the following excerpts is belonging, whether it is Bill's temporary experience in the military, Mike's "respect" as the neighborhood heroin dealer, Fred's knowledge of community played out in bars and pool rooms, or Gus's recovery that brings him back into the Indian community. While the theme of work is strong for each man, it served as the final line between alcoholic and "skid row bum" for both Mike and Bill. For Fred, work is a way to make money for his family, but his family, the mental health of his children, is far more important, and he searches for ways to extend what he has for his kids to other kids, kids like him, growing up without parents. And work for work's sake is expendable when a more connective environment is present for Gus.

Mike: "Satisfying a way to feel good about myself"

Mike relates his heroin experiences in the Mexican community on Milwaukee's south side when he "was a Mexican." Mike's "Mexican years" started in the 1960s with his introduction to Nick Zoric's, a neighborhood Serbian bar, by his maternal uncle, "the original Indian Mike." By the time Mike met his second wife, a woman of mixed Puerto Rican heritage, he was well into cocaine and moving quickly toward heroin.

> Up until I met the person who is now my second wife, I think I felt like most mainstream people felt about drugs other than alcohol. It was like all part of an evil force, whereas being an alcoholic was okay. I liked cocaine. I had been smoking pot on and off and I had sampled amphetamines and life in the circus. Maybe I would have gotten into those if I knew who to see, how to go about it, but alcohol pretty much did the job for what I wanted. It was handy and legal; it worked for me. And then pot smoking was . . . kind of a social happening. I got to where I used it fairly frequently during the prime of my use of drugs, when I used a combination of alcohol and cocaine and marijuana to reach Nirvana . . . the Creator, or God, or some other force. I think I'd converse with the refrigerator because I felt sure it was trying to make contact with me [Mike laughs]. I thought [cocaine] gave me the ability to perceive things that other people couldn't, that I was in a place above the average person that didn't have this ability . . . a way to satisfy a need to feel good about myself.

His rationalized goal—a "codependency thing"—was to help this petite, young, vulnerable woman, ten years his junior, to overcome her addiction to heroin by gradually weaning her off the drug, rather than substituting methadone for her heroin addiction. He made a contact for heroin and found out how easy it was to sell the first ounce, and before she was detoxed, he was buying and selling another ounce, escalating a process that was a boon to his ego.

> And it was fitting in with the lifestyle as I did my socializing in the Mexican neighborhood, drank in a lot of my favorite bars, kind of was accepted in that portion of the Mexican community. . . . But again, it came to pass that I was really getting off, for lack of a better term, in being a dealer, a drug dealer. In my warped way of thinking it was the closest thing that I'd ever get to respect. People were almost adoring me. I wasn't getting rich, but I was being enriched by people treating me in a way I felt I always should have been enriched. . . . It was really a feeling of power. . . . When I stopped, I ended up going back into it. Maybe money was an excuse; it was just that I was really enjoying the position I had gotten for myself.

The position of "respect" lasted for almost seven years. Although he didn't use heroin to begin with, he gradually substituted heroin for cocaine, lost the ambition to sell and eventually lost his clients. His heroin addiction got him further into trouble. His wife was leaving for weeks at a time to feed her own addiction. He pretended to care for his preadolescent daughters, trying to maintain the image of a working man. He eventually ended up in jail, arguing that he belonged in the hospital when he experienced withdrawal. "It was the middle of July and I was walking along with an old blanket around myself. The only thing I could eat comfortably, that made me feel good, was an orange." This jail withdrawal took place in the early 1980s and closed a period of dealing that started in 1975. The low point for him was not heroin addiction, however, but the potential loss of his job. Throughout this period, he continued shift work for A. O. Smith, a company that made automotive frames for trucks and sporting vehicles at that time.

> I always [thought] holding a job [was] number one, 'cause I know without that I would be a skid row bum. I would be that wino that people always think of an alcoholic being, rather than the alcoholic that I was. I had that phony front of being a worker and being a homeowner and having my life in order. So I knew without the job that I would be there. It was important for me, important for my family.

Bill: Recognizing "problem people" and feeling like "I belonged"

> With all the drinking I've done, I mean the years pass so quick, you'd never even know the year is gone. It's just existence. I didn't really keep track of time, because I had nobody. I've gone all over, mainly by myself, but I felt like going some place. . . . I have relatives, but I never see them. . . . None

of my relatives are close to me. I go wherever I feel like going. I have no, you know, sense of belonging. I've met so many people, I have some memories of some people I've met, and then some are just forgotten. They were unimportant people, nothing significant in my life.

Bill traces his addiction to alcohol back to an early work environment at age twenty-one or twenty-two and excuses his earlier experiences with alcohol in the Air Force as "fun." Finding a place of belonging is relevant here. The military experience included training as a military policeman and six months in the stockade for breaking into the bowling alley on base to steal two cases of beer in preparation for a birthday bash he never had. He spent time in a military rehabilitation center in Texas with heavy-drinking demoted sergeants as mentors. He recognized these men as "problem people," yet he felt like he "belonged" to this group of "old veterans" who "honored" him and other young recruits by letting them sit and drink in their company. He continued drinking while being assigned duties as a staff car driver. A bad conduct discharge soon followed.

Bill was an Indian man living off the streets of Milwaukee in the 1970s and 1980s. He can talk about poverty, traveling and hitchhiking, conning, junking, being a trustee in lockup, how drinking "makes the years pass so that you can't tell when one has ended or another year has begun." He'd stayed with his sister, who graduated from Haskell Indian School in Lawrence, Kansas. In Milwaukee, he'd stayed with his dad, who was then an Alcoholics Anonymous (AA) counselor, and now, nearing seventy, "pushes change" at the tribal casino in Green Bay. Twenty-three years ago, Bill had a "detox wedding" to Ann, his non-Indian partner. He can talk about the decline of his health as he turned to a diet of straight liquor—the blood in his stools, the pain in his gut. He tried to separate himself from "the rest of the drunks and the homeless" through his ability to work. But only when Bill could see himself as one of them did his vulnerability to death the doctors predicted finally become real. He decided that he wanted to live, so he stopped drinking.

Now Bill works in an Indian agency in Milwaukee, but his connectedness to the Indian community is not clear. His peers are Indian people, but his only interaction with them is at work. He spends much of his time alone or with Ann. His real focus is money, not relationships. His goal is to work as much overtime as he can to build up his paycheck, but he spends money as fast as he makes it. His connection to his tribe has been tenuous, and he sees this primarily as insurance against being abandoned in his old age. Lately, he's been thinking about his Oneida relatives. He attended a funeral recently, received a warm reception, and his aunt asked him why he never came up to see them. He paused to seriously think about that, and then added, "Maybe I should."

Fred: "Just fitting in"
Earlier in his life, pool was not only Fred's economic lifeline, but also "the highlight" of life. "I was just fitting in maybe, fitting in because I never really had nothing." Part

of his decision to quit drinking centered on the amount of money he spent for a weekend of drinking. He was tired of not having anything. His friends had jobs, had money. He saw them taking their kids to the circus, taking their wives to nice clubs, while he was rationing his income, money for gas and Kentucky Fried Chicken.

Fred's wife quit drinking a couple of years before. Now they would argue about old patterns—he was never home and was always at the bar drinking. At work, Fred was carrying bottles of Rupplemint under the seat of his truck. In his promise to quit drinking, he switched to vodka, something his wife could not smell on his breath. He started with a shot of vodka and a soda, graduated to small beer glasses of vodka, and then exchanged the Rupplemint for bottles of vodka. Soon the vodka had no effect, and he could feel the full impact of the arguments with his wife about his drinking.

> And one time I was kind of buzzed up, just sitting there [at the bar], and these nice young-looking kids . . . came in looking for their mother. And their mother is all drunk with this other guy. . . . "Can you come home?" The girl was about fourteen, asking her mother to come home cause her kid needs milk and he ain't eat yet, and here, her mother's sitting in the bar all drunk, hanging on this other guy and she ain't got no money. I went out-side and the girl is sitting there crying . . . and she had this little rug rat sit-ting with her. So I felt sorry for her . . . and gave her five dollars.

To avoid this scene, Fred crossed the street to another bar. When he returned later, he lambasted the woman, "You are up and sad. Your kids is out here starving and they are crying and they want you to come home and you're sitting in a bar." When the man she was "hanging on" finally passed out, the woman approached Fred, "hugging on me and stuff." "You would make a good father cause you take care of kids and every-thing," she told him. "Hey, get away from me, man!" Fred responded. But what hap-pened that afternoon opened his awareness to his own behavior as a father.

> And that was the first time it really started to dawn on me. . . . My kids would call, "When are you coming home?" I see them kids coming in looking for their parents all the time. I seemed like I was changing. "I ain't going nowhere. Here's a couple of dollars. Get the hell out of here!" And then I was taking my kid to the bar and he was really start-ing to like to be in the bar. I would go to the bar on Saturdays, he would be up before me—Boom! and ready to go. Now my son is going to be in the bar and he is going to have his life being in the bar, not worrying about nobody else. I don't want my kids to have a life like I grew up—hard, sitting in a bar, wasting your life.

Yet the bar is what Fred knows. The familiarity of the bar offered temporary ac-quaintances and, occasionally, a good friend; but it is pool that remained Fred's sol-ace. If his mother or somebody died, he says, he'd go to a bar where no one knows him and play pool. But things have changed. The solitary pool player is inviting trouble in bars where people now carry concealed guns. Now Fred plays pool in a league twice a week for relaxation, as his "time-out." Another thing that has changed, observed Fred, is that there are more nondrinkers in pool leagues than ever before.

Fred has always wanted to own a bar and community has influenced him. Fred wants to share what he has in the one way he knows how. He and his wife have talked about buying a bar and creating a community center/bar for families where adolescents can play video games and adults can play pool. Adolescents would have teen nights where they can enjoy an alcohol- and drug-free night of dancing and meeting one another. Would alcohol be served? Probably, but no one would be allowed to get drunk.

Gus: "I did it the Indian way"

While Gus was in college, his four-year marriage was rocky, the drinking was heavy, and the values were polar. His wife whipped him with her words, and he hit her back. They saw counselors, they went to AA, and they even had another child, a little girl. He slapped her daughters when they didn't obey him, and they told him to "go to hell." He even tried to "capture lost glories" by rekindling the band, but the "whole thing did not come out right." Gus dropped out of college for a year to take care of this. Eventually he was living off the couch of a friend, drinking a twelve-pack a day "easily," smoking more pot, doing a little coke.

"At this time, I got pulled over for drunk driving, lost my license, and I had to take my kids, go pick them up, on the bus through cold, through rain, through blazing hot, and I was paying the price. And I got my license back. . . . Then, I did the same exact thing over again." Gus argued with himself for twenty-four hours. Images of his own childhood replayed in his mind. He didn't want his kids to "go through the same crap he did." He didn't want his wife to talk to his kids about him the way she talked about her "ex." That was it, the first step in his decision process. "I would drink no more, still smoke, but I would drink no more." Later, he gathered the strands of the "internal argument" into a song called "Traveling Thunder."

An alcohol assessment was court ordered for the third Driving While Intoxicated (DWI) charge in four years. The counselor at the DePaul Treatment Center told him he was alcoholic. "No shit," he replied. He was required to take antabuse, and he refused "a drug to take me off drugs." He decided he'd do this the "Indian way" and headed for the Indian Health Board.

> Part of the political thing . . . was meeting different people that had been through the alcohol, people who were more spiritually attuned. . . . I never really thought about spirituality as a form of coming away from drinking or talking about it. . . . I made the physical, the mental and spiritual decision to go back to where I had come from, back . . . with the people. . . . I did it all because I did it here.

For three months Gus and the Indian female counselor met weekly. They would "smudge" before each session with sweet grass. Gus would explore his reality while carrying a stone in his hand. "We were learning, listening and talking, speaking freely, not judged." It was the nonjudgmental approach that attracted him—there is stigma in a non-Indian treatment program, "having someone tell you something you already know." His recovery turned to volunteer work in the Indian community—step two of his healing.

> I had to make myself useful. This is what I needed to do. I needed to work in the Indian community. So many in our community have the same problem, so you weren't judged by whether or not you are an alcoholic, because it's a fact of life. You were judged by who you were, what you did, you were accepted, you know? . . . And that was very spiritual. . . . We all make mistakes, but you are still one of us. You belong to these people.

Gus defines spirituality as "the sense of belonging, a sense of knowing where you come from, where you belong. To me, being in this place [teaching] is spiritual, 'cause I belong here. I am connected here. I am more connected with kids than I am with adults." He doesn't get wrapped up in things he cannot control. Gus understands that there are different ways kids learn and wants flexibility in dealing with student's education and discipline. Suspension, for example, is useless as a tool of discipline because it only serves to isolate a youth from community, instead of supporting him and telling the youth he is cared for, which is something the youth needs to know.

Conclusion

Developmentally, the men in these stories are at different places. Mike, the oldest, is actively looking for ways to serve the Indian community, but is not confident of his leadership abilities for fear of making mistakes. He wants to be heard, but wonders if he has anything useful to say sometimes. Mike, in spite of his strained relationship with "the woman I am married to" and the throes and woes of his postadolescent daughters, now drives to pow-wows by himself and seeks companionship with other Indian men in the community who are involved with spiritual leadership. Bill is self-focused, but thinking about his relatives "up north." He counts his money and spends it. He thinks about self-improvement, and it appears there is no action. Then one is reminded that five years ago Bill was "on the streets" and drinking every day.

The written transcripts for Fred in the last two interviews reveal a man thinking his way through his relationships with his children, with his daily life, the Indian part of him, and his future, without much room for probing questions. At one point, Fred scans the bookshelves in my office and asks, "What is an Indian?" The question is returned, "Fred, what does 'Indian' mean to you?" "I don't know," he answers, "I just figured that if you've read this many books, you would know."

Of the four men, Gus demonstrates the fullest integration of spirituality, work, and relationships. The integration is not uninterrupted by life's impediments: illnesses, work upheaval, uncertainties. Still, he is connected through his teaching and work with students. He is connected through his writing and in involvement in his community. He is connected through his relationship with his children and his partner. And he is connected through his knowledge of who he is. Gus quotes a line from a war movie spoken by a black soldier, "I don't care for a lot, but what I do care for, I care for a lot." His spirituality is expressed in the time he gives his partner, in telling the kids at school that they are doing good work, listening to those who need to be listened to, and "watching a bird once in a while." The "world tilted for him"—he quotes Vizenor—when he learned to laugh at himself and his own stupidity, the owning of himself, recognizing that denial is, perhaps, "the privilege of men." He still has an addictive personality, he admits. He doesn't drink or smoke anymore, but he plays Star Wars on his computer. It's one way of handling stress. "Absolutely," Gus says with a smile, "I can still blast the hell out of the Empire!"

Notes

1. Gerald Vizenor, *Crossbloods: Bone Courts, Bingo and Other Reports* (Minneapolis: University of Minnesota Press, 1990).

2. Ibid., viii.

3. B. A. Christenson, N. J. Kanaskie, D. J. Landry, and D. P. Slesinger, *American Indians in Wisconsin, 1980,* Populations Series 80-4, Department of Rural Sociology (Madison: Applied Population Laboratory, University of Wisconsin-Madison, 1985).

excerpt from a work in progress

PARRIS BUTLER

travel has always been
will always be an act of breathing
the rhythm of strides
the rhythm of breath
drawn out over time and horizons

the trail comes into being
just beyond the moment of desire
of intent
of recognition
like the path of the arrow
conjured by the heart
and the need to take nourishment
set in place by the hunter's eye

the road flows out like a wind
crossing distant points on the horizons
drawn by the rhythm of strides and breath
toward the feet of the runner
each footfall following the rhythm of songs
emitted at the beginning of time
thus transplanted
into my urban mode
as breath flows on the wind
filaments of being drifting
across time and horizons
to this place
where in the cold light of dawn
in that moment where years fold open
and depths of oceans are revealed
amidst concrete
and cloud reflections

usurped by the asphalt grid
and the mortality of contrived intent
roads radiate and converge
caught up in the serpentine flow
we walk among millions we
trace the ritual course
of our day to day as it plays out
across the matrix
infinite
so intricate
asphalt and concrete
concrete and cloud reflections
the masses in the rain
rain on the canyon floor
on grey concrete
footsteps leave no track
no trace

"Mattie Goes Traveling" © by Hulleah J. Tsinhnahjinnie

Index

Numbers in bold indicate artwork.

Abrams, Ruth Ann, 112n6
Acarí, 11
acculturation in urban areas, xiii, 97, 125n2,
    259, 263n38
addiction, among Native Americans,
    277–90
addicts. *See* alcoholics and addicts
agriculture, evolution of, 8–9
Aguilar, Dugan, 4, 27
Alarcon, Francisco, 263n30
Alcatraz occupation, xii, 80, 88, 150
alcoholics and addicts: belonging of,
    284–90; rejection of, 278, 280–84
alcoholism, among Native Americans, 29,
    43, 92, 99, 165, 198, 237, 251, 252,
    277–90
alcoholism and addiction, causes of,
    279–84, 286
Alexie, Sherman, 89
alienation, of Native Americans, x, 76,
    271–73. *See also* American writing
All Tribes American Indian Center, 87, 90,
    91, 92, 93, 110n1, 158
American Anthropological Association, xi, xii
American Indian, legal definitions of, 180,
    182. *See also* Native American
American Indian Alliance (AIA), 249, 250
American Indian Center. *See* All Tribes
    American Indian Center
American Indian Culture and Research Journal, xi,
    xii, xiii, xv, 203

American Indian Film Festival, 79
American Indian heritage. *See* ethnic identity
    of Native Americans
American Indian Holocaust, 249, 250, 251,
    256, 261
American Indian Holocaust Exhibit, 249;
    healing through, 249, 251, 252, 255,
    257, 263n29
American Indian Movement (AIM), 88,
    105
American Indian Policy Review
    Commission, 86, 181
American Indian studies, influence of
    anthropology on, xiv
American writing: alienation in, 33;
    contradiction in, 32–34; Eurocentric
    view in, 32–33
Americans for Indian Opportunity (AIO),
    159
ancestry and ethnicity. *See* ethnicity, ancestry
    and Aspero, 9, 11
assimilation, of Native Americans, xiii, 77,
    82, 86, 97, 130, 131, 178, 197

Banderas, Juan, 53
Barth, Fredrick, 172
Basso, Keith, 34, 76
Beane, Syd, 138–39
Beck, David R. M., 71, 72, 155
Behar, Ruth, 263n31
Belin, Esther, 165, 167

Credits

(p. ix) "Foreword" by Donald L. Fixico © 1999.

(p. xi) "Introduction" by Susan Lobo © 1999.

(p. xvii) "The Path to the Milky Way Leads through Los Angeles" © Joy Harjo. Reprinted from *A Map to the Next World, Poems and Tales* (W. W. Norton, 2000) with permission of Joy Harjo.

(pp. 3, 71, 165) "Introduction" (to parts I, II, and III) by Susan Lobo © 2000.

(p. 5) "The Urban Tradition among Native Americans" by Jack Forbes. An earlier version appeared in the *American Indian Culture and Research Journal*, vol. 22, no. 4, 1998. Reprinted by permission of the American Indian Studies Center, UCLA. © Regents of the University of California.

(p. 29) "Telling the Indian Urban: Representations in American Indian Fiction" by Carol Miller. An earlier version appeared in the *American Indian Culture and Research Journal*, vol. 22, no. 4, 1998. Reprinted by permission of the American Indian Studies Center, UCLA. © Regents of the University of California.

(p. 49) "Yaqui Culture and Language through a History of Urbanization" by Octaviana V. Trujillo. Originally printed as "The Yaqui of Guadalupe, Arizona: A Century of Cultural Survival through Trilingualism" in the *American Indian Culture and Research Journal*, vol. 22, no. 4, 1998. Reprinted by permission of the American Indian Studies Center, UCLA. © Regents of the University of California.

(p. 73) "Is Urban a Person or a Place? Characteristics of Urban Indian Country" by Susan Lobo. An earlier version appeared in the *American Indian Culture and Research Journal*, vol. 22, no. 4, 1998. Reprinted by permission of the American Indian Studies Center, UCLA. © Regents of the University of California.

(p. 84) Figures on page 84 are in the public domain and housed in the Community History Project Archives of the Intertribal Friendship House, Oakland, California.

(p. 85) "Retribalization in Urban Indian Communities" by Terry Straus and Debra Valentino. An earlier version appeared in the *American Indian Culture and Research Journal*, vol. 22, no. 4, 1998. Reprinted by permission of the American Indian Studies Center, UCLA. © Regents of the University of California.

About the Contributors

Dugan Aguilar is a Native California photographer whose work has been shown at the Hearst Museum and throughout California. He specializes in photographing Native California get-togethers, Big Times, and people such as basket weavers, traditional dancers, and other cultural specialists. His work is published often in the magazine *News from Native California.*

David R. M. Beck is an associate professor in the Native American Studies department at the University of Montana. He also serves as senior faculty for the Americans for Indian Opportunity (AIO) Ambassador Program. He has studied and published articles on the Chicago American Indian community, American Indian education, and the Menominee Indian nation, and published a bibliography on the Chicago Indian community.

Esther Belin is a writer raised in Los Angeles. Her first book of poetry, *From the Belly of My Beauty,* which received the American Book Award from the Before Columbus Foundation, was published by the University of Arizona Press in 1999. A second-generation off-reservation Navajo (Diné), she lives in Durango, Colorado, about two hours from her homeland.

Victoria Bomberry (Muscogee/Lenape) was born and raised in Oklahoma. She obtained her Ph.D. in Modern Thought and Literature at Stanford University in 2000. Prior to entering the Ph.D. program she was a lecturer in the Native American Studies Program at California State University, Sonoma. She is the recipient of the Bannerman Fellowship, a national award, for her contributions to community organizing.

Pena Bonita was born and raised in New Mexico. She has lived in New York since 1979 and has a bachelor's of fine arts and a master's degree from Hunter College in New York City. She has worked in the collections at the Thunder Bay Museum in Ontario, Canada, with the Joffrey Ballet Company, at Long Island University, Marvel Comics, Washington State Council on the Arts, and the Heard Museum. "I first began taking photos with the family Brownie camera. However, photography is only one of the artistic expressions or mediums used in the artwork I have created, and it is just a tool in the process of a final piece most of the time."

Parris Butler (Mohave/Cherokee) is a writer and artist currently living in the San Francisco Bay Area. He received fine arts degrees from the Institute of American Indian Arts in both two-dimensional arts and creative writing. He works in various media including pen and ink, acrylic and oils on canvas, ceramic, stone sculpture, wood inlay and lathe, and a number of printmaking techniques. He did the cover art and illustrations for the book *Native American Voices: A Reader.*

John Collier Jr. began a long and distinguished photographic career as a photographer for Roy Stryker of the Farm Security Administration in the 1930s. He went on to work with such artists and scholars as Dorthea Lange and Alexander Leighton, and with indigenous communities from Peru to Alaska. He taught for many decades at San Francisco State University and the San Francisco Art Institute, and is considered to be the founder of visual anthropology. His publications include *Visual Anthropology: Photography as a Research Method* (University of New Mexico Press, 1967/1986), *Alaskan Eskimo Education: A Film Analysis of Cultural Confrontation in Schools* (Holt, Rinehart and Winston, 1973), and *The Awakening Valley* (Chicago University Press, 1949).

Jimmy Curtiss is a well-known country western singer and songwriter who often collaborates with Floyd Red Crow Westerman.

Donald L. Fixico (Sac & Fox/Muscogee Creek/Shawnee/Seminole) is professor of history and director of the Indigenous Nations Studies Program at the University of Kansas. His publications include *Termination and Relocation: Federal Indian Policy, 1945–1960* (1986); *Urban Indians* (1991); *The Invasion of Indian Country in the Twentieth Century: American Capitalism and Tribal Natural Resources* (1998); and the forthcoming *The Urban Indian Experience in America* (2000). He also edited *An Anthology of Western Great Lakes Indian History* (1988) and *Rethinking American Indian History* (1997).

Jack Forbes (Powhatan/Delaware) is author of many books including *Africans and Native Americans, Only Approved Indians,* and *Red Blood: A Novel.* He is cofounder of Native American Studies as a field and of D-Q University. He is currently teaching at the University of California at Berkeley and at Davis.

Taweah Garcia (Mono/Pit River) was in the fifth grade and at a poetry workshop at Hintil Ku Caa when she wrote "My Uncle." She is now twenty-three years old. She attended Hintil until sixth grade and is currently a student at Merritt Community College. Her plan is to transfer to San Francisco State University to major in social work. She dances traditional Pomo and Aztec dance.

Angela A. Gonzales (Hopi from the village of Shungopavi—Spider clan) is a visiting assistant professor in rural sociology at Cornell University. A Ph.D. candidate in sociology at Harvard University, her dissertation is "American Indian Identity Matters: The Political Economy of Ethnic Boundaries." She has a B.A. in sociology from the University of California Riverside and two M.A. degrees from Harvard University, in education and sociology. She has been the recipient of the Katrin H. Lamon Resident Scholar, School of American Research, Santa Fe, New Mexico (1997–98), National Research Council, Ford Foundation Pre-Doctoral Fellowship (1992–95), and Harvard Prize Fellowship (1990–present), and she is the former director of the Hopi Tribe Grant and Scholarship and Adult Vocational Training Programs.

Joy Harjo, an enrolled member of the Muscogee Nation, has published many books of poetry, including *In Mad Love and War* and *The Woman Who Fell from the Sky*, and recently co-edited an anthology of Native women's writing, *Reinventing the Enemy's Language*. Her most recent book is *A Map to the Next World: Poems and Tales*. She plays saxophone and performs her poetry with her band, Joy Harjo & Poetic Justice, whose recent CD release, *Letter from the End of the Twentieth Century*, won several awards.

Päivi Hoikkala received her Ph.D. from Arizona State University. She is a lecturer in the history department at California State Polytechnic University at Pomona where she also directs a grant program that provides professional development for elementary school teachers. Her research and publications focus on twentieth-century Indian women's issues.

Deborah Davis Jackson is an assistant professor in the Sociology/Anthropology department at Earlham College. She is currently conducting research on older American Indians as a part of a program on applied issues of aging.

Edgar Jackson/Anawrok is Inupiat, from the village of Unalakleet on the Norton Sound Coast of Alaska. He was raised by his grandfather, Oliver Anawrok, under whose teachings he learned the traditions of his people, which he tries to keep alive in his writings. He attended the University of Alaska and worked for the Fairbanks Native Association. His poetry has appeared in *The Clouds Threw This Light, Voices from the Inside, In the Dreamlight: 22 Alaskan Writers, The Prison Writing Review, New Letters, Lemon Creek Gold*, and *Alaska Today*.

Zig Jackson (Mandan/Hidatsa/Arikara) was raised at Fort Berthold Indian Reservation in western North Dakota. He has taught photography at the Institute of American Indian Arts in Santa Fe, at San Francisco State University, the University of California at Davis, and the Savannah College of Art and Design. His work has been shown extensively throughout the United States, and he is currently working on a photographic book, "Buffalo Getting Up in the Grass." E-mail: mandan@sirius.com

Alex Julca was born in Huanuco, Peru. "I came to this world accompanied by Isreal, my twin brother. Due to my peripatetic parents, I have a sister born in Cerro de Pasco (Andean town), two sisters born in Chimbote (a northern coastal town), and a younger brother born in Lima. Obdulia, my mother, was born in Cayran, and Alejo, my father, was born in Conchamarca, both small Andean villages outside of Huanuco.

Most of my primary studies were in Chimbote, and later in Lima I studied political economy at San Marcos University and business administration at the Escuela Superio de Administracion de Negocios. I got my Ph.D. in Economics from the New School for Social Research in New York in 1997 and currently work as a consultant for the United Nations."

Chris LaMarr is Paiute/Pit River from Susanville, California. He received a B.A. in Native American Studies from the University of California at Berkeley and a J.D. from the University of Colorado at Boulder School of Law. While at law school he was the director of the Native American Prison Project and the Denver Project for the Indian Law Clinic at CU-Boulder. Chris is also the lead singer and producer of the Native American rap group WithOut Rezervation and is the owner of an all-Native record label called WithOut Rez Productions.

Julian Lang (Karuk) is a writer, visual artist, and has recently become a director of shadow plays based upon the creation stories of northern California. He is the director of the Institute of Native Knowledge and is a scholar of the language and culture of his tribe. He resides in Humboldt County California. E-mail: irahiv@hotmail.com

Susan Lobo, trained as a cultural anthropologist, is a consultant, emphasizing research, advocacy, and project design, working primarily for American Indian tribes and community organizations in the United States and Central and South America. Since 1978 she has been the coordinator of the Community History Project located at Intertribal Friendship House in Oakland and has taught at the University of California at Berkeley and at Davis. Her publications include *A House of My Own: Social Organization in the Squatter Settlements of Peru* and *Native American Voices: A Reader.* E-mail: SLobo333@aol.com

Christine T. Lowery is a Laguna-Hopi from Paguate, New Mexico. She is an associate professor and does qualitative research with American Indians. She teaches graduate and undergraduate courses at the University of Wisconsin–Milwaukee School of Social Welfare. E-mail: ctlowery@aol.com

L. Frank Manriquez (Tongva/Acjachmem) is an artist and writer who is also active on a number of fronts in the cultural revitalization currently taking place throughout Native California. Her drawings, which frequently include Deer and Coyote in many guises, are often seen in *News from Native California.*

Carol Miller is an associate professor in the Program in American Studies and the Department of American Indian Studies at the University of Minnesota. She is a member of the Cherokee Nation of Oklahoma.

Kurt M. Peters (Blackfeet/Powhatan) is assistant professor of Native American and comparative ethnic studies at Oregon State University. He earned his doctorate at the University of California–Berkeley and focuses his research primarily on the twentieth-century Native American experience and Native American wage labor.

Darby Li Po Price is an assistant professor of American Studies at DePaul University in Chicago and earned his Ph.D. in Ethnic Studies at the University of California at Berkeley. He is finishing his book, *Mixed Laughter: Multiracial Identities and American Comedy,* and has published essays in *The American Indian Culture and Research Journal, Amerasia Journal, Critical Mass,* and several edited works.

Renya Ramirez is an enrolled member of the Winnebago tribe of Nebraska. She is an assistant professor of American studies at the University of California at Santa Cruz. She received her Ph.D. from Stanford University and is currently working on turning her dissertation, "Healing through Grief: Native Americans Reimagining Culture, Community and Citizenship in San Jose, California," into a book.

Carter Revard/Nompewathe is Osage from Oklahoma. He grew up on the Osage reservation there, went to the Buck Creek School and then took degrees from the University of Tulsa, Oxford, and Yale. He has been a Gourd Dancer since 1977. He comments, "My Ponca, Osage, and Irish folks get into my poems along with scissortails, mockingbirds, coyotes and other relatives." *Winning the Dust Bowl,* a gathering of his poems and essays, will be published in 2000 by the University of Arizona Press.

Larry Rodriguez Sr. (Luiseño, Rincon Reservation) has a teaching credential from the University of the Pacific and has served as educational director on the Rincon Indian Reservation, located in northern San Diego County. He has exhibited his drawings and ceramic sculptures throughout northern California and is currently working as an arts and crafts instructor for the California Youth Authority. "Although I am an enrolled member of my rez, I grew up in an urban environment, and my work reflects contemporary and traditional themes as seen through the eyes of an Urban Indian." He has shown his work at Chaw'se State Indian Museum and in group shows at the American Indian Contemporary Art Gallery, San Francisco

Mike Rodriguez's (Luiseño) work is often political. His media range from acrylic to spray paint, and works includes murals, prints, and sculpture. He currently lives in Sacramento and has shown throughout northern California including at the State Capital Gallery, Chaw'se, Golden State Museum, Native Ground, and "other spots that aren't necessarily legal." He is currently putting out a magazine, *Heretik,* and can be reached via the web at www.hunwutarts.com.

Terry Straus is professorial lecturer in the Master of Arts Program in Social Sciences at the University of Chicago and has been working in the Chicago Indian community for more than twenty years. Her most recent book is *Native Chicago.*

Michael Thompson (Muskogee Creek) is head of the English department at Bloomfield High School and a member/supporter of the Iron Circle Nation, a prison support group for Native Americans in Los Angeles.

Octaviana V. Trujillo, a former chairwoman of the Pascua Yaqui tribe of Arizona, was born and raised in Guadalupe, Arizona. She is the director of the Center for Indian Education and editor of the *Journal of American Indian Education* at Arizona State University. Dr. Trujillo teaches in the interdisciplinary American Indian Studies program and she works in multicultural education and international indigenous peoples' language and literacy development.

Hulleah Tsinhnahjinnie (Seminole/Creek/Navajo) is a photographer/writer/artist currently living and working in Rough Rock, Arizona. She attended the Institute of American Indian Art, Santa Fe, and the California College of Arts and Crafts. She has shown her work extensively, both nationally and internationally. Over a twenty-year period from 1978 to 1998 she photographed throughout the Bay Area Indian community.

Debra Valentino, an enrolled Oneida, is founding director of the Native American Urban Indian Retreat organization in Chicago.

Joan Weibel-Orlando received a Ph.D. from the Department of Anthropology of the University of California at Los Angeles in 1977. Currently an associate professor in the Department of Anthropology at the University of Southern California in Los Angeles, she is the author of *Indian Country, L.A.: Maintaining Ethnic Community in Complex Society* (1999) and over thirty articles and book chapters about the contemporary Native American experience. She can be contacted electronically at weibel@mizar.usc.edu.

Floyd Red Crow Westerman (Dakota) is well known throughout Indian Country as a singer and performer, an activist, and an international ambassador for indigenous rights. For many years he has traveled throughout the hemisphere and internationally, singing and bringing a message of hope and understanding to Indians and non-Indians—like the *eyapaha*, the crier of old who summoned the camp to action. He is the culture and good-will ambassador for the International Indian Treaty Council. Many remember him as Ten Bears, the part he played in the film *Dances with Wolves*, one of the many movies he has appeared in. More recently he has appeared in a number of television programs, including *The X Files* and *Walker, Texas Ranger.*